THE GREAT THINKERS

THE
GREAT
THINKERS

RUPERT LODGE

Professor of Philosophy, Queen's University
Kingston, Ontario

FREDERICK UNGAR PUBLISHING CO.
NEW YORK

Republished 1964
by arrangement with Routledge & Kegan Paul Ltd

First published 1949

Printed in the United States of America

Library of Congress Catalog Card No. 64-25560

Contents

Contents

Contents

Contents

Preface

IN the history of mankind there have been, in every field of experience, a few men who stand out as "great." There are many famous poets, but very few are pre-eminent: Homer, Dante, Shakespeare, and some few others. There are many well-known painters, but very few whose greatness is unquestioned: Michelangelo, Leonardo, Rembrandt, and some few others. There are many celebrated musicians, but very few who stand head and shoulders above the rest: Bach, Beethoven, and—are there any others who rank with these? So also in the field of thought. There are many thinkers whose names are widely known, but very few whose essential greatness is universally conceded: Plato, Aristotle, perhaps also Plotinus, in the ancient world; Descartes, Leibniz, and Spinoza in the dawn of our modern age, with Locke, Berkeley, and Hume as lesser luminaries, persisting at least in their afterglow; and above all, Kant and his immediate successors, who are still creative influences in our present-day thinking. The work of these ten thinkers constitutes the main stream of European philosophy.

If we judge greatness by vitality and creative influence, the four greatest works in the field of thought are Plato's *Republic*, Descartes' *Method and Meditations*, Locke's *Essay*, and Kant's *Critique of Pure Reason*. The two greatest are the *Republic* and the *Critique*. If asked which is the greatest single work in the whole range of thought, many present-day thinkers would name the *Critique*. I should myself name Plato's *Republic*. It ranks with the achievements of Shakespeare and Beethoven, and is still a well-spring of inspiration. More widely known than the poems of Homer and Dante, it is read as no other book in the literature of the world is read, with the exception of the Bible and the plays of Shakespeare.

In the pages which follow I shall deal, as simply as I can, with the life and work of the ten thinkers I have named. In the case of each, I shall try to show in what his essential greatness consists. I ask my readers to place themselves with me, at the creative point of view, and to experience the life and growth of European philosophy from the inside.

RUPERT LODGE

Kingston, 1949

Acknowledgments

MY obligations are many and various; primarily to the Great Thinkers themselves, and to all translators and commentators who have helped to render their books more accessible and more intelligible to present-day readers. I am also much indebted to past teachers and to friends past and present,—with whom I have been privileged to discuss the work of the Great Thinkers. Among such friends I would count many generations of students.

In particular I desire to express my thanks to publishers who have granted permission to quote from works of which they hold the copyright: to the Clarendon Press, Oxford, for permission to quote from the translation of Aristotle of which they are the publishers; to the Houghton Mifflin Company, for permission to quote from certain translations in *Modern Classical Philosophers* (Rand); to the Macmillan Company, for permission to quote from *Contemporary American Philosophy*; to the D. Appleton-Century Croft Co., for permission to quote from J. L. Childs, *Education and the Philosophy of Experimentalism*; and to Longmans Green & Company, for permission to quote from *Whither Mankind?* (ed. C. Beard).

It should perhaps be added that my obligations are equally deep to many from whom I have no occasion to make exact quotations. They and their friends will, I am sure, not fail to recognize the extent to which their influence has pervaded this book.

Chapter I

PLATO 428-348 B.C.

O F the details of Plato's life, little is known, but that little is
significant. Born at Athens in 428 B.C., he lived his long life
in a city of great memories but no prospects. Its brief period
of external power was over, and the leaders who had unified and
directed its policies were no more. Pericles had died before Plato
was born. Alcibiades died in exile while Plato was still a young
man; and the remaining politicians, less brilliant than Alcibiades,
but hardly less unscrupulous, were little more than gang-leaders
fighting among themselves for shadows whose substance had
departed. In this meaningless see-saw of petty politics there
was no place and no attraction for an aristocratic spirit like
Plato's.

His family were conventional aristocrats of long standing with
a pronounced tendency towards direct action. The notorious
Critias, prominent at the time of the "Terror," was his uncle; and
there can be little doubt that the picture, in the *Republic*, of the
family influences brought to bear upon young men of promise, to
induce them to enter public life, is drawn from his own experience.
That something within him responded to this call to leadership is
also undoubted. But the fate of Critias, and the anti-aristocratic
bias of the times, must have made it impossible for any member of
his family to enter upon the usual avenue of service.

His education, up to a point, was the conventional education of
his class. Like Critias, he studied under a sophist and dabbled in
literature. Like Alcibiades, as well as Critias, he became an associate of Socrates, his senior by some forty years, and was initiated
into the fashionable pastime of dialectical refutation. It was not,
however, only for his dialectical acumen and his enigmatic and
attractive personality that Plato admired Socrates, but especially
for his sincerity and moral earnestness; and it was undoubtedly the
greatest shock of his life when the aged Socrates was put to death
by the new democracy. Plato withdrew altogether from Athens,

and spent his early thirties in travel, visiting Egypt, Magna Graecia, and Sicily, acquainting himself with Pythagorean science and forming friendships with idealistic statesmen, until the wound was partly healed over.

Eventually he returned to Athens: to establish, in his Academy, an institution of higher learning; devoting himself to education, and seeking in the world of ideas for the true source of unity and power. His aim was to stimulate and develop leaders and advisers, so trained in mathematics, science, and philosophy as to be entirely superior to political intrigue and self-interest. It was expected by him that they would work towards the establishment, upon earth, of some approximation to the ideal republic whose home is "in heaven." In this, wisdom would rule, disciplined courage would enforce the decrees of wisdom, and harmony would bind together all classes of citizens into a perfect, quasi-family unity. Each member of this family would perform, in the service of the whole, that function for which, by nature and education, he was best fitted, and thus ideal justice, "God's plan for humanity," would be realized.

Such was the ideal to which Plato looked for the salvation of mankind from the gathering storms of social and political disintegration. It was an ideal intended, not for the many, but for the few. In the last resort, Plato depended, for putting it into practice, upon what we should call the "enlightened dictator." Ever since the time of the "seven wise men of Greece" there had been such persons. Athens had its Solon, and Sparta its Lycurgus. There were few cities which did not owe their constitutions to some great lawgiver, and Plato's hope was that somewhere, some time, a ruler would become imbued with the spirit of philosophy, or perhaps some modern "wise man" would be invited to rule, or at least to act as adviser to some ruler. In this hope, he established the advanced studies of his Academy, and published, from time to time, works which were masterpieces of insight and wisdom.

In Plato's later years, Dionysius, a younger man who had acquired power in Syracuse, and conceived himself to be precisely such an "enlightened dictator," did actually invite him to come to Sicily and assist in establishing there the ideal city of his dreams. Plato accepted the invitation and commenced to initiate the dictator into his philosophy. But he also attempted, at the same time, to push the fortunes of a young idealist who was a friend of his.

Local jealousies and intrigues soon produced their usual crop of misunderstandings. The precise details of Plato's adventures, and of his journeyings to and from Syracuse, are obscure and uncertain. In particular, it is hard to believe that he was actually sold into slavery. The story that a former student saw his "old professor" in this condition on the streets of Aegina, bought him up cheap, and sent him back to his teaching again in the Academy, is a little too much for our credulity. But, whatever the details, the attempt, or attempts, resulted in complete failure; and, the adventure over, Plato spent the remainder of his life in the Academy, teaching and writing. His last work, the *Laws*, which was left unfinished, represents a "wise man's" idea of a constitution suitable for some new colony. Philosophical preambles, and considerations of a historical nature, are interspersed throughout the work: and the detailed laws actually formulated combine a regard for the practical with insight into the ideal. These laws have nowhere been adopted *in toto*. But the hope of creating some sort of "Platonopolis" has animated and sustained the efforts of many a reformer; and such legislation, due to the continuing influence of these writings, has left its mark even upon the constitutions of our own day.

The writings attributed to Plato fall into two main groups. His "juvenilia," not seriously different from the juvenilia of other young men with a taste for writing, were apparently burned when he came under the influence of Socrates; and for the rest of his life literary creativity was regarded by him as subordinate to the work of teaching. In connection with his teaching work as head of the Academy, he wrote (1) *Epistles* and (2) *Dialogues*; and what has come down to us under these two heads is regarded by scholars as partly genuine, partly spurious.

Let us glance briefly at the *Epistles*. It is not unreasonable to suppose that, like most men who have spent some years in travel and are administering an institution of higher learning, Plato wrote a number of letters. He would keep in touch with friends of ideas in other parts of the world. He would report upon his plans, would give advice, and would recommend recent graduates of ability. Certain letters of this sort have come down to us, with Plato's name attached to them. Two of them are of some importance: especially the seventh, which contains the account of his relations with Dionysius. But most of them are entirely commonplace, and might have been written by *anyone*. They are without the depth and sympathetic insight which we associate with Plato's genius. And the important letters exhibit such a degree of egoism that scholars are reluctant to suppose that they can have come from the mind which is the source of such sympathetic and artistically finished works as the *Phaedo, Symposium, Republic,* and *Phaedrus.* They are not authenticated by contemporary references; and it is well known that most of the " epistles " attributed to the great men of antiquity are late forgeries. In the past, therefore, it has been the tendency of scholars to regard *all* such epistles, including those attributed to Plato, as spurious.

At the present day, however, it is recognized that such letters as we have might well have come from the somewhat dogmatic and dis-illusioned mind which is the source of the *Laws,* and there is a certain tendency among scholars to accept, wherever possible, rather than to reject. Philosophically, the letters are without impor-tance, except, perhaps, in the passage which speaks of "Plato's secret," which cannot be told in words, even by Plato himself, and certainly not by disciples who, like Dionysius, imperfectly under-stand the Master.

But the great body of the Platonic writings, published by Plato himself, and preserved and interpreted for generations by his successors in the conduct of the Academy, consists of the so-called *Dialogues.* Of those which have come down to us, one or two were recognized as spurious, even in antiquity; and one or two, possibly authenticated by not very convincing references in Aristotle, can only be accepted if we regard them as "early essays" or "imperfect sketches" which reveal the "prentice hand." It is perhaps too much to expect that *all* Plato's genuine writings should be masterpieces. But so very many of them are precisely that that most scholars are quite content to regard mastery of thought and expression as the only adequate criteria of a genuine Platonic Dialogue.[1] Plato invented the genre, and is easily the greatest master of the philo-sophic Dialogue which the world has ever seen.

A Platonic Dialogue has often been compared to a Greek tragedy. As an artist, Plato was obviously influenced by the tragic form. Like the typical tragedy of his time, the typical Dialogue has a prologue,

---

[1] The *Parmenides,* for example, is not authenticated by contemporary references; and its interpretation tends to puzzle and embarrass the most loyal Platonist. But it is a great work, such as no one but Plato could have written. Plato could have written it; and the ancients, accordingly, accepted it as Platonic—and so do most moderns.

an *agon* or contest, with long speeches followed by rapid inter-change of short questions and answers, a variety of episodes, often associated with the introduction of a new interlocutor, sometimes a "messenger"-like report, and usually a termination from which the thought of a "myth" or some overhanging fate, or other sub-stitute for a *Deus ex machina*, is seldom far absent. Most of the Dialogues have a tragic hero; but, unlike the typical heroes of antiquity, the Platonic hero (Socrates) is always a good man. The contest is between good and evil, reason and chaos, rather than merely between personalities; and there is no weeping and wailing, or any undignified behaviour, except on the part of minor charac-ters. Of these differences, Plato was well aware. They are deliberate; and he quite expected that his *Dialogues* would take, in educational institutions, the place occupied, in his own time, by the writings of the Greek tragedians.

CLE. To what pattern should the law-guardian look in deciding what young citizens may or may not study?

ATH. What pattern? The words we have just been speaking [i.e. Plato's *Laws*]. I cannot imagine a better pattern for the law-guardian who is the minister of education. He should prescribe these words, and others like them, as teaching material. He will first compel the teachers to study and approve them, and will commit to such teachers, and such teachers only, the education of the young citizens.[1]

The question is often asked why it is that no one but Plato has been able to write philosophic masterpieces in dialogue form. In the case of other literary forms invented by the Greeks, the epic, the drama, the lyric, the novel, and history, modern literary artists, down to our own times, have been entirely successful. Their works still live and stir us by their consummate art. In philosophy also there have been great and vital thinkers since Plato. But the great thinkers have not written in dialogue form; and as to the writers of philosophy who *have* selected this form, it must be confessed that their dialogues are, in the main, unreadable. They are pedantic, frigid, and dull, even when attempts are made to lighten their heaviness by mixing in literature and wit. Who, without forcing himself, can read Athenaeus or Macrobius? Who can read the dialogues of Bruno without translating them into doctrinal lectures?

[1] *Laws*, 811b–812a, highly condensed. This includes, not only the Platonic *Dialogues*, but works expressing similar sentiments in Hellenic literature, including poetry as well as prose.

And even then . . . And does anyone at all read the modern imitations of Lucian? Even in those whom we recognize as great writers, do we not pass over, as quickly as possible, the pages in which conversation becomes tinged with philosophy? In Balzac's *Études philosophiques*, is it not the narrative which makes the conversations at all tolerable? And in Anatole France, is it not the brevity, quite as much as the wit, which enables us to swallow his propaganda, when this is presented in dialogueform? Even in the case of Plato himself, some of the dialogues are less readable than others. Why is this?

There are a number of reasons, chiefly historical. The Greeks were a nation of talkers, and loved discussion—at least, in Periclean Athens—for its own sake. In the modern world, we have lost the art of philosophic conversation. We have conversation, and we have philosophy; but the two do not, with us, really mix. There is a time, in the middle and later teens, when it seems natural to a few of us to discuss ideas freely. But the time is brief, the numbers are few, and genuine artists who love and can create free discussion in a way which does not bore others are, with us, non-existent. The conditions have changed and we have changed with them. The age of philosophic dialogue is past; and that is why our modern dialogues, even at their best, are unnatural and forced.

Then again, in Plato we find a genuine flow of dialectic. The ideas grow and develop and live before us. They have a vital and dramatic quality, and we live and thrill and grow as we participate, by reading, in their life and growth. But in modern writing, this Platonic art has vanished. Our moderns substitute logic, with its sharp distinctions and classifications, for dialectic. Their ideas are clear and distinct. Each is its own self, and stands out in sharp contrast against the others. The modern artist seems unable to introduce them to one another. They refuse to mix, to live and to grow together. And the result, as in many a formal reception, is a brilliant kaleidoscope, a mosaic whose parts are bright, but the whole is without life. In the plays of Shaw, as long as the intellect holds the stage, nothing happens. It is only when the brilliance has subsided that vital forces, impervious to the shafts of his or anyone else's logic, succeed in dragging in a conclusion *ex machina*. In our modern writers it is what Santayana calls "animal faith" and not "reason" which gets things done. We have the great practical advantages which attach to a highly developed logical technique.

6

But something has been lost; and when our logicians attempt to construct dialogues without the dramatic life-flow which characterized the older dialectic, the results are, as dialogues, failures. Finally, what makes Plato's works so impressive and so humanly attractive is his hero, Socrates. The obvious worth of the man, his sterling character and his tragic destiny, lend to the compositions in which he appears a reality and significance which we seek in vain in our modern dialogues. Many men have lived well, and many men have died well. The age of heroes is always with us. But it is very seldom that such a combination of circumstances occurs as to make an actual human being, in his sincere and noble living and dying, become to us across the centuries an imperishable symbol of ideal truth and absolute justice. So rare, in fact, is such a combination of qualities and events that we have to look to religious martyrdom for a parallel, and indeed to most of us only one such parallel occurs. By the Christian generations which succeeded the decline of Greek civilization, the passage in which Plato describes the fate of the ideally just man in the *Republic*, "scourged, tormented, . . . and last of all, crucified,"[1] was regarded as directly prophetic, the product of an inspiration transcending the resources even of dialectic. Be that as it may, it is undoubtedly the presence of Socrates which lends to the better-known Dialogues their human interest and their universal significance. Dialogues in which he is absent, as in the *Laws*, or is present only as an auditor, as in the *Timaeus* and *Sophistes*, seem relatively dull by comparison with the Dialogues in which he occupies the centre of the stage, and of technical, rather than of general, significance.

Plato's expectation that his *Dialogues* "and other works like them" would take, in institutional education, the place occupied in his own time by selections from the Greek tragedies, has been partly fulfilled. The great tragedies are, indeed, still read, and read with genuine enjoyment by the cultured few, both in school and out of school. This or that great speech is still learnt by heart and also this or that choric ode. A few of the dramas are "revived" now and then, and performed, whether in school or out of school, upon our modern stage. The sculptural beauty of Aeschylus, and the mysterious destiny which broods over his kingly houses, are still found impressive. Euripides, at his best, is almost a modern;

---

[1] *Rep.*, 361e. The word translated (in most English versions) crucified, means literally *impaled*.

and at least one play of Sophocles still draws fair-sized audiences.[1] All persons of education know something of the sorrows of Hecuba, the vengeance of Medea, and the fate of Oedipus. But, for one person familiar with the actual plays, there must be ten who have read the *Defence of Socrates*, and thirty or forty who have studied the *Republic*. The "Socratic Method" has for centuries been a byword in education, and "Platonic Idealism", or "Platonic Realism" is an ever-recurring type, with its adherents even in our most modern philosophizing.

When we look at the contemporary situation, it is with rather more hesitation that we formulate a conclusion. The plays of Shakespeare, both in school and out of school, are far more widely known than the works of Plato or of any other philosophical writer, ancient or modern; and it is easy to jump to the conclusion that "the many," as Plato himself says, are not in any esoteric sense philosophically minded. And yet, as Plato also says, we must beware how we bring such a charge against the public. In fact, if we can bring ourselves to look at the situation less technically, do we not all know that there is much philosophy in Shakespeare, and that many of our most highly gifted modern writers are philosophers, who use the dramatic form largely as a medium for self-expression? A writer like Shaw is a philosopher at least as much as he is a dramatist. We know that he prefers to be treated as a philosopher. Many a page of his plays is almost pure philosophic dialogue, especially if we consider not merely what the characters say, but also what they suggest and imply. The same is partly true of Galsworthy, and at least equally true of an older writer like Ibsen, whose dramas are still influential. It is ideas, even more than persons, whose conflict really makes up the dramatic action in a modern play; and what is left with the modern audience is a germ whose growth is in the direction of philosophic reflection rather than of play-acting. As Shaw says of *Mrs. Warren's Profession*, his plays are fundamentally "sermons," although of an unconventional, or even anti-conventional, type.

And if, in our pursuit of non-technical philosophizing, we go further and consider sermons which *are* of conventional type, we find that the sermons and readings from the Bible which constitute so large a part of the content of our church services are not merely

[1] About as large as the audiences at the plays of Ibsen or Shaw, and with much the same personnel.

philosophic, but almost Platonic. Certain parts of the Gospels and Epistles, both in tone and content, remind us of much that we read in the *Dialogues*. No less an authority than Dean Inge affirms that a great deal of Platonism, especially in its later and more mystical form, has passed over and been taken up into Christianity; and Christianity, as Schopenhauer has told us, is at least "popular philosophy." It is the only philosophy which has ever been genuinely popular, and it has certainly, for a variety of reasons, been more widely influential than the dramas of Shakespeare, Ibsen, and Shaw put together.

On the whole, then, if we are to include non-technical philosophizing under the head of "other works like" the Platonic *Dialogues*, we conclude that Plato's expectation of a very great extension of "philosophy" as an instrument in education has been largely realized. It has been realized, however, not by the comparative extinction of rival art-forms, but by an expansion of philosophy itself so as to lend background and significance to the other forms of imaginative art. We do not nowadays feel that the reflective and the creative spirit are hostile to one another. We do not believe that the reflective spirit is essentially critical, acting as an absolute censor, and laying down the law to creative artists.[1] With us, the two have become organically interwoven, so that our most characteristic modern creations are reflective in tone and outlook.

Let us now approach our subject more closely. One of the *Letters* maintains that the *Dialogues* are essentially dramatic, and present, not "opinions of Plato," but "Socrates made young and handsome." Whether he takes part in the discussion, or merely listens to it, Socrates is always the dominant figure. Let us therefore, with Plato, follow Socrates about and see him at work, among the sophists, among the citizens, among the scientists, and among the philosophers. In this way we shall gradually put ourselves into a position to understand "Plato's secret."

If Plato or any other young man about town wanted to find Socrates, all he had to do was to go wherever young men of ability were congregating: to the Lyceum, to the home of Callias the millionaire, or to the banquet in honour of some prize-winning poet. Wherever such youths were gathered together, Socrates was sure to be found in the midst of them—and almost always, as was

---

[1] As Plato thinks should be done. Cf. *Rep.*, 377b f., 386b f.; *Laws*, 801cd, 817d, 829d.

9

observed, close to the most notable of them. As an older man who had won distinction as a citizen both at home and in the field, he loved to keep in touch with the more promising members of the rising generation, and by his conversation to initiate them into his own kind of reflective citizenship. In this capacity, he was always welcome.

The Lyceum, in the time of Socrates, corresponded roughly to what we should call an athletic club. There were courts in which the young men exercised and played games under professional instructors; and there was a sort of lounge where, in between games, they would sit and converse. As with us, older men, usually *emeriti*, would sit in the lounge and take part in the conversations.[1] When the famous Socrates appeared, the young men gathered around to hear him talk; and his talk was of manliness, self-mastery, the friendship of man with man, and the like. He would select some gifted youth as his interlocutor and ask him questions: bringing out his views and testing their consistency, interesting, and, indeed, educating the entire group so that it would become more reflective, more aware of the problems lurking in connection with the "self," more aware of the necessity of knowledge as a guide to action.

Many of these conversations begin on the way to or from some such club,[2] or on the way to or from some other gathering-place of the young men. Some striking event furnishes the occasion: a torchlight procession, an exhibition-fight in armour, a demonstration of the new rhetoric, or the visit to Athens of some distinguished stranger. The millionaire, Callias, was what we should call a lion-hunter. He collected distinguished foreign intellectuals as other men collect rare books or trophies of the chase. His *salon* was the scene of many a famous debate. One such is preserved for us by Plato in the *Protagoras*.

Callias was entertaining, on this occasion, a large number of visiting lecturers (called "sophists"—the usual term for lecturers), including the great Protagoras, their acknowledged leader, who had just arrived. A certain young man hears of his arrival late that night, and is so eager to study under the distinguished sophist

[1] At Sparta the rule was "Either change into athletic costume, or depart!" but at Athens lounging was customary.
[2] There were, in addition to the Lyceum, a number of such clubs, usually known by the name of the club professional, as in the case of the "Club of Taureas." Sometimes Plato leaves the club unnamed, his interest being in the conversation rather than in its surroundings.

that he calls on Socrates, even before daybreak, to beg him to introduce him to Protagoras, and to urge Protagoras to accept him as a pupil. When it is late enough for a proper call, Socrates takes him to the home of Callias, introduces him as a prospective pupil, and requests Protagoras to explain what, precisely, his teaching will do for the young man. Flattered at being singled out in the presence of so many of his brother professionals, Protagoras proceeds to give what is really an exhibition of his powers. He delivers a long and beautiful set speech in the form of a myth, discusses the interpretation of a poem, and the nature and interrelation of the virtues. The prospective pupil drops into the background, and the conversation is carried on for us by Protagoras and Socrates, with the rest, including ourselves, as interested auditors.

As the younger man, Socrates is always urbane and deferential, asking the gifted professional to help in solving the difficulties in which Socrates, as an amateur, finds himself involved. Protagoras, as the senior man and more experienced teacher, always maintains his prestige, even when congratulating Socrates on what really amounts to a victory over himself. For, in spite of the scrupulous observance of the forms of politeness, it is soon evident, as we see from the remarks of the auditors, as well as of Protagoras, that we are really present at a duel, and a duel between masters, in which something more than personal prestige is at stake.

It is a duel, not merely between Protagoras and Socrates, but between all they stand for. It is more than the older versus the younger generation, the foreigner versus the native son, and the professional lecturer versus the amateur dialectician. It is something far deeper than a conflict between techniques. What Protagoras stands for, although he is a member of the older generation, is *the new humanism* which has swept the intellectuals off their feet: the conviction that not the "reality" of the physical scientists, with their resolution of everything into earth, water, fire, and air, and not the "gods" of poetic tradition, with their imagined caprices and intrigues, but that man himself, with his senses and desires, is to be taken as the standard or measure of values. Protagoras champions the "modern" movement, which regards all standards as postulates, all sciences as arts, and the art of persuasion, of influencing others by rhetoric and psychology, as fundamental. What he, as a teacher, passes on to his pupils is this insight, which makes them at home in the "modern" world, and also the tricks of public speaking and practical psychology, which give them mastery over their fellows. No wonder that his services were in great demand, and that he died a man of wealth.

What Socrates stands for is something far different from the die-hard conservatism which distrusted and loathed Protagoras and all his works. Socrates understands that the hands of the clock cannot simply be put back, and that enlightenment and scepticism have come to stay. Science *is* in its infancy, contentedly playing with its blocks. Religion *is* local and elusive, poetry crystallized by priestcraft into rites and ceremonies. But he understands also that the new humanism is little more than a resurfacing, a cultural veneer which leaves the oldest game in the world, the crude game of beggar-my-neighbour, going on much as before. What Socrates stands for is a scepticism truly radical, an enlightenment so penetrating that it calls, not for a new deal, but for a new kind of game. He challenges the new humanists to show their credentials. Have they the insight into principle which alone could justify their claim to leadership? Or are they, after all, blind leaders of blind followers, seeking only a redistribution of the loaves and fishes of this world?

The new game demanded by Socrates is the game of absolute, never-yielding idealism. To practical psychology and the arts of public speaking, he opposes his vision of ideal co-operation and the dialectical method of pure reason. What the vision requires in detail, Socrates knows that he does not know. But he does know that his method, when brought to bear against those who deny his vision, never fails him. It helps him to think and to speak. In controversy with the sophists, who accept the *status quo* and attempt to justify its lack of principle, he always finds that his appeal to the formal demands of the ideal shows up the essentially chaotic nature of their position. When they speak of the "virtues" in the plural, he always brings up the question of virtue-as-such, the "idea" of virtue. Is not the ideal really one rather than many, a principle essentially single? Is it not impossible to recognize a multiplicity, if one denies, or fails to recognize, unity? How can the sophists speak of "virtues" if they are without insight into virtue itself? How can they speak of beautiful objects if they are without insight into beauty, or of true statements if they deny truth? If consistent orderliness, systematic unity, and self-sufficing finality are inseparable from any attempt to live a rational life, the psychology which ignores them can hardly be so very "practical"

Plato

after all; and if the world is fundamentally rational, the cleverness of the sophist who succeeds in seeing irrationalities everywhere has merely cut him loose from reality. In the end, he is a man without a country, a foreigner in his own home town.

By these and similar questionings, some obviously sincere and others looking at first sight like clever fencing tricks, Socrates leaves the sophists intellectually discredited. They pose as leaders, but have no real knowledge, and are interested in netting fees rather than in discovering truth. They have a certain gift as teachers, but misuse this gift in the interests of an unscrupulous salesmanship. The sophist's "pedigree" is declared to be as follows:[1]

He belongs to the money-making class. His professional skill is in disputation, contention, and controversy. As a debater, he fights for victory. As an artist, he belongs in the class which causes self-contradiction, imitates appearances, and specializes in word-juggling. His creativity is uninspired, all-too-human.

Largely as a result of Socrates' criticism, the word *sophistes* lost its original meaning of "wise man" and acquired the derogatory sense which it has retained to our own time. The professional sophists at Athens lost the honoured status accorded to distinguished visiting lecturers and sank to the position of dependent aliens, eking out a precarious existence by teaching whatever they could induce their pupils to pay for.

In an ancient community, the status of the professional teacher was not high. The nurses, playground attendants, and the "pedagogues" whose original function was to conduct the child to and from school, belonged of course to the class of personal attendants or household servants. The professionals attached to the athletic clubs, who trained pupils in the elements of hygiene, physical sport, and setting-up drill, belonged equally of course to a class whose status was lower than that of the full citizen. The same was true of the teachers of the elements of reading and writing, and of the technicians who drilled children in the rudiments of practical music. Such professionals, one and all, represented an extension of the playground attendant idea. Their function was to train in gymnastics and music, by the method of organized play.

It is to this class of professionals, "foreigners attracted by pay," that the Socratic criticism relegates the sophists. They become poor dependants, occupying an ambiguous position: higher than

[1] Condensed from *Soph.*, 226a, 268c.

13

the household servants whose status is at least definite and certain, but lower than even the least important of the official citizens. Any citizen who may disapprove of the method or content of their instruction is permitted to correct and, if he thinks fit, to strike them. As dependent aliens, they have no legal redress.[1] Like Juvenal's *Graeculus esuriens*, the teacher teaches to order. He is a mere amplifier of his master's voice.[2] The community authorities require the teaching of arts and sciences in order to liberate the minds and characters of the young citizens-to-be. Respect for spiritual freedom and genuine love of truth and beauty are, in the ideal community, a fundamental part of the social background and outlook. They are expected of all citizens. But they are not expected of the teacher. He has before him the humbler ideal of service. Like the poet, who also has gifts which he is not himself competent to direct aright,[3] the sophist, in Socrates' judgment, must submit himself in all things to his betters, the philosophers.

Let us now take a look at Socrates among his fellow-citizens. To the older members of the community, he always appears something of an enigma. They know of his distinguished conduct on the battlefield, and of his independent and conscientious performance of other civic duties. But he stands out as somehow different from the rest. He does nothing positive to advance his own fortunes. Public life he leaves alone, as much as he can; and in private life he has a peculiar tendency to put people to the question. No one who is outstanding, whether in the field of action or in the field of thought and artistic expression, can escape him for long. He is an expert in the new game of questions and answers, and insists upon playing it on all occasions, not only with distinguished foreigners, but with the better-known native sons as well. Just because a citizen

[1] Cf. *Laws*, 808e–809a.
[2] Cf. *Laws*, 811c–812a (cited above, p. 5). Cf. also *Rep.*, 493 (condensed): "The hirelings called 'Sophists' teach nothing beyond the opinion of the many, in convention assembled. This is the entirety of their wisdom. Imagine the keeper of a mighty beast, who feeds him. They are like that. The keeper learns how to approach the beast, how to handle him; what makes him dangerous, and when; what his cries mean; what sounds irritate or soothe him. So the sophist, by continual attention, perfects himself in this sort of thing. He calls his knowledge 'wisdom,' and makes of it a 'system,' an 'art,' which he proceeds to teach. 'Honourable' and 'dishonourable,' 'good' and 'evil,' are (as he believes) simply what agrees with the tastes and tempers of the beast. He cannot give any other account of them. What a teacher!"
[3] Cf. *Rep.*, 377b f., 378e ff., 383c, 386 ff., 392b f., 401b f.; *Laws*, 719b–c, 800b ff., 817d–e; cf. *Phaedr.* 260 f., 262a–c, 274e f., 277c f.

has made a name for himself as a successful general, merchant, lawyer, public speaker, or poet, it does not follow that he is able to define his purpose and function in the community in words which will prove immune to the shafts of the new dialectic; and such citizens, when put to the question by Socrates, find their faculties benumbed and paralysed, as if by an electric shock.

Some of them take this in good part, but others feel that their reputation, which they value highly, is being undermined in some insidious way, and they lose their tempers. When they find that Socrates asks equally awkward questions about the great men of the past, Themistocles, Miltiades, Cimon, and Pericles, conservative-minded citizens rather easily conclude that Socrates is a kind of extreme sophist and radical, and that his perpetually questioning attitude is not only an offence to the old, but a bad influence upon the young. In this way there arises a wave of prejudice against Socrates which makes things difficult for him when he is eventually put on trial for his life.

One, a politician, had a reputation for wisdom. But, as I talked with him, I could not help thinking him not really wise. I explained to him that he thought himself wise, but was really not. What was the consequence? I made several enemies among those who heard me.

After the politicians, I went to the poets. On the strength of their poetry (the meaning of which they did not understand), they believed themselves very wise in other matters—in which they were not wise.

At last I came to the artisans. They were indeed good workmen, but thought that, because of this, they also had knowledge of all sorts of important things—a weakness that overshadowed their wisdom.

This questioning led to my making many enemies: dangerous enemies.[1]

The younger members of the community, on the other hand, like to follow Socrates around and watch him at work. It amuses them to see great reputations and legends-in-the-making being "debunked," and they do not mind his critical method being turned, at times, upon themselves. They feel that Socrates takes a genuine interest in the younger generation, and that his method helps them to reflect, to think for themselves, and to develop the power which comes with self-knowledge. They are themselves passing through the questioning stage, and see nothing either inappropriate or dangerous in a way of questioning which leads to a more reflective type of citizenship than they find exemplified in

[1] *Apol.*, 21c–23a, highly condensed.

the older generation. The seriousness of Socrates impresses and attracts them. He is, in some sort, their leader and spokesman, and they are his willing disciples.

So much for the ways in which his fellow-citizens regard Socrates. How does he regard them, and what does he wish to make of them, with his many questionings? His own way of stating his "mission" in life is in relation to the Delphic Oracle that "Socrates is the wisest of the Greeks." Conscious that his own knowledge and wisdom hardly rises above the zero level, he wonders whether "Apollo" means that the other Greeks, whose knowledge of the arts and sciences is so much greater than his own, may in some sense know even less than himself. Accordingly he conceives it his mission to question those who seem to know most, in order to find out whether their knowledge is, or is not, genuine. He finds no really grounded knowledge in them, and concludes that, in mistakenly supposing that they know, they are, in truth, less wise than himself. For he at least is under no illusion as to his own lack of positive knowledge.

My questioning has encouraged calumny. My hearers call me "wise" —fancying that the wisdom I find lacking in others, I myself possess. But what is the truth? Only God is wise. What does the oracular response mean? Surely, that the wisdom of man is little worth. Apollo does not mean that Socrates is wise. Using my name to illustrate, his point is that a wise man is one who (like Socrates) knows how truly worthless his "wisdom" is.

And so I go up and down, examining the "wisdom" of anyone who is thought wise: vindicating the oracle by showing that he is not wise— where that is the case. My unceasing practice is to teach philosophy. I exhort my hearers to care more for wisdom, for truth and improvement of the soul, and to be ashamed of heaping up riches and honour and reputation. If a man says he does care for wisdom, I put him to the question; and if I think he has no virtue in him, but only says he has, I reproach him. This is what I say to everyone, and especially to my fellow-citizens who are my brothers. This is what Apollo commands; and I believe that my service to the God is the greatest good which has happened to Athens.

What I do is to persuade you all, in the first place, to have care for the soul and its improvement. I tell you that virtue is not given by money. Virtue is the source of all other goods, private or public. This is my "doctrine." I am a sort of gadfly divinely attached to Athens. All day long I fasten upon you . . .[1]

[1] *Apol.*, 22e–31a, condensed.

Plato

In dealing with the younger generation, his position is that, being in a state of ignorance, he questions them in the hope of having his ignorance replaced by knowledge. When they admit their own ignorance, he induces them to join him in a co-operative quest: they are to furnish the positive suggestions, and he will test them by his dialectical questionings. The results are, as a rule, negative, but the conclusion is, not that knowledge is unattainable, but that renewed and more persistent efforts are needed. In dealing with the younger men, then, he tends to make them more self-critical, more persistently reflective, in a word, philosophers.

This is my art of midwifery: Like midwives, I am myself barren. The God compels me to be a midwife, but does not allow me to bear children myself. I am not wise. I have nothing to show which is the creation or birth of my own soul. It is the souls of others upon which I attend: of men, when their souls are in labour. I examine the thought which the young are bringing to birth, to see if it is true and noble.

Those who converse with me sometimes seem dull enough at first. But as our acquaintance matures, they progress astonishingly, if the God is gracious. From me they learn nothing. The fine discoveries to which they hold fast are all of their own making. It is their delivery that they owe to me (and to the God).[1]

He does not, however, expect them to become philosophers like himself, mere questioners, spiritual "gadflies" to their fellow-citizens; but rather that, by looking always for further positive suggestions, they should eventually discover the elements of positive truth which lie deep down in their own nature. It is significant that his better-known pupils developed along different lines: all, however, in directions which would be called positive. He helped them to be their genuine selves, and to have a very clear idea as to what they could contribute to the life of the community. Before his questioning, they merely wished, in a vague general way, to have a good time, and to do well for themselves and their friends in the community. After his questioning, they were very clearly and distinctly aware of their detailed powers and limitations, and thought of the community as a sphere in which, while being completely themselves, they might find and occupy a place which would be of positive social value, co-operating with their fellows in making the life of the group as a whole thoroughly worth while.

[1] *Theaet.*, 150b–d, condensed and partly transposed.

The Great Thinkers

Let us now consider Plato's portrait of Socrates among the scientists. As a young man, Socrates is represented as "prodigiously interested" in the work of the Ionian scientists. Like them, he wondered whether fire, or air, or water was the underlying substance whose changes produced the various phenomena of nature. In particular, he asked himself how change and growth of all sorts was to be explained. As he was puzzling over these questions, he heard someone reading, from a book by Anaxagoras, that the ultimate principle was really Mind. This intrigued him to such an extent that he secured a copy of the book and read it eagerly. He expected that Anaxagoras would show that the elements and their interactions in the universe depended upon some "principle of the best," and this would have completely satisfied him. But he was terribly disillusioned to find that Anaxagoras was just another physicist, having recourse to mechanical principles wherever possible. In his disillusionment, he withdrew from concrete inquiries into physical science, and devoted himself to ethical inquiries, in which the "principle of the best" was obviously the dominant principle. This became his major occupation, but in later life he was still competent to listen with enjoyment to a philosophic scientist's account of creation, and we find him, in Plato's picture, understanding perfectly such scientific applications of the "principle of the best" as are expounded in the *Timaeus*.

The study of science has for Socrates, as we learn from the *Republic*, an educational value which is entirely distinct from the theoretical interest in the discovery of concrete laws, and also from the practical value of applied science to the community. It liberates the minds of students from excessive preoccupation with practical needs and with the sensory side of experience. The pure scientist lives in a world of ideal formulations and laws which transcend everyday interests and sensory experience. Prolonged study of science familiarizes the student with intellectual ideas, and especially with the disinterested ideal of truth as a dominant motive in human life. The study of science thus has an effect upon character which is permanent and is of great importance in the development of citizens who are swayed by far-reaching ideals rather than immediate impulses.

While scientific study, as such, has this educational value, Socrates further recognizes two ways of studying science. The first is empirical, starting from a foundation in sensory observation and
18

experimentation, and is illustrated by the practice of the "so-called Pythagoreans." This method leads to the discovery of empirical laws, which are then systematized, and, in accordance with the nature of the mathematical system employed, are formulated with an abstract exactitude which goes a little further than sensory experimentation can entirely verify. Here Pythagorean science stops. It has two sources, (1) sensation, and (2) the demands of systematic formulation in terms of mathematics. The two are not entirely in harmony, but the Pythagorean scientist remains satisfied with giving to his empirical observations a mathematical form. It is, however, not hard to see that there is a possibility of going further. The demands of system, which are only incompletely met by the Pythagorean physicist, culminate in the gradual establishment of a number of systems, imperfectly integrated and not in complete harmony with one another. If we could discover a single ultimate principle which went a little beyond the principles used by the scientists, it might be possible to harmonize the principles and results of all the sciences, and to convert them all into parts of a single, perfectly harmonious system of knowledge. In this way, in place of physics, we should have metaphysics, the ultimate account of reality.

Students of such sciences as arithmetic and geometry *assume* "odd," "even," "figures," three kinds of "angle," and suchlike. These are their "hypotheses." Everyone is supposed to know them. In their scientific reasonings, what they think of is not the actual figures drawn on paper. They are trying to intuit what can only be seen with the mind's eye, the things themselves: the absolute square, the absolute diameter, etc.

But such reasonings, where the starting-point is merely assumed without rising to a principle, are not the work of the *higher* reason. It is only when a first principle is added that the higher reason comes into play. The higher reason uses such assumptions (not as something you just take for granted, but) as steps, points of departure into a world which is above hypotheses. By this method the soul is able to soar above its assumptions to the first principle of the whole. Holding fast to this principle and to what is immediately dependent upon it, and taking successive steps, the soul descends again, without the aid of sense-perceivable diagrams. It starts from absolute ideas. It proceeds from one such idea to another throughout; and it is without leaving the field of absolute ideas that its procedure terminates. This is a tremendous task.[1]

[1] *Rep.*, 510c–511d, condensed.

Such a principle Socrates formulates, in the *Republic*, as the "idea of good." It transcends the possibility of verification in terms of sensory experience, and the ideal realm in which, with its aid, the dialectician makes himself at home, is explored, not by science, but by philosophy. Starting with the idea of good, i.e. the principle of the best, the philosopher constructs a system of ideally perfect concepts, and never descends to the empirical world at all. As a philosopher, he remains for ever in "the true Above."

The second way of studying science is when the philosopher, deserting his purely deductive system, proceeds to apply his vision to the details of the actual world, mingling pure thought and sensuous observation, whether in the field of physical or of social science. This "descent into the cave," or mingling of transcendental and empirical, is spoken of as "employment of the philosopher's leisure," when applied to the field of physics. It is a "noble employment," but, as compared with his primary task of exploring the ideal realm itself, is of secondary significance. When applied to the field of social science, the "descent into the cave" is, from the philosopher's standpoint, of equally secondary significance. But the philosopher is not only a pure thinker. He is also a man, living with other men, subject to human needs and social pressure; and it is to his interest, as a man and a citizen, to see that the community of which he is a member is well administered. From Socrates' standpoint, such a man is drafted into the service of the community, and is induced, by social pressure, to apply his powers to the empirical art of government. Social science is applied philosophy, and the results, while the best attainable in a given *milieu*, are never, of course, as exact as the results attained when thought is confined to the ideal realm of philosophy.

Socrates thus recognizes two sorts of scientist: (1) those who have not yet realized the philosopher's vision, but are interested in making generalizations and discovering detailed laws which do not depart any great distance from their base in sensory experience; and (2) philosophic scientists, who apply their transcendental insight to empirical situations, and bring system to bear upon particular cases, in spite of the gap between the ideal and the merely actual. Socrates desires the education of the select students, who are to furnish the leadership material for the community, to be conducted under the supervision of those who have achieved philosophic insight. His aim is to turn out not empirical scientists, men of the Pythagorean stamp, but "wise men," men who are not only masters of science, but are also masters of the arts needed in guiding a community aright.

Mathematical sciences only dream about *being*. As long as they employ assumptions accepted without examination, they cannot behold the waking reality. When a man's first principle is unknown by him, and when his conclusion, and the steps leading to it, are constructed out of—he knows not what: how can such a web of convention ever become true science?

Dialectic is the only science which does away with assumptions in order to make the ground secure. It uses the mathematical sciences as ancillary to its purposes. The dialectician attains a conception of the essence of each thing; and he is able to impart this concept. Until we can abstract and define the idea of good rationally, we apprehend only a shadow. Dialectic is the keystone of the arch of the sciences, the *ne plus ultra* of knowledge.[1]

Let us now picture Socrates among the philosophers. In Plato's pages, he is represented as associated somewhat closely with members of the Pythagorean Brotherhood, and as sympathetically disposed towards their cult on its more mystical side. Their other-worldliness, their tendency to regard the body as the "sepulchre of the soul," and their belief that the philosopher's business is to study how to die to the empirical world of the senses, in order to live as a member of the transcendental realm, is akin to something in Socrates'ı own nature. That is to say, the religious and social side of Pythagoreanism has a definite attraction for him. But when we inquire into the intellectual basis of his beliefs, we find it represented unequivocally as original. "Tell me, Socrates," asks the aged Parmenides, "was this theory your own idea?" "Yes," is the reply.

The reference here is to the "theory of ideas" usually associated with the name of Plato. In this theory, Socrates definitely rejects the Pythagorean doctrine as to the status of the actual world experienced via the senses. The Pythagoreans taught that our life on earth was a mere shadow, an illusory appearance, an image devoid of reality. It copied or "imitated" transcendental existence, but was essentially empty and meaningless. All that a man of

---

[1] *Rep.*, 533c–534e, considerably condensed.

intelligence could do with this life on earth was to see through its pretences and allurements, and withdraw from it, to flee t the transcendental realm and never return.

What Socrates did was to substitute, for this theory of "imitation," his theory of "participation." According to Socrates, our life can participate or share directly in the reality of the transcendental realm of ideal patterns. Our actions in social living here on earth, in the family, in society, and in politics, if we form them upon the pattern of ideal justice, participate, to precisely that extent, in ideal justice, and become truly and really just. Our productions in the field of art, in dancing, in music, in poetry, in painting and the other plastic arts, in so far as they are formed upon the pattern of ideal beauty, acquire a genuine share of ideal beauty, and become, to precisely that extent, really and truly beautiful. Life so formed upon ideal patterns thus becomes more than the Pythagoreans supposed. It becomes more than an empty image, mirroring, but in no sense taking up into itself, the reality of the transcendental world. By participating in ideal reality, our life becomes actually, to that precise extent, really based and truly vital. If all we can say of a man is that he is "an Athenian," "a Theban," or "a Spartan," he is, of course, little more than a geographic expression, one more figure in the census returns for his locality. But if we can say that he lives in the spirit of ideal citizenship, then, whatever his earthly city, he is a marked man, with a reality and value superior to the accidents of time and place.

It is in this life of reflective citizenship that Socrates is interested, and he believes that the road which terminates in this way of living is the road which has passed through the territory of philosophy. Philosophy, for Socrates and those like him,[1] is essentially reflection upon the nature, both in principle and in detail, of the ideal realm. On its theoretical side, such philosophizing culminates in a thorough grasp of the principle of this realm, the principle of ideality or systematic unity, referred to in the *Dialogues* as the "principle of the best," or "idea of good." On its practical side, philosophy is an art. Pure philosophy is the art of creative reflection, exploring dialectically the possibilities open to speculative

[1] Plato makes a sharp distinction between men whom we should call "crass materialists," who are completely unphilosophical, and those whom he calls "friends of ideas." Under the term "friends of ideas," I understand Plato to include *all* whom he recognizes as "philosophers," namely, Socrates and those like him, whether they are also members of the Pythagorean, Eleatic, Academic, or any other "school."

thought, and constructing the formal outlines of an ideally perfect world. This is the metaphysical world presupposed by pure mathematics, pure physics, pure ethics, and pure civics. An ideally perfect physical world would be a world constructed out of elements themselves ideally perfect, the tetrahedra, octohedra, eikosihedra, and cubes discovered as ideal type-forms by (Pythagorean) mathematics. These elements would be thought of as enclosed within an ideally perfect (Parmenidean) sphere, and as working upon one another in accordance with laws of motion derived ultimately from the eternal rotation of the sphere. An ideally perfect social world would be a community constructed out of the type-forms ideally inherent in humanity, the philosophers, fighters, and workers of all sorts required in an ideally perfect community, interacting in such ways and such numbers as are needed for the maximal realization of the potentialities of physical, moral, and spiritual life.

Such exploration and such construction are the specific business of the philosopher, and there are further problems inherent in his activity, problems indicated and touched upon by Socrates and his fellow-seekers, but not receiving exhaustive treatment. How are the ideas related to numbers and to active causes? How far is there a principle of difference and variety, as well as of identity and simplicity, inherent in philosophic reason itself? How far is the principle of ideality susceptible of application to the ignoble, the ugly, and the insignificant? How is the philosopher to account for the misuse of reason, for atheism, and for the existence of evil? Such problems are not only severe in quality, but are inexhaustible in number; and the task before the pure philosopher is thus not only important, but also unending.

In addition to the severe discipline of pure philosophy, there is also the lighter, but not less intriguing, task of applied philosophy which coincides largely with applied science. Just as there is applied mathematics, so there are applied physics, applied ethics, and applied civics. The mingling of pure thinking and sensory experience which occurs when we endeavour to apply, under the conditions of concrete empirical living, the theoretical deductions of pure philosophy, can never be exact and theoretically satisfying. In the actual universe, as opposed to the realm conceived in pure thought, there is always a chaotic and untamed residue. The actual world in which we live our earthly life may have somehow taken on some approximation to the mathematically satisfactory shapes of the tetrahedra and cubes of pure physics. But behind those smooth surfaces there continues to lurk something non-rational, something wild and barbaric, something liable, at times, to burst out and overwhelm the neat and orderly, small-town Hellenic system.

So too in the social field. It is possible to think out, in abstraction from the conditions of actual living, an ideal social system, a pure community in which ideal selves would be able to co-operate for the best. But actual, flesh-and-blood men and women are so far from perfection that they can never be expected, in practice, to live up to the ideal regulations of such a system. There is, in men, a wild and untamable element. In the best of us, according to Socrates, it merely pushes to the surface in forbidden wish-dreams.[1] But in most of us, however well-behaved and cultured we may appear in public and on formal occasions, it torments and plagues unceasingly, and takes every opportunity it can to thwart and make a mock of the ideals of perfect reason. This struggle between the forces of reason and unreason, between Hellenism and Barbarism, is unending; and, while it is a conflict in which the philosopher, like other merely human beings, is inevitably involved, it does not satisfy the demands of his nature for perfect self-realization. Only the ideal would do that. Applied philosophy, then, while inevitable, is always felt by the philosopher to be of secondary value and interest, as contrasted with pure philosophy. It is better to guide human effort by philosophy than to leave it to unguided instinct; but even the best of us can never, in practice (as opposed to theory), attain finally to a position *au dessus de la mêlée*.

In Plato's *Dialogues*, Socrates is pictured, for the most part, as in the human arena, playing a man's part in this unending struggle between the forces of ideal good and the forces which make for chaos and unreason. When the discussion rises to the heights of pure philosophy, Socrates usually shows that he has himself wrestled, and wrestled not unsuccessfully, with the problems involved. But his characteristic modesty frequently, and especially in the later *Dialogues*, reduces him to silence. He listens to the arguments of more technical philosophers, and says not a word, or speaks only formally. But his silence, however appreciative, does not represent incompetence. Socrates silent is still Socrates; and we always feel his presence, not only with its magnetism and intellectual sympathy, but also with its tendency in the direction of

[1] *Rep.*, 571c f.

stubborn criticism. When the great Parmenides discourses upon his theme of "the One," who is there who is not conscious of the criticism, as well as of the admiration, although it remains unspoken? When the Eleatic Stranger lays hands upon "his father, Parmenides," or forces the keen wedge of his analytic distinctions through series after series of technical dichotomies, who does not feel that the new technique derives its importance and philosophic significance, not from itself, but from the fact that it is being applied, in Socrates' presence, to an extension of Socrates' own problems? What is Plato's metaphysics of the "soul" but an extension of Socrates' insistence upon the importance of cultivating a reflective self, and what is his "royal science" but an extension of Socrates' struggle to improve the character of government in his beloved Athens?

We are now in a position to approach what has been called "Plato's secret." Concretely, this is, of course, "Socrates made young and handsome," Socrates living and working, philosophizing and turning others into philosophers, passing on to them the spirit of self-criticism and creative speculation, and turning them into "friends of ideas." The "secret" is neither more nor less than the Socratic spirit, passed on from generation to generation, not by some symbolic laying on of hands, but by living and working with the Master.

On the essence of my philosophy, a good deal has been written: by pupils of mine, by pupils of other teachers, and by some who think they have found out my secret by themselves. Of all such I have this to say: It does not matter who they are or what they write—and this applies to the future quite as much as to the past—the mere attempt to reduce my teaching to a formula, to write it down in words, demonstrates complete and utter misunderstanding. For the thing simply cannot be done. I have never attempted it myself, and I never shall; for philosophy is not like other things that men study. In other fields there is a definite content which can be set down in words and so passed on from teacher to pupil. But the spirit of philosophy is not a content. It cannot be reduced to any verbal formula. When teacher and pupils of philosophy associate intimately in their researches, so that their life is one life: in this continuous merger of personality, something happens. As an inner glow kindles and becomes a leaping flame: even so the philosophic spirit within the soul comes to a spontaneous birth; and it develops and grows by self-nurture.[1]

[1] *Epist.*, 341b f.; cf. *Phaedr.*, 276b f.; *Laws*, 968d f.

That is why Plato uses, as his medium of expression, not description or narration, but dramatic representation: so that we too can live and work with the Master, sharing his experiences and participating in his spirit. That is why, even at the present day, whether we are ourselves learning to appreciate the philosophic spirit, or to pass it on to our pupils, enriched, as it is, by so many centuries of continuous reflection and speculation, co-operative personal intercourse seems so essential; and that is why, if we are thrown upon books rather than persons, we find few books in philosophic literature so helpful as precisely these dramatic portrayals in which Socrates converses and still lives. Plato's secret is a living and personal secret. But is it necessarily confined to Socrates and his contemporaries? Is it not imparted to all those readers of the *Dialogues* to whom Plato still does something, kindling anew in them the philosophic spirit?

A different way in which Plato's secret receives expression is in such formulations of the highest good as "goodness of character," "the life of the philosophic guardian," "philosophy," and "the life of the mind," "happiness," "religion," and "participation in the life of the immortals." Such formulations, in the *Dialogues*, represent, one and all, the living spirit of philosophy, which may be passed on to others and possessed by them. These formulations contain no explicit reference to the historic Socrates; and yet they. clearly remain concrete qualities of living persons. Does not this mean that "Socrates and those like him," i.e. all persons who live in the spirit of philosophy, are in possession, whether aware of it or not, of Plato's secret?

And here a further question will be asked. Cannot this process of abstraction be carried even further? Cannot logical analysis abstract entirely from the personality, whether of Socrates or of any other subjective individual, and formulate in objective and impersonal concepts the fundamental elements involved in "the philosophic spirit" as such? It should not be beyond the range of our powers to discover a scientific definition of the essence of happiness, mind, guardianship, immortality, and the rest. A good deal of Plato's work in the *Dialogues* consists, surely, in defining, at least approximately, just these terms. In fact, to put the matter in a nutshell, the principle of ideality, or "idea of good," formulated abstractly in the Sixth Book of the *Republic*, has usually been regarded as the essence of "Plato's secret." And when we look closely into the matter, we seem to discover that abstract formulations of "the mean" and "the excellence of the whole" can be equated with the principle of ideality. In the end, we cannot deny that the principle of ideality is manifested in every single "idea," and the question forces itself upon us as to whether, if we have eyes to see, Plato's "secret" does not smile out at us from every page of his writings, even when the discussion is impersonal and abstract.

To this question, the answer is not entirely simple. It is true that, if we have eyes to see, i.e. if we are endowed with the Socratic spirit, Plato's secret smiles out at us from every page of his writings. But it is a secret smile, visible only to initiates, to those who are truly friends of ideas. The logical analyst, as such, with his external and impersonal technique, notes that Socrates attempts to discover logical definitions, impersonal formulations of this or that virtue or excellence. He may even, as Aristotle does, think that the search for concepts and definitions, in the limited field of ethics, constitutes the characteristic activity of Socrates. But if he is merely a logician, his investigations conclude with the strange result that Socrates' attempt always ends in failure. If the *Charmides* represents an attempt to discover a logical definition of "temperance" or "self-knowledge," it certainly ends in admitted failure. If the *Laches* is understood as the attempt to define "courage," it too ends in admitted failure. So too the First Book of the *Republic* registers a failure to define the nature of justice; the *Theaetetus* registers failure after failure to define the nature of knowledge; and every one of the characteristic "Socratic Dialogues" concludes with a similar confession of "Socratic ignorance," an admitted failure to establish logical definitions of the excellences investigated.

This is an astonishing result, so astonishing that nine-tenths of Plato's modern interpreters refuse to accept it. They prefer to assume that Socrates is being "ironical," that he really knows the answers to his questions, and does not need the co-operation of his interlocutors to help him out. They treat him as the ideal teacher, who encourages the pupil to think for himself, and never "tells" him the answer. In some cases, they make no pronouncement about *Socrates*, but are convinced that *Plato* knows the answer, and that he furnishes hints which are intended to indicate, to the careful reader, just what the right answer is.

The assumption, which lies at the base of all such interpretations,

The Great Thinkers

that a writer like Plato has constructed a text-book of elementary
philosophy, consisting of problems or questions to which there are
"right" answers, and that a modern teacher can publish a "key
to Plato," a set of right answers, to be pasted into the back of the
book and utilized tutorially, is a typical example of what might be
called "the schoolmaster's fallacy." The whole attitude of mind
involved is alien to Plato's spirit. We can see this when we realize
that, even where an answer which the commentator regards as
"right" is given, it is treated by Socrates in exactly the same way
as any other answer. The interest is not in the answers or definitions put forward, but in the discussion; not in the rightness or
wrongness of the conclusions, but in the spiritual growth effected
by co-operation in research, in the life of Socratic friendship.

It takes something more than logical analysis, however shrewd
and thorough, to realize that the essence so vainly sought in the
quest for formal definitions is so completely present in the persons
of those engaged in the quest. Not only is Socrates himself a perfect
living example of the excellence in question; but those engaged
with him in the quest, his philosophic comrades, are also living
examples of the vital qualities which can never be depersonalized.
Charmides, discussing "modesty" with Socrates, participates
directly in the idea of modesty; and in their conjoint search
for self-knowledge, he is already in process of becoming reflective. Laches and Nicias, joining with Socrates in the search for
the essence of courage, while failing to agree upon an impersonally
satisfactory formula, are clearly developing and deepening their
own participation in the living essence of courage. Theaetetus,
unable, like Socrates, to define "knowledge" in a way which will
withstand criticism, is, even as he fails, almost the personification of
the knowledge-seeking and knowledge-finding spirit, entering into
the deepening process of shared experience which is the living
essence of knowing.

Plato's secret, which cannot be told, is like a virtue which cannot
be defined. It is what links Socrates and his interlocutors, as they
develop and grow before our eyes, and indeed add us to their
number, when we too fall under the spell. Plato's secret is not
abstract and logical, a definition in words, but is concrete and vital,
the spiritual growth which comes with the deepening of shared
philosophic experience. To the reading of Plato's *Dialogues* we
may come as strangers. But when we have once yielded to their

28

charm and have become, like Plato himself, disciples of Socrates and interlocutors in his conversations, we too have become initiates. We too have become members of that spiritual Academy of Friends whose creation is, precisely, Plato's secret and his great achievement. Wherever there is shared philosophic experience, wherever mind meets with mind in spiritual growth, whether in reading the *Republic* and *Theaetetus*, or (tell it softly) in studying the *Essay on Human Understanding* and the *Critique of Pure Reason*, Plato's secret still exercises its power and leads us more deeply into the life of the real spirit.

Chapter II

ARISTOTLE 380-317 B.C.

As the fame of Plato's Academy spread, students from all over the Hellenic world were attracted to the new fellowship, and grouped themselves, as disciples and associates, under the Master. Amongst others, a young man from Macedonia took an enthusiastic part in the life of Platonic friendship, with its intimate discussions and inspired publications. From his seventeenth to his thirty-seventh year, Aristotle was a disciple of Plato, and when, after Plato's death, he withdrew to the Troad and associated himself with a few of the Friends there, he still considered himself an undoubted Platonist, continuing, without a break, the work inspired by Plato's leadership.

But of what Plato was he the disciple? Not the writer of the great *Dialogues* upon which Plato's fame in the later world chiefly rests. The *Symposium*, *Phaedo*, and *Republic* were all in the past. The vein of Socratic inspiration which had carried Plato through the creation of masterpiece after masterpiece was being abandoned in favour of critical reflection and dialectical discussion. Plato had become a teacher rather than a writer. In his later years, he would subject the most intimate and passionate creations of his genius to the cool analysis of his students, illustrating the principles of speech-making in quasi-text-book fashion, and criticizing the value of the written word *überhaupt*. Are there, he further asks, such entities as "Platonic (or Socratic) Ideas," or can this view be neglected or refuted? Are the hypotheses and methods of other schools in a stronger position? Is mathematics, perhaps, the truly fundamental science, fundamental for the understanding, not only of nature, but also of mind and the "ideas"? If sensory observation is discarded, can reality be caught in a network of categories and dialectical subdivision of concepts, with standards of measurement which are purely ideal, or are concepts separate and apart from reality? Is the gap between ideal and actual such that it can only be bridged by *force majeure*, a dictator on earth and a Divine Artificer in heaven?

30

The students who participated in these and similar discussions were very different from what Plato had been in his youth. Detached and coolly impersonal, the enthusiasm of the rising generation was given, not to the Socrates whom they had not known, but to some idealized Anaxagoras or Pythagoras, who seemed to them to personify the spirit of methodic, rational inquiry. If Plato was their spiritual father, and their fellow-students were their brethren, it was the new science which was their mother; and while all believed in some transcendental principle, some metaphysical purpose in the ultimate realms of thought, it was in saving the appearances in the realm of sense, in understanding in detail the world around them, that most of them were especially interested. In the midst of corruption and social disintegration, science alone seemed pure and solid. Its triumphs were permanent, and their fellowship in the work of scientific discovery seemed to offer to each of them opportunities and vistas to which there was no limit.

In the teaching of the Academy, it was not necessary, for the most part, for the disciples to agree with their master. Socrates had never tried to turn his adherents into little replicas of himself. He helped them to become, more completely than would otherwise have been possible, their own selves. So too with Plato. For himself, Plato continued to believe in some quasi-mathematical basis for the "ideas" of his Socratic period. As the numbers of arithmetic are carved out of some "indeterminate twoness" or plurality by successive applications of the determining principle of unity, so each "idea" represents the application, to the matter of knowledge, which, *per se*, is unlimited or infinite, of the principle of the limit; and if mathematics is the fundamental science, it may well be, he thought, that all "ideas," in whatever field of inquiry, are ultimately reducible, without remainder, to mathematics. But while some such belief was maintained, to the end, by Plato, it was always left open to his students "in friendly rivalry" to adopt, after discussion, alternative hypotheses. Eudoxus, who, as an independent scientist, associated himself with the life and work of the Academy, never accepted many of the Platonic tenets; Speusippus, who succeeded Plato in the work of guiding the researches of the Friends, followed the gleam cast by some mythical Pythagoras-figure into a realm of mathematical speculation upon the properties of the first four numbers, in a way peculiar to himself. Aristotle, apparently from the first, found his realist temperament offended by what seemed to him the gratuitous hypothesis of "ideas" which were separate from matter and inaccessible to empirical observation. But these differences, fundamental as they were to prove in the end, did not at first seem sufficient to divide Aristotle from the rest of the Friends, and for many years he continued to write as one entitled to regard himself as a genuine disciple of Plato.

During his years as a member of the Academy, Aristotle published a number of quasi-Platonic Dialogues, known as his "exoteric" works, in some of which he himself figured as an interlocutor. The remains which have come down to us of the *Protrepticus* or *Invitation to Philosophy*, as well as of the *Dialogue on Philosophy*, reveal an enthusiast for the new science whose personal religious problem seems solved by adherence to the transcendental portions of Platonism. Indeed, the note of sustained religious enthusiasm sounds oddly in the ears of those to whom Aristotle represents the impersonal spirit of inquiry *par excellence*. It seems, however, entirely genuine, and shows that Aristotle's God, "pure thought thinking itself," the "unmoved mover" who draws the world "as the beloved draws the lover," is the twin brother of Plato's "idea of good" or "principle of the best" when viewed under the (Aristotelian) category of Substance. This adherence to the principle of ultimate, transcendental purpose in the world remains to the end characteristic of one side of Aristotle's life and thought, even when his interest in scientific detail appears, in terms of a more modern logic, to demand revision or rejection of anything savouring of transcendentalism.

During Aristotle's stay at Assos in the Troad, and later in Macedonia, where he was appointed tutor to Alexander, the criticisms and counter-criticisms which passed between himself and the Academy gradually estranged him more and more. At first, he regarded himself as the exponent of true Platonism, after the ideal theory was rejected; but gradually he came to regard Platonism, not only in the form lent to it by Speusippus and Xenocrates, but in its original form which rested, as he understood it, on a complete separation of the "idea" from actuality, as mistaken. Plato had supposed that the only alternative to transcendental idealism was sensuous materialism of a somewhat crude type. Aristotle believed that he had discovered a new alternative, a realm of forms not separate from, but incorporated in, matter. For him, the beautiful realm in which the soul of man is at home was thus not the transcendental, but the actual empirical world, containing "forms" which are not a few abstract types, but are strictly concrete, and are discovered to be more and more numerous.

After this discovery, the work of Aristotle falls, roughly speaking, into two parts. First, he constructs a philosophy of concrete forms, criticizing Plato's ideal abstractions and reducing them without remainder to concrete concepts. Where Plato suggests the vision of an ideal city "in heaven," to guide the administrative work of his philosopher-kings, Aristotle constructs a composite picture of the ways in which actual human beings most efficiently deal with their concrete problems.

In the light of the constitutions we have collected, let us study what sorts of influence preserve and destroy states, and what sorts preserve or destroy the particular kinds of constitution, and to what causes it is due that some are well and others ill administered. When these have been studied we shall perhaps be more likely to see with a comprehensive view which constitution is best, and how each must be ordered, and what laws and customs it must use, if it is to be at its best.[1]

Where Plato holds up the ideal of insight to a level at which it is identical with an ideal wisdom which none can hope to realize, Aristotle analyses the term into the grasp of practical handling of general problems, which makes a man a good householder and citizen, or, in extreme form, a good political counsellor.

Philosophic wisdom is different from practical wisdom. Anaxagoras, Thales, and men like them have philosophic, but not practical wisdom. They know things that are remarkable, admirable, difficult, and divine —but useless, because it is not human goods that they seek. Practical wisdom on the other hand is concerned with things human, things about which it is possible to deliberate, goods that can be brought about by action, particular concrete things, and not merely with universal principles. For practice is concerned with particulars; and that is why men who have experience are sometimes more practical than theorists, whose knowledge is confined to universal principles. Practical wisdom needs both knowledge of principles and experience of particulars; but of the two, experience is the more important.

Practical wisdom is identified especially with realizing what is good for oneself. Other species of it are concerned with the management of a

[1] *Eth. Nic.*, 1181b 16–23, tr. W. D. Ross. In citing passages from Aristotle, I quote or in certain cases condense from the complete English translation published by the Clarendon Press, Oxford (with permission).

household, with the judicial function, with the legislative function, and with deliberation upon general policies. All these need concrete experience, as well as abstract knowledge of principles; and that is why practical wisdom is of slow growth.[1]

Where Plato suggests to us a metaphysically mystical vision of ultimate causation, Aristotle gives us his doctrine of the four causes, material, formal, and efficient, as well as final, which can be used in the concrete by scientific investigators. It must, however, be admitted that, while characteristically substituting such empirical forms of the ways in which things actually behave, for the ideals envisaged by Plato, Aristotle himself always retains his belief in an ultimate purpose which is as transcendental as any Platonist could desire.

In the second place, Aristotle sets himself and his students, in the years which remained to him as head of the Lyceum at Athens, to trace out the lines of actual happening in all fields of knowledge. This led, gradually and without spiritual break, to the characteristic work of the University of Alexandria in a later generation. It is significant, however, that Aristotle constructs the principles of metaphysics before working out the details of physical science, and the principles of social and political philosophy before applying himself and his students to the detailed investigation of the actual constitution of Athens and of the other States known to the Greek world. So too he constructs his theory of dramatic poetry before compiling a detailed history of the dramatists and their plays, and a theory of philosophy before setting his pupil, Theophrastus, to compile a history of actual philosophers and their philosophies.

Aristotle's personal development thus passes through a curve which, at first sight, might seem to embody and illustrate the three stages recognized by Auguste Comte: from religion to metaphysics, and from metaphysics to positivism. But, when looked at more closely, the metaphysics are seen to centre in vivid faith in a God or Divine Principle of Reason; and this is not merely immanent in the world, but is also transcendent; and the final observation of detailed forms, however scientific, never separates itself, in Aristotle's mind, from the transcendental thought of a purposive Creator.

Such is the First Mover: a principle upon which depend the heavens and the world of nature. Its life is such as the best which we enjoy:

[1] *Eth. Nic.*, 1141a 28–1142a 15, condensed.

waking, perceiving, and thinking; and its thought, which is thought in the fullest sense, deals with that which is best in the fullest sense. It is an active contemplation, in which it contemplates itself: thought and its object being here identical. God's essential actuality is thus life at its very best; and this state persists for ever. We say therefore that God is a living being, eternal, and most good.[1]

It may be that, in terms of present-day logic, cataloguing the forms of the actual world is essentially alien to any kind of transcendentalism whatsoever. But to Aristotle himself, as to so many philosophers, the immanent principles discovered by observation and experimentation, seem to be portions of a great pattern whose origin and ultimate explanation lie outside the field in which the arts of the cataloguer prevail. To the end, Aristotle is a convinced teleologist; and it is his faith that somewhere, beyond and behind the varieties of sense-experience, the detail of phenomena is all caught up in some vital principle of unity akin to the human experience of love. It is this faith of his, quite as much as his industrious cataloguing of detailed forms, which has made his work, first to the Stoic and later to the Christian world, a pattern of human philosophy at its best.

The writings of Aristotle, as they have come down to us, are not, with the exception of the "exoteric" works, in a form suitable for publication. Except in so far as they quote directly from his published works, or contain fragments which are clearly *rifacimenti*, they consist chiefly of a professor's notes, suitable for expansion into lectures to be delivered to classes, or of students' notes of precisely such lectures. On the face of them, all bear evident marks of editorial arrangement. The language is frequently abbreviated and technical, with classifications and analyses which are at times hasty and provisional. They are, however, as a rule, exceedingly clear, and, especially from the standpoint of objectivity, leave little to be desired. Aristotle rarely thrusts himself into the picture, except for polemical purposes, or to explain some point in method. While it is true that, by Stoics and Scholastics alike, these lecture-notes were reduced to a closed system of philosophy, to the present-day reader they bear all the marks of episodes, separate problems treated originally for their own sake and at different times. They seem only very partially and externally unified, and suggest an openness of mind to new evidence which is opposed to closed systems and is

[1] *Metaphys.*, 1072b 10–29, condensed.

also rare in any age. Aristotle's interest was clearly in the co-operative work of actual research in his Lyceum. He was only to a very slight extent concerned with writing and publishing for the outside world. In this, he merely carried further the interest in teaching which we saw to be a mark of Plato also in his later years; and it is because of this interest that Aristotle has come to be regarded as "the professor" *par excellence*, "the master of them that know," an "authority" whose *ex cathedra* statements are accepted docilely and with enthusiasm by successive generations, almost down to our own time.

So far, we have been considering Aristotle as he was for Aristotle, for his estranged Friends in the Academy, and for his industrious students in the Lyceum. But, if we are to consider Aristotle as a great thinker, we cannot confine ourselves to his own times. The true life of a professor is in his teaching, in his interactivity with his students, and his greatness is a function of his students, no less than of himself. In the case of a philosopher like Aristotle, it is not until the prestige of the Macedonian party, and the hostility it awakened among the Athenian Democrats, have passed away with the man himself, that the activity of later students and commentators brings out the real significance of his work for humanity, and his true greatness begins to show. For many centuries, Western civilization has gone to school to his works. His logic, psychology, ethics, politics, and metaphysics have continued to stimulate the intensive thinking of students, right down to our own times; and, by the activity of so many generations, they have been turned into a vehicle for stabilizing and systematizing the spiritual achievement of countless leaders of light and learning. Over the details of his scientific treatises, now, of course, little read, many a battle has been fought between the forces of obscurantism and of enlightenment. But the study of all such problems in terms of his own penetrating technology, with its distinctions of "form" and "matter," "potentiality" and "actuality," "substance" and "accident," "universal" and "particular," and the "four causes," has given to the European mind a uniformity of structure and functioning whose value, for the spiritual development of the West, has been incalculable.

In what follows, then, we shall set forth his philosophy, as this has come to be understood in interactivity with the minds of succeeding generations, in spite of knowing that it did not have, for Aristotle himself, quite the emphases and systematic implications which we shall give to it. It is Aristotelia*nism*, rather than the personal thinking of Aristotle, in which we are interested; and we believe that, in setting forth the essential features of Aristotelianism, we are not being unfair to a thinker who, almost above all other thinkers, sank his personality in his work.

In the first place, then, Aristotle's philosophy, the science of "being" as such, is a philosophy of the concrete forms which Aristotle finds in reality; and the interesting thing about them is that they are not isolated and devoid of systematic implications. Each and every form discovered is, for Aristotle, a step upward upon a ladder of forms which is based upon matter and leads towards God. Wherever Aristotle turns his scientific eye, he observes this ladder-like structure of forms. Each science, and each part of each science, has its own ladder; and each rung on each ladder, when examined minutely, is seen to have similar structure. Whether ultimately all such ladders are rungs on a single great ladder is a question which, as Aristotle would say, belongs to another inquiry; but later ages have not hesitated to answer this question in the affirmative; and part of Aristotle's great influence in the Middle Ages is undoubtedly due to their feeling able to give this affirmative answer.

Let us illustrate a few of the better-known ladders of forms. In biological psychology, the lowest rung of the ladder there discovered is the animating principle of plant life, with its characteristic functions of nutrition, growth, and reproduction. Its second great rung is the animating principle of animal life, with the further functions of movement from place to place, and sensation. The third rung is the animating principle of human life, with the still further function of generalization and reasoning; and beyond that we come finally to the animating principle of the Divine Life, with its further function of "pure" reasoning, thought which apprehends and thinks its own self. These are all rungs or steps upward upon a single ladder. There are no separate animating principles. There is, in the end, only one principle which animates the whole of nature: the Divine principle of Reason, expressed in varying degrees or stages.

Let us turn to the narrower field of psychology proper, and examine the successive steps of the ladder of percipience or apprehension, some of which we share with the animals, although they cannot mount as high as we. The lowest rung is the sensation of touch, of being in physical contact with physical bodies. All the other sensations represent higher forms of the primitive sensation of contact. They are extensions and refinements of this sense, developing by the intervention, in each case, of a more refined medium of connection between the body of the percipient and the physical object perceived.

Taste, for example, apprehends the savoury properties of bodies, through the intermediation of moisture, in which small particles of the bodies are conveyed to our sense-organs, and by them to the seat of animation within the body. Smell apprehends the odorous properties, conveyed through the air. Hearing apprehends the audible properties, conveyed through a sonorous medium; and vision apprehends the properties conveyed through a "diaphanous medium" by the intervention of light.

Each step upon this ladder of sensation is a step from matter towards form, a form already present in matter, but disengaged, in the sensory process, more and more from the matter in which it is embodied. The properties apprehended, even in touch, are never the particular matter of the object, but are already "formed." We apprehend partially generalized or universalized qualities, the rough*ness*, loud*ness*, and red*ness* of this or that physical object; and the role of the objective stimulus in sensation is thus, even at its lowest, to permit us to enter the world of forms. We never, in sensation, apprehend bare matter, but always matter as formed in this or that specific way, as tasty, shaped, and coloured.

Our sense-organs, for Aristotle, are thus always "receptive of form." Mediating between extremes, they take on the form of the object, without its matter. The hand, immersed in water, takes on the form of warmth, adapting itself to the warmth of the water, between the extremes of too hot and too cold. The organs within the ear take on the form of the sounds impinging upon them, within the limits of too loud and too soft. The eye takes on the lightness or darkness, and the coloration, of objects, within the extremes which are too bright or too obscure to act upon our organs. What is selected and apprehended by our sense-organs is thus always, not the matter, but the form of physical objects; and Aristotle's way of expressing this is to say that sense "apprehends the universal."

Omitting "common" sensation, the apprehension of the properties of one and the same object, but perceived through more than one sense, as when we see an object which we also touch or hear, we pass to the next rung upon the ladder of knowledge, which, like sensation, is common to both men and animals. This is imagination, and the growling of dogs when asleep indicates that they dream much as men do. Imagination furnishes us with the same forms as we apprehend in sensation, but is one step further removed from matter, as it functions in the absence of the physical object. It is also more free in its ability to combine the properties of objects in ways which are new and have not been observed in nature, as we see in the imaginative creations of poets, their "centaurs" and "harpies."

The next rung is constituted by the highly complex faculty of memory, in which also animals, as well as men, participate. Like sensation and imagination, it has two sides or aspects. It is partly receptive or passive, accepting from the physical world without, the content of what it remembers. But partly, as a faculty of the principle which animates us, it is also active and selective. It can select the form-element which is common to many sensory experiences, e.g. the dog-form which is common to many dogs seen by us, and is thus not only one step further from particular matter, but one step nearer to a sort of generalization. Its selective power amounts, at times, almost to a sort of analysis. But by Aristotle it is thought of as a faculty closely associated with sense, and thus as lower than the rational and discriminative powers peculiar to man.

The next rung on the ladder upward is furnished by the passive reason. The characteristic activity of reason is to generalize, to extract the logical meaning-essence from the forms furnished by sensation, imagination, and memory. With this faculty, we part company with the animals, and begin to enter upon the domain specifically reserved for man as the "rational animal." Generalization results in concepts, primarily empirical concepts such as "man," "ox," and "house," whose formal content is derived wholly from common, sensory experiences, but leads, by almost imperceptible gradations, to concepts of a more obviously formal type, e.g. such concepts as "substance," "accident," "property," and "relations" of time and space. These concepts, and their interrelations, furnish forth the realm of knowledge in which man is peculiarly at home.

It is by this power that man builds up his social traditions, and especially the body of knowledge which Aristotle and his school took for their province, the systematic knowledge which constitutes "science," both in its secondary, more receptive phase in the departmental sciences, and in its primary, more originative and speculative phase as metaphysics or philosophy, sometimes referred to by Aristotle as "theology."

Here, however, we begin to come upon a difficulty. We have spoken of "passive" reason. But, like memory and the earlier faculties, reason has an "active" side as well; and, especially since there is a gap in Aristotle's chief account of the active reason, it is hard to be entirely certain of his meaning. It is possible to maintain that here, as in the case of the earlier faculties, the distinction of "passive and active" is merely the distinction between the faculty taken in relation to its content or "matter"—a relation in which the faculty is of course passive in the sense of "receptive of form"—and the same faculty taken as "active," i.e. as in operation. When we exercise our power of sensation, or memory, or reason, we are, of course, active and selective. But the content which we perceive or remember or reason about is something which we do not invent or create, but discover and accept, from the hand of nature. We are active in so far as *we* perceive or reason; but passive in so far as we perceive or reason about what is there, *in rerum natura*, to be perceived or reasoned about. When our generalizing reason constructs the concept of "arthropod," the crayfish, lobster, spider, and insects generally, which we actively unify as all "possessing jointed legs," are furnished us by nature; in relation to them, we are receptive and passive, rather than originative and creative. It might indeed be urged that it is the duty of the scientist to restrict his own activity precisely to apprehending what is there to be apprehended, never to go beyond the evidence of his senses, and never to permit his tendency to generalize to carry him beyond the facts.

Such is one characteristic interpretation of Aristotle's account of the active reason. It is regarded as, in fact, the passive reason in operation, actively apprehending and systematizing what is there to be apprehended and systematized, but never "speculating" and adding something of its own to the forms furnished by our senses.

On the other hand, in Aristotle's writings there is plenty of evidence which leads, almost irresistibly, to another conclusion. In the first place, we have noted the power of the selective imagination to go beyond the evidence of combinations of forms occurring *in rerum natura.* Imagination constructs all the creations of all the arts: the light that never was on sea or land, the figures of romance and mythology. Imagination also constructs the rules of all games, of social living, and perhaps even of scientific and philosophical construction. Imagination thus leads us beyond the mere cataloguing of actual phenomena. It remains true, however, that it does not give us new elements, new forms or contents wholly originated from within itself and in no sense borrowed from nature.

But in the case of reason, it looks as though there is a possibility of going further. Above each rung of the ladder of knowledge, there has always been yet another. Each step we have taken has been away from matter and receptivity, and towards form and the origination of combinations not accepted from nature. It is possible to go beyond the thought of a reason which is passive and obedient to nature, and to think of a reason which is wholly active, and dictates to nature: a thought which thinks itself and is self-generative, pure and unmixed with sensory experience.

Such self-initiating activity Aristotle actually attributes to reason at its highest level, where it is identified with the mind of God. But, since all reason, like all life, is ultimately one, and since the contemplation which characterizes God's mind eternally is participated in by human reason for a few moments, when it is at its best, it is possible to go beyond the earlier interpretations, and to assert that when reason is supremely active, as in philosophers, we see as God sees, although we remain, doubtless, without His specifically creative power over nature.

Our human power of creation and initiation is limited to the fields of art and science. As artists, we can "remedy the deficiencies of nature." That is to say, by apprehending the principle which natural objects are trying to follow, if they, through some deficiency, are failing to become themselves, we can step in and help them to realize the potentialities which God has placed within them. We can prop up a tree until it is strong enough to grow of itself. We can protect and teach a child until he becomes a self-determining man. We can construct a play in which poetic justice will produce an ending more in consonance with the moral law than what we find exemplified in the actual history of men and women. That is, we can assist nature to be itself. But we cannot dictate to nature what its self shall be. That remains the prerogative of God.

So far, we have been illustrating the way in which Aristotle, by using his conception of a ladder of forms leading upward, from matter towards God, systematizes and makes sense of the different fields of experience. We could prolong such illustrations indefinitely: for they are characteristic of Aristotle's way of looking at *any* field of experience. But we shall now rather direct our inquiry to the question how this ladder is to be understood. For this will lead us directly towards the central essence of Aristotelianism.

Technically, in terms of abstract logic, the forms on one and the same ladder are related as "genus" and "species." Life is the generic quality manifested by plants. Its essence consists of its faculties of nutrition, growth, and reproduction. When it exercises these faculties, the plant is alive, and when it is alive, it exercises these faculties, nutrition being the most fundamental and generic. The animal possesses these generic properties, but is specifically distinct from the plant, in that it possesses the additional faculties of motion from place to place, and sense-perception, with a certain degree of imagination and memory. It is thus a kind of higher species of plant, or the plant can be regarded as a kind of lower species of animal. So too man is said to be half-way between a brute and a god. He is a "rational animal." Animality represents his genus, and rationality his specific difference. If he were all reason, he would be God; if he were all animal, he would never be God.

Here a question can at once be asked. Which is the more vital and important, the generic or the specifically differentiating qualities? Is it more important for an animal to live the life of nutrition, growth, and reproduction, i.e. the life of a vegetable, or to aim at developing its powers of movement and perception? So too is it more important for a man to be perpetually hustling from place to place and living the life of the senses, or to be exercising "the smallest part of him," his reason? For Aristotle, the usual answer, stated emphatically throughout the whole range of his works, from the *Protrepticus* to the final book of the *Nichomachean Ethics*, is that this part, although the smallest, is infinitely the most important, and that human beings should try to live a divine, rather than a merely human, life.

If reason is divine in comparison with man, the life according to reason is divine in comparison with human life. But we must not follow those who advise us, being men, to think of human things, and, being mortal, of mortal things. So far as we can, we must make ourselves immortal, and strain every nerve to live in accordance with the best thing in us;

42

for even if it be small in bulk, much more does it in power and worth surpass everything. Reason is the authoritative and better part of a man. More than anything else, reason is the man himself; and thus life according to reason is the best life for man.[1]

The evidence adduced to support this view is that "actuality" is the realization of "potentiality," and that a man whose reasoning powers are merely latent and potential is like a man asleep when he might be awake. Life, for Aristotle, is, at its best, emphatically the exercise of our highest powers; and the life of reason, as lived by the philosopher, is life *par excellence*, the life which is as "divine" as possible.

We have already seen that the animating principle is one and the same throughout all its stages. It aims at its own fullest development, not only in man, but throughout the range of biology. Thus, men try to live the life of gods; animals are trying, in their unconscious way, to live like men, as we see in the case of monkeys, dogs, and a few other animals; and certain plants are trying to develop powers of sensation and free movement. Throughout the whole range of existence there is thus a *nisus*, a dumb effort, working in the upward direction. But its source is not in matter, but in form, and is divine, the element of reason which expresses itself in the highest form of which this or that species is capable. The perfection of a plant is to become something more than a plant, and of an animal to become something more than an animal. We have already noticed that the quasi-generalizing principle of memory is not very far removed from logical generalization. The animal, at its best, almost overcomes this difference, just as man, at his best, almost becomes, for the time being, divine.

From this point of view, the movement upward is a negation of the limiting elements of the preceding stage. Man tries to transcend and leave behind him his animality, his grosser nature. Like the animal, he tries to leave altogether upon one side the vegetative side of his nature, the business of mere nutrition and reproduction, while he becomes more spiritual, more absorbed in the higher processes of knowledge, refining his senses and his memory into something more intellectual, something more utterly pure and transcendental. In the case of human beings, the process results first in scientific, and lastly in philosophic contemplation; and Aristotle is undoubtedly sincere in regarding the chief good for

[1] *Nic. Eth.*, 1177b 29–1178a 8, condensed.

man as consisting in philosophy, in withdrawing from the life of the senses and emotions, from the instinctive and social habits of men in cities, and seeking in the life of the intellect, with its limitless sweep and penetration, the highest and most enjoyable happiness. The view is expressed in his latest, no less than in his earliest, works; and there is no reason to doubt that it expresses his considered judgment upon what is really worth while.

Activity of the most divine element in us will be perfect happiness. This activity is contemplative. Contemplative activity is the best, the most continuous, the pleasantest of virtuous activities; the most nearly self-sufficient, the most leisurely, the most lovable for its own sake. It follows that contemplative activity of reason will be the complete happiness of man, if it be allowed a complete term of life.[1]

But if, setting aside Aristotle's undoubted personal bias in favour of philosophic contemplation, we consider the logic of the evidence revealed in his writings, we shall find traces of another, philosophically deeper, view. To grow upward, towards the light, if at the expense of the lower faculties of nutrition and physical growth, is a kind of etiolation, a pathological process; and to endeavour to transcend the genus to which one belongs, in one's pursuit of the last refinements of specific differentiation, is a kind of perversion. Happiness is, after all, something which involves the well-being of man as a whole, in his eating, sleeping, exercising, and resting, in his sensuous and emotional, no less than in his intellectual, living. If he persists in withdrawing from the general activities of the genus of which he is a member, then, however excellent he may become on the exclusively intellectual side, he will miss the deep, abiding sources of human and animal happiness; and the loss will be sufficient to mar the quality of his more technical, intellectual joy.

If, accordingly, we look a little deeper, we shall find, in Aristotle's writings, plenty of evidence that the higher forms develop, not at the expense of the lower forms, and not by withdrawing from the genus, but by perfecting the lower forms until, without loss of any kind, there emerges a form which is higher. Each step upward contains everything of genuine value in the lower steps; but, by developing further, it transforms and transmutes the lower forms, taking their value up into the higher form without loss.

A plant, for example, represents a certain organization of the

[1] *Eth. Nic.*, 1177a 16–1177b 25, condensed.

forces which make for life. The animating principle penetrates just so far into matter as to render it animate in the way characteristic of plants. The further penetration which results in an animal, with the higher values associated with free motion from place to place, and with direct sensation, accompanied by a little imagination and memory, does not need to interfere with the nutrition, growth, and reproduction, i.e. the vegetative side, of the animal. The powers of refined discrimination associated with consciousness may indeed lead to greater perfection of the vegetative functions. The animal may, in fact, be a more perfect living organism than the plant.

In the same way, when the animating principle has penetrated yet further in its reorganization of matter, there is no reason in the nature of things why an intelligent human being should not be more perfect, as a living organism, than any plant or any animal. Certain organs may not be directly retained in the higher organisms. The chlorophyll cell of the typical plant may disappear as we ascend the higher steps of the ladder of living forms. So too certain organs of digestion and reproduction, as well as of sensation and motion, which are characteristic of animals whose mode of living is very different from ours, may disappear or become vestigial in the human form. But there is compensation for these functions, when the animating principle introduces a higher degree of organization into matter. The methods of living and reacting upon the biological and physical environment may thus be different. It is Aristotle's belief that they are not only different, but also essentially superior. Intelligence, as a force in directing one's life, is superior to instinct, and reason is essentially superior to habit.

From this standpoint, which we find adopted without hesitation throughout the writings of Aristotle and his school, including not only the philosophical, but the definitely scientific treatises, we conclude that the logic of the Aristotelian thought regards the ladder of forms as ascending from an infinite, but unrealized, potentiality, called "matter," and culminating in a no less infinite, but entirely realized, group of powers. These powers function actually, and without loss of any kind, constituting an Absolute Substance, or what the later schoolmen call an *ens realissimum*. This is the typical metaphysician's way of regarding what popular thinking calls "God."

When Aristotle declares that God is "pure actuality," "pure form," "pure thought thinking itself," etc., he does not mean that ultimate reality is a thin, etiolated stream of introverted intellectualism, a kind of mystically ingrowing soul, or an "unearthly ballet of bloodless categories." He means, rather, that God or Reality is the full and entire realization of all the powers which might otherwise have lain slumbering in the bosom of not-being or bare potentiality. God is matter so permeated with form that there is no part left which is not completely and perfectly formed. God is the whole of what is animated by the animating principle, as well as the animating principle itself. God is the whole of the forms, *plus* the formative, creative principle. He is thus not only nature, but life and mind, all unified in a single, all-inclusive focus of reflective, self-generative consciousness.

It is this position which makes Aristotle so acceptable to the systematic, religious thought of the Middle Ages. From this standpoint, the philosopher is not a one-sided intellectualist, withdrawn from the life of the senses and emotions, from everything which smacks of his animal origin, but lives the fullest and completest life humanly conceivable. The life of reason does not exclude, but includes, the lower faculties, and includes them at their best. The good man's life is the actualization of all his potentialities, under the direction of practical, no less than theoretical, insight, and represents the completest development of the powers of humanity. To live the god-like life, for Aristotle, means not to become something less than human, but to grow into something higher by becoming perfectly human, as vital and real in every fibre of his being as a man can be. This ideal of the perfectly well-rounded life, as controlled and directed by reason, has always been considered in accordance with common sense, as well as satisfying the highest aspirations of humanity. Later ages have tended to accept this as the true expression of Aristotelian thought, although it is beyond doubt that Aristotle himself preferred the theoretical to the practical life, and personally praised the one-sided, intellectualist development which we have referred to as etiolation.

There is a further side of the logic of the Aristotelian ladder of forms which has especially appealed to posterity. It has frequently been supposed that matter is something in its own right, possessed of $a, b, c, \ldots n \ldots$ qualities, in the form of objective but undeveloped potentialities. It has been supposed, e.g., that matter, as such, occupies space, and is thus possessed of three dimensions, together with all the other attributes which follow from the nature of three-dimensional extension. It has been supposed that matter possesses quantity, and that the quantity of matter in nature is indestructible. It has further been supposed that the business of reason, when faced with these objective possibilities, is to sink itself into the objective facts and their laws, and, by apprehending what is there to be apprehended, namely, the substances and relations lying dormant *in rerum natura*, to play, eventually, the part of a "servant and interpreter of nature," as Bacon puts it. That is to say, the function of reason is to assist these objective potentialities to become what they have it in them to become: to assist the boy to become a man, the acorn to become an oak, and the iron to become an axe-head. The function of reason is thus "to remedy the deficiencies of nature," to render explicit what is already implicit, and to bring out what is already in matter. The forms thus belong, not to reason, but to matter.

This simple materialism does not, however, express Aristotle's view. It is too one-sided. Considered by itself, matter, for Aristotle, is always identical with "not-being." This does not mean that it is absolutely nothing. Matter is always the correlate of form, and is capable of taking on the form of an oak, an axe, or a statue. But these differentiations represent distinctions of form rather than differences within matter, and in no sense belong to matter exclusively, in its own right.

Aristotle takes care, however, to avoid the other extreme also, the extreme of simple formalism. The correlation is strict. Matter needs form, but form also needs matter. The formative principle cannot produce oaks or axes all by itself. It needs matter. It also needs something further: at least an efficient cause. One of Aristotle's chief objections to Plato's "ideas" is that, as he understands them, they are purely formal, and cannot actually cause this or that concrete thing to come into existence. For such causation, even Plato had need of an efficient cause, a philosopher-king on earth, or a Divine Artificer in heaven. As Aristotle understands it, the efficient cause is anything which can bring about physical movement in the physical world. Working in bronze, the artist, who, together with his mallet and chisel, represents the efficient cause, can produce a bronze oak, a bronze axe, and a bronze statue. Working with the living forces of nature, the parent oak can produce an acorn, canine parents can produce a puppy, and human parents a child. But the material with which these efficient causes operate has already been formed in such a way that it is capable of receiving this further formation; and the ultimate reason for this takes us into the realm of final causation, the realm of meaning, end, and purpose.

In this way, Aristotle avoids extreme materialism, which would refer all existence and change to matter alone. He avoids formalism, which would refer everything to form alone. He also avoids all kinds of pragmatism which refer all explanation to efficient causes alone. And, lastly, he avoids extreme finalism, which would explain everything in terms of some ultimate purpose or end, and nothing else. By insisting upon the fourfold nature of causation, he has won the admiration of commonsense, as well as of deeper, thinkers; and by regarding the final cause, i.e. in the end, God, as the most ultimate of the four, he has won the admiration of theologians.

Here, however, a question will be asked. We all understand what is meant by a material cause. We all understand that a formal cause is like the blueprint specifications from which a builder constructs a house. The efficient cause is obvious to us: for we are all efficient causes during most of our lives. But the final cause requires explanation. How does it really operate?

In the case of human beings, Aristotle gives a few commonplace examples, which are satisfactory as far as they go. The final cause of going for a walk, he tells us, may be health. The final cause of an artisan's work may be, under the conditions of our social and economic life, money. The final cause of an artist's work may be beauty; for beauty is something desirable for its own sake, as an end in itself. But when it is said that God is the final cause, just what is meant?

God is said to be the final cause of nature, of all the movements, e.g., of the planets. Does this mean that God is an efficient cause, like Plato's Divine Artificer? Not at all. God is not a physical cause, although He does cause physical movements. He is, in Aristotelian terminology, the "unmoved Mover." He is a "First Cause," i.e. a cause, not in a proximate, but in an ultimate sense, and He moves, while being outside the regular chain of causes and effects, by "being" rather than by "doing."

We have stated above that the animating principle seeks to be perfectly itself, to develop itself to the utmost. This seeking or desire on the part of the vital principle embodied in all living things is likened, by Aristotle, in his latest as well as in his earliest works, to the action of human desire and human love. Empedocles, the popularizer of science before the time of Socrates, had already suggested that love was a cosmic principle, and played a part in physical, as well as social, phenomena. Aristotle carries this further. When *A* is in love with *B*, *A* does a great many things which he would otherwise not do. He tries to make himself similar to *B*, to realize, in his own character, *B*'s nature, as we see in hero-worship. As Plato had already pointed out, the worshippers of Zeus tried to make themselves like Zeus, and the worshippers of Apollo like Apollo. What is sought is a complementation, an enlargement, of the self; and this is essential to true friendship and true love.

Let us apply this. The planet, on Aristotle's view, tries to perfect itself, to be a perfect planet, to be, if we may so express it, a God-like planet. It tries, with its potentialities, to make itself like God, and to live the God-like life. But God's life consists in "pure thought thinking itself," to use, without explanation, the words of Aristotle's definition. That is to say, God's thought is what logicians call "circular." It thinks its thinking, and it thinks its thinking eternally. Now, what is a planet to do? It cannot think; but it can move. It therefore moves, as like the movement of God's thinking as is possible for it: it moves in circles, returning eternally upon its own movement. It is in this sense, then, that God is the final cause of its eternal, circular motion.

The first heavens must be eternal, and their movement, being unceasing, must be circular motion. That which keeps them in motion must itself be a mover which moves without being moved: being eternal, substance, and actuality. The object of desire and the object of thought move in this way—without being moved. The final cause, then, produces motion by being loved; and by that which it moves, it moves all other things. Motion in space is the first of the kinds of change, and motion in a circle is the first kind of spatial motion; and this is what the First Mover produces.[1]

So too man, in trying to live the God-like life, develops, refines, and unifies the whole of his many-sided nature, under the direction of philosophic contemplation. He becomes, as nearly as possible, pure reflection, thought thinking itself: the forms of reality all become focused in a self, and become self-conscious. The divine

[1] *Metaphys.*, 1072a 21–1072b 10, condensed.

principle which animates man, together with the rest of nature, thus, in perfect self-love, endeavours to realize to the full all the values of that nature. With Aristotle, it is not a poet's exaggeration, but literal truth, to say that "it's love which makes the world go round." No wonder that the medieval world, when it read Aristotle, and found that this doctrine could be regarded as an expression of the Christian view of God as Love, adopted Aristotle almost in his entirety, and fused his work, for teaching purposes, with the doctrines of the Church![1]

"God's life is a thinking of thinking. The Thinker and the object of His thinking are one and the same." What does this mean? Aristotle teaches that the forms which thinking apprehends are always concrete, embodied forms. How can there be a thinking of thinking itself?

We are unable to learn or understand without sensuous perception. When we contemplate mentally, we do so necessarily in conjunction with an internal image. These images are like sensations; we apprehend in them the specific forms (visual, auditory, etc., aspects) in separation from their embodiment in material objects. Reason, however, is different from sensuous experience. (1) It is not specific, but universal; and (2) it apprehends not merely this or that aspect (visual, auditory, etc.) of objects, but their essential nature, their conceptual essence or notion. Furthermore (3) it can combine concepts to form a judgment, judgments to form a syllogism, and syllogisms to form a demonstration. It can also make itself and its own processes the objects of its thinking.[2]

One answer consists in taking first the thinking characteristic of the mathematician, the logician, and the metaphysician, e.g. the average serious student in Aristotle's Lyceum. Such a student thoroughly understands that while the passive reason apprehends forms which are concrete, vouched for by sensory experience, it is possible, once such forms are obtained, to ask questions which refer, not to their embodied character, as such, but to their formal side. All concepts, such as "man," "ox," and "house," represent unifications of experience, and refer to many experiences of men, oxen, and houses. Analysis and synthesis have been at work, and

[1] It should be noted, however, that there is a difference. The lover acts as he does, whether his love is returned or not, and even when it is ignored, as we sometimes see in hero-worship. Aristotle's God does not return human love. We are unworthy of His notice. He loves only Himself. He never stoops beneath His own level, as the Christian God does.
[2] Condensed from *De Anima*, Bk. III, Chapters iv–viii.

Aristotle

the resulting concepts are standardized for social and scientific purposes. He understands perfectly that the structure of scientific systematization can be studied as a formal science, in fact, the science of Logic, or "analytic," of which Aristotle is himself the founder. Thinking about concepts and propositions and the syllogistic technique, and truth and reality, or about numbers, lines, and surfaces, as standardized in mathematics, is not primary thinking, thinking about the objects of sensory experience, but is "thinking of second intention," thinking about the operations of thinking itself.

Can this be the kind of thinking in which God's life consists? Are we to think of God as a kind of perfected Aristotelian student, thinking the whole world in a single all-embracing, eternal intuition, but at second hand, as it were? Is He like the professor who accepts the results of an army oi specialized students, merely as results, and works them up into a systematic treatise covering the whole field? The answer is, of course, No. For this thinking is a thinking about thinking in the concrete, not a thinking which has its very self for its object.

Here the interpreters part company, and take one of two ways. Those who follow the pathway of what we have called "etiolation" observe that the metaphysician's grasp upon concrete reality is genuinely at second hand, as he builds up the outlines of a science which embraces the whole of "being" as such, a being which, of course, it transcends his powers to apprehend completely at first hand. They believe that when the metaphysician becomes reflective, aware of his own mind as itself generating the standards of unity, order, and system with which he systematizes the forms passed over to him by the various field-workers of the school, he then becomes like God. God's thinking is reflective, aware of itself as generating its own standards, and aware of the formal, standardizing element present in all its concepts. They are all, on their formal side, particular applications of the mind's ideal of unity order, and perfect system. The human scientist is usually aware of them as glimpses and intimations, arising in contrast to the fragmentary experiences which he is seeking to unify and systematize in this or that concrete science. But God is aware of them in their fulness and perfection. The network of categories which embraces the whole of reality in principle is the original outcome of His own mind, in its reflective self-activity. He does not have to take the

51

scientist's long way round, via sensory and emotional experience, working gradually up to the relative standardizations of the passive reason. His active reason apprehends the full conceptual aspect of whatever can be apprehended, in a perfect logical system, and apprehends it as the creation of His own reflective activity.

This is called "etiolation," because the divine intuition of the world as a self, and the self as identical with its world, never descends to the level of humanity, but omits and abstracts from the rich experience of sensation, of emotion, and of the co-operative struggle upwards towards the light of truth, which characterizes the work of science. The divine intuition is all-inclusive, but cold and inhuman, self-contained in effortless superiority. God does nothing but be Himself, know Himself, and love Himself.

The other, more concrete way of interpreting the logic of Aristotelianism insists that God's awareness of the world of forms, while identical with His awareness of self, is in no sense "at second hand." The ultimate reflective self-activity, in which consists the life of God's mind, embraces the concrete richness of *all* experience, sensuous and emotional, no less than intellectual. The perfect intuition is, for this way of thinking, strictly *all*-inclusive. It contains, not only the principle, but every last detail, of experience. It is experience itself, raised indeed to the *n*th power, as it were, but omitting nothing, nothing whatever, of the content of every experience anywhere experiencible.

So far, we have been writing somewhat in the spirit of Aristotle in his earlier years, when metaphysics for him meant "theology," rather than the science of "being, as such." We have done so because it is on this side that his greatness, in influencing helpfully the thought and life of so many subsequent centuries, has been especially conspicuous. But we shall not be doing justice, either to Aristotle himself or to his influence upon later times, unless we emphasize also the later aspect of his thought, from which the theology is almost missing—although it is never explicitly rejected —and the almost "positivist" investigation of the detail of phenomena is especially in evidence.

Experimental, objective observation of sense-perceivable detail for its own sake, the objective description of phenomena without any imputation of underlying meaning or purpose, owes a great deal to Aristotle in his later years. His insatiable curiosity, his instinctive reaching out after knowledge of all sorts, to the exclusion of all immediate practical and emotional interests and evaluations, has meant a great deal to the development of botany, zoology, and almost every one of the sciences of nature, as well as to historical, literary, and philological research. The establishment of fact, in whatever field, is so important to him in his later years that the work of his school, in many instances, leaves the modern student wondering at the courage and single-mindedness which could initiate and carry on such researches in such times. The openness to fact in almost all his treatises, the readiness to neglect mere system in the effort to include more and more detail, the willingness, at every point, to raise new questions and formulate problems for further research, the amazing fertility and comprehensiveness of his genius, no less than his methodic rigour, make many a page worth reading at the present day, even in treatises whose truths have long since passed into the impersonality of common knowledge.

Because of these characteristics, and the illuminating *aperçus* which abound in his writing, few, if any, later treatises upon moral experience have proved as perpetually stimulating as his *Nichomachean Ethics*. Few, if any, later treatises upon the methods of logical thinking have proved as stimulating as the *Prior* and *Posterior Analytics*. And among present-day philosophers there are not a few who owe much to their careful studies of his *De Anima* and *Metaphysics*. Of all the Great Thinkers, he remains outstandingly the one who is "the professor," before whose desk humanity still lingers and learns.

It has been said that we are all born either Platonists or Aristotelians, and there is a kernel of truth in this saying. Let us compare the two great philosophers, who still divide our allegiance. Plato's work falls into two parts. The inspired genius in whose pages Socrates still lives and teaches is the Plato whom most of us know and love. And the call of those pages is to idealism, to throw ourselves open to the forces of the spirit, to learn to see the vision, and for ever after to be members of the devoted band of friends who live in the transcendental realm of ideals, and seek to lead ever greater numbers to the same vision and the same life. But there is another and a later Plato who, while still retaining the vision, equips his students with the weapons of logical analysis and dialectical synthesis, so that they can coolly arm themselves for the *mêlée* of opposing systems, and can apply the technique of mathematics and

53

exact measurement to the world around them. This Plato is less inspiring, somewhat disillusioned, and a little baffled by the actualities of human life. But he still sees in idealism the only hope for the salvation of the race. "Until philosophers become kings, or the kings of this world become endowed with the spirit of philosophy, there is no hope that humanity will cease from its ills." This remains his vision, and we are still awaiting its fulfilment: still dreaming his dreams, and still fighting on with his weapons, trusting in the power of education and enlightenment, but a little dispirited, at times, by the actualities around us.

Aristotle's work also falls into two parts. On the one hand, we have his metaphysical theology, as transcendental a vision as any Platonist could desire. But on the other hand, we have his philosophy of the actual concrete forms, the study and manipulation of the actual world. And both he himself and certainly his followers believe that humanity should busy itself with the study of what *is*, rather than of what *ought* to be. The objective, the factual, the here and now: these are, for him, the substantial things; and it is to the scientist, rather than to the philosopher, that he looks for the amelioration of our human lot. For the rest, he is a realist rather than an idealist, and believes that men are governed by fear rather than love, and by force rather than enlightenment. Plato becomes disillusioned in his old age. Aristotle was born without illusions. His youthful religious enthusiasm once satisfied by a quasi-Platonic vision, he puts all that on one side and devotes the powers of his manhood to investigating dispassionately the world of actual fact. Unlike Plato, he has no hopes for humanity from any sort of idealistic education. It is force and fear, a dictator like Alexander the Great, that will keep humanity in order. More than this is not to be obtained; and to hope for more is to indulge in idle dreams.

When it is said, then, that we are all born Platonists or born Aristotelians, it is meant that we are like Plato in his earlier, or Aristotle in his later, period. Either we are idealists who make our home in the transcendental realm of the spirit, or we are realists who make our home in the actual world around us, accepting it as what it is. The greatness of these two thinkers consists in their giving classic form to these fundamental differences of human outlook. Both help us to realize our own selves, and to take in life a stand which conforms to and expresses the kind of self which intercourse with them reveals as our own.

Chapter III

PLOTINUS A.D. 204-270

THE chief social institution developed by the Greeks was the small, compact city-state: intensely patriotic, narrowly local, essentially static. Arising naturally in its geographical and social environment, it contained within itself a number of potentialities. But one it did not contain: the potentiality of imperialism. The idea of the city-state and the idea of empire were essentially hostile. The small group of freemen, loyal to their community, and the vast, amorphous association of subjects, loyal only to an absolute monarch, had, and could have, nothing in common. When Greek met Barbarian, there could only be war.

In this war, the Greeks, although physically victorious, were spiritually subdued. Spartan hoplites might repel Persian land-forces. Athenian triremes might drive back Persian navies. But to the Persian idea, the city-state capitulated without a single blow. The career of Athens as a would-be imperial state was brilliant, but brief. Just as soon as she ceased to be self-centred, dissolution set in. Through the slits in the statesman's mask appeared the eyes of the bandit; and party differences became the internecine war of gangsters.

Against this social disintegration, Plato sought refuge, not in democratic education, but in aristocratic control. He looked, not to "the many," the original freemen, but to "the one," his philosopher-king. Aristotle demanded only that order should be maintained. He looked to some alien ruler, some Alexander the Great: neither citizen nor philosopher, but emperor; and with the coming of the Roman legions, his vision was soon realized. The free, self-controlled₁ city-state disappeared, and the Greeks became detached provincials, unrespected pawns on the outskirts of the Roman Empire.

As external self-direction vanished, philosophy became more and more an affair of the inner life. Plato had withdrawn to his Academy and Aristotle to his Lyceum. The newer generation withdrew yet further. Stoicism yields completely to the march of events. It restricts human power to granting or withholding a merely inner consent. Epicureanism retires permanently to the suburbs, to cultivate its gardens, to appreciate the lighter forms of literature, to enjoy the milder forms of friendship, to live a refined life of the senses. Satisfying, but futile. Eclecticism selects, from this system and that, whatever appeals to the urge of the moment, and stitches together a patchwork quilt of sentiments, without inner unity or logical control. Scepticism gives up the problem altogether, balances its judgments with meticulous exactitude, and becomes the champion fence-sitter of antiquity.

One step only remains, and it is soon taken: from the subjectivism of thought to the subjectivism of religious emotion. There sweeps over the once Hellenic world wave upon wave of strange cults, un-Greek, Oriental, mystical: religions of escape, of other-worldliness, of purification and ecstatic vision, in which the objective world is utterly and completely lost.

Such is the background against which Neoplatonism develops. Its chief founder, Plotinus, was born in Egypt and studied in Alexandria. He travelled in Persia and settled in Rome. Until the age of thirty-eight, he was a pupil of that nebulous, quasi-Socratic figure, Ammonius of Alexandria, porter and mystic (A.D. 160–242). From the age of forty to the age of sixty-six, when he passed away, he lived at Rome, quietly busy, bringing up the wards committed to his guardianship, studying and discussing philosophy with his disciples, a man without an enemy. His dream was to establish, in some remote and sheltered corner of the Empire, a Platonopolis, where Plato's laws might govern, and Plato's republic might at last become realized, under his own philosophic guardianship, a ward of Rome. Actually, yielding to the affectionate pressure of his students, he committed to writing the thoughts which they discussed together, and, by permitting his students to edit, publish, and defend these writings, he established the Neoplatonic School which gradually, in Rome, in Alexandria, and in Athens, overcame and included opposing schools, and eventually passed, almost without remainder, into the main stream of Christianity.

As a writer, Plotinus exhibits certain well-defined characteristics. Like Locke, he did not write until well over forty, and, like Locke, he knows his own mind. He writes about what he has experienced, read, thought, and discussed. He knows his subject, and is in no uncertainty as to what he intends to say. He grasps precisely his relation to his predecessors and his contemporaries, whether in philosophic schools or in popular and religious movements. He is clear that he is drawing his inspiration chiefly from Plato, and that he is effecting a new synthesis by means of dialectical discussion with his contemporaries in art, science, philosophy, and religion. He is aware that this involves a reorientation and reinterpretation of Plato; but he does not believe that he is at any point introducing innovations alien to Plato's spirit. Just as Plato apparently believed his *Dialogues* to present, not his own opinions, but "Socrates made young and handsome," so Plotinus disclaims all originality, and attributes to his Master the whole value of what he has lived through and is committing to writing.

In the second place, as a man who has not learned to write in his youth, Plotinus exhibits a certain impatience with formal requirements. He has no love for syllogistic logic, for the niceties of grammar, or even—so Porphyry, his pupil and early editor, tells us—for the rules of orthography. He wrote amid interruptions, and, as his eyesight was poor, he never re-read what he had written. After each interruption, he would sit down again, and, knowing clearly what was in his own mind, would simply continue: no doubt, to his own complete satisfaction.

The consequence of this impatience with details is that many sentences are devoid of definite structure. They just run on. Clauses are fitted in very loosely. Connecting particles, and even verbs, are frequently missing. The present participle of the verb "to be" works overtime; and, while we accept with thankfulness anything which looks like a main verb, it is often disconcertingly in the infinitive. We are left to supply our own mood. Porphyry tells us that Plotinus' own pupils, who were familiar with his way of living and expressing himself, could project themselves into his mood, with its transcendence of empirical formality, and were able to understand his writings without difficulty. But strangers, even Plotinus' former fellow-students under Ammonius, men like the great critic Longinus, found the textual difficulties too much for their patience, and returned the manuscript with a request to have it corrected before re-submission. But this, as Porphyry tells us, was the best manuscript. He had already "corrected" it.

Thus we see that, even in antiquity, there never was an original text of Plotinus' writings. The very first publications bore traces of the editorial hand. Porphyry states that, in addition to altering the spelling, he inserted definitions, summaries, and other helps to following the argument. He arranged the various treatises with some rough regard to their subject-matter, in six groups. Noting the great beauty of the number fifty-four, which is the product of the "perfect" numbers, six and nine, he published the works of Plotinus in six books, containing nine treatises each. It is true that Plotinus had not written exactly fifty-four treatises. It is true also that they did not fall naturally into subject-matter groups containing exactly nine treatises each. But by such devices as dividing a long treatise into three short ones, and by lumping together under the title "Miscellaneous" a few odds and ends which he could not fit in anywhere else, the editor proved equal to the occasion; and to this day the works of Plotinus are known as the *Enneads*, i.e. the *Nines*.

Modern editors are subject to the same temptations as Porphyry; but with the additional difficulty that they share the impatience of the great Longinus. It is almost fatally easy to feel that this sentence or that is "not Greek." If this or that paragraph were recast, so as to put its sentences in a more logically compelling order; if this or that explanatory clause, hanging by the loosest of participles, were detached and inserted among the footnotes; if the tendency of adjectives and the odd verb, towards the end of some over-extended sentence, to drop into the neuter and the infinitive, respectively, was checked, and the rules of concordance were less completely disregarded; or if, best of all, some of the longer sentences were split up into half a dozen short ones; the meaning would remain the same, but its expression would be enormously improved.

The temptation to rewrite the text is thus very strong; and, editorial competence being what it is, it is really remarkable that the author has not been "improved" out of all recognition. But the spirit of conservatism has been equally strong; and the pronounced family likeness of the manuscripts which have come down to us—none of them pre-Renaissance—suggests that the early editors have all been extremely patient, and have resisted the natural temptation to rewrite their author. Now and again we still hear that some editor is about to "establish the text." But in view of the obvious facts (1) that all our manuscripts are some eleven or twelve hundred years later than Plotinus' time, and (2) that, in any case, there never was an original text, it is clear that a modest conservatism must continue to be our guide.

Finally, we note that there is a certain consonance between the transcendence of empirical rules which marks Plotinus' sentences, and the transcendence of empirical barriers which marks his thought. If we can project ourselves into his mood and follow the flow of his thought, we shall find that we can follow the flow of his phrases and sentences without much difficulty. There is a formlessness which is inferior to the rules which govern conventional structures. But there is also, in the work of genius, a formlessness which is superior to conventions, and out of the profundity of its own insight generates its own structures, or even, as in the case of Plotinus, generates forms of expression whose structure is lost in the brightness of the vision. To one whose vision is so intense that the things of this world are devoid of permanence, dissolving views which pass into one another and give place to a conception of transcendental law and beauty, and his concepts, in turn, pass into one another and dissolve into an experience which is beyond even conception, it is no wonder that clauses and phrases, and adjectives, nouns, and verbs, should pass into one another and dissolve, in the end, into symbols which suggest something beyond linguistic structure. "He who has seen the vision," writes Plotinus, "will understand what I say"; and it remains true, today as in the time of Porphyry, that those who become disciples seem able to understand, while others, who remain on the outside, can merely repeat the words, and demand that the text should be "corrected" for them.

What, then, is this philosophy which we are invited to understand? In the first place, Plotinus draws his inspiration from Plato. He studies the greater *Dialogues* of Plato's maturity, the *Symposium*, *Phaedo*, *Timaeus*, *Theaetetus*, etc., and, by projecting himself wholeheartedly into their discussions, becomes something of a Platonic *persona*. The effect upon him of this self-projection is precisely analogous to the effect upon the modern reader who similarly seeks inspiration in the *Dialogues*. What emerges from such discussions is always called "Plato," and is honestly so regarded. But it is, of course, a "Plato" interpreted according to the measure of the interpreter. Plato's *Dialogues* constitute a sort of philosopher's mirror, and what thus emerges is always a full-length portrait of the seeker himself. Plato reveals to us the intimate depths and sources of value in what we bring to the interpretation, the depths and sources contained within our own being. Some of us see more in him, and some of us less. But in every case what we get out of him is precisely related to what we put in: idealized, no doubt, and speaking a slightly different language from that of our everyday needs; but essentially and fundamentally, it is our essential and fundamental self.

Natorp sees in Plato an idealized Natorp, the true leader of the Marburg School of Neokantian Idealism. Grote sees in him an idealized Grote, the true Englishman of Victoria's golden age, with his judicious utilitarianism and liberalism, and with his absence of speculative interest. So it goes with the rest of us; and so also with Plotinus. What he sees in Plato is a gentle, serious, refined and profound genius, a sage of almost magical insight into the depths of every phase of experience, accepting joyously everything which sense can apprehend, transmuting it into love, beauty, religion, and philosophy, and culminating in a mystical ecstasy which transmutes the relativities of love, beauty, religion, and philosophy themselves into an Experience which is Absolute.

Thus inspired, Plotinus proceeds to his new synthesis by dialectical discussion with his contemporaries. And first, in respect of art and beauty. The view which he opposes is that beauty of body, soul, and spirit, of the physical environment and of moral and scientific pursuits, is eternally one and the same: namely, the formal element of "symmetry," the proportionate relationship of part to part, and of parts to whole.

If we start empirically and uncritically, it is easy to fall into this mistaken view. We judge that the moonlight brooding over some still lake is beautiful, that the human form, at its best, is beautiful, that the pursuit of truth is beautiful, that religious self-surrender is beautiful. No one really doubts value-judgments of this sort. We can appeal to the poets of all ages, or we can experience them directly ourselves. The next false step is taken when we consider that there must be something common to all these contents in virtue of which we make the same judgment about them, namely, that they are all "beautiful." It is perfectly natural to take a third false step, and to suppose that this "something common" will be something objective, something independent of us and our ways of looking at things, something there in the objects themselves. We apprehend *them* as "beautiful." We do not thrust ourselves into the picture, and create what we are apprehending. It is there, awaiting our apprehension. The moonlight is beautiful even when we are asleep, or not beside the lake. The pursuit of truth is beautiful, and religious self-surrender is beautiful, even in an age of scepticism and cynicism. Anything which is grand, noble, and beautiful is so in its own right; and it is part of the judgment "this is beautiful" to recognize that this is so.

Anyone who has taken these three steps will easily and almost inevitably conclude that the objective element common to such diverse things as moonlight and the pursuit of truth will not be material, something physical belonging to the contents of such judgments on their material side, but will be something structural, formal. A work of art is a unity. It is a totality of diverse parts, whose interrelations may well be thought of as constituting its unity. These structural and formal relations are now conceived as constituting its beauty, and we conclude, falsely but quite simply, that what the Greeks call "symmetry," namely, the proportionate relationship of parts to one another within a unifying whole, is the secret formula of beauty, the formula actually used, with variations designed to suit various fields and media, by the artist.

This view is thus natural, and is not without value. But if we try to think out what it implies, and what it does not say, we find this kind of view unsatisfactory. It does provide answers to such questions as "What is beauty?", "At what does the artist aim?", etc. It thus succeeds in providing a formula which can be applied in practice in many fields, and, when so applied, will be found to work. But, in the first place, it omits something from consideration, and that something is of the essence of the question. It omits the human factor in the value-judgment, the subjective side of the appreciation of beauty. Judgment is an activity of ours. It is synthetic, putting together what nature has not joined. In judging, we do something which would otherwise not be done. When we judge that "moonlight brooding over a still lake is beautiful," what we do is to select, interrelate, emphasize, and systematize the moonlight, the stillness, the brooding, etc. As far as nature is concerned, these elements of the total effect may indeed be "there." But they are not selected, not emphasized, and not unified. No view of art can afford to neglect the artist himself, and no theory of beauty can afford to omit the subjective factors.

In the second place, if we confine ourselves to some such objec-

61

tive formula, we have no answer to such questions as "*Why* should we judge what is symmetrical to be beautiful?", "*Why* should we respond to such-and-such objective factors in such-and-such subjective ways?" We are confronted with a brute fact, and are left without an explanation. In fact, in spite of the three or four steps taken, we have not really moved far. We began by asking "Why do we judge this, that, and the other to be beautiful?", and were told, "Because this, that, and the other are symmetrical unities." But we are still left with the question, "Why do we judge symmetrical unities to be beautiful?" To reply, "Because we do," merely restates the fact to be explained.

If we look more closely at this answer, "Because we do," we find ourselves thinking that there must be something in the self which induces our response, some *nisus* or inner impulse which is for ever seeking its kindred, and feels, in the presence of beauty, some quickening of the spirit, some sense of comradeship in bringing to birth the more vital and transcendental reaches of selfhood. But such thoughts, together with their whole (Platonic) background and outlook, clearly take us right out of the simple, empirical, and would-be objective standpoint from which we started.

Finally, the attempt to reduce the secret essence of beauty to a lifeless formula, supposed to be identical in all cases, breaks down completely as soon as we realize that the "symmetry" which might conceivably be applied to a Greek vase, or to a human face and figure, means nothing in the case of an ethical activity, or of the pursuit of scientific and metaphysical truth. It becomes at once clear that such formulas are pure metaphors, and that it is impossible to assign to them any precise significance applicable, without change, to all cases.

Beauty is thus to be sought, not in the objective world, considered purely in itself, nor in the abstract formulations with which a self-forgetful, contemplative science may amuse its leisure hours. A mountain, a lake, the moonlight, as such and purely in themselves, as fragments of an external world, are devoid of beauty.[1] So too with the realm of mathematical and logical formulations, considered in themselves, as abstractions without life or power. A square,

[1] The modern reader can realize the situation more easily, perhaps, by observing what a difference fashion makes to our ideas of what is beautiful. The object remains what it always was. But, when fashions change, the "beauty" which we once attributed to a dress or hat, to an automobile or a "hog-backed" racing yacht, seems to have faded out. The object has become external to our self, and is seen to possess no beauty *per se*.

straight line, or circle, the concept of genus and species, of whole and parts, and all similar abstractions, considered merely as such, have in them no place where beauty could dwell. For beauty is not a "thing," and it is not an "abstraction." It is a living experience; and, in order to be experienced, it must be lived, and lived by one who has the living idea of beauty as a constituent part of his living self.

The way to understand art and beauty, then, is not to analyse and classify, comparing abstraction with abstraction, after the manner of a narrow, would-be objective logic; but to experience, to experience both creatively and reflectively, from a standpoint which is not sensuous, receptive, and empirical, but dialectical, originative, and transcendental, not physical but metaphysical. We must seek to appreciate and understand, not by constructing an aggregate by adding one external block to another external block, but by envisaging all details in the light of the single, total living experience, which includes the self and all its activities.

Let us begin by creating a sort of ladder leading upward towards beauty, commencing at the bottom rung. At the very bottom of the scale of reality we have, of course, matter. Here Plotinus follows what he takes to be Plato's view, as indicated in the *Timaeus*. Matter, as he understands it,[1] is something far more abstract and remote than space or space-time, which other thinkers have regarded as the ultimate material substratum. For space or extension has its three distinct dimensions, and space-time has its four distinct dimensions. But dimensions are positive forms, apprehended by reason, the same as any other forms, while matter has no form. Absolute matter is the absolutely formless, the formless below form. It has no positive qualities whatever; for these would be so many forms. It is thus not any kind of "being." At the same time, it is not non-being; for non-being is simply nothing, and matter, while not something, is most certainly not nothing. What, then, is it?

In a sense, it would be almost true to say that it is not; for, in itself, it is not anything at all. It can be grasped, however, indirectly, in relation to its correlate. Matter is the correlate of form, and it is from form that it borrows whatever significance it seems to have, namely, when it is formed in this way or that, as a mass of

---

[1] Plotinus does not, of course, use the term "matter" in the sense still popular among us, as equivalent to "substance" or "material substance." Matter is, for him, the antithesis of substance.

marble, a horse, a human being, or a star. In relation to its correlate, then, matter can be described and indicated, though not directly defined. It is the universal receptivity of form, the potentiality of form, the capacity for taking on any and every form. Plato calls it "the receptacle." If we must think of it as a substrate, it is the formless substrate of form, the ultimate condition of the embodiment of form, absolutely indifferent to the forms which may express themselves in material embodiment.

In this relation with form, matter receives everything, and gives nothing. It has nothing which it could give. Even when it receives, it has nothing to receive with, nothing which could, perhaps, benefit by receiving the forms, benefit by being permanently enriched, raised more nearly to the status of form. It is said that a new violin, being played upon by a master, vibrates in harmony with the pure tones which he produces, until the wood of its sounding-box becomes more and more responsive to such tones, and its value is permanently enhanced. It does not lose, but retains the forms impressed upon it. But with matter in the absolute sense, as Plotinus understands it, there is nothing positive enough to be altered, to be impressed, and to retain the impress of the forms it has received. Matter is just not quite nothing, and that is all. Before, during, and after its commerce with forms, matter remains what it was, passive, receptive, but eternally formless, eternally not quite. Its apparent reality is thus always purely illusory, and it never attains to any kind of being. The forms flit in and out, and leave it permanently unaffected.

Matter is expelled from being, utterly separate from being. Incapable of transforming itself, matter remains for all eternity what it was originally, viz. non-being. Originally it was no actual thing, but fell outside all that is; and it has never become actual. Wishing to clothe itself in forms, it has failed to catch even their colouring, and remains what it was: potential existence, a phantom, feeble and without outline, never a form. It is illusion, falsity; and its negative character sets it poles apart from positive reality.[1]

Is matter beautiful? Surely not. It is unsubstantial, and has no qualities whatever. How could it, then, possess the quality of beauty? Beauty is a quality possessed only by substances. Is matter ugly? Again, surely not. Absolute matter, in itself, does not possess the minimum of reality necessary even to be ugly.

[1] *Enn.*, II, v, 5, condensed; cf. III, vi, 10, 11, 16.

There is thus, in matter, taken strictly, no place for either beauty or ugliness. It is beneath both.

And yet, in a certain sense, matter may be pronounced more nearly ugly than beautiful, just as it may be pronounced more nearly evil than good: and Plotinus does not hesitate to apply such terms to it, though hardly in a strict sense. When we look at concrete objects in which some ideal form has become embodied, at a horse, a tree, or a human being, we distinguish between the ideal and its material embodiment. We may say this specimen falls short of the ideal. It is not a true horse, or a true human being. It is deformed. The ideal is almost lost in its material copy or image. The form is dominated by the material in which it is embodied. In fact, the more nearly we approach to pure matter, the more completely does the ideal form fail to stamp its living impress. It becomes effaced and disappears.

Considered from this standpoint, absolute matter is thought of as absolute deformity, absolute failure of the ideal form to register its true self; and deformity in this sense, representing a failure on the part of the ideal form, a loss of power and a sinking into powerlessness, a passive drift towards formlessness, is of the essence of ugliness. And Plotinus, thinking of matter from this point of view, as the last and worst failure of form to be its true self, as the stage at which the vitality of form fades out, and exhausts itself in producing an image which is powerless to create further, but is a fleeting phantom, an aimless and strengthless illusion, speaks of matter as the source of ugliness and indeed as ugly. It is, however, only in relation to form and its failure in vitality that matter is, so called. It is really the deformed image or copy which is ugly. Taken strictly, in itself, absolute matter is *un*formed rather than *de*formed. It is altogether beneath form and deformity, and contains no place for either beauty or ugliness. It is the bottom rung on the ladder which leads towards beauty.

Let us mount the next rung, and consider concrete physical objects, fire, water, earth, air, and their compounds. These are material, and yet they participate in form, in the ideal principle or formula of fire, earth, and air. In so far as they are material, such objects are unsubstantial, illusory, and formless; and in so far, they are not beautiful. In fact, *qua* deformed, they are ugly. But in so far as they participate in the nature of the ideal principle, and are transformed by it into something more nearly resembling the living ideal, they take on the form of beauty, and become images of beauty.

The lake beneath the moon seems beautiful, as we all admit. Considered merely in itself, as a physical object consisting of material water, it is not beautiful. But considered as participating in form, as sharing in the unity, order, and harmonious system which belong to the nature of form, it suggests the idea of beauty to those beholders whose lives participate in that idea. The lake is not beauty. It is an image which stimulates the beholder to realize within himself the ideal form which is beauty. The lake is not even a substance. It is an image, an impress, a copy, whose whole function is to suggest its original, to suggest to the beholder that ideal realm of the spirit which the *nisus* within him is for ever urging him to seek.

We listen, for instance, to a child playing some piece of music. The child makes mistakes, and, if we attend to the mistakes, we shall never realize that he is doing more than making mistakes. He is, however, making music. We can so listen as to hear, through and in spite of the mistakes, the authentic note of the ideal. It is then, and then only, that we realize the beauty of the music, and welcome it as something akin to what it awakens in our own selves. So too when we meet with a fair human form, it awakens in us the expectation of a correspondingly beautiful human spirit; and if it fails to come up to the expectations it awakens, we are disappointed and shocked. With our sense-organs, we see and hear the objects of the physical world; but, in seeing and hearing them, we think of the ideal objects of the spiritual world; and it is only in such cases that we think of the physical objects as beautiful.

Plotinus takes the example of the mystic, who, on beholding the panorama of the physical universe, feels stirred within himself to his very depths. His sense of worship is touched, and he thinks "How beautiful, how wonderful—and how transcendently beautiful its Source, its Original!" Such objects, that is to say, are beautiful, not in their own right, as physical objects, but as participating in form, and as suggesting, to all who have any feeling for the ideal—and who has not?—the transcendental realm of the spirit, and its surpassing values.

The physical world, if it had a voice, would say to us, "God created me. Coming from His hand, I am perfect. I include everything, every species which can be created: plant and animal, gods and spiritual beings innumerable, souls which are good, and men whose virtue makes them blessed. Not only is the land beautified with every plant and animal species. Not only is the sea responsive to my life-giving power. The air also, the ether, and the entire celestial region as well, participate in my power which animates them. In the higher region are all souls which are good. They animate the stars and the eternal sphere of the heavens, whose circular motion around its unchanging centre is a wisely ordered copy of its spiritual model, and is guided by no external attraction. All within me make the good their aim; and every one of them attains his aim, as far as his power extends. The whole heaven is dependent upon the principle of the good. So is the principle which animates me. So are the gods which are in the parts of me. So finally are all animals, plants, and apparently inanimate beings contained within me. The last-mentioned are thought to participate in existence only. Plants participate in life too, and animals in sensation as well; while human beings possess reason, and the gods possess life in its completest extent. And this cannot be otherwise; for unequals could hardly be expected to participate equally."[1]

Let us mount the next rung, and consider the psyche, the animating principle found associated with everything which is alive, from Nature as a whole to the individual men, animals, and plants which people space-time, and, in their interrelations, make it the interesting and active scene that it is. We can consider the vital principle from observing its behaviour, what it does in the space-time world, and thence inferring its nature; or we can go further, and consider it metaphysically, in relation to its source or transcendental origin.

Let us begin by considering the living organism, which represents the vital principle in its embodied aspect, and observing its behaviour. What we see with our eyes is obviously the space-time movements of the organism. But, by interpreting these in the light of our own consciousness of self, we can infer to the nature of the vital principle involved.

In the first place, we observe the unifying, selective, orderly, and systematic nature of organic behaviour. If an organism is mechanically injured, e.g. by a cut of some sort, so long as the organism is alive, we observe the phenomenon of regeneration, the attempt to re-unify the powers of the organism. If we place an organism, or a group of social organisms, in a novel environment, we observe the phenomenon of adaptation, the attempt to react upon the environment in such a way as to live out the life-cycle characteristic of the organism or group of organisms. In fact, the study of biologi-

[1] *Enn.*, III, ii, 3.

cal and social science convinces us that behind the experimental interactivity with the environment in the space-time world, there is a definite, living principle of order and unity. We inevitably infer that life expresses itself by projecting, into the space-time environment, its own inherent forms of unity, building up structures and systems of its own, and using space-time as a medium for its own self-expression. Ants and bees, birds, cattle, and men, all have their characteristic ways of doing this. But behind all the different forms of behaviour created by the various species, it is easy to infer the operation of a fundamental tendency towards unity and the maximal development of systematic order. We deduce, therefore, that this is the function characteristic of living organisms as such, that is to say, of the vital principle which animates them.

In the second place, we observe that, in the exercise of this function, some organisms are more efficient than others, and that one and the same organism varies from time to time. In sickness, and shortly before death, we observe the control or unifying power of the organism to weaken, and we infer that the vital principle is itself, perhaps, weak. It seems as though it may be overwhelmed by material forces, and its tendency towards unity disrupted. As Plotinus understands this phenomenon, we conclude that when fully present, the animating principle animates, unifies, and strengthens in the normal way. But it may be absent, or partly absent. In such cases, the specific unifying tendencies of this or that organic type do not make much impression upon the environment. We infer, then, that the animating principle, considered in itself, has the inherent function of imposing its characteristic unity and order; but, considered in relation to its material embodiment in space-time, it may be not strong enough to dominate, but may be dominated by, the material forces to which organisms are exposed. This naturally suggests a further inquiry, as to what the vital principle is, in itself, or in relation to its source; an inquiry not empirical, not based merely upon observed space-time behaviour, but transcendental, dialectical, and metaphysical.

Let us make this metaphysical inquiry. The source from which the vital principle draws its characteristic powers will obviously be a principle of unity and order considered apart from the space-time conditions which militate against its complete expression. The source from which the animating principle draws its vitality will thus be spirit, the living realm of ideals in their most perfect and transcendental form. Spiritual life is, in itself, the creative self-projection of these ideals, in entire independence upon spatial and temporal conditions, and in accordance only with its own inherent dialectic. Animate life is the projection of these ideals into the space-time world, under the especial conditions of some determinate species, such as the ant, the horse, the human being, or of Nature as a whole. Like Plato, Plotinus thinks of the soul as withdrawing at times from the empirical world of space-time action and reaction, and communing again with the transcendental ideals which are the source of its vitality. It lives in contemplation of the principles of absolute justice, beauty, goodness, and truth, and in that vision renews its vigour and insight. Eventually, clad in shining armour and with a new edge to its weapons, it returns again to the space-time conflict in which it realizes its especial function.

Plotinus considers the animating principle from two standpoints, and at times speaks as if there were two such principles, a higher and a lower. (1) In relation to its source, the realm of pure ideals, from which it can never be completely severed, the vital principle can be regarded as the spearhead of the ideal realm, directed towards space-time, maintaining contact with its source, and never losing itself in the details of mundane existence. (2) In relation to its space-time activities, i.e. in its lower aspect, the vital principle is spoken of as though the living organism could lose sight of its connection with ideals, and could sink into the region of particular details and purely local interests; as though it could use its powers of unifying and organizing in the service, not of the higher ideals, but of a narrow and ultimately visionless selfishness. This is seen when human beings lay up for themselves treasure upon earth, and lose themselves in futile conflicts with other human beings, rather than co-operate with others towards the realization of the common realm of transcendental ideals.

Students of Plotinus sometimes think that the soul, in so far as it directs its activities upon the space-time world, is essentially degenerate, and falls below its inherent station. They believe that only when it turns its back upon the space-time world, and withdraws towards union with the ideal visions, does it become regenerate. For this view, there is undoubted evidence in the work of Plotinus. His final attitude, however, is expressed in his image of the teacher. The ideal teacher passes on his spirit to his pupils, kindling in them insight and love, a vital acceptance of the ideal realm. He does not withdraw himself from them, but gives all that he has in him to give. Yet, in so giving, his spirit does not lose its vision, or weary of well-doing. It gives of its abundance, yet loses nothing of its power. The pupils take what it is in them to take from him; but it is not a physical taking, that it should use up the supply. Spiritual power is a source which is inexhaustible. It can be passed on from generation to generation, spreading as it passes. Not only is there no weakening, no dilution, but its strength seems to increase, as we see when we consider the history of culture. This is, in fact, the ideal task of the spirit, and of the soul in so far as it co-operates with the spirit: to enlighten others, to kindle kindred fire in their inmost souls, to spread illumination abroad without limit, until the space-time world has become radiant with spiritual light, and has become transmuted, without remainder, into the ideal realm.

The animating principle gives to body all that body is competent to receive from soul. It gives without toil, without planning, without directing and without correcting. In contemplating what is prior to itself (namely, Spirit), it orders all things with marvellous power. Its increase in beauty and might is proportioned to its devotion to contemplation. From contemplation it draws all that it has, all that it gives to what comes after it (i.e. to body). The radiance which it spreads around it is drawn from that eternally radiant source (viz. Spirit).[1]

Thus understood, how is the soul, or animating principle, related to beauty? In so far as the soul realizes ideals, reshaping the space-time world in accordance with the soul's desire for a completer unity and co-operation, its activity succeeds in creating space-time images of beauty. This creative activity is clearly itself beautiful. But soul is not beautiful in itself, in its own right. It draws its value from a higher source, from the realm of the spirit, from the transcendental ideals which it is realizing in co-operation with others. There are souls which are ugly and vicious, as well as souls which are beautiful and virtuous. But in its inherent nature, as essentially alive and creative of space-time images of value, the soul is more nearly akin to beauty and virtue than to ugliness and vice.

Let us now mount the next rung, the rung occupied by spirit. There are many ways in which we can make clear to ourselves what

[1] *Enn.*, II, ix, 2, condensed.

Plotinus understands by "spirit." It is the intellectual place, the home of ideas and ideals. Go into a library, and pick up any book which it contains: some work of physical or social science, the latest encyclopaedia, the plays of Shakespeare or Shaw, what you will. It is already contained in the spirit: only in more perfect form. In the libraries of the spirit are contained all the works, written and unwritten, dreamt of and not yet dreamt of, past, present, and future. All are there, and in perfect form. Go into any art gallery, and survey the masterpieces of Leonardo, Raphael, Rembrandt, Rubens, whom you will. They are already contained in the art galleries of the spirit, along with the work of secessionists, cubists, futurists, and what not: only, in the art galleries of the spirit, they are present in perfect form. Go into the concert halls of the world, and listen to the sonatas of Beethoven, the symphonies of Schubert, the operas of Wagner. In the concert halls of the spirit they are already present: only, in those halls, Beethoven's latest sonata has its final movement, Schubert's unfinished symphony is completed, Wagner's early operas are rewritten. The puzzles are solved. The misunderstandings have disappeared.

How are these "present to" or "contained in" spirit? Not, of course, as volumes are placed side by side on shelves, each excluding the others from the space which it occupies, but implicitly, in power, and in idea. For spirit transcends both space and time. In fact, library books, paintings, and tone-poems are all space-time images, copies of some idea, expressions of ideals which exist in transcendental form, in the realms of the spirit, mind, or reason. This is true, not only of art-works, but also of the works of nature, whether animate or inanimate. In the spirit are the ideas of every genus, every species, and every individual animal or plant, every rock, every breath which moves over the face of the waters, every star in the heavens. Just as the mind of an architect contains ideas which will one day issue into the space-time world as blue-prints, designs to be executed in steel and stone, so does the creative spirit contain within itself all the ideas for everything which can be created. It contains them in the creative germ, and can make any part of them explicit, when it wills. Spirit is the place of plans; and all the little plans are related to a single, all-embracing plan. In this there is a place for everything, and everything is in the place ideally best for it, nature, art, science, religion, and philosophy: all forming part of a single harmonious system, the outcome

71

and self-expression of a cosmic, and more than cosmic, Reason or Spirit.

Suppose we ask, "In *whose* mind or spirit do these ideas exist?" the answer is not difficult. It is easy to realize that the ideas of Beethoven's symphonies and Leonardo's paintings once existed in the minds of Beethoven and Leonardo. It is not difficult to realize that we can make them exist in our minds, too; that they are there, implicit, requiring only a certain stimulus to bring them out. When we attend a concert, a lecture, or a sermon, we find ourselves capable of criticizing, from an inner source, what we hear. We criticize the relation of its parts, its inherent excellence, its idea, as well as its space-time performance. This inner source is the spirit. It is within our selves, or perhaps we should say, our selves are within it. If we ask, "In whose mind is the great, all-inclusive, ideal plan?", the simplest answer is to say, "in God's mind." In point of fact, Plotinus does speak of the ideas as existing in God's mind, as though God and spirit were identical, that is to say, as though what the ordinary man thinks of as "God," and what Plotinus thinks of as "spirit," were at least co-extensive.

But this is not the whole truth. The ideas exist in *our* minds, as well as in "God's" mind. This does not mean that "we" and "God" are regarded by Plotinus as self-subsistent substances, introspecting and reporting upon their own contents. His view is less personal. We see Plato the high-born Athenian disappearing into Plato the philosopher, and ultimately into philosophy itself. We see Beethoven the struggling Rhenish composer turning into Beethoven the musical artist, and ultimately into music itself. As we ourselves enter more deeply into the life of the spirit, we become less and less merely empirical selves, and more and more spiritual selves, and ultimately we disappear into spirit.[1]

And this leads us to our last point. Spirit is not abstract and dry-as-dust, a collection of formulas, idealized blue-prints, and what not. Soul and Spirit are, rather, stages of life and experience. We can live at the level of the instincts, senses, and emotions. That is life or experience at the space-time level of animation. Or we can so develop that we live at a high level, the life of the scientist, artist, priest, and philosopher, at the level of reason. This is the life of the spirit. It is the same life as space-time animation, in the

---

[1] So, in everyday conversation, we hear that "John is the embodiment of courage," and "Mary is kindness personified."

sense that nothing vital has been lost. But it is infinitely more real, infinitely more alive. It has greater range, and greater depth, is superior to space-time considerations, and is through and through creative and active. At this level of experience, we understand everything in principle. We sympathize with, and are united in feeling with, everything. Our self becomes, in principle, all-inclusive. And yet, it still remains a self. It remains subjective, and does not utterly vanish into the object of our activity. We remain scientists, artists, philosophers, and do not entirely disappear into science, art, and philosophy, although such self-transcendence is plainly our goal.

So much for what Plotinus understands by "spirit." How is this related to beauty and creative art? Spirit is the home of beauty, the creative source from which issue, not only the art-works which we admire in our space-time world, and which make us reflect upon their creative source, but the ideas of those works, and indeed the idea of beauty itself. It is the spirit which unifies and organizes, and, by so doing, gives us, in place of chaos, a cosmos in which new values come to life. The creation of such values is the function of art, the self-expression of the idea of the beautiful.

The ideas, the source of all beauty in the world, spring from the very substance of spirit. And above and beyond beauty we see goodness—the so-called "idea of good"—for beauty is a projection of goodness, and lies at its threshold. In one word: Beauty is ultimate. It is not physical, but spiritual. We first identify beauty with goodness. But, if we must distinguish in the realm of spirit, beauty is where the ideas are at home, while goodness lies beyond, and is the fountain-head and origin of beauty.[1]

One further question remains. What is the relation of beauty to the other value-experiences, goodness, wisdom, worship? In the Platonic school, there was a tendency to regard beauty as essentially subordinate to goodness, goodness as essentially subordinate to wisdom, and wisdom to worship. It was believed that the master had taught that sex-love is an imperfect experience which reaches complete fulfilment when it leads the lover into the realm of the beautiful, that beauty is an imperfect experience which reaches its completion when it passes over into the realm of moral values, that moral experience is also imperfect, and leads to its own transcendence in spiritual wisdom, and that wisdom too, in the end,

[1] *Enn.*, I, vi, 9, *ad fin.*

73

culminates in something higher even than wisdom, namely, in mystical worship. In an earlier treatise Plotinus shows the influence of this school tradition. But his maturer attitude towards the question is determined by his distinction between lower and higher levels of experience, and his recognition that each of these values has a definite place at each level of experience.

At the space-time level, we have physical love, physical beauty, physical goodness: mere images or rough copies of love, beauty, and goodness at the spiritual level. At the physical level, these value-experiences are relatively separate and distinct. Sex-attraction is not necessarily connected with love of the good, the beautiful, and the true; and an interest in a simple ethics or a simple establishment of scientific facts may have little in common with aesthetics, or with a love of one's fellows. But as we advance to the higher levels, these values not only deepen in meaning, but converge, and tend to fuse together. Spiritual love cannot be dissociated from beauty, goodness, and truth. Spiritual truth cannot be dissociated from beauty, goodness, and love. At the highest level of all, in mystical experience, the fusion is complete. But even at the intermediate or spiritual level, he who has attained to one, has attained to something of the others also.

Thus, whatever the lower starting-point, our experience, from Plotinus' maturer standpoint, as we advance towards the higher levels, becomes not only deepened, but broadened, more nearly all-inclusive. Ordinary everyday goodness may be a stepping-stone to the whole spiritual level: to beauty and truth at that level, as well as to ideal goodness. So too the space-time images of beauty, which make us reflect and create in our minds the ideal of beauty, awaken also the ideals of goodness, love, and truth; and the ordinary observed truths of the world of sense can, if dealt with sincerely, call into activity, not merely the ideal of truth-as-such, but the whole range of spiritual values.

Let us now consider briefly another class of values, the virtues or moral values. Here again, Plotinus finds himself in conflict with the empirical view, which regards the virtues as social phenomena, based upon instinctive tendencies, but developing, in human intercourse, and especially in the highly organized city-state, into their highest form, as the "civic" virtues. These are, e.g., military courage in the service of the community, justice in the sense of honesty as between citizens, temperance or self-control in eating, drinking, and sex, in accordance with the conventions approved by the community, and prudence or intelligent direction of domestic and civic planning, within the outlook of ordinary community life. The virtues are, in fact, largely so understood at the present day, and are justified, as a rule, on hedonistic and utilitarian considerations, much as in Plotinus' time, namely, as leading to "happiness," ordinary, human happiness.

He is equally opposed to the contemporary alternative, namely, the abstract and rigid logic of the Stoic school, which identified Nature and Reason, and made a virtue of necessity, treating the virtues as external necessities inwardly accepted. There is something humanly revolting in Epictetus' acceptance of humiliation, pain and disease as the necessary human lot, and in Marcus Aurelius' "cheerful contemplation of his own dissolution," and his slogan, "Thy will, O world, is my will!" Human civilization has developed only upon the contrary hypothesis, upon refusal to accept intolerable conditions. The Stoic doctrine of "inner consent" is, in fact, the rationalization of impotence.

As against these views, Plotinus puts forward his own doctrine, characteristically as an interpretation of certain passages from Plato's *Dialogues*, especially the *Phaedo* and *Theaetetus*. He treats the virtues as essentially "purifications," withdrawals from hedonistic and space-time considerations altogether, into a superior realm. This superior realm is, of course, the realm of spirit, the true source and home of ideals, the home from which issue those self-projections into the space-time world which make of it a place worth living in by spiritual beings.

Here too, as in the case of beauty, hasty readers have supposed that Plotinus counsels withdrawal from the world we live in, from the warm human contacts which make life a thing of comfort and joy, into a strange realm; a realm in which mystics luxuriate in their private and personal emotions, and succeed in shutting out the thought of everything unpleasant, as being somehow "unreal." The truth is, that it is only in opposition to other schools that he stresses the "withdrawal." His real emphasis is not upon the withdrawal, as such, but rather upon the positive nature of the spiritual realm to which we withdraw. For in that realm the seeker obtains what he really desires, namely, clear and sound ideals of conduct based, not upon empirical trial-and-error, but upon transcendental order and system, and associated with an experience of life which is not superficial, a mere matter of neural stimulus and reaction as the be-all and end-all of existence, but life understood in its deepest and most spiritual sense.

Just as Plato's philosopher-kings withdraw from the world to refresh their idealism, and then return to their task of administrative and educative activity in the space-time world, so too of Plotinus' doctrine. What he teaches is the doctrine of *reculer pour mieux sauter*. It is in opposition to other schools that he emphasizes the element of *reculer*. But the positive purpose behind the withdrawal is there, if we read carefully. The line of progress leads, never backwards, but always forwards. But it is advisable, at times, to withdraw from excessive preoccupation with space-time, and to reflect upon the line of progress, if the movements we make are to lead truly forward.

So too we might consider the truth-values, and might bring out Plotinus' opposition to a merely empirical science, which limits itself to the work of a curator, blindly cataloguing the objective particulars which it observes, in favour of a study permeated by metaphysical insight into the living spiritual source of scientific discovery. Or we might consider the religious values, and might bring out Plotinus' opposition to the empirical acceptance of some religious creed because of its psychological thrills, or its flattering promises, so easily misunderstood by the ignorant and only half-initiated neophyte. We might investigate what he himself favours, a way of living radiant through and through with the inner glow of the deepest mystical insight and love. Or we might consider his philosophy of nature, animate and inanimate, or his social philosophy, or even his spiritual psychology. In each and every case we should find the same opposition to a visionless empiricism which, in Plotinus' thought, is identified with a cheap and easy materialism; and we should find the same clear distinction between lower and higher levels of experience, starting with matter and space-time, and passing through soul and spirit to a final view of experience as absolute. But perhaps it is time now to take these for granted and to advance, as far as we can, along the path which leads upwards from the realm of spirit to the ultimate source of neo-Platonic mysticism.

Spirit is fair, of all realities the fairest. In the pure light, the spotless radiance in which it reposes, it embraces all that truly exists. Our empirical world, fair as it is, is but a shadow cast in its semblance; and as, when we look up into the heavens and behold the pure light of the stars, we are put in mind of their Creator and seek after Him: even so we feel a need to search out the Creator who has wrought the reality of the spiritual realm, the Father who has begotten this Son who is Spirit, so fair in plenitude, with a plenitude coming from the Father. The nature of this higher Creator, His abode and mode of operation, become our quest. For the transcendental Creator is assuredly other than Spirit and its plenitude, seeing that He is prior to both. They are indeed posterior to Him, and need Him to form them into Spirit and to fulfil them with His plenitude. They are near neighbours of the principle which transcends all need, even all activity of thought; and they possess veritable plenitude and veritable thought-activity, because their possession is an unmediated heritage from the good. But the principle which is prior to them transcends both possession and need; for it is absolute, ultimate goodness.[1]

It will be remembered that Plato's "idea of good" occupies a peculiar position in Plato's thought. It is seen last of all in the ideal world, and even then only with an effort. It is in fact left so obscure that modern, as well as ancient, writers do not hesitate to identify it with "Plato's secret"; and the interpretations which they offer, in so far as they do not give up the riddle altogether, diverge. Plato himself suggests that the way to it is "by destroying the hypotheses" upon which the work of the departmental sciences rests. It is thus not so much *an* idea as *the* idea, the principle of ideality itself, experience at a level which transcends the conceptual instruments of the scientist; and in our study of Plato we have so interpreted it.

Plotinus' approach to his highest and holiest is somewhat similar. For him too it represents that which is implicit, only partially revealed, in the lower levels of experience, in space-time existence, in animate creativity, in spiritual activity; and it can be approached by following this path still further. What stands out, as we progress from lower to higher levels of experience, is (1) an approximation to an all-inclusive unity which brings new spiritual values into being, and (2) an increase in comprehensiveness, depth, and vitality. Accordingly Plotinus defines his highest stage, the goal towards which development in spirituality points, as "the one," and makes it abundantly plain that he does not mean arithmetical unity, or some abstract point of concentration around which experiences may be methodically grouped, but a concrete and vital experience. He

[1] *Enn.*, III, viii, 11.

means an experience which includes everything of value in animate existence, but fused together in a new way, which makes of it all something transcendently wonderful, transcendently alive and creative, beyond sensation, beyond thought, and beyond self.

In our search for this underlying and all-containing unity, which is to render intelligible in a new and finally satisfying way the plurality and manifoldness of our empirical experiences, we advance from the space-time multiplicity of objects, horses, dogs, etc., to their unifying principle in the class-concept, "the horse," "the dog," and from the multiplicity of class-concepts to their unity in the ideal plan which exists in the spirit. But when we have reached this spiritual level itself, we still find a last residue of dualism, which we seem unable to overcome: the dualism of subject and object. This ideal plan is a plan made for a self and by a self; and the self exists over and above the plan. It is, and remains, distinct.

Just as, in the field of action, there seem to be always (1) the person who acts, the agent, and (2) other things or persons upon, with, or against which or whom the agent acts; so in the field of knowledge there are always (1) the knower and (2) the known. The dualism does not vanish. We cannot conjure it away. It seems to be inherent in knowing, as such. The philosopher who remains at the level of spirit does not disappear finally into philosophy, for all that he feels and realizes that this is his goal. The artist does not disappear into his art, the scientist into his science, the priest into his religion, the lover into his loving. The subject-object relation remains obstinately dual. No rational procedure can reduce it to unity.

The ordinary attempts at such unity consist in trying to reduce one of the two factors to a phase of the other. Materialists construct their purely objective world, and find they have left the self out. They try, simply enough, to put it into the world, holus-bolus, to make of it one of the objects which it constructs and considers. But everyone except the materialist himself can see the illogical nature of this procedure. Spiritualists, on the other hand, try to treat the world as a kind of self, and put everything on the side of the thinker: so that, when we think, our thoughts are somehow alive with a life which is their own. They are subjective, self-centred existences. They think, therefore they exist. But everyone except the spiritualist can see the flaw in this method.

The attempt thus seems hopeless. At the spiritual level of experience we are faced with what is called "bifurcation," and we remain unable to solve the puzzles it entails. This level of experience, like those below it, seems, in the end, not free from contradiction, not quite rational. The position is most unsatisfactory.

It is easy to see that our search must be for a kind of experience which will overcome this conflict and opposition, and attain to a level of unity which is above dualism, above contradiction of all sorts. If spirit and reason have failed us, then we must search for a kind of experience which is above the rational level. What we seek must contain everything positive, everything of value in rational experience. It must be spiritual through and through. But it must be above the thought of self and above the thought of a world. It must not be subjective, and it must not be objective. It must succeed in transcending this distinction altogether. To succeed, it may have to become something more than experience; more, but not less.

We have discussed matter, the formless below form. Supreme reality will be at least its antithesis: the formless which is above form. Balzac tells the story of an artist who rebelled against the natural limitations of his art, and kept on painting out all sharp outlines, trying to suggest the living form by subtleties of shading. When his picture was finished, the spectator, if exceptionally sympathetic and imaginative, could catch a suggestion of a vision of a living form, but could never attach it definitely to the canvas. Unsympathetic spectators, and those who examined the canvas with empirical eyes rather than with the creative imagination, saw nothing, no trace or suggestion of any figure whatsoever. It is the same with Plotinus' ultimate vision. We can use words in such a way as to suggest what it would look like, if we could see it. We understand it to be the reality, the wholeness, the ideally creative unity which lies back of experience. We understand that it transcends all empirical space-time images, all ideal concepts, thoughts, or plans; that it transcends life as we know it, and even the idea of life; that it transcends love, and beauty, and goodness, and truth as we know them, and even the idea of love and truth; that it transcends all the historical figures worshipped in the historical creeds, and even the ideal figure which we might conceive to be the true object of religious worship, as such.

We can say all this, and much more, about "the one," or the

ultimate, the final, the absolute. But when we have said it all, when we have gone over Plotinus' arguments, and have replied to all criticisms; when we admit that it is all true and undeniable, that there must be some ultra-logical reality, ultra-metaphysical, even, if we follow philosophy whither it leads—do we, when we attempt to go further, and seek to enter the sanctuary which we have built up, stone by stone of pure white marble, find within what we should find, what we have deduced should be there? Do we find something beyond experience, the infinite, absolute, ultra-living, more-than reality, of which our best and surest experiences are but a palely illumined copy, shining by reflected light? Do we bathe joyously in the radiance of those ultra-spectral beams, permeated with such transcendent clarity that we lose our self-centred being, and become absolutely one with the vision? Do we cease to be merely human beings, living, as well as we can, a god-like existence, and become divine, with no part of us not in intimate contact with divinity? Or do we, after arousing our expectations to the aching-point, find the interior of the holy of holies to be an aching void, absolutely and painfully empty? Do we find Everything or—nothing?

That is the question. If we are mystics, we answer in the affirmative. We describe, as well as we can, using words as symbols to suggest far more than words can ever express, the glory, the beauty, the majesty, the wonder, of this more-than experience which is occasionally vouchsafed to us. For ever after, if we are mystics, we walk through the world with eyes turned inward and upward, aglow with our inner vision, seeing things differently from our fellow-mortals, but understanding and sympathizing with their blindness, even with their criticisms and mistrust of our glorious certainties. To us there are no more riddles. All mysteries are solved. The world is once again the Garden of Eden, and again, in love and reverence, we walk with God.

But if we are not mystics, we answer in the negative. We have strained and tormented our poor human faculties beyond what they can bear, and we have seen—nothing. Not that there is nothing there; on the contrary, we are assured that, back of experience, there *is* something, something which our experience only partly reveals. But we conclude that it lies beyond human power to see the ultimate. How can human beings, we ask, put off their humanity? How can we experience what is not an object of experience? How can we imagine what is not an image, or conceive what is beyond conception? The thing simply cannot be done. We admit that the dualism of the subject-object relation is unsatisfactory. We admit that there may be a formless which is above form, as there is a formless which is beneath form. We admit, with unwincing logic, that these are not identical, but are antitheses, the one as transcendently real as the other is unreal. But yet, what we believe in as a logical and metaphysical construction, we fail to grasp in any mystical, intuitive, self-validating ecstasy; and, as honest men, if we are not mystics, we not merely admit our failure, but we scrutinize a little closely the mentality and morality of those who insist that they have succeeded where we have failed, and that, where we have registered a blank, they have seen the vision.

It is usual for critics to point to the negative element in Plotinus' depiction of the ultimate. The "one" is *not* this, *not* that, *not* the other thing. And it is usual to stress the image of flight, of turning away from the world, the isolation of the process, the "flight of the alone to the Alone," as it is sometimes translated. The criticism, however, probably goes too far. The mystic withdraws, not from the world, but from a superficial and fragmentary attitude towards the world. He withdraws to a source which is deep, full, refreshing, vital, and completely satisfying. To walk with God is not to be isolated, but to understand and sympathize with all things. To be conscious of unity is the direct antithesis of loneliness; and the mystic of Plotinus' stamp is not lonely. He is absolutely at home in the universe. And as to "negation": to one who has felt the truth of Plotinus' view, negation of the determinations which might be applied to the ultimate leads, not to nothingness, but to Everything. What it negates is the fragmentary, the merely empirical, the meaningless. Negation, in Plotinus' hands, is the sculptor's chisel which, stroke by stroke, strips off this and that chip of extrinsic and adventitious marble, and thus reveals the perfect, living statue. It is the negation of negativity.

To behold, we must turn to ourselves and look within. If we do not at once see beauty in ourselves, then, like the sculptor of a statue which is to be beautiful, who gradually, by chiselling off, scraping, polishing, and wiping clean, brings to light a face of beauty within the marble, we must work away at our selves, chiselling away what is superfluous, rectifying what is awry, scouring what is soiled until it shines again: not ceasing from our sculpturing until the divine brightness of virtue flashes forth, and we behold temperance seated upon a sacred throne.

When we meet with the self thus purified, and behold the entire self as a single, veritable radiance, a radiance beyond measure, altogether transcending quantity, the vision has come. Even while here below, we have reached the heights, and need no further guidance.[1]

The conclusion to which our study points is the acceptance of a moderate, mitigated mysticism. Behind the differences and disagreements of life, behind its difficulties and unsolved conflicts, we all feel that there is a basic, vital unity; a sense of comradeship in a common spiritual endeavour. We all feel, and believe, that life is more than appears on the surface, that its values are deeper than a shallow empiricism can reach. The adoption of such a view, even though we do not see, and do not hope to see, the visions which extreme mystics describe for us, is helpful and self-validating; and it is into this sane and mitigated mysticism that Plotinus initiates us.

He failed to found, within the Roman Empire, a temporal "City of Plato." He succeeded in founding, with the co-operation of St. Augustine, St. Bonaventura, and St. Thomas, a spiritual city, before which temporality bows humbly, the City of God. The life-giving waters from his inmost shrine have been blessed and freely mingled with the waters of the Christian font; and it is as the father of all subsequent mysticism, the greatest mystic of all time, that we take our leave of Plotinus.

[1] *Enn.*, I, vi, 9, condensed.

Chapter IV

DESCARTES 1596-1650

AFTER the inroads of the barbarians had destroyed the military and civil organization of the long-moribund Roman Empire, it fell to the Church to claim and exercise jurisdiction, primarily spiritual but also in an ancillary sense temporal, over the bewildered child-mind of medieval Europe; and the Church became mother, nurse, and tutor to unquestioning millions. Under her authoritative care, Christianity was gradually reduced to text-book form by the question-and-answer method adopted by Scholasticism: an approved catechism extending into many volumes. The language was first that of Platonism, and subsequently of Aristotelianism. But the voice was throughout the voice of ecclesiastical dogma, of unquestionable authority. Humanity was instructed in what it should think, say, and do, on all occasions of birth, life, death, and indeed afterwards.[1]

Under this beneficent tutelage, the child-mind grew and throve and eventually reached adolescence. And then began, as might have been foreseen, a certain chafing against its mother's indulgent but powerful apron-strings. The bad boy of the family, Giordano Bruno (1548–1600), ran away from his monastery to be the prophet of the new science. He escaped into the chill atmosphere of northern freedom and, after bewildering but not attracting his contemporaries, was reclaimed and severely punished, to discourage others from playing truant. Good sons of the Church gradually acquainted themselves with the spirit and details of the new science; and it fell to one who never officially broke away to initiate and guide the great change from adolescence to manhood, from obedience to the free life of reason, and to become the founder of modern philosophy.

René des Cartes was a young man of good family and good education. But he deserted his family and disowned his education.

---

[1] St. Augustine is the great Church Father who fused Neoplatonism with Christianity (354–430). St. Thomas Aquinas is the great scholastic whose *Summa Theologica* became the authoritative basis of "orthodox" theology (1225–74).

After concluding his studies in the Jesuit college of la Flêche, he entered upon the usual period of adolescent questioning, and found no satisfactory answer to the doubts which beset all intelligent youth. He had been instructed in a number of elementary techniques: the classical languages and the literary accomplishments associated with them, mathematics and their simpler military and scientific applications, a little philosophy and a little theology: just enough to make him more than a little doubtful as to their value.

> From my childhood I have been familiar with letters; and as I was given to believe that by their help a clear and certain knowledge of all that is useful in life might be acquired, I was ardently desirous of instruction. But as soon as I had finished the entire course of study, at the close of which it is customary to be admitted into the order of the learned, I completely changed my opinion. For I found myself involved in so many doubts and errors, that I was convinced I had advanced no farther in all my attempts at learning, than the discovery at every turn of my own ignorance.[1]

Did these studies lead to ideas so clear and distinct as to exclude all scepticism? Did they rest upon a basis so firm as to be proof against a young man's obstinate questionings? Had they anything at all to do with the discovery of genuine truth, or were they just words, words, words, the relics of a dead-and-gone social culture? To a young man of René's penetration, there could only be one answer. So far as he could see, all that he had learnt was waste time, or practically so. He would need to reject it and make a fresh start and effect an entirely new synthesis, before he could satisfy the impulses within him. If he could only discover a good starting-point and devise a satisfactory method! But it was hard. He was young and inexperienced. His family wanted to make a man of him by marrying him off, so that he could settle down to live the life of his social class. What was he to do?

Eventually he decided to postpone his sceptical inquiry until he should have become a man of judgment, an experienced man of the world. So he did the then equivalent of making the Grand Tour. He went to the wars as a gentleman volunteer, paying his own charges, living independently in camp, taking part in military engagements, and associating with the adventurous men of his own class.

[1] *Discourse on Method* (1637, tr. Veitch, 1850), Part I.

Descartes

As soon as my age permitted me to pass from under the control of my instructors, I entirely abandoned the study of letters, and resolved no longer to seek any other science than the knowledge of myself, or of the great book of the world. I spent the remainder of my youth in travelling, in visiting courts and armies, in holding intercourse with men of different dispositions and ranks, in collecting varied experience, in proving myself in the different situations into which fortune threw me, and, above all, in making such reflection on the matter of my experience as to secure my improvement.[1]

But one night he went out of his tent, the loneliest man in the whole army. The germ of a new idea, of a method which would enable him to investigate and attain to truth, to discoveries in the field of science, and perhaps in other fields as well, came to him in the long night-watches. The more he thought it over, the more convinced he became that here at last he had hit upon what he had always wanted.

What was he doing in this army, with all these simple-minded men of action around him? He felt an absolute stranger to them and their whole set of ideas and plans. As soon as he could complete his arrangements, he returned to Paris and devoted himself to studying, in an obscure quarter, the details and consequences of his new method.

Like one walking alone and in the dark, I resolved to proceed so slowly and with such circumspection, that if I did not advance far, I would at least guard against falling. I did not even choose to dismiss summarily any of the opinions that had crept into my belief without having been introduced by Reason, but first of all took sufficient time carefully to satisfy myself of the general nature of the task I was setting myself, and ascertain the true Method by which to arrive at the knowledge of whatever lay within the compass of my powers.

Accident restored him for a brief period to his family. But their ideas of a young marquis's social duties were incompatible with his determined scientific temperament; and he separated himself deliberately from them, and from all influences which migh interrupt his fundamental enthusiasm. Whatever he might have lost, he had certainly found—himself; and he was determined to stick to what he had found.

[1] Ibid. The selections which follow are from the same work.

85

What precisely was this method he had discovered, this method of rightly conducting the reason in its search for truth? With characteristic caution, Descartes set himself to elaborate its principles, to work out its details, backwards and forwards, to consider it from a number of points of view and, further, to apply it in practice to the fields of physical and biological science, before he felt ready to initiate his contemporaries into the new art. Eventually he published his *Discourse on Method*, and the matter was then out of his hands.

This work begins autobiographically and shows how the author came to his ideas. It then states four fundamental propositions which formulate the principal features of the new method. It concludes with appendices showing how its author had himself used it in the sciences and had succeeded in making discoveries which were both new and well grounded. He composed further descriptions of his method in works which remained unpublished until long after Cartesianism had passed into history; and he answered the questions of a number of correspondents, giving further accounts and specimens of his way of guiding the reason aright. From all of these, put together, there is no difficulty in discovering clearly and distinctly in what his method consisted.

The method is connected with his own discovery of analytic geometry, i.e. his discovery that the method of algebra could be extended to embrace the truths of a different branch of science. Fundamentally it is a generalization, an extension of mathematical method into non-mathematical fields. It is a kind of quasi-mathematical logic. As Descartes understood it, mathematics proceeds by long chains of argumentation, deductive or inductive, from step A to step B, from step B to step C, and so on. The chain may be long, so long that no one is able to hold the whole of it before his mind at any one time. But if the first step was correct, and if each subsequent step or transition was correct, the conclusion is also correct. The vital point is thus to be found at the first step, and at each subsequent transition; and Descartes focused his attention upon these.

What makes us say that "two straight lines cannot enclose a space"? This is not a matter of lengthy argumentation, but of intuition, simple inspection. We just see it. When we have the case before our minds, we apprehend what is there to be apprehended; and we apprehend it clearly and distinctly, so much so as to exclude all possibility of doubt. What we thus apprehend is not matter of opinion, indirect, subject to challenge and deliberation. It is matter of knowledge: self-evident, certain. We know, and we know that we know. Reasoning thus consists of a chain of direct, intuitive apprehensions; and each individual step of deductive and inductive argumentation rests upon intuition, upon the clear and distinct apprehension that this is—whatever it is.

In the case of lengthy arguments, we may not have the whole clearly and distinctly present to our minds. But we remember that we have tested each link with our intuitive criterion, and have found it to be well and truly argued; and our knowledge as a whole thus rests partly upon our memories, but ultimately upon the natural light, the unquestionable, clear and distinct idea, intuitively apprehended.

With these beliefs in mind, Descartes sets forth his four principles. The first was

> Never to accept anything for true which I did not clearly know to be such; that is to say, carefully to avoid precipitancy and prejudice, and to comprise nothing more in my judgment than what was presented to my mind so clearly and distinctly as to exclude all ground of doubt.

This applies to the starting-point, to each link in the reasoning, and to the conclusion. Every proposition whatever which does not satisfy this primary requirement is to be regarded with methodic scepticism, whether it forms the beginning, the middle, or the ending of any process of reasoning. This principle further involves the complete rejection of all book-knowledge, all school-knowledge, all belief upon someone else's say-so; and it is as alien to the medieval outlook upon life as it is possible to be.

This principle formulates the resolution of adolescent doubt in all ages: the resolution to experience for oneself, to make up one's own mind, to refuse to be fobbed off with the alleged superior wisdom of elders-and-betters. It formulates the methodic scepticism which is so pronounced a feature of scientific inquiry: the determination to be objective at all costs, to establish contact with reality, with things as they are in themselves, independently of what anyone might prefer to have said about them. It formulates the ultimate assumption of logic, the possibility of an unquestionable simple apprehension. Once formulated, this principle has been a corner-stone of almost all subsequent philosophic edifices, and its fundamental importance has been stressed in recent treatises on the principles of logic.

In the second place, Descartes formulates the principle of methodic analysis:

> To divide each of the difficulties under examination into as many parts as possible, i.e. as might be necessary for its adequate solution.

To break up, that is to say, large questions into a number of small ones, so simple that they can easily be apprehended by the natural light, and the interrelations of their few parts thoroughly grasped. This obviously rests upon the first principle, which accepts the possibility of forming clear and distinct ideas of everything. It also plainly presupposes that in the analytic reduction of a complex problem to a number of simple issues, nothing of importance is lost. Objectivity is somehow safeguarded. If this is sound, Descartes has here formulated a principle accepted by common sense and indispensable to science. Analysis, if thoroughly reliable, is one of man's most valuable weapons in the unending battle with ignorance, and is a fundamental part of all modern logic.

In the third place, he formulates the principle of methodic synthesis:

> To conduct my thoughts in such order that, by commencing with objects the simplest, i.e. easiest to know, I might ascend by little and little, and, as it were, step by step, to the knowledge of the more complex; assigning in thought a certain order even to those objects which in their own nature do not stand in a relation of antecedence and sequence.

To link together, that is to say, the small questions, the clear and distinct ideas into which analysis has broken up the large question, and to proceed from the simple to the complex, grasping each step of the procedure, until the whole is reconstituted and understood in every detail. This also plainly rests upon the two preceding principles, especially the first. It also rests upon a further presupposition, namely that, without prejudice to objectivity and without introducing anything new and unforeseen, it is possible to put together any given number of simple apprehensions and thus to construct a totality which is thoroughly intelligible.

The aim of synthesis, resting upon its two forerunners, is thus to reduce a large question to a number of small ones, each clearly and distinctly apprehended, not only in itself, but also in each of its relations to each one of the rest. This is a very ambitious aim.

It has been accepted as an ideal principle to guide scientific research. But it has been actually realized (if at all) more in the mathematical than in the physical, biological, and social sciences.

And here it is necessary to explain a point which easily puzzles the modern reader, who naturally supposes that he understands what is meant by "proceeding from the simple to the complex." Since the time of Aristotle philosophers have used, and still use, these words in two distinct senses, only one of which is familiar to most of us. A conception can be "simple" (1) *in relation to us*: that is to say, psychologically, in relation to our present state of knowledge. What is simple to an adult, in this sense, may be quite a puzzle to a child; and what is simple to a child may seem quite complicated to one who has forgotten his childhood. This is the sense which we all understand, and it is utilized in text-books written for teaching purposes, which start with what the pupil may be supposed to know beforehand, and then gradually build upon that knowledge, introducing further complications as the exposition proceeds. But this is not the sense in which Descartes is using the term.

In the philosophic sense (2) a conception is "simple" *in itself*: that is to say, logically or metaphysically, when it states a presupposition, an axiom or higher principle, upon which the later propositions which constitute the body of a science depend. The propositions of Euclid's *Elements of Geometry*, for instance, were regarded in Descartes' time as arranged in an order which passed from the simple to the complex. But the order was not psychological, but logical. Descartes regarded as the really simple thing in geometry that which the whole science presupposes, namely, the nature of space. In itself, or "in the order of nature" (as opposed to an order based upon the relations to the immature human mind), space is logically prior to triangles, straight lines, and points, and is thus "simple." Two-dimensional space was thought to be "simpler" than three-dimensional space, and one-dimensional space was considered still "simpler." The "objective" way of studying science (as opposed to the psychological method) was thus to arrange the propositions in which its ascertained truths were expressed in such an order that the earlier propositions were presupposed by, and were logically prior to, the later propositions.

When Descartes, then, speaks of the synthetic method as "proceeding from the simple to the complex" he means proceeding from what is simpler in itself, or logically, or in the order of nature.

That is to say, he means starting from fundamental or very general concepts and working gradually to consequences and details which are "complex" as being meeting-points for several principles. Principles and general axioms are thus "simple ideas," of the kind which can be clearly and distinctly apprehended when analysis has separated them out from the complicated empirical environment in which they are found. The synthetic method proceeds step by step, investigating what happens, i.e. what can be deduced clearly and distinctly, when you add idea A to idea B or to idea C.

A correct specimen of the Cartesian method is given by Descartes himself. When asked why he did not write his philosophy in accordance with his own method, he admitted the justice of the criticism and appended a concrete specimen of how he would follow his own method. Spinoza, in one of his earlier publications, completed the work along the lines indicated by Descartes, and afterwards wrote his own chief work in the same way, starting with definitions of *God*, *Substance*, *Attribute*, etc., as ideas which are "simple and general," i.e. fundamental.

This explains why Descartes believes it possible to analyse and synthesize without prejudice to objectivity, to the order of nature. Analysis gives us not just ideas which are small in extent, so small that the mind can grasp their structure in a single intuition, but ideas which are fundamental in the order of nature. Analysis reveals the objective structure of the phenomena analysed. So too synthesis, in constructing the complicated phenomena of nature out of the objective ideas which are "simple" in the sense of "fundamental," basic in the order of nature, terminates in giving us an idea which is not merely clear and distinct, with each part of its structure apprehended with intuitive certainty, but an idea whose structure is objective, and follows the lines of nature itself. For, in the end, as Descartes understands it, nature and God's plan, the creative plan of nature, are identical; and when we have succeeded in educating ourselves out of the fanciful, subjective, and merely psychological way of taking ideas apart and putting them together: when we have schooled ourselves to follow the order of logic which is also the order of nature, our thought is objective through and through. It is beyond the possibility of doubt, and has attained to complete certitude.

The fourth and final precept of the Cartesian method is, "in every case to make enumerations so complete, and reviews so general, that I might be assured that nothing was omitted." That is to say, to review the ideas, and make sure that each is sufficiently clear and distinct, i.e. sufficiently objective; to review the chains of reasoning, both analytic and synthetic, and make sure, not merely that each step is clearly and distinctly, i.e. objectively, apprehended, but also that no objectively necessary step has been omitted, and that nothing ungrounded has been introduced. That is to say, it is the principle of going over one's reasoning, and testing each link of each chain, so as to make sure that the conclusions rest, not upon anything subjective and merely psychological, but upon connections and conceptions which are objective, fundamental, and undoubtedly in the order of logic which is the order of nature.

This last principle is not a criterion or test of truth, different from the reasoning which is being tested. It is simply the reasoning process itself, repeated and re-viewed, to make sure that it is all evident, all objective, and all certain, i.e. that it has all been reasoned out in accordance with the three preceding principles.

Thus we see how Descartes passed from adolescent doubt to the construction of a method which he was assured would enable him to reach certitude and truth. It rests upon the conviction that intuition, or simple apprehension, with its clearness and distinctness, is able to exclude doubt for ever. It is a method which is itself clear and distinct, and in the passage from adolescence to manhood has been found helpful by many a young thinker, not merely in Descartes' own time, but in all succeeding times down to our own day. There is something in it of eternal youth, and it is as a symbol of the youth movement that the *Discourse on Method* still proves attractive to modern readers. It typifies the spirit of independence, of self-reliance, of confident adventure, of faith in the resources of reason. It calls to eager youth to follow, to think for itself, to co-operate in constructing science, to be clear, distinct, and objective, to be methodical and systematic. As such, it has been, and still is, an important influence upon modern thinking.

But after this work was published, Descartes' scepticism again awoke. He had published a method for banishing doubt, and yet doubt refused to be banished. He had developed the trick of meditating as he lay in bed. That is to say, he did not relax, and disperse his attention, as most of us do. He concentrated, brought all his mental powers to bear, as he reviewed, point by point, what he had written and published and, indeed, successfully used.

As he meditated, it occurred to him that certain assumptions of his method were exceedingly ambitious. "I am constrained," he writes,[1] "at last to avow that there is nothing of all that I formerly believed to be true of which it is impossible to doubt, and that not through thoughtlessness or levity, but from cogent and maturely considered reasons." An idea could be both clear and distinct, so much so as to exclude all doubt. But, after all, was not this subjective rather than objective certainty? For instance, as he meditated, he would sometimes drop off to sleep and would dream that he was meditating, would dream that he was awake and concentrating. His idea of himself would be clear and distinct. He would have no doubt as to its certainty. But then| he would wake up, and would find that he had really been dreaming. It was thus possible to have ideas which were clear and distinct, but false, out of touch with the order of nature, not conveying information objectively reliable. Even in the field of mathematics, where it had seemed to him that doubt was absolutely excluded, he could now see that it was possible to be sincerely in error. He needed, in a word, something more than his own powers of clear and distinct intuition to be assured that his thinking was objectively true. It might be that "some malignant demon" delighted in deceiving him, in encouraging him to think clear and distinct ideas which were false.

Accordingly, he reconstructed his thinking in the light of the further wave of doubt, and eventually published his *Metaphysical Meditations*, having copies distributed to the foremost thinkers of Europe, with a request for criticisms. The criticisms received, he considered them carefully, and published them, together with his replies to the objections. In some cases, he admitted the justice of the objections, and did his best to improve his manner of statement. In others, as in the case of the philosopher Hobbes, he coldly drew attention to the difference of their presuppositions, and, on the ground that they were discussing different propositions, he refused, somewhat abruptly, to enter upon a controversy.

Famous and influential as the *Discourse on Method* has been, the *Metaphysical Meditations* has been even more famous and influential. This treatise is like the earlier work, in that it is a treatise upon doubt and its presuppositions, and points the way to certitude. But the scepticism is more comprehensive and more thorough; the simple, i.e. fundamental, ideas revealed by analysis as involved in

[1] *Meditationes de prima Philosophiae*, Paris, 1641; *Med.* I, tr. John Veitch, 1853.

doubting, are set forth with extreme clearness and distinctness; and the synthetic part, pointing the way to scientific research by experiments which are rational rather than sensuous and empirical, is so distinctive as to be a pattern for all future rationalism. Henceforth, as far as Descartes himself was concerned, his mind was made up. He had found himself completely, was sure of the ultimate presuppositions upon which his thinking rested, and was able to devote himself to more synthetic work, in the field, chiefly, of physical science. His third great work, the *Principia Philosophiae*, is an example of mathematical physics which rests, without hesitation, upon the principles enunciated in the *Metaphysical Meditations*, and proceeds, with admirable clearness and distinctness, to unfold and develop the consequences of those principles. A fourth work, still read, is his treatise *On the Soul*, which proceeds upon the assumption of dualism, namely that there are two independent "substances," body and mind, and that body is the subject studied in physics, and mind the subject studied in psychology. It raises the problem of the relation between these two independent substances, and the problem thus raised, together with the further question as to how these two are related to a third ultimate substance, God, furnishes the chief starting-point for the further development of characteristically modern philosophy.

Let us consider the teaching of the *Metaphysical Meditations*. It begins with a meditation upon the nature and extent of doubt, and finds, soundly enough, that most so-called knowledge rests upon sensuous experience and memory. But it is obvious that the senses sometimes deceive us, and the same is true of memory also. It follows that eternal scepticism should attach to all knowledge resting upon so doubtful a basis. "All that I have, up to this moment," he writes,[1] "accepted as possessed of the highest truth and certainty, I received either from or through the senses. I observed, however, that these sometimes misled us; and it is the part of prudence not to place absolute confidence in that by which we have even once been deceived." The other basis of knowledge is thought or reasoning, especially as exemplified in mathematics; and many thinkers in Descartes' time, as at the present day, supposed it possible to cure the maladies of the senses by doses of infallible mathematics. But Descartes enunciates a new methodic rule against prejudice. When we believe something clearly and dis-

[1] Ibid.

tinctly, and feel no doubt at all, it is wise to construct artificially a counter-balancing prejudice, so as to free the judgment from all bias, and permit our minds to form clear and distinct ideas which are objectively, rather than subjectively, controlled. "I am persuaded," he says, "that I shall not be doing wrong, if, taking an opposite judgment of deliberate design, I become my own deceiver, by supposing, for a time, that all those opinions are entirely false and imaginary, until at length, having thus balanced my old by my new prejudices, my judgment shall no longer be turned aside by perverted usage from the path that may conduct to the perception of truth." This methodic rule has been adopted by many later thinkers and scientists, down to and including the present day, and certainly provides an additional safeguard against error. Descartes therefore applies his artificial prejudice in favour of the malignant demon who delights in deceiving him, even in the field of mathematics, and thus proceeds with an even greater degree of scepticism than before.

He proceeds by inquiring whether there is anything at all not open to doubt. Earlier sceptics, who asked themselves the same question, tended to conclude that "they knew that they did not know." This has been analysed and explained on the analogy of the paradoxes of one of the Socratic schools, e.g. "All Chians are liars; but I am a Chian; therefore, I am a liar. Therefore, when I say, 'All Chians are liars,' I am lying. Therefore, not all Chians are liars; so perhaps I am telling the truth after all; in which case . . ." There are many such paradoxes, on the edge of what can be thought and of what cannot be thought; and they are usually explained by saying that there is a contradiction between the form and the content. The form asserts a positive belief, but the content consists in denying positive belief altogether. Thus, to assert "I know . . ." suggests, in form, belief in positive knowledge; but the content, "that I know nothing," or "that I do not know," denies the possibility of positive knowledge; the argument thus contains a contradiction. It is usual to deduce from this that the position of scepticism is untenable, and that positive knowledge is therefore presupposed, as a possibility, in all assertion whatsoever.

Descartes avoids this well-known paradox by concentrating upon the subjective side of the subject-object relation. Nothing can stop the inquiring mind from inquiring, from questioning, from doubting. That is its essential nature. Inquiry is not something which comes to an end. It is of the essence of thinking that it should continue to raise questions and should subject all answers to further questioning. This is, so far, logically incompatible with the possession of knowledge which transcends the possibility of criticism. *All* so-called knowledge is, and can be, only a provisional summary, a cross-section indicating the present stage of inquiry. This position is, and remains for Descartes, fundamental; and it is of the essence of all characteristically "modern" thought.

When, therefore, Descartes pushes his question, "Is there anything about which the inquiring, doubting mind cannot doubt?" he finds that it accepts, affirms, and asserts *itself*, namely: inquiry, doubt, scepticism. I cannot doubt that I am doubting. The form of our thought is positive and determinate. It is true that there may be a contradiction between the *form* of thinking, which always connotes inquiry, and the *content* of our thinking, which tries to assert itself as though it were raised above further inquiry. But it is characteristic of Descartes and of modern philosophy to believe that mind is essentially an animated question-mark; and that no content, however clear and distinct, can raise itself above the possibility of being asked to give an account of itself, and of losing for ever the divine right of factuality. By changing the account of the nature of the mind from contemplative acceptance and worship to inquiry and theoretic investigation, Descartes at one stroke exchanges supposed fact for self-conscious questioning, and the medieval for the modern outlook.

Descartes has now succeeded in finding himself and in making this self, the inquiring and thinking self, the starting-point for his further thought. His way of expressing this, his fundamental formula, is well known. Regarding "doubting" as a species of "thinking," he formulates his sceptical position as *cogito, ergo sum*, "I think, therefore I am." "Thinking," he writes,[1] "is an attribute of the soul which properly belongs to myself. This alone is inseparable from me. I am—I exist: this is certain; but how often? As often as I think. I am, precisely speaking, a mind, understanding, or reason, a thinking thing."

Many readers suppose that Descartes passes, by an unconscious transition, from "I think" to "I am," i.e. from the subjective to the objective side of the subject-object relation, and thus ends with a philosophy of "being," of objective reality, consisting of substances

[1] *Meditation*, II, condensed.

95

interrelated in some ultimate, self-existing world. Some of these substances possess the attribute of thinking, whereas others are doubtless unthinking. In this way it is supposed that we have here an ontology, a metaphysics of "being," rather than a metaphysic of thinking, of mind, investigation, doubt, and inquiry.

This, however, is a mistake. One of Descartes' correspondents, naturally enough, raised this very question. He was informed that the *ergo*, the "therefore" of the famous formula, did not mean, for Descartes himself, what others took it to mean. "I think, *therefore* I am" looked like a deduction: as who should say, "I think; but, in order to think, I must first exist; my existence is thus prior to and independent of my thinking," and thus proceed to consider "existence" out of connection with "thinking." But what Descartes personally means is "I think. I am." These are two ways of saying the same thing: namely, that the kind of being which Descartes enjoys is the kind of being which consists in thinking. It is an intuition, a clear and distinct thought, that Descartes is essentially an inquirer, a doubter, a thinker. Expressed universally, it is the view that mind is essentially sceptical and inquiring. The Cartesian metaphysic thus remains, in the opinion of its founder, a metaphysic of inquiry as such, of scepticism *par excellence*, of unending doubt, thoroughly convinced of its own nature.

From this as a basis, how does Descartes proceed further? In accordance with the precepts of his own method, he reviews the situation and establishes the precise significance of his central thought. With thoroughgoing rationalism, he shows that "thinking" is the essential element in every phase of consciousness; not merely in logical and mathematical processes, but in emotional and sensuous processes; not merely in knowing, but in every form of experience. "I think. I am," he writes.[1]

What, then, am I? A thinking thing, it has been said. But what is a thinking thing? It is a thing that doubts, understands [conceives], affirms, denies, wills, refuses, that imagines also, and perceives. Assuredly it is not little, if all these properties belong to my nature. But why should they not belong to it? Am I not that very being who now doubts of almost everything; who, for all that, understands and conceives certain things; who affirms one alone as true, and denies the others; who desires to know more of them, and does not wish to be deceived; who imagines many things, sometimes even despite his will; and ˙is likewise percipient of

[1] *Meditation*, II.

many, as if through the medium of the senses. Is there nothing of all this as true as that I am, even although I should be always dreaming, and although he who gave me being employed all his ingenuity to deceive me? Is there also any one of these attributes that can be properly distinguished from my thought, or that can be said to be separate from myself? For it is of itself so evident that it is I who doubt, I who understand, and I who desire, that it is here unnecessary to add anything by way of rendering it more clear. And I am as certainly the same being who imagines; for, although it may be (as I before supposed) that nothing I imagine is true, still the power of imagination does not cease really to exist in me and to form part of my thought. In fine, I am the same being who perceives, that is, who apprehends certain objects as by the organs of sense, since, in truth, I see light, hear a noise, and feel heat. But it will be said that these presentations are false, and that I am dreaming. Let it be so. At all events it is certain that I seem to see light, hear a noise, and feel heat; this cannot be false, and this is what in me is properly called perceiving (*sentire*), which is *nothing else than thinking*. From this I begin to know what I am with somewhat greater clearness and distinctness than heretofore.

To the present-day psychologist, it is almost axiomatic that it is problems, questions, puzzles, which awaken the mind to activity, and that "thinking" is essentially the raising and solving of problems, both practical and theoretical. But towards the end of the Middle Ages, while the question-and-answer method inherited from the Socratic *Dialogues* of Plato was still used, it had degenerated into a mere external trick of pedagogic method. The emphasis was all upon contemplative acceptance and worship. And to find Descartes substituting inquiry for acceptance, and critical questioning for authoritative pronouncements, must have produced the effect of throwing open the windows of a room which has been too long closed up. Philosophy had been too long like an airman confined to ground-work. The work was important, and doubtless necessary. But what a relief, what a release, when the airman is allowed to take the controls and fly in the free air! The modern mind has taken the controls and has flown ever since.

From this point, Descartes proceeds by asking what the inquiring mind, now that it is free to inquire, really knows. In the first place, it knows itself. It experiments with its efforts after knowledge, analyses down to fundamental ideas, and then, by synthetic constructions, proceeds to expand what it knows into further, more developed knowledge. The most fundamental and most central of its ideas is mind itself: thinking, reasoning, doubting, asking itself questions and testing the answers it gives to its own questions. In this work, it asks its own questions, sets its own standards, and is always creative, originative, never satisfied with anything external, foreign to itself.

The first of the further developments of what it finds implicit in its own being is the development of the conception of a perfect mind, a mind which is all mind, unhampered by space-time conditions, by biological conditions: a mind which is pure thought, logic or dialectic personified. This is the Mind of an Ideal Thinker, an Infinite Intelligence, which asks all conceivable questions, faces all conceivable problems, and embraces within its comprehensive reflection everything which can be conceived or imagined.

Descartes calls this ideal intelligence "God." He constructs this ideal concept by taking the various excellences which analysis reveals in the limited, human form of intelligence, and thinking of them as released from human limitations, as unlimited in power. He also considers that an infinite mind would possess, not only the relatively few powers of the human mind, but an unlimited number of further powers. God or Infinite Mind is thus the human mind freed from all human limitations: each power is raised to infinity, and there is an infinity of such powers, many, indeed most, of which surpass our span of comprehension.

The idea of a being supremely perfect, and infinite, is in the highest degree true. It is likewise clear and distinct in the highest degree, since whatever the mind clearly and distinctly conceives as real or true, and as implying any perfection, is contained entire in this idea. And this is true, nevertheless, although I do not comprehend the infinite, and although there may be in God an infinity of things that I cannot comprehend, nor perhaps even compass by thought in any way; for it is of the nature of the infinite that it should not be comprehended by the finite; and it is enough that I rightly understand this, and judge that all which I clearly perceive, and in which I know there is some perfection, and perhaps also an infinity of properties of which I am ignorant, are formally or eminently in God, in order that the idea I have of him may become the most true, clear, and distinct of all the ideas in my mind.[1]

He finds the infinite mind implied by the limitations of the finite mind, the human intelligence which each of us knows. The question arises as to whether the infinite mind is imaginary, an abstraction

[1] *Meditation*, III.

constructed by our idealizing hopes—as we think of the perfect street-car, always there when we want it, or the perfect dictionary, always open at the right word—or whether it is real, perhaps more real than our own finite minds. To Descartes, it is obvious that for a finite mind, with its limited experience, to succeed in transcending its limitations and conceiving an infinite mind whose experience is unlimited, would involve a logical contradiction. It simply could not be done. He feels intuitively that the infinite is more real than the finite, the perfect than the imperfect, the ideal than the merely actual. He therefore accepts without hesitation the ontological argument associated with the name of St. Anselm, viz. that the ideal of perfection includes all thinkable perfections, and thus includes, as a necessary part of itself, the actuality of existence, of perfect existence, as well as, and along with, all other excellences. But the kind of existence which the perfect mind possesses is not, of course, a merely sense-perceivable existence. It is a perfect, ideal, thinkable and more than thinkable kind of existence, namely, the existence-for-self bound up with reflection. He writes:

When I make myself the object of reflection, I not only find that I am an incomplete, [imperfect] and dependent being, and one who unceasingly aspires after something better and greater than he is; but, at the same time, I am assured likewise that he upon whom I am dependent possesses in himself all the goods after which I aspire, [and the ideas of which I find in my mind] and that not merely indefinitely and potentially, but infinitely and actually, and that he is thus God. And the whole force of the argument of which I have here availed myself to establish the existence of God, consists in this, that I perceive I could not possibly be of such a nature as I am, and yet have in my mind the idea of a God, if God did not in reality exist.[1]

God, then, as the perfection of reflective intelligence implied in all intelligence, exists, and exists in the highest conceivable degree.

To Descartes this is important, because he has discovered that his finite mind is fallible; for it forms ideas which may be clear and distinct, and may seem indubitable, and yet turn out to be false. A perfect intelligence would, obviously, be absolutely infallible; and if we can subject our minds to the rules of perfect intelligence, we shall see as God sees, and thus our best and most methodic thinking will be infallible too. For instance, in regarding the self

[1] Ibid.

as fundamental, in treating the reflective, questioning mind as absolutely central in experience, and in regarding God, i.e. the ideal reflective mind, as ideally existent, Descartes cannot possibly be in error. These are ideas which are not merely clear and distinct. We have to assume them, if we are to think at all. They are thus self-evident, self-guaranteeing; and thinking which lives up to the standards of ideal reflection can never deceive, but is certainly to be accepted as objectively sound. God, as the most ultimate concept which can be thought, is what guarantees us against the deceptions of the malignant demon; and all knowledge which is based upon reflectively critical standards is free from error.

Let us pass to consider such knowledge, the content of the mathematical and physical sciences. We look at, e.g., a piece of wax. We enumerate its qualities. It is hard, white, has a certain smell and taste. When struck, it gives out a dull sound. It has such and such a size and shape. Now, melt the wax. It is no longer hard, its colour changes, its smell and taste become intensified. When struck, it gives out no sound. Its size and shape are no longer what they were. Its qualities have all changed. Yet we speak of it as the same substance, wax. Why? Sensation cannot assure us of its substantial identity. In fact, for sensation, its qualities are all different. Our minds think of it as identical. Its identity as a substance persisting under change is an ideal, a reflectively created concept. And it is this which is to be accepted in our thinking as permanent and true.

I must admit that I cannot even comprehend by imagination what the piece of wax is, and that it is the mind alone (*mens*, Lat., *entendement*, F.) which perceives it. But what is the piece of wax that can be perceived only by the [understanding or] mind? It is certainly the same which I see, touch, imagine; and, in fine, it is the same which, from the beginning, I believed it to be. But (and this it is of moment to observe) the perception of it is neither an act of sight, of touch, nor of imagination, and never was either of these, though it might formerly seem so, but is simply an intuition (*inspectio*) of the mind, which may be very clear and distinct, according as the attention is directed to the elements which it contains, and of which it is composed.[2]

We construct mathematical physics. This is not an absolutely pure science, like logic or metaphysics. The objects with which we deal, the "bodies" or corporeal substances whose motions we

[1] *Meditation*, II.

study, are not treated as things in themselves, as realities in their own right. They are treated in relation to our mathematical system, the system of three-dimensional geometry. "Body" is defined in terms of "extension," three-dimensional extension, and it is with the geometrical interrelations of the concepts thus constructed that mathematical physics concerns itself. What we know of them is thus not what they may perhaps be in their own right, but what the mind has constructed, namely, the network of geometrical propositions and ideas, a mind-made system which obeys the standards of an ideally reflective intelligence. So too the mathematics we use cannot be regarded as an absolutely pure science. Three-dimensional geometry is already adapted to dealing with a definite type of object, the type of object handled in Cartesian physics. Thus handled, physics constitutes an entirely mechanical science, applying under rigid conditions to geometrically extended objects affecting one another in a three-dimensional continuum by transmitting motion by impact.

The details of this science belong to the history of physics, and do not concern us here. What we are concerned with is to note (1) the rigidly mechanical nature of the Cartesian system, its complete avoidance of anything savouring of purpose or design, and (2) its complete rationalism, its thoroughgoing avoidance of appeals to sensuous experience, or trial and error as an experimental method. Rational analysis and synthesis are, indeed, experimental. If you put A, B, and C, as clear and distinct ideas, together in order to see what happens, this is an experiment; but it is a *rational* experiment. You construct the totality and see intuitively what the synthesis leads to. But you "see" by the natural light of reason, and not by the eyes or other sense-organs. What you "see" is not so much a fact as a conclusion which you deduce from premises. It is a "trial," if you will, but, if you follow the Cartesian method strictly, it is a trial without error. Cartesian physics is thus experimental, in so far as it is synthetic; but its method is deductive and rational, rather than sensuous and empirical.

From Descartes' standpoint, this is only to be expected. We know mind better than we know matter. "It is now manifest to me," he writes,[1] "that bodies themselves are not properly perceived by the senses nor by the imagination, but *by the intellect alone*; and since they are not perceived because they are seen and touched,

[1] Ibid. (italics mine).

but only because they are understood [or rightly comprehended by thought], I readily discover that there is nothing more easily or clearly apprehended than my own mind." We know God better than we know the world. That is to say, logic, mathematics, and metaphysics are prior to, presupposed by, physics. Pure philosophy is prior to applied philosophy; and rational methods, while undeniably experimental, are, for scientific purposes, of more fundamental importance than groping, empirical, and sensuous methods.

Descartes, himself a great discoverer in the field of science, thus remains obstinately a rationalist rather than an empiricist; and to this day he has his followers, physicists of great eminence who are mathematicians rather than laboratory experimenters; that is to say, men whose experimentation is of the nature of rational synthesis, prolonged reasoning, rather than of an appeal to the senses by trial and error. They take as their starting-point the most general and universal conceptions, and from these deduce the pervasive characters of reality. From these they deduce synthetically the more specific characters of this or that field of study, until finally they approximate to applying the whole system of their thought to an individual case. To this day rational or deductive philosophizing of this type is characteristic of the type of thinking we associate with educated Frenchmen, not only in science, but in art, in morals, in statesmanship, and in all practical affairs. That is what gives to their proposals in every field an air of necessity, of inevitability, of self-evidence; of something which has only to be stated clearly and distinctly to be admitted and accepted. It also gives to them a certain suggestion of mechanism, of rigidity, with perhaps more of narrow logic than of deep insight.

With this in mind, it is customary for students of philosophy to draw attention to what they consider Descartes' narrowness. They point out that his ideas are indeed clear and distinct, and that his logic, within its field, is excellent. But they also point out that the field is extremely narrow. What it leaves out is the whole of morality, in the sense of warm human interrelations, the whole of art, the whole of culture, the whole of religion and the life of the soul. It is practically restricted to science, and to a somewhat narrowly understood, purely theoretic science at that. The field of Cartesian philosophizing is thus, they think, dangerously narrow; so narrow that it stultifies itself, and concentrates upon a small part as if it were the whole. It is usual to go further, and to compare Cartesianism with that "positivism" which attempts to negate every human activity except a narrowly understood devotion to laboratory work in the physical sciences, and is associated with the general attitude of mind called variously "agnosticism" and "atheism."

As far as some modern thinkers are concerned, it is possible that this criticism contains more than a germ of truth. We have all met persons whose outlook is narrow, in the sense indicated. But, to tell the truth, narrowness is not confined to workers in the field of natural science. There are narrow moralists, narrow religionists, and, indeed, narrow culturists and narrow artists. The objection is thus to narrowness rather than to science, and it is universal in its application.

But as far as Descartes himself is concerned, it is possible that the criticism goes too far. It is true that Descartes withdrew from all influences which interfered with his work. He withdrew from his family, from his country, and from the great network of social ties which bind most of us to a single locality, in a spiritual, if not also in a geographical sense. But we find in his work two lines of thought which indicate all the breadth we could desire, in place of the narrowness which the critics deprecate.

In the first place, in his *Discourse on Method*, he states quite definitely that his "re-view" should extend so as to include, some day, morality and religion. But, his chief present interest being in science, he postpones the further inquiry until he is ready for it. Meanwhile, unlike many young men whose thinking is somewhat radical, he is perfectly willing and ready to accept and abide by the conventional rules of morality and established religious practice. If these statements are sincere, and there is no objective evidence that they are not, this means that Descartes took along with him, in his life, the great support which comes from conformity to established usage, from belonging to a definite social group, in this wide and important field. He behaved with the dignity associated with his rank. He had taken part in the wars. He had travelled extensively. He had arranged matters so as to live well within his income. He was *persona grata* to all persons with a claim to be regarded as intellectual leaders, whether royal, ecclesiastical, or commoners. He did harm to none, and he devoted himself to making the greatest contribution to human development of which he was capable. So far, his life was not narrow, or an influence making for narrowness in others.

In the second place, it is easily forgotten by modern readers that Descartes had received a very good general education. He was like a good many contemporary scientists who, in advising the young, suggest that time spent upon ancient Greek, or upon modern poetry, would be spent to better advantage in the scientific laboratory. As we all know, such advisers can, upon occasion, rattle off the paradigms of the verbs in -*mi* as well as any Grecian, and can quote the latest fashionable verse with taste and discernment. We can see that they enjoy their Homer as much as we do ourselves, and can cite their Shakespeare or their Bible at least as appositely as we can. Descartes belongs in this class. He does not feel the need of a professedly cultural education, because he has already received it. He has been through the mill. All this is a part of his background, as it is part of the social background of the men amongst whom he moves. It would hardly occur to him that there could ever be persons without it, efficient but uncultured technicians in some narrow field of applied science. We should not, then, regard him as really narrow, either in himself or in his intentional influence upon others.

We come now to the Cartesian psychology, especially as elaborated in the treatise *On the Soul*. As far as the physical side of life is concerned, Descartes, as a mathematical physicist, is as mechanistic and as rigidly deductive in his self-restricted field as any modern physiologist could desire. He treats animals in general as so many purely physical mechanisms, to be examined carefully and reported upon as so much machinery, wound up by nature (or the Deity) to run for just so long, and to react to stimulation in such and such precise ways. Animals have no "immortal souls," and no place, in their mechanisms, for any such thing. Human beings too are treated, as far as possible, on the same hypothesis.

But in the case of human beings, there is a recognized difference, and it goes very deep. Not only are we assured, by high authority, that human beings differ from the brutes that perish, by having been given immortal souls; we can also, by dissection, discover for ourselves the place in their mechanism where this reflective intelligence is probably located, the seat of the soul.

This is a small gland towards the base of the brain, centrally located. Its precise function was unknown in Descartes' time. It is still a matter of some doubt. Some present-day scientists suppose the "pineal gland" corresponds to the "pineal eye," a kind of third visual organ located beneath the horn-layer on the top of the head in certain prehistoric lizards, whose remains have come down to us. Others suppose it to be the last vestige of what corresponds to the swimming bladder in herrings, pike, and other fish. Descartes supposed, partly from its convenient central location, partly from the fact that the bodily nerves in general may be said to lead upwards in its direction, and partly because it is, as he understands it, a single organ, not in any way double, like the eyes, ears, and hands—that it was a kind of monastic cell, which received and originated messages. Messages, he thought, were transmitted to it from the rest of the body, when stimulated. Further messages, he supposed, issued from it by way of reply, directing the consequent motions of the hands, feet, and other parts of the body. Motions which were physical extended as far as to the walls of this gland within the brain. They were transmitted in the form of pressure or impact, in accordance with his general standpoint in physics, and brought pressure to bear upon the walls of the gland. But within the gland was the soul, a substance of a different order, reflecting, questioning, planning, directing; taking account of the various pressures, and indicating the most suitable responses.

These audacious speculations at once raised, in an acute form, a question which philosophers have always considered fundamental. If matter and mind are, as Descartes believes and teaches, two entirely distinct substances, with diverse natures and functions, so that matter is non-purposive, and mind is non-physical, non-mechanical, just precisely how do they intercommunicate and interact? Do not the terms of the definitions themselves exclude any conceivable answer?

Descartes himself tries to present a clear and distinct account of the situation as he sees it. But it must be confessed that the clearness and distinctness apply primarily to the physical side of the mechanism. They accompany our thinking from the impressed surface of the body, via the connecting nerves and tissues, as far as to the external surface of the pineal gland. They conduct us no further. How the physical, while remaining specifically physical, specifically non-psychical, gets translated into terms which are not physical, but psychical: and how, in turn, the psychical, while remaining specifically psychical, specifically non-physical, gets translated into movements which are not psychical, but physical: these are problems to which the answer was not easy for Descartes, and it is not easy for ourselves. Two sovereign and independent substances: how, if at all, can they co-operate? This problem, thus inherited from the seventeenth century in general, and the treatise *On the Soul* in particular, remains to this day unsolved.

At the present day, after exhaustive exploration of all formulations, it is generally believed that the problem cannot possibly be solved in the way in which it was left by Descartes. There is something fundamentally wrong with the Cartesian outlook and the Cartesian terms. It will be necessary to go back, to try to get behind his formulation, to construct new premises, and thus to make a new start. But in the seventeenth century, men were still hopeful of discovering some formula which would prove satisfactory to all parties. To Descartes' successors in philosophy in the seventeenth and eighteenth centuries, this became the central problem of metaphysics. Malebranche, Geulincx, Spinoza, Leibniz, and the rest, all set themselves to invent and formulate solutions of this problem. They were particularly fascinated by the further difficulty of how the two given independent substances, matter and mind, could be related to a third, even more independent and ultimate, the substance known as "God."

Descartes himself, in one of his latest letters, answers this very question, which a correspondent had submitted to him, by suggesting that matter and mind, while independent, mutually exclusive, in relation to each other, were not independent in relation to the all-inclusive substance, God. In this relation, which, for metaphysics, might be regarded as ultimate, matter and mind might be defined as two mutually exclusive aspects or attributes. It remained, however, for others to work out the full consequences suggested by this original formulation. For Descartes himself, shortly afterwards, visiting Sweden in order to instruct Sweden's learned princess in his philosophy, caught a severe chill, and died in Stockholm: not the only victim of the conventional belief that a wish expressed by royalty was the equivalent of an absolute command.

Viewed from the standpoint of the present day, in what does the greatness of Descartes consist? In the first place, in his thoroughgoing modernity: his freedom from prepossessions, his open-minded objectivity, his honest scepticism, his refusal to accept impressive substitutes, however authoritative, for personal investigation. In the second place, in his thoroughgoing criticism: his placing of the self, with its background and outlook, in the centre of the philosophic horizon. Henceforth, no statement can be presented as absolute, in its own right. Every proposition is presented as reflective, as a consequence of the "I think . . ." Not "*A is A*" but "*I think* (that A is A)" is henceforth fundamental for philosophy. From this blossom forth the twin buds of modern epistemology and modern psychology, and the whole revolution in thought which we call "the critical philosophy," as well as much which we still call "scepticism." In the third place, in the Cartesian method, the clear and distinct ideas, the quasi-mathematical logic, whose detailed consequences our latest logicians are still engaged in developing, and whose fascinating simplicity lures many an amateur into the ranks of life-long philosophers today, no less than in the time of John Locke. Finally, his dualism, his setting mind and matter over against each other as two independent substances, has furnished a problem for the thinkers of succeeding centuries, down to and including our own, a problem of fundamental importance, and fruitful in the variety of insights to which it has given, and still gives, occasion. Beside these four fundamental characteristics of his thinking, the detailed discoveries associated with his name become of merely historical value. But in these four ways, René des Cartes is still a living influence, a model, and a stimulus to us all.

Chapter V

SPINOZA 1632-1677

SPINOZA—a seventeenth-century philosopher of whom I know
nothing further," wrote Hilaire Belloc, not many years
ago, and proceeded to justify his *ignorabimus*. Did the
rest of us know much more? We all knew that he was an
obscure Jew, member of a Spanish family (Espinosa) living in exile
in Holland. We knew that he was expelled from his synagogue on
the charge of "atheism," that he was satisfied to earn a modest
livelihood by polishing optical lenses with his hands, while he
meditated, with his head, upon philosophical topics. We knew that
he would discuss his thoughts with a few quiet friends, of an
evening, and that eventually he committed his thoughts to writing,
at first in Dutch and later, as he became convinced of the importance of his work, in the language of scholars, Latin. Such, in
summary, was the knowledge of most of us, at that time. Spinoza's
Works contained, besides a systematization of the philosophy of
Descartes, a study of metaphysical concepts, a couple of "tractates,"
one theological, the other theologico-political, and then came that
strange publication in five "Books," springing to life in complete
armour, like Athene from the head of her creator in the old myth,
the *Ethics*, "demonstrated by the geometric method": a work
without parallel in the history of thought. His honours: a visit from
the great Leibniz, incognito, of course; the offer of a German
professorship, which he declined lest it interfere with his complete
liberty of thought and expression; and, in general, a reputation
such that his books were proscribed, and "Spinozism" was long
regarded as synonymous with "atheism."

Why should we seek to know more? A Cartesian. Has he anything to add to our modern outlook, or is Descartes enough? A
mystic. Has he anything to add to our insight, or is Plotinus
enough? A Jew. Has the Jew anything of his own to contribute,
or would the history of philosophy and our modern outlook have
been the same if he had never lived? If the second of these alternatives is sound, Hilaire Belloc is justified. If not, let us examine and
discover what we have to learn.

Spinoza

It is the *Ethics*, with its every proposition "demonstrated," which has proved the intriguing, mysterious, and challenging work. How such a book, so complete in every detail, so apparently logical and systematic throughout, so dogmatic, and yet at the same time so modern in tone, came to be written was, until very recently, a puzzle. No one knew, or even guessed, the answer. What were the influences upon Spinoza's thinking? The Cartesian influences were obvious to all. The "geometric method" clearly originates with Descartes, and it is in systematizing the work of Descartes that Spinoza has learnt to express himself geometrically. Many of his metaphysical concepts, Substance, God, Existence, Freedom, may well have originated as a result of reflection upon the thought of Descartes. The problem of mind and matter, and its importance for philosophy, certainly originates with Descartes; and even the solution offered by Spinoza might, with an effort, be regarded as originating in certain suggestions of Descartes, although certain of its traits are characteristically Spinozistic. Even the mystical facing away from the good things of life, love, happiness, power, and wealth, might at least be compared with the way in which Descartes withdrew from his family and early ambitions of worldly experience. But the difference is here too great for such an explanation to be altogether satisfactory.

It is, however, when we come to what is obviously Spinoza's central thought, the yearning to advance beyond science, and to lose himself entirely in the "intellectual love of God," with all which this involves, that we realize sharply that we are face to face with mystery, something which we cannot explain by reference to Descartes or indeed any thinker of the generation immediately preceding Spinoza. As soon as our scepticism is thus thoroughly awakened, and we look more critically behind the form of expression which Spinoza employs, we begin to realize how entirely alien his thought is. His psychology is startlingly original. The nearest parallel to it is not the Cartesian treatise *On the Soul*, but rather something like Freud's *Interpretation of Dreams*, a work not written till centuries later. His physics, complete in outline, is also startlingly full of ideas and principles which are original; and his metaphysics; now that we look over them again, with an eye freed from the prejudice of Cartesian interpretation, they are seen to have nothing fundamental to do with the great French thinker. In fact, the geometric method, like the Latin language which Spinoza uses, now seems something completely external, something deliberately acquired as a medium of communication to others, expressing thoughts which have nothing to do either with the Cartesian philosophy or with the language of European scholars.

What, then, can be the central influence upon Spinoza's thinking? Spontaneous, entirely self-created, it cannot be. For the philosophy is not a few individual *aperçus*, but is obviously the result of centuries of developing thought. Its background, as well as its outlook, is plainly systematic and co-operative rather than merely individual. Spinoza is a Jew and a mystic. Can it be that he rests upon Hebrew thinkers, and is there, perhaps, some line of influence which connects him with Plotinus? This question, not raised until comparatively recently, has led to considerable historical research, and has eventually been answered in the affirmative. Spinoza rests upon a chain of medieval Jewish writers, whose doctrines have been traced back as far as the work of Plotinus. All that remains is to add that there are indirect traces of a slightly older writer, Philo the Jew of Alexandria, whose mysticism is in many respects like that of Plotinus: so much so that it has been largely overlooked by historians of philosophy. In short, just as the Renaissance in general goes back to Greek culture, so the great outlines of modern philosophy, in spite of the insistence upon a new beginning in the case of Bacon, Hobbes, Descartes, and Locke, go back, via the thought of Spinoza, to the long development of philosophy in Greece and Alexandria. But while the background is ancient, the outlook is entirely and characteristically modern, bound up with the thought of the self, of the importance of science, of the liberation from authority, and of the free creation of a new world.

Metaphysically, Spinoza is convinced, like Plotinus and indeed like all mystics, of the fundamental unity of experience. We are too prone to regard as individual and fragmentary, split up into disconnected little bits, what is really one great living pattern. It is a mistake to think of (1) God, (2) the world created by God, and (3) man—created by God so as to be able to live, temporarily, in the world, but essentially a being not of the world at all—as three distinct, individual kinds of being. God is not separate from the world of nature. Nature is not separate from God. They are one and the same reality, envisaged, doubtless, from different points of view. Spinoza employs his Latin, with its distinction between the present participle active and the perfect participle passive, to illustrate his meaning. God is nature in the creative sense, *natura naturans*. If we try to think of nature fragmentarily and abstractly, losing sight of its connection with activity, we speak of it as the creation, *natura naturata*. But essentially "natura" is identical with "deus," and should be so understood. Spinoza thus entitles the First Book of his *Ethics, De Deo sive Natura*.

This title, as well as the content of the book, produced, however, an effect which Spinoza could hardly have foreseen. The cry of "pantheism" was at once raised. A pantheist, it is true, is a thinker who identifies the Creator with his creation, *natura naturans* with *natura naturata*, instead of keeping them sharply distinct, and regarding the Creator as greater than what he creates, viz. his world. If the slogan "Spinoza is a pantheist" is understood in this sense, as a descriptive label, it is thus doubtless correct. But if it is understood, as it usually is, as a term of reproach, we must permit ourselves to observe a certain distinction. In philosophy, as such, "pantheism" is simply one of several ways of viewing the world of experience. It is perfectly possible to think of a creator as immanent in his work. It is doubtless possible also to think of him as transcending his work. For a philosophy without prejudices, these are two alternative hypotheses, equally legitimate in themselves, and neither to be used, *ohne Weiteres*, as a term of reproach. Further investigation may, indeed, succeed in discovering one of the two to be preferable, as a hypothesis which helps us to understand experience, to realize its utter intelligibility; but philosophy is interested mainly in the further investigation, and meanwhile keeps an open mind as to the value of such alternatives.

It is from the standpoint of a different discipline, namely theology, and indeed one particular theology, the theology associated with the names of St. Thomas Aquinas and his followers, that pantheism is regarded, not as a possible principle of explanation, but as a term of reproach. From the standpoint of this particular type of theology, God is not merely immanent, but also transcendent. He is distinct from, and infinitely greater than, His creation; and it is a serious error, fraught with moral as well as intellectual consequences, if we presume to limit God's power to what He has created. From this standpoint, to call a thinker a pantheist is to put him beyond the pale. It is a criticism, a gesture of rejection, rejection without further consideration. It is thus incumbent upon us to point out that the criticism is of theological rather than philosophical importance, and that in a difference of opinion as to first principles, it is hardly fitting for us to decide arbitrarily either in favour of Spinoza or in favour of St. Thomas.

To resume. As, for Spinoza, nature and God are inseparable, two ways of viewing one and the same reality, so also of man. Man cannot be separated from nature. He is a part of nature, through and through, entirely, both in principle and in detail, of a piece with the rest of the creation. Men are not cut off from the things of this world as with a hatchet. They are physically and spiritually members of the realm of nature. If dogs and horses are brutes that perish, man is a brute that perishes. If dogs and horses are mechanisms wound up by God to run for just so long, and to respond to stimulation in such and such ways, the same is true of man. Conversely, if man not only occupies space, but also thinks, dogs and horses not merely occupy space, but also think. If there is something eternal about man, there is something eternal about horses and dogs. Man is utterly and completely, without reservation of any kind, of a piece with the rest of nature.

He is also inseparable from God. Man is not an independent, self-subsistent substance in his own right, a being endowed with individual powers of thinking, willing, and acting. Just as the space he occupies is not something separate and individual, belonging to him personally, but is a part of space-in-general: so the thoughts he thinks are not something separate and individual, belonging to him personally, but are integral parts of thought-in-general. Many a writer supposes that his thoughts are somehow his very own, created by himself. But we all recognize that he is really a creature of his age, and that he no more creates, in any ultimate sense, the thoughts to which he gives expression than he creates the words and grammar in which he expresses them. Thought, like language, is something over-individual, a social creation of which the contributions of individuals are fragmentary parts.

Spinoza's way of putting this is to say that our ideas are "modes" of God's thinking, i.e. of thinking in general. And, in order to make clear his feeling of the ultimate unity of all things, Spinoza makes use of the technical distinction of modes and substances. "Substances" are self-subsistent. They can, according to the seventeenth century, exist in themselves and can be thought by themselves. "Modes" are more adjectival. They stand in need of a substance upon which they can depend, to which they can attach themselves, and of which they can be the modifications. Apart from substance, they have no meaning or existence. Human beings are of this dependent type. They are floating adjectives seeking to attach themselves to a permanent reality, isolated fragments in search of a synthesis which will give them a place within a vital whole, waifs and strays looking for a home life, for a family which will take them in and give to each a meaning and a value which they can only dimly conceive.

The essence of man is constituted by certain modifications of the attributes of God. For the being of substance does not belong to the essence of man. That essence therefore is something which is in God, and without God can neither be nor be conceived, whether it be a modification or a mode which expresses God's nature in a certain conditioned manner.[1]

What is the substance to which man seeks to attach himself? Nothing less than the whole of nature, the whole of reality, the whole of the only ultimate substance there is. Spinoza calls this "God." The tissue of biological and social stimuli and reactions which looms so large upon the horizon of each one of us, and indeed, for many, represents the only reality of which we need take account, is, for Spinoza, the merest fragment. Life, love, the pursuit of happiness and power, are, for him, superficial, one-sided, transient episodes upon the surface of experience. To take them for the whole of what experience has to offer implies a tragic blindness to the real riches of experience, a blindness not less tragic because it is so widespread. Faith in the unity of experience is common, perhaps, to all mystics. The hunger for an experienced reality is something more. It is the core of the modern rejection of authority, of words and rituals, in favour of a direct, personal experience.

As the love of God is man's highest happiness and blessedness, and the ultimate end and aim of all human actions, it follows that he alone lives by the Divine law who loves God not from fear of punishment, or from love of any other object, such as sensual pleasure, fame, or the like; but solely because he has knowledge of God, or is convinced that the knowledge and love of God is the highest good. The sum and chief precept, then, of the Divine law is to love God as the highest good, namely, as we have said, not from fear of any pains and penalties, or from the love of any other object in which we desire to take pleasure. The idea of God lays down the rule that God is our highest good—in other words, that the

[1] *Ethics*, II, x, Corollary.

knowledge and love of God is the ultimate aim to which all our actions should be directed. The worldling cannot understand these things, they appear foolishness to him, because he has too meagre a knowledge of God, and also because in this highest good he can discover nothing which he can handle or eat, or which affects the fleshly appetites wherein he chiefly delights, for it consists solely in thought and the pure reason. They, on the other hand, who know that they possess no greater gift than intellect and sound reason, will doubtless accept what I have said without question. . . .[1]

Let us consider this further. If God and nature are identical, and man and nature are inseparable, then, surely, God and man are inseparable. But if so, why does man hunger for what, surely, he already possesses? Here we come upon what looks like a difficulty in Spinoza's thinking. It is solved by recognizing a distinction between two standpoints. From the standpoint of God, i.e. of ultimate reality, it is true that man cannot lose contact with God. Nature, or reality, or the world, or God, plainly includes and comprehends every detail of our living, moving, and thinking. Eternity includes, in principle, every moment of time, past, present, and future. Outside of reality, indeed, where could we look for an explanation of the details of our living and thinking? But from the standpoint of the individual man or woman, eternity seems remote, and the present moment seems all. The individual sees in part. He sees especially that part of the whole by which he is immediately surrounded, and he sees it from his own limited point of view. Consequently, he does not realize the true nature of the whole, of which he is a part, or the true nature of himself.

Man thinks of himself as a self-subsistent, self-directing free agent, and takes credit to himself for all he, in his sovereign wisdom, thinks, says, and does. The fragment masquerades as the whole, the mode regards itself as a substance, and treats its every phase as real and important. If man thinks of reality as a whole at all, he thinks of it from the modal point of view, for which God is a quasi-human self, a very modal substance, with wants and desires and a will which plans, treasuring up His bright designs and working His sovereign will, carrying out definite purposes, and subject, in so doing, to human prayer, human promises, and human rituals. But all this is merely modal, anthropomorphic, and, in the end, illusory.

[1] *The Improvement of the Understanding: Works* (Bohn), vol. I, p. 60.

Men think themselves free inasmuch as they are conscious of their volitions and desires, and never even dream, in their ignorance, of the causes which have disposed them so to wish and desire. Secondly, men do all things for an end, namely for that which is useful to them, and which they seek. Thus it comes to pass that they only look for a knowledge of the final causes of events, and when these are learned, they are content, as having no cause for further doubt. If they cannot learn such causes from external sources, they are compelled to turn to considering themselves, and reflecting what end would have induced them personally to bring about the given event, and thus they necessarily judge other natures by their own. Further, as they find in themselves and outside themselves many means which assist them not a little in their search for what is useful, for instance, eyes for seeing, teeth for chewing, herbs and animals for yielding food, the sun for giving light, the sea for breeding fish, etc., they come to look on the whole of nature as a means for obtaining such conveniences. Now as they are aware that they found these conveniences and did not make them, they think they have cause for believing that some other being has made them for their use. As they look upon things as means, they cannot believe them to be self-created; but, judging from the means which they are accustomed to prepare for themselves, they are bound to believe in some ruler or rulers of the universe endowed with human freedom, who have arranged and adapted everything for human use. They are bound to estimate the nature of such rulers (having no information on the subject) in accordance with their own nature, and therefore they assert that the gods ordained everything for the use of man, in order to bind man to themselves and obtain from him the highest honour. Hence also it follows, that everyone thought out for himself, according to his abilities, a different way of worshipping God, so that God might love him more than his fellows, and direct the whole course of nature for the satisfaction of his blind cupidity and insatiable avarice. Thus the prejudice developed into superstition, and took deep root in the human mind; and for this reason everyone strove most zealously to understand and explain the final causes of things; but in their endeavour to show that nature does nothing in vain, i.e. nothing which is useless to man, they only seem to have demonstrated that nature, the gods, and man are all mad together.[1]

We can distinguish three levels of experience. The first and lowest, the most superficial form of experience, is perception through the senses. Spinoza calls it "imagination," and includes both direct sensory awareness, and the images in which we represent to ourselves, in reverie and in memory, in planning and in acting upon

[1] *Ethics*, Part I, Appendix.

the space-time world, the realities of human experience. Imagination is both spatial and temporal. It cannot go beyond a reality which can be reduced, without remainder, to pictures. From the pictorial point of view, "God" means to many what the term meant to the poet Heine: the image of an old man with a long beard, sitting on a damp cloud and looking down, with a frown, at little Heine, when he had done something naughty. In fact, many persons live in such a picture-world all their lives, and are unable to apprehend any experience which cannot be translated into such imagery. To such persons the world of the senses, of the emotions, and of the will, so far as it is individual and personal, means everything. The world of pure science and metaphysics, the attempt to penetrate, with refined instruments devised by the intellect, to a standpoint which is impersonal and universal, and from this standpoint to reinterpret the whole of experience, means little or nothing. In fact, persons who live primarily at the biological and social level tend to regard the scientific and metaphysical level as something to be avoided, a mistake, the vicious substitution of abstractions and unrealities for the actions and reactions which constitute the pictorial mind's whole world.

The second level of experience recognized by Spinoza is what he understands as the level exemplified by the scientific habit of mind, the level at which experience is envisaged as law and order: as universals, principles capable of mathematical expression and manipulation. The two widest-reaching of these universals are extension and thought. Extension is the form under which the physicist views the world of experience. From his standpoint, whatever *is*, is spatial, and its activities can be described, without remainder, in terms of two or three dimensions. Thought is the form under which the psychologist views the world of experience. From his standpoint, whatever *is*, is a thought of some sort, an idea or concept, the crystallized expression of a living mind. From this standpoint, the behaviour of whatever *is* can be described without remainder in terms of concepts and their systematic inter-implications. How completely this differs from the "imagination"-level of experience can be realized by considering an example.

At the imagination-level, Mary is, to John, an image, the picture of his ideal woman. Her picture haunts him, day and night. What Mary may be in herself, John neither knows nor, indeed, cares. To him, she is a picture, and, as long as he lives in a world of pictures, she is the most satisfying of images. Indeed, for biological and social purposes, it may be that no further questions need be asked. But when John reaches the level of understanding or intellect, he views his beloved dispassionately and impersonally, from the standpoint of the physicist or psychologist. From the standpoint of the physicist, Mary represents so much "extension." She occupies so and so much of space. Her outline, in trhee dimensions, is such and such. If she springs down the steps to meet him, she moves with such and such an accelerating velocity per second, until she reaches the ground. If she rests upon him with her full weight, it will require so and so much energy to support her in the style to which she is accustomed, etc., all a matter of deduction from principles whose scope is universal and strictly impersonal. So too from the standpoint of psychology. From this standpoint, Mary is the "idea" of her physical conformation, the consciousness which runs parallel to the motions registered by the physicist. She is limited by her antecedents and her environment, and her mental processes can be traced, without remainder, as consequences of those antecedents and that environment. In a word, considered from the second level of experience, Mary is just so much applied physics and applied psychology: the meeting-point of a number of laws, all impersonal and all susceptible of mathematical formulation and proof.

Is there anything unsatisfactory about this scientific level, which urges Spinoza to seek for a higher kind of knowledge? To the mystic, it is obvious that it is grotesque to treat spiritual beings, even modes, as though they were merely so much mathematics. The standpoint is doubtless scientific; but it is too abstractly universal, too impersonal and external, to do full justice to its object. To Spinoza, with his feeling for the spiritual unity which underlies all distinctions and differences, it is thus plain that there must be a higher level of experience, which will see reality as it really is— not as the abstracting scientist, with his narrow purposes, views it, but as God sees it, as it is in itself—with an apprehension which does full justice to its living unity. This third and ultimate level Spinoza calls "intuition."

We, in many cases, perceive and form our general notions: (1) From particular things represented to our intellect fragmentarily, confusedly, and without order through our senses; I have settled to call such perceptions by the name of knowledge from the mere suggestions of experience.

(2) From symbols, e.g. from the fact of having read or heard certain words we remember things and form certain ideas concerning them, similar to those through which we imagine things. I shall call both these ways of regarding things *knowledge of the first kind, opinion,* or *imagination.* (3) From the fact that we have notions common to all men, and adequate ideas of the properties of things; this I call *reason* and *knowledge of the second kind.* Besides these two kinds of knowledge, there is a third kind of knowledge, which we will call *intuition.* This kind of knowledge proceeds from an adequate idea of the absolute essence of certain attributes of God to the adequate knowledge of the essence of things.[1]

If John could see Mary from this final level, he would see her as God sees her, not from his own impassioned point of view, nor even with the impersonal interest of the pure scientist, but from the standpoint of eternity, as Spinoza puts it. He would see her through and through, with all her thoughts and motives, her hopes and fears, her background and outlook, her past, present, and future, all transparent to his intuitive apprehension: not as so much space-time detail, but in principle, as involved in her living personality, in that spark of the divine fire which makes her what she truly is: a particular centre of experience, God Himself becoming apparent from a particular spiritual perspective, the infinite and ultimate reality expressing itself in a particular space-time form.

The human mind is part of the infinite intellect of God; thus when we say that the human mind perceives this or that, we make the assertion that God has this or that idea, not in so far as he is infinite, but in so far as he is displayed through the nature of the human mind, or in so far as he constitutes the essence of the human mind.[2]

He would realize further that all that he saw was merely a "mode," an adjective, a non-substantial form of experience; that Mary, at her worst, tries to conceive herself to be a self-dependent being, cut off from John and from God; but that, at her best, Mary gives herself up wholly, in a last and complete sacrifice of self, to the love of God: becoming real as she yields to reality, and divine as she accepts the ultimate Divinity behind all particulars.

That is to say, when John looks at Mary with the eyes of intuitive

[1] *Ethics,* Part II, Prop. XL, Note ii. In his admiration for the fashionable Cartesian Method, Spinoza illustrates his meaning by examples exclusively mathematical. But the content of much of his work (e.g. of most of Book V of the *Ethics*) plainly deals with just such problems as the one mentioned in the text.

[2] Ibid., Prop. XI, Corollary.

insight, what he sees is not so much Mary, as God. It is God (or Nature or Reality) which is the truly real thing about Mary, as about everything else which is "modal." What he values and responds to in Mary is thus something more than what is merely biological and social. It is the divine in him responding to the divine in her. Deep calls to deep, and reality to reality, and in their life together they can, if they reach the level of intuitive insight, develop away from all narrowness, all preoccupation with self, and their love can become, not merely attraction for one another, but also something more universal: love of the divine in one another, and ultimately the intellectual love of God.

Intuitive insight, for Spinoza, is essentially reflective. It is the way in which the divine in us appreciates the divine in everything which *is*. It is the way in which we become aware of our true nature and of our place in reality. It is the way in which God is aware of Himself. It is an activity which is all joy. It is intellectual, and it is bound up with the thought of reality or God as its object. It is accordingly defined by Spinoza as identical with the intellectual love of God.

In respect of emotion, passion, sensuous feeling, we are carried away and are passive, not masters but servants, not substances but unsubstantial modes, fleeting phantoms, unable to lay hold upon true existence. It is only in so far as we learn to master our emotions, to control our passions, to become active and intellectual, to exchange the modal for the intuitive and substantial point of view, that we give up our subjectivity, and become objective and truly real.

Thus we see that there is an opposition between finite and infinite, between mode and substance, between appearance and reality, between man and God. The part which endeavours to remain a part, the fragment which refuses to merge its identity in the whole, the human being who insists upon remaining human, upon being master of his fate and captain of his soul, is fighting against the fundamental law, the unity of all modes in the one ultimate substance. Conversely, from the standpoint of the whole, the parts have no meaning or value of their own. Their only reality consists in their being parts-of-the-whole. It is only the whole which is truly and entirely real.

This, however, raises a problem. Boys will be boys, women will be women, men will be men, and modes will be modes. In their blindness, they persist in trying to be their empirical selves. John has a weakness for Mary. It is all a matter of passion, imagination and illusion, no doubt. But, as the poet says, the weakness is so strong. The passion draws him along with it. How can he learn to master his weakness, to control his passion and spiritualize his senses, so as to sublimate his whole nature until it becomes intellectual love of the divine?

But, in order that this power of the mind over the emotions may be better understood, it should be specially observed that the emotions are called by us strong, when we compare the emotion of one man with the emotion of another, and see that one man is more troubled than another by the same emotion; or when we are comparing the various emotions of the same man one with another, and find that he is more affected or stirred by one emotion than by another. For the strength of every emotion is defined by a comparison of our own power with the power of an external cause. Now the power of the mind is defined by knowledge only, and its infirmity or passion is defined by the privation of knowledge only: it therefore follows, that that mind is most passive, whose greatest part is made up of inadequate ideas, so that it may be characterized more readily by its passive states than by its activities; on the other hand, that mind is most active, whose greatest part is made up of adequate ideas, so that, although it may contain as many inadequate ideas as the former mind, it may yet be more easily characterized by ideas attributable to human virtue, than by ideas which tell of human infirmity. Again, it must be observed, that spiritual unhealthiness and misfortunes can generally be traced to excessive love for something which is subject to many variations, and which we can never become masters of. For no one is solicitous or anxious about anything, unless he loves it; neither do wrongs, suspicions, enmities, etc., arise, except in regard to things whereof no one can be really master.[1]

In solving the problem thus raised, Spinoza develops a whole psychology, analogous to the clinical psychology associated with the school of Freud. He appeals to the intellectualist method of Descartes, and he does not appeal in vain. Substitute clear and distinct ideas for the confused feelings of the passionate side of our nature, and the thing is, in principle, done. As we all know, since Freud has made it so familiar, our biological emotions are often extremely obscure and confused. The "complexes" to which they give rise can be mastered precisely in so far as we clear up the obscurities and confusions, and face clearly and distinctly the issues involved, raising each factor from the emotional to the intellectual level.

[1] *Ethics*, Part V, Prop. xx, Note.

Spinoza

Analyse a feeling, bring out into the open every factor involved, and subject it to your mental microscope: in doing this, you are changing your whole attitude from one of feeling, in which you are submerged in the feeling, to an attitude of scientific and logical thinking, in which you stand out as your self, coolly critical. The more we do this, as we all know, the greater our control over the emotions; and, in actual fact, the substitution of the intellectual for the emotional attitude tends to make the emotion disappear altogether. The intellectual analyst eliminates the emotion, and leaves in its place a logical concept.

We may thus readily conceive the power which clear and distinct knowledge, and especially that third kind of knowledge, founded on the actual knowledge of God, possesses over the emotions: if it does not absolutely destroy them, in so far as they are passions; at any rate, it causes them to occupy a very small part of the mind. Further, it begets a love towards a thing immutable and eternal, whereof we may really enter into possession; neither can it be defiled with those faults which are inherent in ordinary love; but it may grow from strength to strength, and may engross the greater part of the mind, and deeply penetrate it.[1]

In practice, we can all do this if the pain we are analysing is slight, or the emotion is of recent growth. If the pain is severe, or the emotion has become chronic, our intellectual analysis is not quite so successful. Sometimes we repeat the spell, reciting the verbal formula which indicates clear and convincing analysis, but the emotion remains an emotion, and smiles at our efforts to change its form. In such cases, analysis looks like the hocus-pocus and abracadabra of the amateur conjurer. However, if we persist, and especially if we secure assistance from experts in intellectualist technique, the method appears, in principle, and indeed, in the end, in fact too, successful. The feeling is brought under control, and may be completely eliminated.

A second method consists in substituting, for the original object of the emotion, a different one, bringing about what Freud calls "transference." With Freud, the new object is usually the clinician himself who is directing the course of the psychoanalytic treatments. With Spinoza, the new object is always the universal and ideal object: God, or ultimate reality as a whole. Thus, if John brings his weakness for Mary to a Spinozistic physician, he will be

[1] Ibid.

121

urged, after forming all the clear and distinct ideas which seem to meet the case, to detach his urgent yearnings from the image of Mary, considering that she is but an unsubstantial and illusory mode, and to attach them to the true reality, the substance of which Mary, like John himself, is an infinitesimal modification, namely, God or ultimate reality. Instead of letting himself be haunted, day and night, by the image of Mary, he will devote his powers of cool analysis into clear and distinct ideas, to expounding to himself the main features of the Spinozistic philosophy, culminating always in intuitive insight directed towards contemplation and love of God. In this way he will learn to overcome his empirical weakness, and will grow, slowly but surely, towards the higher mysticism.

I have now gone through all the remedies against the emotions, or all that mind, considered in itself alone, can do against them. Whence it appears that the mind's power over the emotions consists:

I. In the actual knowledge of the emotions.

II. In the fact that it separates the emotions from the thought of an external cause, which we conceive confusedly.

III. In the fact that, in respect to time, the emotions referred to things, which we distinctly understand, surpass those referred to what we conceive in a confused and fragmentary manner.

IV. In the number of causes whereby those modifications are fostered, which have regard to the common properties of things or to God.

V. Lastly, in the order wherein the mind can arrange and associate, one with another, its own emotions.

The highest virtue of the mind, that is the power, or nature, or highest endeavour of the mind, is to understand things by the third kind of knowledge.[1]

And here we must, as a matter of historical accuracy, draw attention to the fact that Spinoza does not aim at educating and refining the emotion itself, so that John and Mary continue to love one another empirically as well as mystically, in a way which blends both. Empirical feeling is a passivity, a weakness, an unreality, an illusion. It must be rooted out entirely, so that nothing of it remains, nothing whatever. From Spinoza's standpoint, John's love for Mary, and her love for him, are not perfect until their love of the divine in one another has completely taken the place of biological and social feeling. When the level of intuitive insight has really

[1] *Ethics*, Part V, Prop. xx, Note, and Prop. xxv, Proof, condensed.

been reached, so that John and Mary see one another as "modes," they see each other as God sees them, and they love one another as God loves them, and in no other way. Each now realizes that the mode is nothing, but God is everything. In proportion as they learn to fix their affections upon God, all human passion for one another vanishes; and in the end they regard one another as God regards a human being, or a tree, or a rock, or, for the matter of that, an idea or a triangle: namely, as infinitesimal portions of that totality of experience which alone holds their love.

The mind's essence consists in knowledge; therefore, in proportion as the mind understands more things by the second and third kinds of knowledge, the greater will be the part of it that endures, and, consequently, the greater will be the part that is not touched by the emotions, which are contrary to our nature, or in other words, evil. Thus, in proportion as the mind understands more things by the second and third kinds of knowledge, the greater will be the part of it that remains unimpaired, and, consequently, less subject to emotions.[1]

For, let us consider a little further. The mode may learn to love God, but how about God? Does nature love her children? Does the world itself love its various parts? Does God love His own innumerable, infinitesimal modifications? Or is not all this anthropomorphic, modal, illusory? The Christian God, we are assured, loves us, as a father loves his children, in spite of their imperfections. But Aristotle's God, that pure thinking which thinks only itself, loves only what is worthy of such love, what is absolutely and entirely perfect, namely, Aristotle's God. With which of these opposite extremes are we to rank the mystical ultimate expounded for us by Spinoza?

Strictly speaking, God does not love or hate anyone. For God is not affected by any emotion of pleasure or pain, consequently he does not love or hate anyone.[2]

Spinoza sides with Aristotle. He is not a Christian, or a practising member of any historic creed. His view rests upon the (to him) invincible logic which identifies God with perfection. It would involve a logical contradiction if perfection loved imperfection, if the divine substance condescended to love its own unworthy modes.

---

[1] Ibid., Prop. xxxviii, Proof.   [2] Ibid., Prop. xvii, Corollary.

Spinoza so loves the whole that he rigorously excludes from it everything which is partial, fragmentary, incomplete, less than the one all-inclusive totality. Spinoza's God loves Himself with the same intellectual love with which the mystic learns to regard Him. But it is as a single, all-inclusive, absolutely unified totality that He loves Himself, and not as an aggregation or bundle of disconnected fragments. He loves each part, it is true, but not as a part. He loves John and Mary, but not in so far as they are John and Mary, imperfect modes struggling to make themselves more worthy of substantial regard. He loves them only in so far as they transcend their imperfections, their modal existence, and cease to be their empirical selves. He loves them only in so far as they cease to be John and Mary, and become entirely merged in God, so that their separate identity completely disappears, and is as if it had never been.

God, in so far as he loves himself, loves man, and, consequently, the love of God towards men and the intellectual love of the mind towards God are identical.[1]

All this follows from Spinoza's logic. He is so convinced of the necessary unity of all things, of the unique and all-inclusive nature of the sole real substance, that he regards all partial and finite judgments as infected with negativity. "All determination is negation," as he puts it. Particular judgments give us something less than the whole. The more particular they are, the less meaning, the less positivity, they express. "Mary is coming." Such a judgment means very little in itself. It is when we see it in its context, as part of a growing system of experience, that it begins to acquire significance. For John, waiting under the clock, in accordance with a prearranged plan, it means a good deal. Seen in the light of the full history of both John and Mary, and the background and outlook of their social stratum and century, it means much more.

Even the judgments of the scientist, universal in form though they may seem, are all partial and finite. Science is the gradual systematization of an indefinite number of such judgments. But compare a total system of such finite, mutually exclusive judgments with the single intuitive self-regard with which the mystic, or God,

---

[1] *Ethics*, Part V, Prop. xxxvi, Corollary.

apprehends all that can be apprehended. The divine intuition is infinitely positive, while the scientist's judgments, both in principle and in detail, necessarily fall short of complete positivity.

The scientist explains *A* as following upon *B*, *B* as following upon *C*, and so on, indefinitely. His explanation pushes back our ignorance a little way, but never reaches the full stop of complete comprehension. The true reason of *A* is not *B* or *B* and *C*, or any other number of finite antecedents. The real explanation of any detail is to be sought by learning to see it as God sees it, as a part completely contained within and belonging to the absolute whole. All attempts of any kind of experience, whether modal or intellectual, which falls short of the mystical intuition or divine experience, are thus infected with negativity. They may be socially convenient and useful. But they fall short of truth. No amount of linking finite view to finite view can ever succeed in giving us the infinite view. Our experience, in so far as it is finite, thus negates infinity, reality, God. And conversely: God, in so far as He is infinite, transcends everything which is finite, modal, and merely human.

Things are conceived by us as actual in two ways; either as existing in relation to a given time and place, or as contained in God and following from the necessity of the divine nature. Whatsoever we conceive in this second way as true or real, we conceive under the form of eternity, and their ideas involve the eternal and infinite essence of God.[1]

What, then, is God, the mystical object of our intellectual love? In the first place, God is entirely positive, experience at its fullest and best. God transcends imperfections of all sorts, and is, in every respect, infinitely perfect. Let us consider two of these respects, which fall partially within our human experience. Our experience has, as Descartes pointed out, two chief sides or aspects: the aspect of extension, and the aspect of thought.

On the side of extension, our experiences are finite: we occupy space in our home, on a street which leads to other homes, and to another street with shops, a post-office, and a railway station. The post-office and railway station connect us with other similar places, all extended and all equally finite. The divine experience contains this aspect of extension, but not as an aggregation of finite extensions. God's experience is infinite and perfect. God includes the

[1] Ibid., Part II, Prop. XXIX, Note.

world, and is in principle identical with it. But the world He includes is more than the world as we know it. It is an infinitely extended and an infinitely perfect world.

So too our human experience contains thoughts, all, of course, finite. We think of what we shall eat, what we shall drink, where-withal we shall be clothed. We perform laboratory experiments and formulate the outcome in terms of our logical and mathematical techniques. The result we call science. We think of pictures, poems, music. The result we call art. We plan rules for individual and social behaviour. The result we call morality. We formulate rituals and creeds, and call the result religion. So, with us, thinking goes on. But God's thought is not like ours, all details, gropings, experiments, tentative formulations with high-sounding titles. God's thought is perfect, complete, all-inclusive, utterly reflective: a single perfect self-apprehending intuition.

The attributes of thought and extension, which in us are finite and imperfect, are thus, in God, infinite and perfect. But what of the rest? Are thought and extension the only attributes of God's essence, or are there others? For Spinoza, as for Descartes, it is obvious that, in constructing an ideal of absolute perfection, we cannot, if we have any regard for logic, limit our concept of perfection to the attributes exhibited by humanity. God, in order to be perfect, must possess, in His essence, all the attributes there are; and, since we have no reason to limit those attributes to any finite number, we pronounce that God consists of an infinite number of attributes, of which each expresses infinite perfection. We admit that of these further attributes, which transcend our human experience, we are unable to comprehend their specific nature. But we are convinced that they are infinite, and that each is, in its own way, infinitely perfect.

By *God*, I mean a being absolutely infinite—that is, a substance consisting in infinite attributes, of which each expresses eternal and infinite essentiality.[1]

And here a further question arises. How are these attributes related to one another? How is thought related to extension, and how are both related to the rest? This brings us to a fundamental position in the philosophy of Spinoza, his solution of the relation of mind and matter, or of thought and extension in God.

[1] *Ethics*, Part I, Def. vi.

Spinoza

A great deal of Spinoza's philosophy is built around his dictum that "The order and connection of ideas is the same as the order and connection of things." God or ultimate reality is one and the same, whether viewed under the attribute of thought, or under the attribute of extension, or indeed under any other attribute. Each attribute is infinite after its kind, and while the attributes differ in kind, they agree in all being infinite, i.e. in being coextensive in relation to God. It follows from this that, while each is distinct from the rest, a certain parallelism may be deduced in their structural interrelations.

God acts. Viewed under the attribute of thought, God's act is a concept or proposition *A*, following upon another concept or proposition *B*, which in turn follows upon another concept or proposition *C*, etc. Viewed under the attribute of extension, God's act is a physical event *a*, following upon another such event *b*, which in turn follows upon another such event *c*, etc. Viewed under any other attribute, God's act is characteristically different, but follows the selfsame order, *alpha* following upon *beta*, *beta* upon *gamma*, and so on.

Whatsoever can be perceived by the infinite intellect as constituting the essence of substance, belongs altogether only to one substance: consequently, substance thinking and substance extended are one and the same substance, comprehended now through one attribute, now through the other. So, also, a mode of extension and the idea of that mode are one and the same thing, though expressed in two ways. For instance, a circle existing in nature, and the idea of a circle existing, which is also in God, are one and the same thing displayed through different attributes. Thus, whether we conceive nature under the attribute of extension, or under the attribute of thought, or under any other attribute, we shall find the same order, *or one and the same chain of causes*—that is, the same things following in either case.

I said that God is the cause of an idea—for instance, of the idea of a circle—in so far as he is a thinking thing; and of a circle, in so far as he is an extended thing, simply because the actual being of the idea of a circle can only be perceived as a proximate cause through another mode of thinking, and that again through another, and so on to infinity; so that, so long as we consider things as modes of thinking, we must explain the order of the whole of nature, or the whole chain of causes, through the attribute of thought only. And, in so far as we consider things as modes of extension, we must explain the order of the whole of nature through the attribute of extension only; and so on, in the case of other attributes. Wherefore of things as they are in themselves God is really the cause, inasmuch as he consists of infinite attributes.[1]

The parallelism is complete, both in principle and in detail. In principle, just as two parallel lines do not meet, although their parts have a one-to-one correspondence, so you can never explain what takes place under the attribute of thought except in terms of logic and psychology. It will not do to try to fill in a gap in the chain of thoughts by inserting an event taken from under the attribute of physical extension, or from some other attribute. In the same way, in physical science, you cannot explain a missing link in the chain of physical causation by inserting a link from the chain of thoughts, or from the chain of connections under some other attribute. Each attribute keeps itself to itself, and cannot, at any point, be exchanged for any other attribute.

In detail, again, however far down your analysis of order and connection may go, you will always find a precise and exact parallelism. To every thought, however fanciful and however minute, there corresponds some specific change in the physical order, and in the other attributes; and to every change in the realm of extension, however great or however small, there corresponds some definite and specific change in the realm of thought. The mind of a human being is the idea-side of his body; and conversely, the muscles, glands, and nervous system of such an organism are the extension-side of its mental processes.

These views of Spinoza's are developed in the attempt to solve the problem bequeathed to modern philosophy by Descartes, namely, the problem as to the relation of matter, mind, and God. It is usual to refer to Spinoza's solution as the hypothesis of psycho-physical parallelism, or of psycho-physiological parallelism. Thus understood, it has been of great importance in the psychology of the last generation. It was found helpful by G. F. Stout,[2] in his *Analytic Psychology*, for many years accepted as a standard work, and by very many others. It was thought to provide philosophical justification—if any was needed—for the clinical hypothesis, "No psychosis without a neurosis," which was fundamental in the treatment of mental disease.

But, while such has undoubtedly been its use in the history of

---

[1] *Ethics*, Part II, Prop. VII, Note.

[2] Stout published two papers on Spinoza's doctrine in *Proceedings of the Aristotelian Society*.

thought, and while Spinoza himself clearly makes full use of the psycho-physical deductions in many parts of his *Ethics*, especially in Book Five, which deals with the power of human reason over its ideas; the principle, in Spinoza's work, is primarily of metaphysical import. It applies explicitly, not only to the detailed interrelations of psychical and physical phenomena or modes, but to the detailed interrelations of phenomena under an infinity of attributes. Of these attributes, thought and extension are merely two, the two with which human beings happen to be partly familiar. But the reasoning applies to all attributes, without limitation to human or any other experience.

The propositions we have advanced hitherto have been entirely general, applying not more to men than to other individual things, all of which, though in different degrees, are animated. For of everything there is necessarily an idea in God, of which God is the cause, in the same way as there is an idea of the human body; thus whatever we have asserted of the idea of the human body must necessarily also be asserted of the idea of everything else.[1]

It is plainly one thing to regard the mental and physical changes of one and the same organism as "parallel," that is to say, as corresponding roughly and upon the whole. It is possible, even, to apply in practice some belief in a more minute and detailed, one-to-one correspondence between conscious thoughts and neural changes: to apply it, that is to say, as a heuristic principle, a hypothesis to guide further empirical research, but not to dictate beforehand to that research what it will find. It is plainly something very different, something infinitely further-reaching, to maintain that, in principle, for every lightning-flash, for every curve of every wavelet in the seven seas, for every eddy of every wind that breathes upon the face of the waters, there must be, actually existing, some precisely and exactly corresponding movement of thought, and something precisely corresponding under each one of an infinity of other attributes, whose nature completely transcends our human experience. It is this last, however, which Spinoza maintains, and its import, for him, is not primarily scientific, but mystical, inducing a feeling of satisfaction in the ultimate unity which he believes to underlie all forms of experience.

God, then, is substance or reality, whose changes, whether regarded under this, that, or the other attribute, are fundamentally

---

1 *Ethics*, Part II, Prop. XIII, Note.

the same series of changes. Let us ask, further, about this series of changes. How is it initiated? Upon what principle does it proceed, how far is it purposive, intelligent, subject to deliberation and perhaps co-operation? How, further, is it related to the thinking and willing of finite modes, such as human beings?

Such questions are, obviously, not only of fundamental importance, but of great difficulty. Consider the present state of the universe. For Spinoza, this is to be envisaged as a whole. Call the present state A, and the antecedent state B. A is accounted for as a consequence logically implicit in B, taken as a whole. B is similarly explained as a consequence of C, taken as a whole, and so on and so forth, to infinity.

We have just shown that solely from the necessity of the divine nature, or, what is the same thing, solely from the laws of his nature, an infinite number of things absolutely follow in an infinite number of ways; and we proved that without God nothing can be nor be conceived; but that all things are in God. Wherefore nothing can exist outside himself, whereby he can be conditioned or constrained to act. Wherefore God acts solely by the laws of his own nature, and is not constrained by anyone.

Corollary I. It follows: 1. That there can be no cause which, either extrinsically or intrinsically, besides the perfection of his own nature, moves God to act.

Corollary II. It follows: 2. That God is the sole free cause. For God alone exists by the sole necessity of his nature and acts by the sole necessity of his nature, wherefore God is the sole free cause.[1]

John says to Mary, when they approximate to reaching the stage of mystical intuition: "The meaning of the universe is expressed in its history; and the last stage of that history, the ultimate in the self-expression which constitutes the meaning of the universe, is our love for one another." "Yes," comes the reply, "but is it not something more, even, than our love? Is not our love a part, and only a small part, of the universe at present? Is it not the universe taken as a whole, and not with especial reference to two simple modes, which is the important thing? And will not the next stage, and the next, of the universe as a whole, come into being, not merely through our love, great as that is, but through all the rest of the universe, taken as a whole?" The world rolls on, spiritually as well as physically. What makes it roll? What guides its move-

[1]*Ethics*, Part I, Prop. XVII, Proof.

ment as a whole? Surely, not the hopes and fears of two or three of its innumerable modifications.

Can such a question really be answered? The whole is, at every stage, perfect. It cannot be regarded as changing to anything more perfect, or less perfect, without some flaw appearing in the logic which maintains such a view. To regard the series of changes (if any) as initiated by an intelligence which deliberates, plans, and possibly co-operates with other similar intelligences, is to speak of the whole as if it were a mode, a finite individual operating in association with other finite individuals. It reflects, no doubt, a certain credit upon the idealizing powers of the mode which thus conceives of the whole as a perfect imperfect, an infinite finite, a substantial mode. But the point of view remains modal, and the logical contradiction involved is incapable of solution. That way, perplexity lies.

To apprehend the truth about the whole, then, we must learn to transcend the standpoint of the finite mode altogether and adopt the intuitive standpoint of the mystic, the intellectual self-love with which God, as a whole, views Himself as a whole. From this standpoint, we must altogether give up that mode of thought which inquires after purpose, design, intelligent planning. We must realize that God is His own Interpreter, and that to non-mystics He will *not* make it plain. All we can assure ourselves is that the whole is what it is because of what it is. It is self-caused, self-initiated, as the self is generated in that kind of thinking which we call "reflection." In reflection, the self comes into being, and generates itself, both as subject and as object of its reflection. The activity is unique, not to be explained in terms of mathematics and physics. Yet we are all capable of understanding what is meant, and of performing the experiment for ourselves.

God, then, or nature, or the world as a whole, is self-caused, self-initiated, not merely originally, but continuously, in respect of every change, if indeed there is change in perfection. He could at no time be other than He is: viz. the whole of reality, the totality of perfection, the sole substance, whose essence involves, not only existence in general, but the specific kind of existence which the whole enjoys. To try to think of a reality which is unreal, and does not include the reality of its own existence, to attempt to think of a God whose essence is not identical with His existence, to try to think of the whole as other than self-caused, not only in principle, but in respect of every detail, is to try to think the unthinkable, and to fall into a clear and obvious self-contradiction.

All things necessarily follow from the nature of God and by the nature of God are conditioned to exist and act in a particular way. If things, therefore, could have been of a different nature, or have been conditioned to act in a different way, so that the order of nature would have been different, God's nature would also have been able to be different from what it now is; and therefore that different nature also would have perforce existed, and consequently there would have been able to be two or more Gods. This is absurd. Therefore things could not have been brought into being by God in any other manner.[1]

Let us answer, now, the questions raised above. God, viewed as a series of changes, as an "order and connection" which, under attribute *A* is a chain of thoughts, under attribute *B* is a chain of physical events, and under other aspects is a nexus of different sorts, but substantially the self-same nexus—God is self-caused, self-initiated, self-originated, at every such stage. As to the principle upon which God proceeds, this is plainly the unity of the whole, the reflective principle of maximal perfection, of self-regard and intuitive or intellectual self-love. This transcends altogether what we call "purpose" and "intelligence." It is above deliberation, planning, choice, and co-operation of any sort.

The multitude understand by the power of God the free will of God, and the right over all things that exist, which latter are accordingly generally considered as contingent. For it is said that God has the power to destroy all things, and to reduce them to nothing. Further, the power of God is very often likened to the power of kings. But this doctrine we have refuted and we have shown that God acts by the same necessity as that by which he understands himself; in other words, as it follows from the necessity of the divine nature (as all admit), that God understands himself, so also does it follow by the same necessity that God performs infinite acts in infinite ways. We further showed that God's power is identical with God's essence in action; therefore it is as impossible for us to conceive God as not acting, as to conceive him as non-existent. If we might pursue the subject further, I could point out, that the power which is commonly attributed to God is not only human (as showing that God is conceived by the multitude as a man, or in the likeness of a man), but involves a negation of power. However, I am unwilling to go over the

[1] *Ethics*, Part I, Prop. xxxiii, Proof.

same ground so often. I would only beg the reader again and again, to turn over frequently in his mind what I have said in Part I from Prop. XVI to the end. No one will be able to follow my meaning, unless he is scrupulously careful not to confound the power of God with the human power and right of kings.[1]

To the thinking and willing of finite modes, it is related in the sense of containing and transcending them all. If the whole, both in principle and in detail, could not be otherwise than as it is, it should be plain that the activities of the modes, as expressed in such concepts as finite thinking and willing, could also not be other than they are. The modal point of view, which flatters itself as to its own self-dependence, both in thinking and in willing, is thus completely illusory. In Spinoza's mystical metaphysics there is no place for human freedom. Human beings are in exactly the same position as wave-beats upon the strand, or triangles and circles in the works of Euclid. There is, perhaps, this difference to be recorded: namely, that the waves and triangles are at least under no illusion on the subject of freedom. They persist in their own kind of being, it is true. But that is because it is impossible for them to be, in any respect, different from what they are.

But, it will be asked, is not this going too far? Does Spinoza, in his mystical absorption in the whole, in attributing to the whole all power, might, majesty, dominion, and glory, leave nothing over to the parts, absolutely nothing, except to be parts in a whole which completely transcends them, a whole in which they utterly and completely lose every semblance of independent reality? Does not this involve, to use Spinoza's Cartesian method, a contradiction, if we try to construct a whole which is so much of a whole that it has no real parts at all? Are not the concepts of "whole" and "part" so interrelated that each by itself is imperfect, and stands in need of its correlate, its other half? So that, if we try to do away with the whole, we destroy, in the end, the parts also; and if we try to do away with the parts, we destroy, in the end, the whole too?

We have here a famous crux, a fundamental difficulty in Spinoza's position. Logicians who refuse to succumb to the charms of mysticism maintain that, in fact, Spinoza rests, in the end, upon an absolute self-contradiction. Everything is explained in terms of the whole, and the whole turns out, when you come to it, to be

[1] Ibid., Part II, Prop. III, Note.

self-contradictory and meaningless, a totality which in trying to be absolutely All, and in negating everything other than itself, succeeds in becoming absolutely nothing. And it is no answer to this objection (the logician continues) to refer to the exaltation of mystical feeling. The point of the objection is that, as logic, Spinoza's position is unreasonable and untenable.

To this objection, the Spinozist can, indeed, reply only by reasserting his position. For the mystic, the parts are, of course, modes; but even the merest of mere modes is more than just nothing. A mode is always a mode *of substance*, a modification *of reality*. There is always something substantial and real about it, although it is true that this does not, as a rule, lie upon the surface. A triangle and a square are modes of extension. It is true that extension in general is indifferent to such figures, whether regular or irregular. But such figures are more than just nothing. An acute-angled triangle is really different from an obtuse-angled triangle, and both are really different from a square. What makes these differences possible is the nature of extension, and it is this which is real and fundamental in such figures.

In the same way, God's nature is indifferent to the forms assumed by its modifications. Whether John loves Mary, or hates her, makes no real difference to God. But it is God's nature, the divine element in John and in Mary, which makes them capable of loving or of hating; and this element is real and fundamental in such beings. As we all know, whether they love or hate each other, John and Mary live in a state of almost complete illusion about one another. Yet, transient and deceptive as such modes of experience are, they have behind them something which is permanent and true: and it is with this divine element of value that Spinoza's mysticism seeks to establish contact. Who shall say that he is not on the right track?

As to the problem of free-will, from Spinoza's standpoint, this is almost wholly a matter of illusion. The more people try to be self-willed, to give themselves up to biological loves and hates, to follow narrow lines of social ambition, the more, he believes, they are unfree, flotsam and jetsam upon the gulf-stream of biological instinct. It is only in so far as this blind self-will transcends itself, ceases to push and pull in these directions, and surrenders to intuitive insight, to the intellectual self-love which characterizes God, and thus identifies itself with what is ultimate in experience, that it knows serenity, security, and joy. It is true that this is an exalted, mystical, state. But is it not better than its alternative, the endless puzzles in which the non-mystical logician enfolds himself as well as others? For he too is unable to solve this problem, of which his logic makes so much, the problem of freedom.

The highest virtue of the mind is to know God or to understand things by the third kind of knowledge and this virtue is greater in proportion as the mind knows things more by the said kind of knowledge: consequently, he who knows things by this kind of knowledge passes to the summit of human perfection, and is therefore affected by the highest pleasure, such pleasure being accompanied by the idea of himself and his own virtue; thus from this kind of knowledge arises the highest possible acquiescence.[1]

And now we come to consider briefly Spinoza's philosophy of social life, as set forth in the *Ethics* and in the *Theological-political Tractate*. This has puzzled the interpreters not a little, chiefly, perhaps, because they are so anxious to connect it with the philosophy of Thomas Hobbes. Hobbes had said that "good" is of subjective, rather than of objective, significance. It is not because something is really good that we want it, but on the contrary; it is because we want it that we call it "good." Spinoza says the same kind of thing; and interpreters accordingly assume that he is "influenced" by Hobbes, and is "borrowing" from the older thinker. But the positions of the two thinkers are somewhat different. Hobbes, a realist in politics, describing what he has seen and felt during the Cavalier-Roundhead wars, states roundly that there is nothing good or bad in itself. Before the State is established, "good" is what anyone wants, independently of whether anyone else wants it or not. But after the State is established, "good" is what is established by agreement, by convention and the law of the land, and enforced by the full power of the sovereign. Hobbes so hates war that he is all for the establishment of law and order. In the case of Spinoza, we have something whose roots are entirely different: an almost typical form of what is sometimes called "Hebrew radicalism," that tendency to see behind such high-sounding terms as "patriotism," "public spirit," and civic ideals generally, the self-interested ambition of leading citizens. It is "radicalism" of this kind which sometimes makes the Hebrew suspect to his fellow-citizens, who agree, for reasons

[1] *Ethics*, Part V, Prop. xxvii, Proof.

doubtless satisfactory to themselves, to resent any probing beneath the surface of civic life.

Spinoza's view is akin to the view of conduct made popular in our time through the work of the Freudian school. The view is that we "rationalize" our wants, and that conventional ideals are always disguised expressions of rather simple, biological and social, desires,[1] roundabout ways in which frustrated sex-impulse and thwarted ambition seek to attain their objects. Propaganda takes the place which might conceivably have been devoted to the pursuit of truth, and each citizen supports the accepted conventions, because he secretly thinks that he is clever enough to "work" them in his own personal interest.

This view fits in with Spinoza's whole philosophy. The citizens are, of course, "modes," and it is characteristic of the mode to pursue its own pathway. The triangle remains a triangle, John remains John, and Mary remains Mary. The positive *conatus* within them, the divine spark which makes each mode what it is, aims primarily at maintaining itself, at continuing its own specific modality. What each thus, because of its nature, pursues, it regards as its "good," namely, what it wants, in entire independence of inquiry into its objective value. Whether it will really be good for John and Mary to link their lives is a question which, with their biological and social bias, they are unable to face in the spirit of impartial and dispassionate investigation. Living at the modal level, carried away by these simple impulses, the citizens are very simple modes, and the State, with its titles and rewards for civic, military, and ecclesiastical ambition, is merely a meeting-ground for the maximal realization of self-interest and self-development. The citizens are not really free, but are bound in the chains of blind ignorance and impulse.

The pursuit of honours and riches is very absorbing, especially if such objects be sought simply for their own sake, inasmuch as they are then supposed to constitute the highest good. In the case of fame the mind is still more absorbed, for fame is conceived as always good for its own sake, and as the ultimate end to which all actions are directed. Further, the attainment of riches and fame is not followed as in the case of sensual pleasures by repentance, but, the more we acquire, the greater is our

[1] For instance, this school would "explain" such a mysticism as Spinoza's as a substitute satisfaction for thwarted sex-impulse and social ambition: a kind of "sour grapes" philosophy, possibly with the hope of its making him famous, so that wealth, power, admiration, and love would come to him, after all.

delight, and, consequently, the more are we incited to increase both the one and the other; on the other hand, if our hopes happen to be frustrated we are plunged into the deepest sadness. Fame has the further drawback that it compels its votaries to order their lives according to the opinions of their fellow-men, shunning what they usually shun, and seeking what they usually seek.[1]

The philosopher Hobbes approves of this sort of State: organized selfishness resting largely upon fear and hatred of war and social chaos. The philosopher Spinoza regards the whole tissue of views connected with social and civic life as modal and illusory. People do actually think and act as Hobbes supposes. But they are mistaken in so thinking and acting. There is a better way. From this blind following after ambitions as fundamentally petty and illusory as they are simple, the mystic turns away, not without a sigh for human absurdity. He believes that he is pursuing and finding truth, experiencing objective reality, in itself, and escaping from the net of illusion in which his fellow-citizens are taken captive. The mystic prefers open eyes to grasping hands, and the love of God to a worldly success which is a cheat and a delusion. He is kindly and sympathetic to his fellow-men; but between him and them there is a great gulf fixed. And the best thing he can do is to withdraw from the universal competition, to show by his life that he utterly disregards wealth, excitement, and worldly honours, and by his writing and conversation to preach what he practises: the better way, the quiet serenity of a mind at peace with itself, the transforming power of a love which is not of this world, but, in transcendental intuition, has become the intellectual love of God.

Such is the philosophy of Spinoza: a mystic, a Hebrew Plotinus, if you will, in our modern world: speaking the language of Descartes, and correcting the social gospel according to the materialist Hobbes. But, while partly "explained" by such historical references, his synthesis contains something more, something original, something which, while much neglected in our modern living, philosophy needs for its complete fulfilment.

We have with us science, art, commerce, religion. We have competing philosophies of science, of art, of commerce, and of religion. But we need also something which only Spinoza can set before us. Hilaire Belloc was mistaken. We need Spinoza's peace,

[1] *On the Improvement of the Understanding: Works* (Bohn), vol. II, p. 4.

his serenity, his faith, his love. We need, for a time, to withdraw from the business of modern living, in all its forms, and to listen, with respect, and hope, and growing insight, to the still, small voice which is, and remains, the great challenge to the blatant satisfaction of our modern worship of success: Is it really worth while, or is there not something deeper, the love, not of sex, not of power, not of action, but of God?

Chapter VI

LEIBNIZ 1646-1716

THE seventeenth century, which produced Spinoza, produced also a thinker far more typical of his time and place in Europe: the great intellectual, Leibniz. Modern among moderns, yet thoroughly conservative in temperament, linguist among linguists, scientist among scientists, diplomat among diplomats, courtier among courtiers, this self-taught son of a professor of moral philosophy became, and remained his whole life long, a narrow schemer among narrow schemers, an apologist of the established order, a man convinced that a world which had a place at the top for such a one as himself was the best world which God or man could conceive.

First, as to his gifts of intellect, natural and acquired. Before he was ten, Gottfried Wilhelm, a German of Polish ancestry, was reading, with ease, what books in Latin and French his father's capacious library afforded. History, scholastic philosophy, and medieval books first; then, at the age of fifteen, Descartes, Bacon, Bruno, and the moderns, contrasting them, at every point, with Aristotle and the scholastics: trying to formulate, for his own satisfaction, the essential characteristics of his own times, and to find out how far the modern method was truly superior to what he could read in Aristotle. His curiosity was unbounded, and his ability equal to his curiosity. His head simply teemed with intellectual projects, all new, all exciting, and all likely to prove profitable in advancing the ambitious worldling. He discovered the Calculus, both Integral and Differential. He dreamt of creating a universal logic, a generalized mathematics, and actually constructed a calculating machine which would add, subtract, multiply, divide, and extract roots. He could conceive and plan diplomatic and military campaigns with any man of affairs of his century. He could and did advise authorities, princes of church and state, as to how they could advance their own ambitious projects. He discovered so much of the secret society of the Rosicrucians that they, under the impression that the brilliant young man was one of themselves, actually elected him their secretary. He could and did advise scientists, in almost every field, of new conceptions which, when worked out, would advance them in their discoveries. In short, he was almost a universal genius in the field of intellectual knowledge.

With such gifts, what was a young man to do, in the seventeenth century? A prodigy, if ever there was one, not only during his childhood and youth, but throughout his entire life? Nowadays, such a man would tend to become a university professor, probably also an author, devoting himself to research and publication, doing a little teaching as well, so as to train others to continue along the paths he had opened to them. If anxious to get on in the world, he might study law, and might throw himself into organizing work, becoming an administrator, a well-paid executive. Or possibly he might become a consultant and advocate, placing his abilities at the service of such corporations and individuals as would be best able to requite those services with wealth and distinction.

Except that the field of service was far narrower in the seventeenth century, the choice, for an outstanding intellectual, was much the same as it is now. Gottfried Wilhelm was offered a German professorship before he was twenty-one. He declined it, because the opportunities for advancement seemed too narrow to him. At a still earlier age, he prepared himself for a degree in law, with the idea of obtaining the post of Assessor in his home town. Professional jealousy on the part of older competitors prevented him from obtaining the degree locally, and thus obtaining the local Assessorship. As the reason alleged was merely his extreme youth, he took the degree elsewhere, left home for ever, and devoted himself, for the rest of his life, to the service of dukes and princes. He lived among the great ones of the earth, acting as their advocate, adviser, and executive; writing, with immense industry, histories in support of ducal claims, briefs in favour of this or that ambitious plan of action; and moving from one service to another, according as he considered it to his advantage to do so: somewhat as a young intellectual in our own times might move from one university to another, according as his services met with a greater meed of recognition.

Throughout his life, however, surrounded though he was by men of the narrowest personal ambitions, he kept in touch with intellectual movements in almost every field of science. A Fellow of the Royal Society in England at the age of twenty-seven, a Foreign Member of the French Academy, he founded and was Life President of the Berlin Academy, and was zealous in promoting such co-operative projects. There were indeed few learned bodies in Europe which did not enrol him among their members, at least *honoris causa*, and did not look to him for benevolent patronage, as well as for intellectual contributions and the appearance, at any rate, of scientific leadership.

The position of Baron of the Empire—so that he became Gottfried Wilhelm *von* Leibniz—was conferred upon him, however, only partly in recognition of his distinction as an intellectual. It was chiefly his services to the powers that were, that is to say, his abilities as an advocate, adviser, and assistant in pushing the fortunes of others, which were responsible for this distinction.

One lesson Leibniz learnt in his teens, and never forgot. Until his home university refused him his law degree, he had naturally supposed that youth and merit can and should receive encouragement when they seek advancement in proportion to their abilities. He learnt, however, by sad experience, that power was usually in the hands of a small ring of older persons, and that what they had, they kept. This made a great impression upon him.

After leaving his home town, he always sought to make himself a member of such small inner rings of powerful persons, and to do unto others as others had done unto him. He sought, that is to say, to refuse recognition, place, and power to younger men; to claim for himself all that he could get; and to associate himself always with the older, more dominant, group, and thus to be a power among the powerful.

Throughout his life he was thus always the great Leibniz: the great intellectual, the great scientist, the great optimist, the great privy councillor: claiming and receiving the greatest honour and respect, and never conceding that possible competitors and critics might also be men of ability. He envisaged himself as the one man who saw everything and understood everyone. In life, as in literature, he felt himself to be a universal genius, who could understand and reconcile all points of view and all sorts of persons: Catholics and Protestants, no less than scientists and politicians. He believed himself to be the great reconciler, the great harmonizer. Others might be one-sided, narrow-minded, blinded by this or that special interest. Leibniz felt himself to be peculiarly all-sided. He could

The Great Thinkers

see, he was sure, the main outlines and tendencies of all ages, past, present, and future, clearly and distinctly.

He had observed, as had his patrons, that for him to throw his immense abilities to this side or that was, as a rule, for this side or that to become the winning side. How could he help regarding himself as a little divinity within his own province, disposing all for the best?[1] It should, however, be added that his province was so wide and many-sided that he felt himself to be a major rather than a minor deity. He treated others as lesser monads, shut up within themselves, without windows opening towards one another:[2] that is to say, as puppets whom, in his superior wisdom, he would adjust, combine, and harmonize, one with another, to the greatest possible advantage of his world as a whole.

The consequence of this policy grew more and more evident as Leibniz reached the threshold of old age. The still older power-holders, with whom he continued to associate himself, gradually, in the course of nature, weakened and passed away. Younger men, who owed nothing to the great Baron of the Empire, and indeed regarded him, for good reason, with unfriendly eyes, ascended, by inheritance, the seats of the mighty; and in his last years the great Leibniz, suffering slightly from his quasi-Messianic complex, the thought that the world could and must be saved by him and by him alone, found himself out of it all: deserted, unregarded, obscure, unknown.

Even the intellectuals, the professors and members of academies, who had, for so long, at least seemed to look up to his greatness, fell away from him; and when he died, only the French Academy, of which he was merely a Foreign Member, pronounced an oration, commemorating his services to the advancement of science. The rest regarded him as what he had gradually proved himself to be: an ultra-conservative, a medievalist in modern garments, a stub-

[1] Cf. *Monadology* (1714, tr. Hedges, 1863), sect. 83: "Among other differences which exist between spirits (rational souls) and ordinary souls, there is also this: that souls in general are living mirrors or images of the universe of creatures, but spirits are, furthermore, images of Divinity itself, capable of knowing the system of the universe and of imitating something of it, each spirit being, as it were, a little divinity in its own department."
[2] Ibid., sect. 7: "The monads have no windows through which anything can enter or go forth." Sect. 51: "There is merely an ideal influence of one monad upon another, and it can have its effect only by the intervention of God, inasmuch as in the ideas of God any monad has a right to demand that God, in regulating the rest, should have regard to it." Sect. 52: "God, comparing two simple substances, finds reasons in each which oblige Him to adapt the one to the other."

born defender of the *ancien régime*, in a word, an *überwundener Standpunkt*. The sun of his greatness thus set in almost universal obscurity and neglect.

And here the question naturally arises as to how any man could manage, for so many years, to keep himself in the forefront of intellectual advance in so many fields. How did a busy man like Leibniz find time to keep abreast of what was being done, and indeed to keep a little ahead of most of his contemporaries? The usual answer consists in referring to his genius and to his industry. The foundations of his education had been well and truly laid, and to build upon the structures established once for all in his youth was not especially difficult. This is doubtless, in part, true. But it was the way in which he read, rather than the actual number of books studied, which furnished him with the kind of reputation he continued to enjoy.

Leibniz never read passively, seeking for information which he would accept, as a docile student consults the latest encyclopedia. He was never a pupil, but was self-taught, self-made: active rather than receptive; critical, creative, originative; projecting himself into the position of each author, and asking himself how far, both in principle and in detail, it might be possible to improve upon the work of that author. His was a lawyer's mind: always a little aloof, always a little on the offensive: a bit of a bully, compelling the witnesses to answer the questions he asked; never letting them tell their story in their own way, but definitely putting them to the question.

An illustration will make clear how he read, and will show that it was more than a technical trick. It was of a piece with his whole attitude towards life and letters. He read the first two "Parts" of Spinoza's *Ethics*, and the whole of Locke's celebrated *Essay on Human Understanding*. It had taken Locke many a long year to write his book, and he had put into it almost his whole life. Leibniz read, and as he read, he took notes, a lawyer's notes, a judge's notes. He set down, for each chapter, Locke's position, and also his own questions, his own critical reaction. At the end of his reading, not only had Locke been tried and condemned. The great Leibniz had written another great book. This work, the *Nouveaux essais sur l'entendement humain*, published much later than Leibniz's time, and still frequently studied, is in four "Books," like the *Essay* itself. But it took the great Leibniz only a little time to complete. The structure, the impulse, the work, indeed, had been done by Locke This does not, however, prevent Leibniz's reactions from being both interesting and important.

His work is not like that of a student writing a "report" upon assigned reading: so many pages of "analysis," so many pages of "original reaction." It is more original, in that (1) it criticizes the views of the author by comparing the views of other authors, and (2) it enables Leibniz to express and emphasize his own characteristic thoughts. It is altogether more like the work of a good book-reviewer, who seems to know more about the subjects he reviews than the men who have spent their lives writing the books. It places him immediately in the position for which he felt himself pre-eminently fitted: the position of a judge, again the "monad of monads," seeing through the one-sidednesses and blindnesses of the witnesses before him, piecing out for himself the totality which none of them could quite see, and setting them all straight, each properly adjusted in relation to his co-workers in the field. Here too Leibniz was a superior being, a divinity, disposing all for the best in this best of possible worlds.

His philosophy proper is to be gathered from a group of works written during his last years. As is well known, books so written may, as a rule, be given the sub-title "My Life: An Exposition and Defence." Leibniz's two volumes of *Œuvres philosophiques* are no exception to this rule. Attempts have been made to understand his "system" objectively, as the logical outcome of certain abstract propositions. But the content, as well as the personal style of his writing, shows, plainly enough, that his philosophy is the genuine expression of his life and character, an autobiographical self-projection masquerading as metaphysics.

It is possible to argue that the "monads" or ultimate units of his system are borrowed (characteristically, without acknowledgment) from the long since dead-and-forgotten Bruno, and to find historical precursors for this and that view which Leibniz acclaims as "new." But a closer reading shows us, in every case, that his synthesis is personal and social in its background and outlook. It is the work of the trained administrator, accepting everything which he finds in the world, because of his supreme confidence in his ability to combine, organize, harmonize, reconcile, and, by readjustment, to make something out of the given material. His philosophy is a faithful picture of the game of the higher-ups in the seventeenth century, as seen by a master-player: at the extremes, the lower-type people, unregarded atoms of power, active indeed, but needing to be directed practically, "indiscernibles" who could be treated, by a competent administrator, as almost "identical." At the centre, of course, the master-organizer, a superior being, an intellectual, who could be to the rest "what a prince is to his subjects," arranging everything in accordance with a principle of "fitness," of "pre-established harmony." Between the extremes, a middle class of quasi-intellectuals, understanding enough of themselves and their place in the whole to co-operate with the master-mind in the execution of his plans.

Spirits [*esprits*] are able to enter into a kind of fellowship with God. In their view he is not merely what an inventor is to his machine (which is the relation of God to other creatures), but also what a prince is to his subjects, and even what a father is to his children.[1]

In fact, a further look at the world thus constructed reveals, at least in its content, nothing whatever which could be called "new." Popes and kings at the centre of power, surrounded by rings of cardinals, bishops, nobles and knights, with an outer mass of laity and villeins, all organized, adjusted, and harmonized in reference to one another so as to realize the administrator's ideal of "the greatest possible variety consistently with the greatest possible unity."[2] What have we here but the medieval picture itself, the feudal system which was really beginning to pass away? How does Leibniz, thus shown as the apologist of the *status quo*, differ from the medieval saint, e.g. from St. Thomas himself?

There are two main differences. In St. Thomas, everything, in the end, rests upon authority, the authority of a divinely organized Church. Reason is "ancillary," a handmaid to authority, and nothing more. Beyond Church Councils, properly convoked and consulted, there is no higher court of appeal. And further, the method is literary, resting upon texts from Holy Writ or the Church Fathers, supported by texts from Aristotle. In Leibniz, we have substantially the same system: but it rests, not upon authority, but upon reason. The function of authority is executive, but the plan is devised by reason. So too the appeal is not to councils, to the divine right of kings and popes; not even to literature, whether sacred or profane: but to rational consistency,

[1] *Monadology*, tr. Hedges, sect. 84.   [2] Cf. ibid., sect. 58.

rational harmony, mathematics and logic. The result is not a priest's world, but an intellectual's world. The details are almost identical; but the method and point of view are so distinct that the one picture can be called medieval, and the other modern. It must, however, be admitted that the modernity tends, in the work of Leibniz, to be overlaid by his incurable conservatism. His confidence in his ability to manage, to arrange everything for the best, blinded him to the necessity of the changes which were, indeed, going on in spite of him.

Just what is this philosophy, the "system" which so fully expresses Leibniz's personality and the outlook of the seventeenth century? In the *Monadology*, a work written, characteristically enough, for the initiation of a noble prince into the new philosophy, Leibniz expounds briefly his metaphysical view of the world. His view is spiritual pluralism. That is to say, he regards the world as an infinity of spiritual units, each viewing the world from his own perspective.

As the same city viewed from different sides appears quite different, and is perspectively multiplied, so, in the infinite number of simple substances, there are given, as it were, so many different worlds, which, nevertheless, are only the perspectives of a single one, according to the different points of view of each Monad.[1]

The "world" so viewed consists, essentially, of all the other units, viewed, however, not from within, but externally. John sees Mary, Bill, and Jane. Mary sees John, Bill, and Jane. Bill's world contains John, Mary, and Jane; and so on. Each, however, sees the rest from his own standpoint, externally. It is only himself that he understands from the inside. These spiritual units, called by Leibniz "monads," are thus independent substances, self-contained conscious beings, each living its own internal life, in accordance with its own internal principle. John lives John's life, not Mary's, or Bill's, or Jane's. He sees everything from an incurably Johnian point of view. Anything that affects John closely he tends to see clearly and distinctly. Anything remote, affecting distant monads, is vague and blurred to him. But each is a living mirror of the whole universe.

1. The Monad is merely a simple substance entering into those which are compound; simple, that is to say, without parts.

[1] *Monadology*, tr. Hedges, sect. 57.

2. And there must be simple substances, since there are compounds; for the compound is only a collection or aggregation of simple things.

3. Where there are no parts, neither extension nor figure, nor divisibility is possible; and these Monads are the veritable atoms of nature and, in a word, the elements of things.

7. There is no intelligible way in which a Monad can be altered or changed in its interior by any other created thing; since it would be impossible to transpose anything in it, or conceive in it any internal movement which could be excited, directed, augmented or diminished within, such as may take place in compound bodies, where there is change of parts.

56. This adaptation of all created things to each, and of each to all, implies in each simple substance relations which express all the rest. Each, accordingly, is a living and perpetual mirror of the universe.[1]

Leibniz's view is, so far, the reverse of Spinoza's. Spinoza made God everything, and the individual John or Mary almost nothing. Leibniz makes of the individuals unique centres of life and energy, each representing the universe in its own unique way. With Spinoza, there is only one substance, God. The rest are "modes," modifications of substance. With Leibniz, there is an infinity of substances, all true substances, all living their own lives. God is the supreme monad, the monad of monads, the master-mind which harmonizes all these independent substances, and guides all their independent energies so that they work together for a common end, although, as individuals, they may not be conscious of this end.

60. We see, moreover, in what I have just stated, the *a priori* reasons why things could not be other than they are. For God, in ordering the whole, has respect to each part, and specifically to each Monad, whose nature being to represent, is by nothing restrained from representing the whole of things, although, it is true, that this representation must needs be confused, as it regards the detail [*le détail*] of the whole universe, and can be distinct only in relation to a small part of things, that is, in relation to those which are nearest, or whose relations to any given Monad are greatest. Otherwise each Monad would be a divinity. The Monads are limited, not in the object, but in the mode of their knowledge of the object. They all tend confusedly towards the infinite, towards the whole; but they are limited and distinguished by the degrees of distinctness in their perceptions.

61. Each soul can read in itself only that which is distinctly represented in it. It cannot unfold its laws at once, for they reach into the infinite.[2]

[1] Ibid.　　[2] Ibid.

The monad is a "substance." What does Leibniz mean by this? It is the most universally accepted ultimate of the seventeenth century, and at the same time the most elusive. Spinoza had defined it as "that which exists in itself, and is understood through itself," i.e. as something unique, inexplicable in terms of anything other than itself. As he admits only one substance, God, it is plain that, with him, substance is a term which it transcends our powers completely to grasp. Leibniz equated substance with "activity," "energy," "force." So far, it left the realms of mysticism, and became of scientific significance. In connection with his infinity of monads, he equates this activity or energy with "percipience," i.e. with that awareness of which consciousness and self-consciousness represent the more general and the more specialized forms, respectively.

13. As all natural changes proceed by degrees, something changes and something remains unchanged, and consequently there must be in the simple substance a plurality of affections and relations, although there are no parts.

14. This shifting state, which involves and represents multiplicity in the unit, or in the simple substance, is nothing but what we call Perception, which must be carefully distinguished from *apperception*, or consciousness, as will appear in the sequel.[1]

What does this mean? Leibniz had discovered what we call "subconsciousness." He calls it "perception" as distinguished from "apperception" (=self-consciousness). The example he gives makes it plain. If you listen to the waves rolling in surf along the beach, you hear a continuous roar. But this roar is made up, physically, of a large number of minute "roars," each caused by a particular wavelet. These minute "roars" are perceived by us, not as the separate individual roars they are, but *en masse*. However, our auditory mechanism must be able to appreciate them somehow, as otherwise we should hardly be able to appreciate the mass effect. There are, then, minute awarenesses, *petites perceptions*, but we are unconscious of them, as such. Leibniz thinks that this may be the normal state of mind of the infinitesimal, "simple" monad. The simple monad represents the multiplicity of other monads, i.e. the universe, indistinctly and confusedly, unconsciously; and its activity, in virtue of which he assigns to it the character of sub-

[1] *Monadology*, tr. Hedges, sect. 57.

stance, consists precisely in this unconscious representation, this mere awareness.

20. We experience in ourselves a state in which we remember nothing, and have no distinct perception; as when we are in a swoon or in a profound or dreamless sleep. In this state the soul does not differ perceptibly from a simple Monad.

21. And it does not by any means follow, in that case, that the simple substance is without perception. That, indeed, is impossible, for the reasons given above; for it cannot perish, neither can it subsist without affection of some kind, which is nothing else than its perception. But where there is a great number of minute perceptions, and where nothing is distinct, one is stunned; as when we turn round and round in continual succession in the same direction, whence arises a vertigo, which may cause us to faint, and which prevents us from distinguishing anything. And possibly death may produce this state for a time in animals.

23. Then, as on waking from a state of stupor, we become conscious of our perceptions, we must have perceptions, although unconscious of them, immediately before awaking. For each perception can have no other natural origin but an antecedent perception, as every motion must be derived from one which preceded it.

24. Thus it appears that if there were no distinction—no relief, so to speak—no enhanced flavour in our perceptions, we should continue forever in a state of stupor; and this is the condition of the naked Monad.[1]

Thus we see that, in viewing the world as an infinity of "substances," Leibniz is regarding it as an infinity of centres of energy, as an infinity of percipient beings, mainly of low-grade consciousness, whose activity and life consists, precisely, in their unique, separate, individual low-grade representation of the activities of all the rest, envisaged by each from its own exclusive point of view.

All this is very easy to understand, if we regard it as a metaphysical projection of social life, as Leibniz observed it in the seventeenth century; with each individual conscious mainly of himself and his wants, and a little deficient in genuine appreciation of his neighbours. The monads correspond, also, to the "atoms" of Cartesian physics, with, however, a certain difference. The "atom" is regarded in a purely external way, as a unit in a physicist's formula, interchangeable in principle with any similarly defined atom, and subject to the mechanism of push and pull, and nothing else. For the physicist, such atoms are indiscernibles, identical points of mathematical

[1] Ibid.

reference, ideally suited to statistical manipulation. Leibniz, on the contrary, claiming that the business of the metaphysician is to remedy the deficiencies of the mere physicist, reduces the physicist's statistical formulas to conventions which hold good in physics, but are not really true. For Leibnizian monads are such that they cannot be interchanged or regarded as identical, or subjected to the external manipulations of the statistician, without grave error.

9. Each Monad must differ from every other, for there are never two beings in nature perfectly alike, and in which it is impossible to find an internal difference, or one founded on some intrinsic denomination.

10. I assume, furthermore, that every created being, and consequently the created Monad, is subject to change; and likewise that this change is continual in each.

11. It follows, from what we have now said, that the natural changes of Monads proceed from an internal principle, since no external cause can influence their interior.[1]

Essentially, their existence is not external, but internal, not spatial, but conscious or percipient, and their activity is governed not by mechanical principles but by the spiritual principle of the choice of the best. It follows that, unless corrected by Leibnizian metaphysics, Cartesian physics is a simple mechanism, resting upon conventions acceptable to low-grade intelligences, but raising merely a superior smile on the face of the master-mind, the true intellectual.

Leibniz recognizes four grades of monadic life. Monads are alike in that all represent or "mirror" everything in the universe. But they differ in the distinctness and completeness with which they exercise this function. At the lowest level, in what Leibniz calls "the bare monad," there is no "enhancement or relief." The images are all at the same level, all dim, unclear, indistinct, as in the state of stupor, vertigo, or the fainting which may precede death. The bare monad is unconscious, or perhaps we should say, subconscious. At the second level, represented by "the animal soul," there is clear and distinct perception over a very small portion of the total field of representation. That is to say, there is the focusing activity of sensation, and there is also association, giving rise to a kind of sensory memory and sensory anticipation:

[1] *Monadology*, tr. Hedges, sect. 57.

as we see in the case of a dog, who, on seeing Leibniz with his cane, whines and runs away.

I am willing that the general name of Monads shall suffice for those simple substances which have perception only, and that the term souls shall be confined to those in which perceptions are more distinct, and accompanied by memory.[1]

At the third level, the level of "mind," there is clear and distinct apprehension of logical concepts. There is philosophic reflection upon the self which thinks and plans, and upon experience as a whole, leading to the mental construction of an ideal self, an ideal God, an ideal world, and an ideal scientific method. This intellectual reflection reveals the nature of mind itself, and shows that it rests upon two fundamental principles, namely, the law of contradiction, and the principle of sufficient reason. This reflection culminates in logic on the one hand, and in a final or metaphysical view of experience on the other.

29. The knowledge of necessary and eternal truths is what distinguishes us from mere animals and furnishes us with *reason* and the sciences, raising us to a knowledge of ourselves and of God. This is what we call in us the rational soul or *spirit*.

30. It is also by the knowledge of necessary truths, and by their abstractions, that we rise to *acts of reflection*, which make us think of that which calls itself "*I*," and to observe that this or that is within *us*: and it is thus that, in thinking of ourselves, we think of being, of substance, simple or compound, of the immaterial and of God himself, conceiving that what is limited in us is in him without limits. And these reflective acts furnish the principal objects of our reasonings.

31. Our reasonings are founded on *two great principles, that of contradiction*, in virtue of which we judge that to be *false* which involves contradiction, and that true which is opposed or contradictory to the false.

32. And *that of sufficient reason*, in virtue of which we hold that no fact can be real or existent, no statement true, unless there be a sufficient reason why it is so and not otherwise, although most often these reasons cannot be known to us.[2]

The last and highest level of all is that of the ultimate substance, God, the monad of monads, i.e. the master-mind who adjusts the others to one another so as to realize their maximal value-potentialities in a single world, the best world which reason can think out, as a consistent totality.

[1] Ibid., sect. 19.   [2] Ibid., tr. Duncan.

The question at once arises, as to how these different grades or stages of development on the part of monads are related to one another. Is it, e.g. possible for a "bare" monad to acquire enhancement and develop into an "animal soul"? Can an "animal soul" develop into a reflectively self-conscious "mind?" And can an intellectual, a "mind" exemplified, e.g. by Leibniz himself, develop into the master-mind, God? Questions of this kind are not answered directly in the *Monadology*. It looks as though Leibniz himself is quite prepared to leave the grand outlines of his world without change, so that, once a bare monad, always a bare monad. A world with a large number of such monads always occupying the lowest position, with the great masses of humanity always in the position of "animal souls," requiring and receiving direction from the higher-ups, and with a place, just under God, for "minds," i.e. for intellectuals like Leibniz himself, who never sink to lower levels, and never rise to the highest level of all, but deliberately co-operate with God in adjusting lower monads to one another so as to bring out the best that is in them, poor things—such a world seems to Leibniz the best world which reason can conceive.

This view is carried further in an interpretation of Leibniz which thinks of the higher monads as relatively composite, as social groups composed of bare monads, in such a way that, while the bare monads A, B, C, . . . , continue to live their own subconscious lives, they may yet, in unconscious adjustment to one another, give rise to something which experiences "enhancement," an approximation to that clearness and distinctness of perception upon which all the higher mental functions seem to depend. This is thought of as analogous to the way in which the biological cells, which together constitute the human body, live, each of them, their own lives, entirely unconscious of the plans and activities of that higher unity, the living human being, to whose life they nevertheless contribute. From this standpoint, God would be the highest unity of all, the monad to whose life all individual monads without exception contribute something, namely, their own individual perspectives, all ultimately harmonized and reduced to a final living world-picture, with every half-thought and every blind groping receiving its complement and its perfect orientation, all ideally focused and concentrated.

What Leibniz himself says on such points comes out in the process of explaining what he means by his celebrated "principle of sufficient reason." This he understands in two senses, (1) logical, and (2) physical and metaphysical. From the standpoint of logic, he maintains that every proposition has a sufficient reason. This means that thought is systematic, that every proposition can be viewed as a conclusion from premisses, or sufficient reasons for its being so and not otherwise. These premisses can in turn be viewed as dependent upon further premisses, or sufficient reasons. When you go back and back, you come, in the end, to propositions which are self-evident, and to axioms which are "primitive" or ultimate, and are so simple as to require no further explanation.

13. Finally, there are simple ideas of which no definition can be given; there are also axioms and postulates, in a word, *ultimate principles*, which cannot and need not be proved. And these are *identical propositions*, the opposite of which contains an express contradiction.[1]

As a whole, however, the system of thought, from its divine-right axioms to its remotest deduced consequences, has a sufficient reason in the self-dependence of thought as a whole, i.e. as a single, deductive, inter-implicative system of propositions. This sufficient reason is to be sought in the divine laws of thought, i.e. in thought itself conceived as a divine, self-creative, and self-justifying activity. It is ideally perfect and, in the end, is identified with the intellectual's God.

So too from the standpoint of physics. Leibniz maintains that there is no fact without its sufficient reason, i.e. without factual antecedents which account for its being so, and not otherwise. This means that the physical world is systematic, and that its fundamental principle is the principle of cause and effect, "cause" being understood as the sufficient reason for the effect. These causes, in turn, are viewed as the effects of yet anterior causes, and, in the end, the whole system of causes and effects, i.e. the universe considered from the standpoint of physics, is regarded as having its sufficient reason in the causal series as a whole, including its ultimate ground. This ultimate ground, the sufficient reason for things being as they are, and caused in the ways in which they are caused, is similarly pronounced to be ultimate reality, the metaphysical substance called God.

[1] *Monadology*, tr. Hedges, sect. 35.

30. There must be a sufficient reason for contingent truths, or truths of fact, that is, for the series of things diffused through the universe of created objects, or else the process of resolving into particular reasons might run into a detail without bounds, on account of the immense variety of things in nature, and the infinite division of bodies. There is an infinity of figures and of movements, present and past, which enter into the efficient cause of my present writing; and there is an infinity of minute inclinations and dispositions of my soul, present and past, which enter into the final cause of it.

37. And as all this *detail* only involves other anterior or more detailed contingencies, each one of which again requires a similar analysis in order to account for it, we have made no advance; and the sufficient or final reason must be outside of the series of this detail of contingencies [i.e. accidental causes], however infinite this series may be.

38. And thus the final reason of things must be found in a necessary substance, in which the detail of changes exists only eminently, as in their source. And this substance we call God.

39. Now this substance being a sufficient reason of all this detail, which also is everywhere linked together, *there is only one God, and this God suffices.*[1]

How does this ultimate substance act? In the first place, it creates the whole infinity of separate monads. The world is plainly full of things which are composite. They are created by putting together things which are not composite, but simple. These simple entities, shown by reason to be implied in the composites we experience, are the monads. These cannot be called into being by any process of building up, but must be created as wholes, called into being all at once. It takes God's power to create the monads, in this way.

There is no way in which a simple substance can begin naturally, since it could not be formed by composition.
Therefore we may say that the Monads can neither begin nor end in any other way than all at once; that is to say, they cannot begin except by creation, nor end except by annihilation; whereas that which is compounded begins and ends by parts.[2]

Furthermore, for a mathematician like Leibniz, "continuity" seems to be composite, made up of a number of separate, isolated moments. He therefore thinks of God's creativity as a momentary

[1] *Monadology*, tr. Hedges, sect. 35.   [2] Ibid., sects. 5–6.

affair, repeated from moment to moment, like lightning flashes, "fulgurations of divinity."

> God alone is the primitive unity, or the original simple substance of which all the created or derived Monads are the products; and they are generated so to speak, by continual fulgurations of the Divinity, from moment to moment, bounded by the receptivity of the creature, of whose existence limitation is an essential condition.[1]

God, by His *fiat*, keeps on creating the whole set of spiritual units, and thus presents the appearance, through unceasing repetition, of continuity in the world thus created. Furthermore, what God thus keeps on creating, as units, elements which are strictly non-composite, cannot be destroyed, except by God's power of annihilation, calling out of being, all at once. The monads thus created are accordingly, in the nature of things, immortal. There will always be an infinity of spiritual perspectives, points of view which supplement one another, but, taken by themselves, are one-sided, limited, and unreliable. It is this infinity of points of view which sustains the modern outlook, the modern universe.

In the second place, God "adjusts" this infinity of isolated points of view to one another. He acts, as do all rational beings, upon the principle of "choice of the best," i.e. the realization of maximal value-potentiality. Left to themselves, and in relation to one another, the lesser monads "have no windows." They cannot see in, and they cannot see out. But in relation to the superior being, God, the monads are all window. God sees right through them, into their most intimate recesses, and understands them and their individual points of view far better than they can ever hope to understand themselves. Left to themselves, they would act blindly and one-sidedly. God sees in Monad *A*, however, the blindness and one-sidedness which would prevent Monad *A* from being a valuable member of the monad-community. He therefore effects the proper adjustment. He associates Monad *A* with Monads *B* and *C*, and thus, by supplementation, harmonizes all three, making their activities, in combination, far more effective and value-producing than they would ever have been in isolation.

Choice of the best, bringing about the greatest variety consistently with the greatest unity, selecting means to ends: such phrases are all, for Leibniz, ways of expressing the principle of sufficient reason.

[1] Ibid., sect. 47.

In relation to God's plan for the universe (the maximal realization of value), Leibniz usually refers to it as the "principle of pre-established harmony."

My hypothesis is, *the way of the harmony pre-established* by a prevenient divine contrivance, which from the beginning has formed each substance in a way so perfect, and regulated with so much accuracy, that merely by following laws of its own, received with its being, it nevertheless agrees with the other, just as if there were mutual influence, or as if God in addition to his general co-operation constantly put his hand thereto. . . .[1]

God harmonizes the monads as a skilful orchestral conductor brings out the best that is in his instrumentalists. God directs the monads as a prince directs his subjects, ruling them, whether they know it or not, in their own best interest, but securing, where possible, their active co-operation.

The soul follows its proper laws, and the body likewise follows those which are proper to it, and they meet in virtue of the pre-established harmony which exists between all substances, as representations of one and the same universe.

Souls act according to the laws of final causes, by appetitions, means, and ends; bodies act according to the laws of efficient causes, or the laws of motion. And the two kingdoms, that of efficient causes and that of final causes, are in harmony with one another.

According to this system, bodies act as if there were no souls, and souls act as if there were no bodies; and yet both act as though the one influenced the other.[2]

God harmonizes mechanism and purpose, the kingdom of nature and the kingdom of grace, rewarding the virtuous and punishing the vicious by the action of natural, as well as of moral, law. In short, God is the ideally skilful administrator, who makes everything in the universe, while carefully preserving its especial and independent way of living and experiencing, work together in such a way as to make of the whole the best of thinkable worlds, i.e. that system in which the greatest possible quantity and quality of value-experience is realized.

87. As we have established above a perfect harmony between the two natural kingdoms—the one of efficient, the other of final causes—it be-

[1] *The Philosophical Works of Leibniz*, tr. Duncan, 1908, p. 99.
[2] *Monadology*, tr. Hedges, sects. 78, 79, 81.

hoves us to notice here also still another harmony between the physical kingdom of nature and the moral kingdom of grace, that is to say, between God considered as the architect of the mechanism [*machine*] of the universe, and God considered as monarch of the divine City of Spirits.

88. This harmony makes all things conduce to grace by natural methods. This globe, for example, must be destroyed and repaired by natural means, at such seasons as the government of spirits may require, for the chastisement of some and recompense of others.

89. We may say, furthermore, that God as architect satisfies entirely God as legislator, and that accordingly, sins must carry their punishment with them in the order of nature, and by virtue even of the mechanical structure of things; and that good deeds in like manner will bring their recompense, through their connection with bodies, although this cannot, and ought not always to happen immediately.[1]

From the standpoint of this or that individual, seeing, in his one-sidedness, only in part, it may well seem that the universe is far from perfect. The victims of an earthquake, a plague, or the chances of a war in which they personally have had no choice, may complain that this is a very imperfect state of things. They may, in their ignorance, feel that their rulers, both ecclesiastical and civil, have shown themselves to be anything but master-minds. They may feel doubtful, even, whether God is really in His heaven, whether all is really right with the world. They may become discontented, and may repine at Providence, or may even doubt whether there is any such thing.

But Leibniz, now standing forth as the great optimist—as which he is indeed best known—is assured that his hypothesis "can now be pronounced established." He is convinced that no individual has a right to expect to find all his blind and one-sided desires satisfied. He is certain that anyone who will study Leibniz's system of pre-established harmony, in which the ideally best place is found for each monad, relatively to all the rest, and upon the whole—will realize, not only that things in general could not, upon any rational principle, be otherwise; but that this actual, every-day world, with its wars, brutalities, injustices, plagues, famines, accidents, and pure stupidities, with its present inheritance-rulers and its ambitious seekers after place and power, is, in point of fact as well as of theory, the best world which, upon the whole, an Infinite Intelligence could think out and, in Its Infinite Goodness, bring into existence.

[1] Ibid.

Under this perfect government, there will be no good deed without its recompense, and no evil deed without its punishment, and all must redound to the advantage of the good, that is to say, of those who are not malcontents, in this great commonwealth, who confide in Providence after having done their duty, and who worthily love and imitate the Author of all good, pleasing themselves with the contemplation of His perfections, following the nature of genuine "pure love," which makes us blest in the happiness of the loved. In this spirit the wise and good labour for that which appears to be conformable to the divine will, presumptive or antecedent, contented the while with all that God brings to pass by his secret, consequent and decisive will, recognizing that if we were sufficiently acquainted with the order of the universe we should find that it surpasses all the wishes of the wisest, and that it could not be made better than it is, not only for all in general, but for ourselves in particular, if we are attached, as is fitting, to the Author of All, not only as the architect and efficient cause of our being, but also as our master and final cause, who ought to be the whole aim of our volition, and who alone can make us blest.[1]

This conviction, needless to say, is far easier to accept if you happen to be one of the higher-ups. If you are one of life's failures, someone who has never had a real chance, physical, mental, moral, social, or economic, but is sensitive, eager, and—in the light of continued misfortune—despairing and defiant, it is hard to accept. Leibniz's philosophy is, it must be admitted, a little complacent. It is suited to the group of higher-ups with whom Leibniz consistently associated himself. It knows nothing, so far as the modern reader can see, either of human sympathy with human weakness, or of the bitterness and poison of continued defeat. Like Pope's *Essay on Man*, it proclaims that whatever *is*, is right. It rejoices in the hard-and-fast logic of rationalism. But to the softer side of human life, to sympathetic insight, to love stronger than death, to simple faith and hope rising above despair, the great optimist has not one word to say that is not trivial, frigid, and insulting. To reduce mathematics to mysticism may be a mistake. But to leave out of the account the whole mystical side of life: to reduce life, without remainder, to integral and differential calculus, is perhaps. after all, no less one-sided. And for a philosophy which proclaims itself peculiarly *all*-sided, such omission, or rather exclusion, is hard to justify. It may be true that Spinoza had much to learn from the great Leibniz. It is certain that the great Leibniz had something to

[1] *Monadology*, tr. Hedges sect. 90.

learn from the Hebrew mystic. Perhaps it is only in both voices, taken in combination, that we hear the authentic note of the seventeenth century.

What would it feel like, to be a member of Leibniz's world, rather than of Spinoza's? Let us imagine a simple discussion. *John*: I am a Leibnizian. I like his system. It gives me a self, with a self-dependent status. I live my own life in my own way. In so living, I make my own definite contribution to the nature of things. There is an infinity of us. We are all different. Taken together, we make up the variegated texture which is modern life. Taken individually, each is precisely his own self, interfering with no one else's intimate life, and interfered with by no one else. No one but God can see inside of me, and can realize fully what I am. My power consists in organizing, in arranging and adjusting my environment, my thoughts, dreams, and plans, for the best In so doing, I am, in my small way, like the Master-mind, God. I should not like to be a Spinozist, to be a mere modification, something not existing in its own right at all: a mere surface-ripple, a Buddhist raindrop. I should not like to think all my notions of self, all my ambitions, plannings, and actings, illusory. They are the real stuff of life; and I like Leibniz, because his system gives them the place they deserve. *Mary*: I am a Spinozist, and am contented with his view. There is in me something deeper than my space-time self. This something, call it Nature, or Life, or God, or what you will, expresses itself through me, as well as through a million other modifications of Reality. This deeper reality is more to me than my surface self. I can trust to its guidance and direction, although I do not fully understand it. It is more than our human plannings and schemings; more, even, than your "Master-Mind," which is, surely, merely a human schemer writ large. Leibniz's world is a glittering kaleidoscope, all bright reflections and facets which are polished and as brilliant as you please. But what is there behind them? Leibniz recognizes the modern infinity of different opinions, all personal and individual, and all different. But what do they really amount to? In seventeenth-century court life, with which Leibniz is doubtless familiar, we have a number of human beings dressing up and pretending to be something worth while. But are they, after all, doing anything beyond dressing up and pretending, dramatizing their own quite superficial selves, rationalizing their own quite simple desires and dreams? So too in our modern reviews, we have a number of clever writers dressing up their own opinions and pretending to be doing something worth while, being truly modern. But are not they too merely dramatizing their own surface selves? Is it not all, in the end, make-believe, childish pretence? To give meaning to his world, does not Leibniz have to go outside his infinite monads, and bring in an old-fashioned *Deus ex machina*? For it is not the monads, but God, who harmonizes, unifies, and lends significance to all this infinity of posturing. And is Leibniz's God really different from Spinoza's, in fundamentals? At least, according to Leibniz, you and I are like two clocks which strike the same hour because, although each has his or her own private set of works, it was the same Master-Workman who fabricated both of us. But a Master-Workman, a harmonizer who adjusts you and me to one another—how does that differ from Spinoza's Nature, from a Life and a Reality for which we are not responsible, but which has created us for one another? I think Leibniz's Master-Mind differs from Spinoza's God mainly in being more like our surface-selves, in having purposes, plans, ambitions, and activities. This, to me, looks like an anthropomorphic, superficial, picture-image way of indicating what Spinoza is seeking to express in a deeper way.

John: I grant that, in many ways, Leibniz and Spinoza seem to be saying much the same thing, in practice. But the great difference is, that Leibniz leaves a place for me and my ambitions, while Spinoza does not. His God occupies the foreground as well as the background, and leaves no room for any real person but himself.

Mary: I think that the self, for which Leibniz leaves a place, is superficial, and that Spinoza is right in suggesting that we should learn to give up a childish self and childish ambitions, and should learn to lose our surface self in the love of a deeper reality, God. For the rest, I doubt whether a God who can and does harmonize and adjust the monads, really leaves them very much place for the exercise of what they would call their free will. It is not difficult to show that, in Leibniz's system, the bare monads are the merest puppets. The higher monads adjust them as they think best. The kings, popes, and intellectuals have their way with them, and it is a question, in my mind, whether the kings, popes, and intellectuals themselves are not, in the end, carried along, willy-nilly, by the forces of Nature, Life, or God, in a sense which leaves them little, if any, genuine powers of self-determination.

This brief discussion serves to bring out the chief point of difference between Leibniz and Spinoza. But further investigation leaves us asking whether, in spite of such differences, Leibniz and Spinoza are not more different from thinkers of the present day than they are from one another. In fact, they seem to belong together, to be seventeenth-century thinkers with seventeenth-century limitations, and their differences, seen in the perspective of three centuries, seem to be only superficial, after all.

This comes out clearly in relation to two issues which are of capital importance. In the first place, in relation to the question of free will. The modern reader finds himself puzzled, on this point, not only by Spinoza, but also by Leibniz. Here we have two thinkers, each of the highest natural ability, each well trained: and yet, neither seems to have our modern feeling for liberty at all. Spinoza, it is true, maintains explicitly that any sort of free will, i.e. any sort of real liberty in the realm of action, is pure illusion, whether we speak of the individual John and Mary, or of the great Substance, God. He maintains, we understand, metaphysical determinism, without compromise of any sort. The world is what it is, in detail as well as in principle; and nothing whatever could have made it different.

All things which are, are in God, and must be conceived through God, therefore God is the cause of those things which are in him. Further, besides God there can be no substance, that is nothing in itself external to God. God, therefore, is the indwelling cause of all things.[1]

John is the mode that he is. He could not possibly have been other than precisely what he is. Every motion he makes in space, every movement he goes through in the world of thought, is a necessary consequence of antecedent movements, all bound up in the nature of the ultimate Substance, God or Nature.

On the other hand, when he is discussing questions of psychology or ethics, Spinoza writes quite simply, as any of us might do, plainly assuming the possibility of choice, e.g. of controlling or not controlling our emotions. He gives us definite rules to follow, which show us how to apply the power of reason over feeling. This certainly presupposes that we are free to be reasonable or to be unreasonable. The modern interpreters of Spinoza find here a notable inconsistency in his thought. How can we be ethically free

[1] *Ethics*, Part I, Prop. xviii, Proof.

if we are metaphysically bound? There is no accepted solution of this difficulty.

Readers of Leibniz seem to find, at first, the exact opposite of Spinoza's metaphysics. The monad lives an inner life, in complete self-determination. John cannot see into Mary, or Mary into John. Each has his own thoughts, and the other cannot in any way direct or alter them. Thought is free, not subject to external control. Each thinks and plans for himself, as he wills. This is true, not only of the "bare" monad, but also of the animal soul, the rational mind, and the Master-Mind, God. Each acts from the principle of sufficient reason, making choice of what it judges to be the best. We do our reasoning for ourselves. No one else can make our choices for us. Each lives out his own life, fully and freely, making his own contribution, such as it is, to reality. In fact, reality is made up of such contributions.

So far, Leibniz seems to be teaching indeterminism, the freedom of self-determination, and many a modern would gladly accept what he says. But, when we come to consider the higher-ups, we find ourselves no longer sure that Leibniz, in spite of his words, has the modern feeling for liberty at all. God, the Master-Mind, adjusts the monads to one another: John is adjusted to Mary, and Mary to John. They do not adjust themselves to each other; for John never really understands Mary, and Mary never really understands John. Their adjustment, or harmonization, is done for them by someone higher up.

We see, moreover, in what I have just stated, the *a priori* reasons why things could not be other than they are.

Each organic living body is a kind of divine machine, or a natural automaton, infinitely surpassing all artificial automata. A machine made by human art is not a machine in all its parts. For example, the tooth of a brass wheel has parts or fragments which are not artificial to us, and which have nothing to mark the machine in relation to the use for which the wheel is designed. But nature's machines, that is, living bodies, are still machines in their minutest parts, *ad infinitum*. This constitutes the difference between nature and art, that is to say, between the divine art and ours.[1]

The same is true of them in all their relations. Politically, they are adjusted by the State; religiously, they are harmonized by the

[1] *Monadology*, sects. 60, 64.

Church; commercially, they are organized by the Guilds. There is no point at which their life is not organized, adjusted, harmonized, wrought into the tissue of this or that system, by spiritual forces over which they exercise no effective control. Even the higher-ups themselves, the leaders like Leibniz, who act "as little divinities within their own departments," are, in practice, confined to co-operating with the Master-Mind. They adopt towards God the attitude of a dutiful subject towards his Prince. That is to say, they are Reality's yes-men. Their freedom is essentially restricted to the freedom of the servant to serve, of the follower to follow. Over all is the trail of a harmony which is foreordained, *pre*-established: an order of things to which the monads have to conform, a system which they have to accept.

It looks, then, as though, in the seventeenth century, the modern problem of liberty was only very partly felt, even by its greatest thinkers: as though, for the vast majority of mankind at any rate, adjustment by higher-ups was universally accepted as part of the pre-established order of things. And here, on this capital issue, Leibniz and Spinoza stand so aloof from us moderns and so close to one another that their differences, important as these doubtless were at the time, appear to us only technical.

In the second place, in relation to the matter-mind problem. Spinoza, accepting the premisses involved in the dualism of Descartes, had invented the hypothesis known as psycho-physical parallelism. That is to say, he had represented thought and extension as co-ordinate attributes of the divine nature, such that to each change in the one, there corresponded some parallel change in the other. John's mind was the idea-side of John's body. Mary's body was the corporeal aspect of Mary's thought. Taken as wholes, each attribute was co-extensive with the whole of God's nature. The alternative hypotheses were interactionism (Descartes), occasionalism (Malebranche, Geulincx), materialism (Hobbes), and spiritualism (Leibniz). These views at the time, and indeed at their revival in nineteenth-century psychology, were clear-cut and startlingly distinct. And yet, from the standpoint of the present-day thinker, they are so hopelessly alien to our ways of looking at the problem involved, so artificial and mistaken in their premisses, which all equally accept from Descartes, that, in spite of these differences, they seem the merest variations upon a common theme. They belong together, back in the seventeenth century.

Leibniz was tremendously proud of his solution, and tried to show how Descartes had almost "hit upon my system," the system, that is to say, of pre-established harmony. In that system, minds act as if there were no bodies, and bodies as if there were no minds. That is to say, minds act upon the principle of sufficient reason, choosing means to the best ends, while bodies act mechanically, by impact. And yet, all are harmonized in the higher unity, and are reconciled in the best conceivable way: so that mechanism serves the interests of purpose. We call Leibniz's view "spiritualism," because he regarded reality as essentially spiritual, as made up of monads living inner lives, without externality in other than a social sense. There are, for Leibniz, no independent, physical, external things, such as bodies, existing in their own right. The external or spatial way of regarding other monads, which characterizes Cartesian physics, is merely a convenient social convention, a way of graphing relations which are essentially not external, but spiritual. It is the internal way of regarding experience, as essentially mind or spirit, which is ultimately true to the facts. John's mind is not truly described as "the idea-side of John's body." It is the real John. John's "body" is a way of referring to John, as a distinct social entity from all other spiritual units, which is convenient for a number of purposes. But his "body" is not the true John, and ultimately, it has no metaphysical status whatever.

Here the modern reader confesses himself puzzled. If matter, for Leibniz, is merely a convenient social fiction, a physicist's technical way of graphing relations which are, in themselves, purely spiritual why is it necessary for Leibniz to appeal to God, the Great Harmonizer, to reconcile the opposition between matter and mind? Metaphysically speaking, if matter is a fiction, a human way of regarding experience, while mind alone is real, there can be no real, genuine, metaphysical, opposition in the case, and no appeal to the Ultimate Monad is necessary. If, however, the opposition is genuine enough to call for the appeal, which Leibniz certainly makes, then matter is surely being regarded as approximately co-ordinate with mind, by Leibniz, no less than by Spinoza, the Occasionalists, and the other followers of Descartes.

The only answer to this puzzle is to regret that Leibniz himself was too busy, throughout his life, to write one single, definitive, metaphysical discussion of all the points in his "system." This answer leaves the puzzle where it was, a point of dissatisfaction, to which no solution is indicated.

But, apart altogether from difficulties in Leibniz's way of expressing his thoughts, there is one point, and it is vital, where Leibniz is absolutely at one with all the rest of his contemporaries and near-contemporaries. They all regard "mind" as objective, as a kind of "thing," at least co-extensive with the physical universe; and it is this which separates them so completely from thinkers of the present day. Of the modern treatment of mind as essentially subjective, as the experienc*ing* side of experience, and not as objective, not as one of the things experienc*ed*, there seems, in all these seventeenth-century thinkers, to be no trace. In spite of their technical differences, in this respect both Leibniz and Spinoza are subject to the general limitations of their age.

One further point should perhaps be mentioned here. It has been thought that neither Spinoza nor Leibniz is altogether serious, that they are so perversely "intellectual" as to amuse themselves by drawing out the consequences of a few definitions which are arbitrary, assumed for their own purposes, but not supposed to be taken as applying to reality. It is admitted that the individual thinker has a right to lay down, for what it is worth, his own personal use of terminology, and this is then applied to Spinoza. Spinoza writes, "By *attribute* I understand . . . by *substance* I understand . . ." this and that; and it has been supposed that Spinoza is, in effect, warning us that what he writes is merely his personal individual reading of experience, and represents the way in which he likes to think of human beings, God, and the rest. But it is impossible to study Spinoza's work without realizing how thoroughly he suppresses his mere individuality, and schools himself to give us, not *his* reading of reality, but his reading of *reality*. He sinks his self completely in his work.

In the same way, it has been thought that Leibniz is entirely arbitrary, playing a kind of intellectual chess-game with himself and his contemporaries, with monads (defined by himself) as pawns, and with the monadic equivalents of knights, bishops, castles, and royalty, all performing in accordance with his definitions, in a tissue of consistent interplay. It has been thought that while Leibniz personally amuses his leisure by this game, here and there he happens to hit upon propositions which are of interest to the rest of humanity also, and that some of these happen to be of great practical importance; but that the whole of his philosophy is, in principle, arbitrary.

There is, however, no sound reason to suppose that the immensely industrious Leibniz is any less serious as a metaphysician than he is as a lawyer, a politician, or a historian. He is not playing at make-believe, although he no doubt takes a human enjoyment in his intellectual superiority, but is presenting mankind with what he takes to be the truth about momentous issues. He is just as serious as Spinoza, although in a different way. In the seventeenth century, theology and metaphysics were ranked among the more serious pursuits, and men of distinction did not spend their valuable time playing chess with themselves. The problems they handled were the kind of problems which have an especial appeal to "intellectuals." But the solutions they offered were meant to be final, and the work of neither can be regarded as, in any especial sense, arbitrary. From Leibniz' standpoint, there are *n* possible worlds, all equally thinkable; but it is a part of his theory that the Master-mind has selected, to create as actual, the best of these possible worlds; and it is to tracing the steps taken by the Master-mind that the philosopher devotes himself.

Why is Leibniz ranked among the great thinkers? In the first place, because he stands out as the classic example of intellectualism. The industry and ability which could achieve what Leibniz achieved constitute a standing challenge to the modern student to beat his record, if the modern student can. His discovery of the calculus, his invention of a calculating machine, his project for the invention of a universal language for science, an algebra of thought, his principle of the identity of indiscernibles, his principle of sufficient reason: all these discoveries and projects are of the first importance in our intellectual life, and all have borne rich fruit since Leibniz's day. Not less important, both as an example of what can be achieved, and as a challenge to all his successors, is his originality. Others have been as erudite, some more so; but to combine such erudition with such unimpaired originative power: to grasp the creative secrets of others, and to feed and develop thereby one's own creativity: this has been granted to very few. With most of us, to grow in breadth is at the expense of depth, and vice versa. We have many academicians, but few creative discoverers. Leibniz's method is, however, clearly before us; and it can be followed, in the twentieth, no less than in the seventeenth, century with success, if we persist.

In the second place, he stands out as the classic example of what the man of affairs, the lawyer, administrator, and judge, can achieve. Relying upon his intellectual insight, Leibniz is the great understander, the great reconciler, the great harmonizer: the great leader whom all can unite in following: for he seeks what is best for all, taken together. He is, in his way, an example of the philosopher-king, or philosophic adviser of kings, the philosophic executive. And here too his work is a challenge to all who are called to administrative positions: a challenge to allow for and preserve diversities of opinion, the independence of individuals, the freedom of citizens to co-operate with the government in their own characteristic ways, to be themselves, self-reliant, self-developing, self-creating. The administrator guides, stimulates, and directs these individual contributions. He weaves with them a single pattern, a tissue infinitely rich, infinitely variegated. But he never allows his feeling for unity and efficiency to obscure the incalculable value of each and every distinctively individual contribution, however humble, however different it may seem from the straight line which traverses the shortest distance in passing from its beginning to its end-point. Each monad mirrors the whole universe; and to neglect one mirroring would be to lose something which can never be made good in the whole.

In the third place, he is the great optimist, the great exponent of the value of things-as-they-are, the great conservative, the opponent of change, as such. Even while doing his utmost, as a modern, to exchange authority for reason, he is anxious to preserve the values which the régime of authority has gradually built up, to maintain the conventions, the outward observances of rank, power, and order for which he is able to find a place in the new world of his vision. With that short-sighted impatience which would scrap the whole cultural achievement of the past, in its eagerness to make a radically new beginning, he has no sympathy whatever. The universality of his outlook can accept much which his less optimistic contemporaries did their best to reject: and for the old, as well as for the new, his optimism can easily find a value and a place which is permanent.

Finally, he is an encouraging example of the modern principle in metaphysics, namely, that metaphysics are something more than "the systematic misuse of a terminology invented for that precise purpose." Metaphysics are a technical expression of the social outlook of an age, and may contain elements of value which far outlive the particular age and the particular interpretation which that age put upon metaphysical propositions. Such elements of value in Leibnizian metaphysics are his spiritual pluralism, his recognition of the function of the self, his definition of substance as activity, energy, force, rather than mere existence, or mere contemplation, and his feeling for the fundamental importance of that energy which expresses itself in the life of the mind.

In a word, it is as the great intellectualist, the great administrator, the great optimist, and the stimulating metaphysician, that Leibniz is ranked among the world's great thinkers.

Chapter VII

LOCKE 1632-1704

To the empiricism characteristic of the British way of looking at things, more than one thinker has made a significant contribution; and while it is usual to regard Locke as its chief founder, he had distinguished predecessors; and of these, each contributed something which, in itself, was not really empirical in spirit, but, when taken with the rest, combined to direct philosophy into the channel historically known as empiricism.

Of these predecessors, Francis Bacon, Lord Verulam (1561–1626), is perhaps the best known. He was a man of affairs, rather than a philosopher, and it was only after he had ceased, abruptly and for ever, to be at the head of affairs, that he wrote the works on which his reputation as a philosopher chiefly rests. He was essentially an ambitious man, a lawyer determined to get on. If he could not longer be Chancellor of England, then he would look about him for a wider realm, and be Chancellor of that. Grandiose to the last, he projected schemes for the advancement of learning, along lines laid down by himself. He outlined a modern university with all its departments devoted to research, research consisting chiefly in collecting materials in this or that specialized field, and carefully refraining from generalizing, constructing hypotheses, and discovering wide-reaching laws.

Experience, when it wanders in its own track, is mere groping in the dark, and confounds men rather than instructs them. But when it shall proceed in accordance with a fixed law, in regular order, and without interruption, then may better things be hoped of knowledge.

But even after such a store of natural history and experience as is required for the work of the understanding, or of philosophy, shall be ready to hand, still the understanding is by no means competent to deal with it off-hand.[1]

[1] *Novum Organum*, Aphorisms c, ci, condensed.

He published what became a fairly popular work on what he called "induction," an induction consisting, precisely, in the self-denying gathering of such materials, and storing them in appropriate museums, until, some fine day, there would be enough material for some master of method to establish a narrow, well-evidenced, generalization.

Then, and then only, may we hope well of the sciences, when in a just scale of ascent, and by successive steps not interrupted or broken, we rise from particulars to lesser axioms; and then to middle axioms, one above the other; and last of all to the most general. For the lowest axioms differ but slightly from bare experience, while the highest and most general (which we now have) are notional and abstract and without solidity. But the middle are the true and solid and living axioms, on which depend the affairs and fortunes of men; and above them again, last of all, those which are indeed the most general; such I mean as are not abstract, but of which those intermediate axioms are really limitations.

The understanding must not be supplied with wings, but rather hung with weights to keep it from leaping and flying. This has never yet been done; when it is done, we may entertain better hopes of the sciences.[1]

Scientists, naturally enough, supposed that Bacon's journalistic enthusiasm had something to do with the cause of scientific investigation, and for many a long year welcomed his co-operation, while well aware that his ideas had very little in common with the methods by which discoveries were really made. But, as the centuries have rolled by, it has become increasingly evident that Bacon had no understanding of science, no appreciation whatever of the nature and function of hypotheses, and no interest in men of science who, like his contemporary, Harvey, were really making discoveries.

Bacon's interest is, in fact, chiefly an interest in the advancement of Bacon, and his method is, when looked at more closely, the method, not of the scientist, but of the lawyer and judge. Used, for so much of his life, to weighing and sifting the legal evidence collected by others and brought to his court for final decision, he imagined things might be much the same in science. He could see himself assigning to field-workers in the different departments the task of collecting material, to be submitted, as evidence, to a weighing and sifting, whose rules of procedure he would himself prescribe. He would then be a kind of Lord Chancellor in the field

[1] *Novum Organum*, Aphorism civ.

of science: "taking all knowledge as his province," and settling all cases brought before him by his humble collaborators. The others should be "pupils of nature"; he would be the judge, the authority on the proper procedure: setting everybody right, and composing the final reports and summaries of the evidence upon which his judicial decision would rest. A pleasant occupation for a highly important Chancellor.

What do such views contribute towards the cause of empiricism? The appeal to "authoritative tables of discovery," i.e. to rules of procedure in weighing and sifting evidence, is a step, not forward, but backward: back towards the medieval love of authority, of highest courts of appeal, and of unquestionable, divine right. But the definition of man as "the servant and interpreter of nature":

> Man, being the servant and interpreter of nature, can do and understand so much and so much only as he has observed in fact or in thought of the course of nature: beyond this he neither knows anything nor can do anything,[1]

the insistence upon factual evidence rather than upon erudition and brilliance of deductive plausibility, and, above all, the conviction that success comes, in the end, to the persistent seeker who uses trial-and-error methods: these are characteristics of British empiricism from the beginning to the present day, and these are formulated and driven home by Bacon's great journalistic skill.

Another of Locke's predecessors was Thomas Hobbes, the shrewd and vigorous philosopher of Malmesbury (1586–1679). As a young man, Hobbes had acted as Bacon's secretary, translating into the language of scholars the grandiose dreams in the mother-tongue with which the great ex-Chancellor sought to disguise his defeat in the world of action. He never mentions Bacon or Bacon's theories, and writes as if no such person had ever existed. Convinced that reasoning consists in adding and subtracting the logical consequences of terms adequately defined, he has no use for Bacon's elaborate demands for factual evidence. His thought moves wholly in the field of consistently constructed edifices of words, of terms carefully purged of all ambiguity; and it would be considered deductive rather than inductive.

Hobbes' work consists of three parts: (1) A mechanical physics, an account of matter in motion, with motions initiated and trans-

---

[1] Ibid., i.

mitted by impact only. (2) A physical psychology, a theory which reduces mental life, without remainder, to physical motions, to physical interaction between a brain and nervous system on the one hand, and a mechanical environment on the other. (3) A social philosophy, which constructs an ideal form of human association, resting upon universal agreement to set up a sovereign leader to enforce, while remaining above, the laws which govern human association. The social philosophy rests upon the individual psychology, and, through it, upon the mechanical physics; and the whole constitutes the most consistent materialist theory which the world has seen.

The appeal to authority is for Hobbes, not a step backward, a step towards recognition of the divine right of kings. Resting, as it does, upon a social contract born of the fears of individuals, it represents, in essence, the only alternative to anarchy, the only safe escape from the chaos and dangers incident, as Hobbes so well knew, to civil war. Hobbes's work, with its constant note of almost anxious polemic, is, in fact, an elaborately disguised confession. The pen is, he hopes, mightier than the sword, and he is declaring his intention to do his personal fighting with the mightier weapon.

During the time men live without a common power to keep them all in awe, they are in that condition which is called war; and such a war, as is of every man, against every man.

In such condition, there is no place for industry, because the fruit thereof is uncertain, and consequently no culture of the earth; no navigation, nor use of the commodities that may be imported by sea; no commodious building; no instruments of moving, and removing, such things as require much force; no knowledge of the face of the earth; no account of time; no arts; no letters; no society; and, which is worst of all, continual fear, and danger of violent death; and the life of man, solitary, poor, nasty, brutish, and short.[1]

What contribution does Hobbes make to British empiricism? (1) His desire to avoid chaos in the field of opinion no less than in the field of action. (2) His reliance upon logic, the logic of implication. His use of words in a definite sense, which is made clear and distinct, with unhesitating acceptance of the consequences implicit in his formulations. (3) His thoroughgoing trust in the might of reason, in the power of thought to continue without deviation upon its self-chosen path. His deductive experimentation, which rests,

[1] *Leviathan*, ch. xiii.

Locke

not upon unstable sensation or flabby emotion, but upon the stark strength of consistency; and the devil take all shifters and weaklings! These contributions also form a part of all subsequent British empiricism, down to and including the present day.

The only way to erect such a common power, as may be able to defend them from the invasion of foreigners, and the injuries of one another, and thereby to secure them in such sort, as that by their own industry, and by the fruits of the earth, they may nourish themselves, and live contentedly; is, to confer all their power and strength upon one man, or upon one assembly of men, that may reduce all their wills, by plurality of voices, unto one will: which is as much as to say, to appoint one man, or assembly of men, to bear their person; and every one to own, and acknowledge himself to be author of whatsoever he that so beareth their person, shall act, or cause to be acted, in those things which concern the common peace and safety; and therein to submit their wills, every one to his will, and their judgments, to his judgment. This is more than consent, or concord; it is a real unity of them all, in one and the same person, made by covenant of every man with every man, in such manner, as if every man should say to every man, *I authorize and give up my right of governing myself, to this man, or to this assembly of men, on this condition, that thou give up thy right to him, and authorize all his actions in like manner.* This done, the multitude so united in one person is called a COMMONWEALTH.[1]

When we come to John Locke, we find united in him the empirical tendencies of both Bacon and Hobbes. On the one hand, he is never tired of urging his readers not to be misled by words, and the conventions of language and logic, but always to "think the things themselves."

Truth is to be found and supported by a mature and due consideration of things themselves, and not by artificial terms and ways of arguing.[2]

This means, not merely to form mental pictures, and to contemplate these rather than to use words hastily, but also to think oneself into the concrete situation symbolized by mental imagery no less than by words. This corresponds to Bacon's demand for factual evidence in place of verbal dexterity. On the other hand, while using many words rather than one only, in order to "suggest, convey, furnish, supply, and provide" ideas for his readers, Locke, like Hobbes, is always careful to avoid the pitfalls incident to

[1] Ibid., ch. xvii.   [2] *Some Thoughts Concerning Education.*

undefined speech, and to utilize the resources of language to establish a single, unmistakable pathway along which thought can advance without having to retrace its footsteps or hesitate in ambiguity and doubt.

John Locke, as becomes the real founder of British empiricism, was a student all his life. After the usual four years at Oxford, he was elected to a "studentship" in his college (Christ Church), which he held indefinitely. There were certain duties nominally attached to it, such as lecturing on Aristotle's *Ethics*; but, by agreement, the studentship could be held *in absentia*, and the "duties" did not, apparently, have to be performed. Having a marked distaste for (scholastic) philosophy, Locke devoted himself to empirical, if not experimental, pursuits: assisting Sydenham in his experimental treatment of fever-patients, acting as secretary in the Shaftesbury family and thus assisting in political activities, functioning as commissioner of the Board of Trade. When he travelled, it was not academic personalities and abstract pursuits which engaged his interest, but things which concerned practical men: new ways of doing business, new kinds of factories; not theories, but things. As secretary of a royal commission, he personally composed most of what was intended as the constitution of the State of Carolina; and he acted as adviser to William of Orange in the matter of reforming the (debased) coinage, and in other entirely practical affairs. He was known as "the judicious Mr. Locke," and the adjective could hardly have been bettered. Toleration, co-operation, commonsense, honesty, and hard work, were what he looked for, in others and in himself.

Intellectually, as librarian in the Shaftesbury family, he read widely, and, as readers did in those days of expensive books, made excerpts of what he read, devising his own method of keeping his commonplace book, with a convenient system of reference and indexing, which he later published. He also felt drawn to the experimental work of the Royal Society, whose Fellows co-opted him as one of themselves; and all his life he continued interested in scientific experimentation. The only degree he ever held was the degree of Doctor of Medicine, conferred upon him late in life by the University of Oxford, *honoris causa*.

What his manner of thinking was, we know from a paper, published in the *Life* by Lord King, entitled "Thus I Think." He thought quite empirically and unsystematically, trying to make up his mind definitely on this point and that, with the idea that, once made up, his mind would have a firm basis for further thought. From Descartes he had acquired the method of clear and distinct ideas; but of that love of system, which would transfer unhesitatingly to fields *A*, *B*, and *C*, what one believed in field *D*, and vice versa, he had no trace whatever. He supposed, indeed, that a thought which was based upon many beginnings, rather than upon a single wide-reaching principle, would, in the end, prove to be consistent with itself; but he supposed this would be because it was, in each case, consistent with the things, and the things constituted, in fact, a single system. He thus studied many things rather than a single system, read many authors, preformed many experiments, all concrete and individual, and avoided wide-sweeping speculation. In a word, he behaved as empiricists have behaved, and continue to behave, all the world over.

Of a piece with this pluralism and attention to concrete detail, which characterized his way of thinking as a young man, is one of the doctrines of his *Thoughts Concerning Education*, which was published in later life, and is still read. He there states it as his conviction that a boy should be educated in the beginnings of many subjects, languages, and sciences, without any systematic ordering of studies. His reason is that life itself, as the boy grows older, will indicate what further development will be required for practical purposes. It is easy to build upon foundations laid down in youth. This is the point of view of a practical man, an experimentalist, guiding himself through life as occasion requires: not at all the point of view of a theoretician, a doctrinaire. He does not think of education as "forming the mind" in this or that desirable mould; but rather as providing a man with instruments which he will use as experience requires: instruments which will make a man's reaction upon the concrete occasions of life more efficient in detail.

The reverse side of this picture is a highly critical attitude towards all pretensions not based upon direct experience. The logic which professes to deal with "universals" and apply general principles to all details which come under those principles, without further detailed investigation, seemed to him, as to Bacon, a mistake.

If the use and end of right reasoning be to have right notions, and a right judgment of things, to distinguish betwixt truth and falsehood, right and wrong, and to act accordingly; be sure not to let your son be bred up in the art and formality of disputing, either practising it himself or admiring it in others; unless, instead of an able man, you desire to have him an insignificant wrangler, opiniator in discourse, and priding himself in contradicting others; or, which is worse, questioning everything, and thinking there is no such thing as truth to be sought, but only victory in disputing.[1]

The syllogism wins assent to the words and propositions; but it leaves the things and concrete situations untouched. It is a useful method of co-ordinating knowledge acquired by direct experience; but it is incapable of making direct discoveries itself. Locke therefore feels a distaste for syllogistic logic, much as has been felt by other experimentalists, down to and including our own time. The forms and structures implicit in language, which influence us to believe and accept what is consistent with them, and not to believe and accept what is new and perhaps inconsistent with them, come under the same critical review; and, as far as possible, Locke keeps his mind clear of all kinds of cant.

But this is not all. In Locke's time, it was widely believed that the human mind contained, implicit in its structure, a number of axioms and principles, such as the Laws of Thought, certain principles of morality, and certain principles of religion, such as the necessary belief in a single eternal, all-powerful God. These claimed the divine right of axioms: to be above questioning and criticism, and to possess a domain at least coextensive with human knowledge.

There is nothing more commonly taken for granted, than that there are certain principles, both speculative and practical (for they speak of both) universally agreed upon by all mankind: which therefore, they argue, must needs be constant impressions which the souls of men receive in their first beings, and which they bring into the world with them, as necessarily and really as they do any of their inherent faculties.[2]

A popular way of referring to them was to call them "innate ideas," and, under this heading, an enormous number of ways of regarding experience, such as faculty psychology, and much popular theology, were widely accepted without criticism. Such "principles" are quite widely believed in and acted upon and preached

[1] *Some Thoughts Concerning Education.*   [2] *Essay*, I, ii, 2.

about at the present day too; and many persons, if asked "How do we remember, or think, or appreciate beauty?", would answer, without guile, "Because we have a faculty of Memory, or Thought, or Aesthetic Appreciation."

Locke, as a convinced empiricist, believing that our knowledge is altogether such as direct experience conveys to us, direct experience via sensation or reflection, regarded such "innate ideas" as the enemy, and conceived and directed a frontal attack upon them, from which they are only just beginning to recover, in our own time.

I take liberty to say, that these propositions are so far from having an universal assent, that there are a great part of mankind to whom they are not so much as known.

For, first, it is evident, that all children and idiots have not the least apprehension or thought of them; and the want of that is enough to destroy that universal assent, which must needs be the necessary concomitant of all innate truths.[1]

As a medical man, he asks if new-born babies have such ideas as "Whatever is, is," "A thing must either be or not-be," etc.; whether they reveal to themselves and others an innate apprehension of the principles of truth and social justice; whether they express clear and distinct ideas upon religious subjects, etc. Critics of Locke have asked, whom he had in mind, and whether any sane person ever maintained such nonsense. It is probable, however, that he is attacking the conception of "innate ideas," maintained on the (then) usual ground of *Quod semper, ubique, ab omnibus,* by indicating the absurdities implicit in such views. It has been thought that he was attacking William of Occam, on whose (abridged) text-books of scholastic philosophy he had been educated; or perhaps Descartes, whose works he read in his fifth or sixth year at Oxford; or possibly the Cambridge Platonists, whose sermons he had attended as an undergraduate, during week-end visits from Oxford. But it is more probable that he was attacking a very widespread attitude towards knowledge, life, and religion: an attitude of acceptance, of laziness, of absence of criticism. Attacking it, because it is essentially opposed to the convictions of the empiricist, namely, that everything worth-while has to be won by work, by investigation and persistent experiment, and never comes unasked-for, as

[1] *Ibid.*, I, ii, 4–5.

a gift of the gods. How important and necessary such an attack can be, we can realize when we remember that in the last generation a distinguished psychologist[1] found it wise to write a slashing attack upon faculty psychology, and that in our own times the development of genuine criticism, which will see through the mass-slogans upon which so much of our so-called "civilization" rests, is regarded as a fundamental task of the modern college and university, all the world over.

Locke's criticism extended further, to include doctrines accepted because maintained by men in high places in Church and State, supposedly beyond question. The characteristic doctrine of Father Malebranche, that we should "see all things in God," certain views of the great Leibniz, the somewhat hasty polemics of the great Trinitarian, Bishop Stillingfleet—such views drew his fire; although he was always careful to observe *les convenances*, and to speak politely of the man, while questioning whether his doctrine really meant anything in terms of direct experience. Part of the time, he might seem to be asking enlightenment as to how he was to understand the linguistic and grammatical implications of an author's words; while in reality he was emphasizing the tremendous difference between the empirical and the dogmatic attitude. What he is really attacking is always some form of "enthusiasm," the uncritical championing of vague and intolerant views.

Reason is natural revelation, whereby the eternal father of light, and fountain of all knowledge, communicates to mankind that portion of truth which he has laid within the reach of their natural faculties: revelation is natural reason enlarged by a new set of discoveries communicated by God immediately, which reason vouches the truth of, by the testimony and proofs it gives, that they come from God. So that he that takes away reason, to make way for revelation, puts out the light of both, and does much-what the same, as if he would persuade a man to put out his eyes the better to receive the remote light of an invisible star by a telescope.

Enthusiasm, though founded neither on reason nor divine revelation, but rising from the conceits of a warmed or over-weening brain, works yet where it once gets footing, more powerfully on the persuasions and actions of men, than either of those two, or both together: men being most forwardly obedient to the impulses they receive from themselves; and the whole man is sure to act more vigorously, where the whole man is carried by a natural motion. For strong conceit, like a new principle, carries all

[1] G. F. Stout, *Manual of Psychology*, Book I, iii.

easily with it, when got above common sense, and freed from all restraint of reason, and check of reflection, it is heightened into a divine authority, in concurrence with our own temper and inclination.

Though the odd opinions and extravagant actions enthusiasm has run men into, were enough to warn them against this wrong principle, so apt to misguide them both in their belief and conduct; yet the love of something extraordinary, the ease and glory it is to be inspired, and be above the common and natural ways of knowledge, so flatters many men's laziness, ignorance, and vanity, that when once they are got into this way of immediate revelation, of illumination without search, and of certainty without proof, and without examination; it is a hard matter to get them out of it.[1]

What he is really defending is always the right and duty of the individual to criticize, question, and discover for himself what this or that problem means in terms of direct experience via the senses or reflection.

Polemics of this kind are part and parcel of Locke's whole attitude as an empiricist. He is opposed to dogmatism and unquestioned authority in every shape and form, and desires to substitute for it common sense, co-operation, judicious trial-and-error. His writings *On Civil Government* have, as their reverse side, a polemic against "paternal authority" on the part of those in high places, an authority championed by Sir Robert Filmer, as well as against the more absolute authority—absolute, although based upon common agreement—advocated by Hobbes. Locke's view is that government should rest always upon the consent of the governed, and he advocates, with reference to William of Orange, the kind of democracy called "constitutional monarchy," the kind of democracy which has in fact become the standard British tradition.

Political power is that power which every man having in the state of nature has given up into the hands of the society, and therein to the governors whom the society hath set over itself, with this express or tacit trust, that it shall be employed for their good and the preservation of their property. Now this power which every man has in the state of nature, and which he parts with to the society in all such cases where the society can secure him, is to use such means for the preserving of his own property as he thinks good and nature allows him, and to punish the breach of the law of nature in others, so as (according to the best of his reason) may most conduce to the preservation of himself and the rest of mankind. So

[1] *Essay*, IV, xix, 1, 7.

that the end and measure of this power, when in every man's hands in the state of nature, being the preservation of all of his society, that is, all mankind in general, it can have no other end or measure when in the hands of the magistrate, but to preserve the members of that society in their lives, liberties, and possessions. And so it cannot be an absolute arbitrary power over their lives and fortunes, which are as much as possible to be preserved, but a power to make laws, and annex such penalties to them, as may tend to the preservation of the whole, by cutting off those parts and those only which are so corrupt that they threaten the sound and healthy, without which no severity is lawful. And this power has its original only from compact and agreement and the mutual consent of those who make up the community.[1]

So too in matters ecclesiastical: his *Letters on Toleration* show opposition, not only to foreign rulers, to popes and cardinals, but also to native sons who assume the authority of civil magistrates on ecclesiastical matters. In their place, he advocates the establishment of that type of administration which we know as "congregationalism."

A church I take to be a voluntary society of men, joining themselves together of their own accord, in order to the public worshipping of God, in such a manner as they judge acceptable to him, and effectual to the salvation of their souls.

The end of a religious society is the public worship of God, and by means thereof the acquisition of eternal life. All discipline ought therefore to tend to that end, and all ecclesiastical laws to be thereunto confined. Nothing ought, nor can be transacted in this society, relating to the possession of civil or worldly goods. No force is here to be made use of, upon any occasion whatsoever; for force belongs wholly to the civil magistrate, and the possession of all outward goods is subject to his jurisdiction.[2]

Reasonableness is thus the dominant note of Locke's life and work, and it might well be thought that he is essentially of a practical, rather than theoretical nature: judicious, competent, honest, but—no philosopher.

This, however, would be a mistake. Locke *is* a man of affairs. But he is also a philosopher, through and through. His insistence upon democracy, upon toleration and co-operation, rests, in the end, upon philosophic conviction. He is convinced that no human being is capable of knowing enough to be "paternal" towards the rest of

[1] *Treatise of Civil Government.*   [2] *Works* (11th edition, 1812), vol. VI.

us. The human understanding is essentially limited, and the best we can do is to recognize our limitations, and co-operate empirically, trusting in one another's practical wisdom, in so far as this is based upon experience.

If we face ultimate questions, we discover that our minds are too weak, too incompetent, to attain to "certain real knowledge." Space and time are "vast oceans, in which our understandings lose themselves." The universe and God constitute subjects "too wide for our minds to compass." Infinity, in every shape and form, is something we are never able to grasp, and represents, when we look at it critically, the "restlessness and impotency" of our minds. Convictions like these, upon which Locke acted all his life, gradually came to a head, and, after occupying the foreground of his attention for many years, issued in the great work upon which his reputation as a technical philosopher chiefly rests, the *Essay On Human Understanding*.

This work, as Voltaire wittily pointed out, is understood by everyone but philosophers. Men of affairs, with a turn for reflection, men of wide and deep experience of life, men, in a word, who are like Locke himself, have never felt any difficulty in understanding him. They realize at once that he is avoiding extremes and standing aloof from all one-sided theories. He has no axe of his own to grind. He is obviously unimaginative, impartial, cool, judicious, reasonable, sound. He clearly takes his stand upon fact, upon the actualities of common experience, and represents, in almost ideal form, the perfection of common sense, sublimated into practical wisdom.

But technical philosophers read the *Essay* technically, attending less to the concrete actualities of common experience, and more to the logical implications of the words and arguments employed. Common experience indicates that our understandings have their limitations. The technical philosopher has here a great many questions to ask. Just what is meant by "understanding"? Does Locke teach that we "understand" something when we have in our minds an "idea" which is a "true copy" of the "something"? Does he teach that what we know immediately is the "idea in our own minds" and that we know the "thing itself" only mediately, by means of an inference from the "idea in our mind" to the "thing" as it exists "outside the mind"?

It is evident the mind knows not things immediately, but only by the intervention of the ideas it has of them. Our knowledge therefore is real, only so far as there is a conformity between our ideas and the reality of things. But what shall be here the criterion? How shall the mind, when it perceives nothing but its own ideas, know that they agree with things themselves?[1]

If the "idea" is different from the "thing," and merely "represents" the "thing" to us indirectly, are we not involved in hopeless difficulties? How do we know a "copy" *is* a copy, unless we also somehow know the original, of which it is a copy, too? There is, in an old number of *Punch*, a picture of two washerwomen, discussing whether a portrait of the Queen of England is a good likeness or not. As they have never seen the Queen, it is obvious that they are hardly in a position to judge. So too with Locke. If all he knows is the "idea" in his mind, how does he know that it represents something outside the mind, or even that there *is* anything outside the mind and its ideas?

Questions like these lead the philosopher Berkeley to reject many of the fundamental beliefs of the *Essay*, and to construct an idealistic theory which does without "things outside the mind" altogether; and philosophers like Sir William Hamilton and Victor Cousin definitely elaborated the implications of Locke's language into a theory known as "representative idealism," in order to provide it with an equally elaborate technical refutation. And it can hardly be denied that Locke's language, if taken strictly, is susceptible of the interpretation which these philosophers place upon it.

At the same time, if we keep an eye upon the concrete situation which Locke is undoubtedly attempting to describe, the technical interpretation seems a little unfair. Locke's language is really not unreasonable, and is not intended to mislead in any way. If we ourselves refer, without prejudice, and in our slightly more modern terminology, to the selfsame knowledge-situation, we find ourselves describing it in much the same sort of way as he does. To any sophisticated student of science, it is obvious that what we really know are not the "secrets of nature," the objective events in themselves. We know, in so far as the objects correspond to the hypotheses we have, up to date, constructed and tried to apply to them. In the end, all we really understand is what Locke calls the

[1] *Essay*, IV, iv, 3.

"nominal essence," the tissue of hypotheses which we have ourselves constructed.

There is an internal constitution of things on which their properties depend. This we call the real essence. There are also certain complex ideas or combinations of these properties in men's minds, to which they commonly annex specific names (man, horse). These complex ideas I have called nominal essences.[1] That whereby we distinguish and rank particular substances into species is not those real essences or internal constitutions, but such combinations of simple ideas as we observe in them.[2] Our ideas of substances, consisting of a collection of simple ideas, supposed taken from the works of nature, may yet vary from them, by having more or different ideas united in them than are to be found united in the things themselves; from whence it comes to pass, that they may and often do fail of being exactly conformable to things themselves.[3]

Science develops by constructing more refined, more consistent, and more comprehensive hypotheses, testing them at this point and that, and trying to bring them into closer correspondence with factual experience. But we could well say, at the present day, that we know things only via our hypotheses, only in so far as scientists have succeeded in constructing what Locke calls "ideas," i.e. mind-made concepts and theories which seem to correspond with the observed behaviour of phenomena.

We understand, e.g., the function of the bast-cells in the bulrush by reference to engineering constructions, such as "trusses" calculated to withstand such-and-such lateral strains. We understand the mechanism involved in hearing by reference to such mind-made constructions as the principle of the telephone or grand piano. There are, no doubt, ultimate difficulties implicit in all our attempts at describing phenomena; but we find ourselves, like Locke, naturally using language which can be construed as implying the position of "representative idealism." Like Locke, we should be surprised to hear ourselves pilloried as "representative idealists," and, like ourselves, Locke would probably protest against the label, when all he is trying to do is to describe, simply and without bias, and in the same kind of language as the rest of us use, what appear to be the facts of a very common concrete situation.

In what follows, we shall accordingly attempt to set forth Locke's philosophical views without crystallizing them into one of the many

[1] *Works*, vol. IV, pp. 87–8.   [2] Ibid., vol. IX, p. 306.   [3] *Essay*, IV, iv, ii.

one-sided theories which have been formulated by systematic metaphysicians, chiefly in order that, as so formulated, they can be demolished *secundum artem*. We shall endeavour, rather, to keep in touch with the concrete situations which Locke plainly has in mind, and to avoid, as far as possible, being misled by the nests of implications so easily discovered by the pure logician.

Locke's work is entitled *Essay on Human Understanding*. It is not intended as a normative science, a systematic study of rules and laws to which thinking should conform, if it wishes to be more than human, e.g. if it wishes to be "pure reason," abstractly rational. It is not even intended as a logical analysis, a setting forth in explicit terms of the elements involved in "understanding" in general, or of "human understanding" in particular, although it does contain a partial analysis of this kind. It is rather a description, with constant reference to concrete experience, of the ways in which human beings actually proceed when they are "thinking" upon the ordinary occasions of life, social, ethical, political, scientific, and religious, in seventeenth-century England. It is a survey, by an inquiring mind, of the nature of human experience, with some reference to its genetic development, and to its limitations, especially to its limitations in respect of knowledge-validity. It is a broad and sweeping attempt at reflective self-criticism, at philosophical stock-taking, by a typical seventeenth-century Englishman. It is a crystal globe in which we see, not so much our own selves as a portrait of England in the process of growing to self-consciousness: honest, straightforward, matter-of-fact, a little puzzled, but judicious, self-reliant, persistent, muddling through.

The book is written, not systematically, not deductively, not with Cartesian or Spinozistic appreciation of the interrelation of parts within a unified totality. It is written piecemeal, inductively, empirically, with an obvious love of detail for its own sake. If the Cartesian method is telescopic, bringing distant horizons close to us, and concentrating vast ranges of experience, Locke's method is microscopic, making details stand out clearly and distinctly, but leaving remoter margins out of focus, vague and blurred. Both rest upon "simple ideas." But to Descartes a "simple" idea is something extremely general, such as God, or thought-in-general, or extension-in-general, while to Locke a "simple" idea is something extremely specific, such as the experience of "red" or "cold" or "smooth."

1. *Uncompounded appearances.*—The better to understand the nature, manner, and extent of our knowledge, one thing is carefully to be observed concerning the ideas we have; and that is, that some of them are *simple*.

Though the qualities that affect our senses are, in the things themselves, so united and blended that there is no separation, no distance between them; yet it is plain the ideas they produce in the mind enter by the senses simple and unmixed. For though the sight and touch often take in from the same object, at the same time, different ideas—as a man sees at once motion and colour, the hand feels softness and warmth in the same piece of wax—yet the simple ideas thus united in the same subject are as perfectly distinct as those that come in by different senses; the coldness and hardness which a man feels in a piece of ice being as distinct ideas in the mind as the smell and whiteness of a lily, or as the taste of sugar and smell of a rose: and there is nothing can be plainer to a man than the clear and distinct perception he has of those simple ideas; which, being each in itself uncompounded, contains in it nothing but one uniform appearance or conception in the mind, and is not distinguishable into different ideas.[1]

Book I is a prelude, a clearing of the decks for action. It contains the overwhelming attack upon the conception of "innate" ideas, upon the conception that what is fundamental for knowledge and action and belief is somehow given to us without our having to work for it, to act as co-labourers, to make our own discoveries by our own efforts. It has been said that in Book I it is the pedagogue rather than the philosopher who speaks. But this is not entirely correct. In the case of British empiricism, and in the case of its founder, John Locke, the "pedagogue" is a philosophical pedagogue, and the "philosopher" is a pedagogic philosopher. British empiricism is essentially practical rather than "pure" reasoning, and Book I is philosophical in this practical sense.

What makes us believe that we should not lie or kill or steal, that we should not fall into inconsistencies and contradictions, is not some heaven-sent intuition, some physically inborn disposition towards goodness and truth, bestowed upon all men at birth, but is acquired and learned by slow experience, by trial-and-error, by appreciation of the practical consequences of lying and stealing. There is no royal road to virtue or to truth or to heaven; and not all the inertia of vested interests should delude us into supposing that it is enough to be born as men, or even as seventeenth-century Englishmen. We have indeed a cultural heritage; but it has been

---

[1] *Essay*, II, ii, 1.

acquired by work, and can be maintained and improved only by further work.

The senses at first let in particular ideas, and furnish the yet empty cabinet; and the mind by degrees growing familiar with some of them, they are lodged in the memory, and names got to them. Afterwards the mind, proceeding farther, abstracts them, and by degrees learns the use of general names. In this manner the mind comes to be furnished with ideas and language, the materials about which to exercise its discursive faculty: and the use of reason becomes daily more visible, as these materials, that give it employment, increase. But though the having of general ideas, and the use of general words and reason, usually grow together; yet, I see not, how this any way proves them innate. The knowledge of some truths, I confess, is very early in the mind; but in a way that shows them not to be innate. For, if we will observe, we shall find it still to be about ideas, not innate, but acquired.[1]

Do we find new-born babies lisping moral maxims or the axioms of Aristotelian logic? Do we find universal agreement as to how our modern problems can best be solved? Have men always thought in the same way in fundamentals? To ask such questions is to realize at once the absurdity of any such suppositions. If they were as supposed, how much simpler life would be than it is! No, it is obvious that it is to experience, to trial-and-error, to the testing of hypotheses by their practical consequences, that we must look as the sources of the degree of civilization which humanity has slowly achieved, and to a more rigorously methodized experience that we must look as our hope for the future.

Book II consists of an analytic-synthetic account of experience, as envisaged by Locke. Experience is, he believes, highly concrete, and he attempts, in his varying descriptions, to be just to its many-sided concreteness, and to avoid falling into one-sided abstractions, as so many philosophers do. The philosopher Hobbes, for instance, like many a present-day neo-realist, regards experience as essentially physical, the interactivity of a brain and nervous system on the one hand, with a texture of "motions" taking place in the physical environment, on the other. The whole affair is a complicated tissue of motions. "Motion produceth nothing but motion," and the ideas in our minds are envisaged by Hobbes as nothing but phases of physical movement.

[1] *Essay*, I, ii, 3.

Locke

The cause of sense, is the external body, or object, which presseth the organ proper to each sense, either immediately, as in the taste and touch; or mediately, as in seeing, hearing, and smelling; which pressure, by the mediation of the nerves, and other strings and membranes of the body, continued inwards to the brain and heart, causeth there a resistance, or counter-pressure or endeavour of the heart to deliver itself, which endeavour, because *outward*, seemeth to be some matter without. And this *seeming*, or *fancy*, is that which men call *sense*; and consisteth, as to the eye, in a *light*, or *colour figured*; to the ear, in a *sound*; to the nostril, in an *odour*; to the tongue and palate, in a *savour*; and to the rest of the body, in *heat, cold, hardness, softness*, and such other qualities as we discern by *feeling*. All which qualities, called *sensible*, are in the object, that causeth them, but so many several motions of the matter, by which it presseth our organs diversely. Neither in us that are pressed, are they anything else, but divers motions; for motion produceth nothing but motion.[1]

Locke, as a student of contemporary physical science, adopts the then accepted atomic hypothesis with characteristic caution as only a hypothesis, and refuses to accept the physicist's account of the tissue of interacting atoms as a final account of human experience. For Locke, human experience is essentially conscious, reflective, cautious, a human, social, seventeenth-century mind busying itself with its human, social, seventeenth-century ideas: looking within and testing what it finds; accepting here and rejecting there, trying out new combinations, standardizing and approving what fits in with the economic, social, political, and religious needs of the times; and conducting itself, in general, coolly, judiciously, and with practical wisdom.

Experience thus has two poles: (1) the busy self or mind, and (2) the material which it finds somehow supplied, furnished, and provided for it to work with. In Book II the treatment of the self or mind, while important and suggestive, is incidental. It is the content of experience, seventeenth-century ideas considered in respect of their material, which occupies the foreground; and the whole of Book II is fundamentally an analytic-synthetic study of the content of experience.

Let us suppose the mind to be, as we say, white paper, void of all characters, without any ideas: How comes it to be furnished? Whence comes it by that vast store, which the busy and boundless fancy of man has painted on it with an almost endless variety? Whence has it all the

[1] *Leviathan*, i.

187

materials of reason and knowledge? To this I answer, in one word, From *experience*. In that all our knowledge is founded, and from that it ultimately derives itself. Our observation, employed either about external sensible objects, or about the internal operations of our minds, perceived and reflected on by ourselves, is that which supplies our understandings with all the materials of thinking. These two are the fountains of knowledge, from whence all the ideas we have, or can naturally have, do spring.[1]

In the first place, this content falls apart naturally into two large groups of ideas, namely, (*a*) ideas of sensation, and (*b*) ideas of reflection. The first group is exemplified by such ideas as hot, round, yellow, loud, and sharp; the second by such ideas as perceiving, believing, recollecting, hoping, and loving. The distinction between these groups is not hard to recognize in a general way, so long as we keep clearly before us the concrete situation envisaged by Locke. But it is difficult to formulate it acceptably, to express it in language which is abstractly exact and not misleading; and Locke's well-meant metaphors have all been found somewhat unsatisfactory by later thinkers.

For instance: to call sensory ideas "external" and the others "internal," and to treat reflection as a kind of "internal *sense*," when it plainly has no specific sense-organs and no specific sensory nerves, has been severely criticized. To treat sensation and reflection as two kinds of "channel" through which ideas are "conveyed, furnished, supplied, and given" to our minds, is, when we look at it closely, just about as absurd as the metaphors in which present-day Freudians refer to these selfsame processes. Freud speaks as though "the mind" had (1) an antechamber, and (2) an interior-presence-room, with a moral censor standing on guard between the two, and letting through only such ideas as manage to disguise themselves sufficiently to pass the censor's inspection. The unsatisfactoriness of all such metaphors seems to suggest that *all* psychological attempts to deal with "consciousness" are foredoomed to failure, and that the only kind of strictly scientific treatment of human behaviour which we can set up will be objective and physical.

The fact thus seems to be that exact definitions of conscious experience and its assumed factors are not to be found. Locke simply supposes that we "go to experience" directly to find out what he is discussing, and that we discover for ourselves a concrete situation corresponding fairly well to his metaphors. He assumes

[1] *Essay*, II, i, 2.

that the correspondence thus apprehended is close enough to prevent us from being misled. We all know what he means, although none of us, including Locke himself, seems able to formulate it in language which is above reproach.

In the second place, the content of experience, i.e. seventeenth-century ideas, are observed to fall apart naturally into two different kinds of grouping. However ideas may come into the mind, some of them (1) are "simple," while others (2) are "complex." As experience comes to us in the concrete it is, of course, highly complicated, a higgledy-piggledy of sensory and reflective processes, all jumbled up, and needing to be sorted out before we can make much of them. The sorting-out process is, of course, the work of the busy seventeenth-century mind, analysing, selecting, and emphasizing this or that idea or group of ideas, according as the interests and practical needs of the seventeenth century make such selection and emphasis seem important.

I think, it will be needless to enumerate all the particular simple ideas belonging to each sense. Nor indeed is it possible, if we would; there being a great many more of them belonging to most of the senses, than we have names for. The variety of smells, which are as many almost, if not more, than species of bodies in the world, do most of them want names. Sweet and stinking commonly serve our turn for these ideas, which in effect is little more than to call them pleasing or displeasing; though the smell of a rose and violet, both sweet, are certainly very distinct ideas. Nor are the different tastes, that by our palates we receive ideas of, much better provided with names. Sweet, bitter, sour, harsh, and salt, are almost all the epithets we have to denominate that numberless variety of relishes, which are to be found distinct, not only in almost every sort of creatures, but in the different parts of the same plant, fruit, or animal. The same may be said of colours and sounds. I shall therefore, in the account of simple ideas I am here giving, content myself to set down only such, as are most material to our present purpose, or are in themselves less apt to be taken notice of, though they are very frequently the ingredients of our complex ideas.[1]

In this process of analysing, of breaking up the complicated jumble of ideas occurring in concrete experience, we come upon certain ideas which, for seventeenth-century purposes, are accepted as ultimate or "simple," not in need of further analysis to make them clearly and distinctly intelligible to the seventeenth-century

[1] Ibid.

mind. Just what does Locke understand by a "simple" idea? In the first place, it is qualitatively simple. It is not only intuitively distinct from other ideas, as "red" is distinct from "blue" or "hot" or "smooth," but it "presents a single, uncompounded appearance to the mind." That is to say, "red" is a simple idea, in contrast with such an idea as "red-hot," which presents the appearance of being composite, a mixture of "red" with another, different idea. So too "perceiving" is simple, as contrasted with such an idea as "remembering" or "expecting," which contain, in addition to the idea of perceiving, a further idea, namely, of past or future time.

In the second place, such ideas may also be quantitatively simple. From this standpoint, the simple idea of red is the *minimum sensible*, the smallest portion of the red-experience which can be appreciated as coloured red. The simple idea of duration is the smallest portion of duration which can be apprehended as enduring. It is called by Locke the "moment," and is that amount of duration which a single idea can be held before the attention. In the modern experiment, in which the two eyes look through a stereoscope and see a piece of red paper with the one eye, and of blue paper with the other, it is possible to concentrate upon the "red" alone, or the "blue" alone, or the combined sensation of "purple" alone, and to test, with appropriate apparatus, the amount of time during which one idea (the red, blue, or purple) can be held before the attention. The time varies from a fraction of a second to a maximum of (it is said) four seconds. It is this varying amount of time which corresponds to what Locke calls the "moment" or psychological duration-unit, the "simple idea of duration." So too the simple idea of space is the smallest portion of space which can be appreciated, by our sense-organs, as spatial; and the simple idea of perceiving is that amount of perceiving which is limited to the apprehension of a single idea such as red or purple. In every field of experience, sensory or reflective, this distinction between ideas which are simple, qualitatively and quantitatively, and ideas which are composite, compounded of one or more simple ideas, such as "red-hot," "running motion," "theft," and "ostracism," will be found to hold good.

These two distinctions, (1) between sensation and reflection, and (2) between ideas which are simple and ideas which are complex, as well as the underlying distinction between mind and its ideas, have all proved of fundamental importance in the history of thought.

It is not that the distinctions, as formulated by Locke, have been accepted. They have not been accepted. But students of Locke have found themselves, when confronted with Locke's formulations on the one hand, and concrete experience on the other, impelled to improve upon what they read in the *Essay*: to be more precise and exact, to devise refined experiments to test the alternatives suggested by Locke's shifting metaphors, to try to account in a more fundamentally satisfactory way for the distinctions which they do find. And it has proved hard to subject Locke's *Essay* to thorough study without the student himself becoming a philosopher with decided views and definitively reasoned hypotheses. Locke's honesty in the face of concrete experience, his refusal to accept this or that facile theory, his insistence upon fidelity to fact, to what he seems to be discovering rather than inventing, lead him into many a perilous field of implication, and indeed into many a plain inconsistency of expression. But out of the study of his unconcealed difficulties and inconsistencies there emerges a new psychology, a new epistemology, a new logic, and a new metaphysic, which have become more and more differentiated as new generations have worked at his problems. Without Locke, no Berkeley, no Hume, and no Kant. Without Locke, empirical psychology would not have taken the course it has followed. Without Locke, the intellectual technique characteristic of the eighteenth century, and indeed the analytic methods characteristic of the twentieth century, could hardly have developed as they have done. And the main lines have diverged from precisely these distinctions between sensation and reflection, between simple and complex ideas, and between the mind and its ideas.

Let us consider briefly how, from Locke's descriptions of the concrete situation, such divergent developments are inevitable. In the distinction between sensation and reflection, it is the description of reflection which at first seems to create difficulties. But, as soon as we begin to study the difficulties, we find that the description of sensation is swept along into the same stream of doubt. As Locke describes the situation, the mind, apart from its analytic-synthetic activity, is entirely receptive. It does not create the simple ideas of "red," "hot," "smooth," and "loud." It may disentangle them from the confused mixtures in which they are first given to us, so that they stand out clearly and distinctly. But the redness of "red," the warmness of "hot," represent something ultimate. The mind does not manufacture these. Experience just brings them to us. We know them intuitively, and accept them unquestioningly. Mind neither makes nor unmakes them. It just apprehends them, without in any way altering their nature. In sensation, they are given to us, and given to us without mediation of any kind.

We have hitherto considered those ideas, in the reception whereof the mind is only passive, which are those simple ones received from sensation and reflection before mentioned, whereof the mind cannot make one to itself, nor have any idea which does not wholly consist of them. But as the mind is wholly passive in the reception of all its simple ideas, so it exerts several acts of its own, whereby out of its simple ideas as the materials and foundations of the rest, the other are framed. The acts of the mind, wherein it exerts its power over its simple ideas, are chiefly these three: 1. Combining several simple ideas into one compound one, and thus all complex ideas are made. 2. The second is bringing two ideas, whether simple or complex, together, and setting them by one another, so as to take a view of them at once, without uniting them into one; by which way it gets all its ideas of relations. 3. The third is separating them from all other ideas that accompany them in their real existence; this is called abstraction: and thus all its general ideas are made. This shows man's power, and its ways of operation, to be much-what the same in the material and intellectual world. For the materials in both being such as he has no power over, either to make or destroy, all that man can do is either to unite them together, or to set them by one another, or wholly separate them.[1]

This description may at first seem reasonable enough; but when we attempt to describe what Locke names "reflection," we come upon difficulties, and difficulties which seem to spread over the whole field of experience, including sensation itself. Reflection, as soon as we try to describe it in Lockian terminology, appears to be secondary. Ideas of reflection cannot be observed until the mind has performed, upon what ideas it has, its characteristic operations. Before we can observe the operations of analysis and synthesis, the mind must have analysed and synthesized. Before we can observe the operations of remembering, studying, hoping, and loving, the mind must have remembered, studied, and loved. And these operations can only be performed when there is something there to operate upon, something given immediately, independently of

[1] *Essay*, II, xii, 1.

the operations themselves. And this can be nothing but the ideas of sensation. Sensation is thus primary, while reflection is secondary.

The other fountain, from which experience furnisheth the understanding with ideas, is the perception of the operations of our own minds within us, as it is employed about the ideas it has got; which operations when the soul comes to reflect on and consider, do furnish the understanding with another set of ideas which could not be had from things without; and such are perception, thinking, doubting, believing, reasoning, knowing, willing, and all the different actings of our own minds; which we, being conscious of, and observing in ourselves, do from these receive into our understandings as distinct ideas, as we do from bodies affecting our senses. This source of ideas every man has wholly in himself.[1]

Precisely here is where the difficulty occurs. If sensation is primary, does this mean that we can have sensation independently of the mental operations of analysis and synthesis, perception, memory, hope, and the rest? And if this seems too much to believe, if sensation is obviously shot through with the selecting, emphasizing, and organizing activities of mind, so that even the simplest sensation is inextricably bound up with reflection, do we not find ourselves describing mental operations, rather than objective qualities, even when we are confining ourselves to ideas of sensation? In which case, what becomes of the famous distinction between sensation and reflection?

Consider the simple experiment with which the student often commences his study of modern psychology. Look, with one eye, at a small piece of black paper lying upon a white background. Observe, with unmoving eye, and describe what you observe. As the eye steadies, you see a white film superinduced upon the black paper, and a black film spreading out into the white background. Seen through these two filmy surfaces, which proceed to mingle as the eye remains steady, the black looks no longer black, and the white looks no longer white. Both look grey. If the eye moves, there is a bright contrast-effect around the edge where the black paper meets the white background. But if the eye remains steady, this effect vanishes, and soon there is present before the eye one field of uniform grey. This does not remain, but changes, so that at times we see the black paper on the white background, at times the uniform grey of the intermingling films, and at times nothing

[1] Ibid., II, ii, 4.

at all. The process of sensation fluctuates, and its content does not remain the same. It is the mind which selects, emphasizes, cuts off part of the fluctuating content and endows it with a fixity, a permanence, which, as experienced through the senses, it does not possess. We pronounce that what we have seen is a piece of black paper on a white ground. But what the eye actually senses is something very different: a fluctuating process in which subjective and objective factors are hopelessly intermingled.

Faced with this sort of situation, some students of Locke follow the pathway taken by Condillac. They try to reduce all mental operations to the single fundamental operation of sensation, and treat this as though it were purely objective, as though the mind, with its analytic-synthetic powers and other activities, were a merely passive receptor; as though it simply apprehended, without alteration, what is there to be apprehended.

If we consider that to remember, compare, judge, discern, imagine, be astonished, have abstract notions, have notions of duration and number, know general and particular truths, are but different modes of attention; that to have passions, to love, to hate, to hope, to fear and to will are but different modes of desire, and that, finally, attention and desire are in their essence but sensation, we shall conclude that sensation calls out all the faculties of the soul.[1]

Other students find themselves following the pathway taken by Kant. Realizing that the sensory processes themselves are conditioned by the mind's ideal of analytic-synthetic unity, and by its persistent search for clearness and distinctness, they regard sensation as a particular species of reflection, as a particular instance of the application of the whole apparatus of mental categories, a part of the life of the mind.

Experience is itself made up of two elements, one received through impressions of sense, and the other supplied from itself by our faculty of knowledge on occasion of those impressions. If that be so, it may take long practice before our attention is drawn to the element added by the mind, and we learn to distinguish and separate it from the material to which it is applied.[2]

These two pathways are not consistent, but divergent. To follow either is to abandon the other. We come at once to the parting of

[1] Condillac, *Treatise on Sensations*, vii, 2.
[2] Kant, *Critique of Pure Reason*, Introduction.

the ways. Other students of Locke refuse to advance at all for a while, and ask instead for further evidence. They devote themselves to the refined techniques of experimental psychology, and come gradually to the opinion that all these puzzles, into which commonsense description inevitably falls, are due to an entirely fallacious faith in the possibility of a genuine introspection, and in the existence of an indescribable and mysterious entity called "consciousness." This faith they give up, and, for the future, they confine themselves, as psychologists, to describing, in strictly objective terms, the "behaviour," i.e. the space–time movements, of the organisms studied, in interaction with their environment.

So too Locke's second distinction, between ideas which are simple and ideas which are complex, has led to a great variety of researches, and to the eventual championing of divergent points of view. Are there "simple ideas," unit-experiences which can be standardized and established by precise measurement, in the fields of the various sensory and affective reactions to stimulation? If so, just how are these related to the more complex experiences in the same fields? For instance, can we establish an intensity-scale of pleasures, in the order 1, 2, 3, 4, 5, 6, 7, . . . , in such a way that a pleasure of intensity "4" will equal two pleasures of intensity "2," or the half of a pleasure of intensity "8," or the fifth of a pleasure of intensity "20"? Can we have a series of negative or minus sensory and affective experiences, e.g. a red sensation of minus two units, or a pleasure of minus ten units? Is the difference between a two-unit and a three-unit experience in these fields the same as the difference between a twenty-unit and a twenty-one unit experience, or is it more like the difference between a twenty-unit and a thirty-unit experience? Or if by introspection alone we prove unable to establish differences of intensity with any such exactitude, can we perhaps establish precise relations between the unit-experience on the one hand, and an exactly measurable amount of objective stimulation on the other, expressible in some such formula as $S = k \log.1$, and from this equation proceed to solve all the problems raised? In this way, thinkers like G. T. Fechner attempt to construct "psycho-physics," a new branch of scientific investigation, all physical and mathematical, and, at the same time, applying, via the formula, to "the mind."

Again, is it possible to discover just what the "simple" experiences are, in any field of experience? For instance, in the field of colour-experience, are the "simple" ideas, of which all the rest are "compounded," to be taken as red, green, and blue, or is yellow to be included as well? With what right are purple and orange treated as compounds? In the series from lightest pink to deepest red, just where is the "simple" idea to be established? Is it a median red, or is it scarlet, or on what principle is this to be determined? So too, in the series of tones, just how is the simple idea to be established? Or are there, perhaps, several simple ideas in this field, as there are "sweet," "bitter," "sour," and "salt" in the field of taste, and "red," "yellow," "green," and "blue" in the fields of vision? And so on and so forth, in the various sensory and affective fields.

Again, Locke states that, while the mind can compound and divide its ideas at will, it cannot, by such devices, manufacture any new simple idea, i.e. any content not directly experienced. Many thinkers have taken up this challenge. Why not? they ask. If our experiences can be arranged in a series, $a, b, c, d, e, f, g, \ldots$, and we have experienced a, b, c, e, f, g, but have not experienced d, is it so very certain, they ask, that we cannot experience a manifest gap at the point d? And is it so very certain that we cannot fill in this gap from contents abstracted from the surrounding fields, at least sufficiently for practical purposes? For example, Helen Keller, whose sensory experience is almost incredibly defective, confined, as it is, to kinaesthetic and touch experiences, has been so marvellously well taught that she can write about the world she does not see, in terms of visual imagery which she does not possess. So too the eyes of each of us contain a "blind spot," which constitutes a demonstrable gap in the field of monocular vision. Yet we all fill in the gap from the surrounding field, and do it so well that most of us, from the cradle to the grave, are unaware that there is any gap in our field of vision. And finally, do not we all believe that many of our ideas are not given to us in any direct experience, but that the mind creates them on the suggestions furnished by this or that experience? Even Locke himself writes as though such ideas as *unity* and *existence* are "suggested" to us.

Existence and unity are two other ideas that are suggested to the understanding by every object without, and every idea within. When ideas are in our minds, we consider them as being actually there, as well as we consider things to be actually without us: which is, that they exist, or have existence: and whatever we can consider as one thing, whether a real being or idea, suggests to the understanding the idea of unity. Besides these there is another idea, which though suggested by our senses, yet is more constantly offered us by what passes in our minds; and that is the idea of succession. For if we look immediately into ourselves, and reflect on what is observable there, we shall find our ideas always, whilst we are awake or have any thought, passing in train, one going and another coming without intermission.[1]

In carrying through researches and speculations of this kind, a divergence of outlook becomes increasingly marked. Some thinkers believe that the simple ideas are our actual starting-points. It is maintained, e.g., that the new-born baby soon learns to recognize and differentiate the experience of red, while other elementary experiences, such as green, blue, and yellow, develop later. Still later there develop such experiences as purple, orange, sky-blue, sea-green, red-hot, etc. As we grow older and more sophisticated, we move less and less amid elementary experiences, and more and more in a world which is almost incredibly complicated. On the other hand, there are thinkers who maintain that experience starts with the complex jumble, the "big, buzzing, booming confusion," and that this becomes very gradually sorted out, and that we never really get down to what could be called a single simple idea, in any field of experience whatever. These two points of view are entirely incompatible, and yet both undoubtedly take their origin from the descriptions of experience found in Locke's *Essay*.

The third distinction of Locke's, between "the mind" and "its ideas," has led to the greatest variety of researches and divergent outlooks. Empiricists tend to treat the ideas as somehow existing in their own right, as entities-in-themselves, as relatively independent contents, and treat "the mind" as merely that which comprehends and is constituted by its contents. Realists like Herbart equate such simple ideas with something derived from Leibniz's description of his "monads." They suppose that if you took two identical twins, and educated the one in Paris, and the other in Baffin Land, their minds, at maturity, would be as diverse as their environments, and could be explained, without remainder, in terms of their diverse contents. On the other hand idealists, and investigators who pay attention to the active processes of "the mind," tend to regard mind as primary, and its constructs, the ideas, as secondary, as applications of its powers to this or that particular field.

[1] *Essay*, II, vi, 7, 9.

From this standpoint, all ideas are alike in being analytic and synthetic, partially unified, systematic, and consistent; and the minds of the two twins would have in common at least all these well-developed powers and would thus be alike in function and to a considerable extent in structure as well, although the details, in operating upon which these minds had developed themselves, might be different. Yet further divergencies develop according as the standpoint accepted is transcendental or empirical, and according as "the mind" is envisaged as contemplative or as active, as a self-creating substance, or as a relation, or as a function, of the factors concerned. In all these ways, then, Book II leads to the development of strikingly divergent schools of thought.

God, having designed man for a sociable creature, made him not only with an inclination, and under a necessity to have fellowship with those of his own kind; but furnished him also with language, which was to be the great instrument and common tie of society.[1]

Book III contains Locke's philosophy of language, and is particularly remarkable for his clear insistence upon the social influences at work in giving unity, consistency, and currency to our words and thoughts.

The comfort and advantage of society not being to be had without communication of thoughts, it was necessary that man should find out some external sensible signs, whereof those invisible ideas, which his thoughts are made up for, might be made known to others. For this purpose nothing was so fit, either for plenty or quickness, as those articulate sounds, which with so much ease and variety he found himself able to make. Thus we may conceive how words which were by nature so well adapted to that purpose, come to be made use of by men, as the signs of their ideas; not by any natural connection that there is between particular articulate sounds and certain ideas, for then there would be but one language amongst all men; but by a voluntary imposition, whereby such a word is made arbitrarily the mark of such an idea.[2]

Such terms as "ostracism" in Greek thought, and "triumph" in Roman thought, show beyond the possibility of doubt that our complex ideas, the ways in which we think of our virtues and vices, or of the objects of which we take notice in our physical environ-

[1] *Essay*, III, i, 1–3.   [2] Ibid.

198

ment, are in no sense entities-in-themselves, in abstraction from their time and place, but are historical phenomena, permeated with social emphasis and meaning, and represent cross-currents through the life and struggles of their epochs. Book III furnishes an extended concrete demonstration that our ideas are, for the most part, complex empirical growths, and the study of all the factors indicates, beyond the possibility of reasonable doubt, that we have no complex ideas which can be regarded as "innate," as in their own right abstracted from the flux of events.

There is indeed a sense in which *simple* ideas might be regarded as innate. For they do not change as humanity progresses from barbarism to civilization, from Baffin Land to Paris or London. They are relative to our human sense-organs and our human span of attention. But, even so, they are a part of the flux of events; a small part, small enough to be apprehended satisfactorily; but not little absolutes, entities-in-themselves. In the case of *complex* ideas, however, although they are built up without remainder out of these simple ideas, Book III shows that they are like fashions in clothes or in social usages. They are groupings of elementary experiences, groupings whose selection and standardization, by naming, is governed by social usefulness and social need. They are essentially local and temporal, not in any sense transcendental and perennial.

These thoughts of Locke on language, like his thoughts on government, have passed over without remainder into the main stream of empiricism. In the vast reaches of that stream they have long since become anonymous, as what is accepted loses its individual identity in proportion as its acceptance is universal.

Book IV, developing further the position established in the preceding three Books, deals with the extent and validity of human knowledge. An empiricist, a seeker, tends everywhere to find probability rather than certainty, and stimulation to further inquiry rather than a conclusion in which the mind can rest. And, having stressed these *motifs* in the preceding three Books, Locke might well be expected, in his fourth and last Book, to reformulate his forward-looking position, to insist upon the movement, change, and growth necessarily inherent in every phase of life, and to state that knowledge and certainty are guiding ideals rather than facts, and are likely for ever to remain so.

This, however, is not what Locke does. There is, beneath

Locke's empiricism, a pronounced realist strain. It will be remembered that in his paper "Thus I think," Locke regarded it as possible, in dealing with elementary and simple questions, to reach answers in which the mind could rest. So here he believes that, in the simple ideas, at any rate, his mind can feel entire confidence. Defining "knowledge" as "perception of the agreement and disagreement of ideas," he proceeds, in Book IV, to inquire into the extent and validity of such knowledge.

As to extent, his conclusions are modest. We cannot perceive agreement beyond the range of our ideas, and, within that range, we can compare ideas directly only in respect of identity and difference. Some ideas are so disparate that they can be compared, if at all, only mediately, by comparing them with some "middle term." But it takes time, ingenuity, and goodwill to discover such middle terms; and, in practice, such mediate or "demonstrative" knowledge is scarcely applicable to any but mathematical relations. It may be that, in time . . . Finally, as to "real existence," we are dependent upon direct sensation, and that extends, as we all know, only a very little way. The extent of human knowledge is thus far narrower, upon the whole, than the range of human ideas.

It is easy to perceive what a darkness we are involved in, how little it is of being, and the things that are, that we are capable to know. And therefore we shall do no injury to our knowledge, when we modestly think with ourselves, that we are so far from being able to comprehend the whole nature of the universe, and all the things contained in it, that we are not capable of a philosophical knowledge of the bodies that are about us, and make a part of us: concerning their secondary qualities, powers, and operations, we can have no universal certainty. Several effects come every day within the notice of our senses, of which we have so far sensitive knowledge; but the causes, manner, and certainty of their production, for the two foregoing reasons, we must be content to be very ignorant of. In these we can go no farther than particular experience informs us of matter of fact, and by analogy to guess what effects the like bodies are, upon other trials, like to produce. But as to a perfect science of natural bodies (not to mention spiritual beings) we are, I think, so far from being capable of any such thing, that I conclude it lost labour to seek after it.[1]

In respect of validity, i.e. "real" or objective certainty, the position is not hopeless. So far as we succeed in analysing our experience into simple ideas, we are, Locke believes, in reliable know-

[1] *Essay*, IV, iii, 30.

ledge-contact with reality. We can then proceed to synthesize these simple ideas, and construct complex units. These complexes are of two kinds. (*a*) They may have no intended relation to reality. We can construct tangents, circles, and other mathematical figures, without expecting to meet their archetypes *in rerum natura*; just as we can construct centaurs, one-eyed giants, and other mythological figures; or as we can construct the virtues and vices of a system of morality, or the correlative attributes of an omnipotent God and weak and guidance-needing human beings, in systematic theology. Such complex systems, like the rules of a chess-game, have their own validity. Confined to specific fields, as long as the system is consistent, it is beyond question; for nothing further is intended. It is even conceivable that, since such systems rest upon simple ideas, some of their consequences, e.g. in the mathematical system, may be applicable beyond the limited range of "pure" thought. But that is a matter for experiment, not for deduction.

All the discourses of the mathematicians about the squaring of a circle, conic sections, or any other part of mathematics, concern not the existence of any of those figures; but their demonstrations, which depend on their ideas, are the same, whether there be any square or circle existing in the world, or no. In the same manner the truth and certainty of moral discourses abstracts from the lives of men, and the existence of those virtues in the world whereof they treat. Nor are Tully's offices less true, because there is nobody in the world that exactly practises his rules, and lives up to that pattern of a virtuous man which he has given us, and which existed nowhere, when he writ, but in idea. If it be true in speculation, i.e. in idea, that murder deserves death, it will also be true in reality of any action that exists conformable to that idea of murder. As for other actions, the truth of that proposition concerns them not. And thus it is of all other species of things, which have no other essences but those ideas, which are in the minds of men.[1]

Other complex units (*b*) may be intended as reproductions or copies of complexes actually observed *in rerum natura*. Our ideas of gold, lead, cows, horses, water, air, etc., are of this kind. In all such cases, the validity of our constructs rests upon the test of further sensory observation, and does not enjoy the autocratic validity of mathematics, ethics, and theology.

To have ideas of *substances* which, by being conformable to things, may afford us real knowledge, it is not enough, as in *modes*, to put together

[1] Ibid., IV, iv, 8.

such ideas as have no inconsistence, though they did never before so exist; e.g. the ideas of sacrilege or perjury, etc., were as real and true ideas before as after the existence of any such fact. But our ideas of substances, being supposed copies, and referred to archetypes without us, must still be taken from something that does or has existed; they must not consist of ideas put together at the pleasure of our thoughts without any real pattern they were taken from, though we can perceive no inconsistence in such a combination. The reason whereof is, because we knowing not what real constitution it is of substances whereon our simple ideas depend, and which really is the cause of the strict union of some of them one with another, and the exclusion of others; there are very few of them that we can be sure are or are not inconsistent in nature, any farther than experience and sensible observation reach.[1]

It was in connection with this last question, referring the validity of such mental constructs to the perception, via the senses, of "substances" existing outside our minds *in rerum natura*, that Locke succeeded, perhaps unintentionally, in profoundly shocking his contemporaries. As our knowledge is confined, primarily, to perceiving the relations of ideas, and ideas are subjective, within our own minds, our knowledge can be objective only in a secondary sense, in so far as these ideas "conform to" or "correspond to" an external reality, a world of substances existing outside our minds. Locke himself believes that the simple ideas "carry with them all the conformity requisite for real knowledge." But since we have no direct knowledge, as Locke sees it, of a reality which is external, outside our minds and therefore beyond direct comparison, he very honestly defines this external reality or substance as "something, I know not what."

He does not doubt its existence, and indeed he explicitly regards it as the (secret, unknown) ground of the coexistences and sequences which we observe in nature. But his contemporaries, reading, over and over again, that "substance" was "something, Locke knew not what," and supposing him to be sarcastic at the expense of "substance," seriously believed him to be excluding "substance" from the realm of knowledge altogether, and thus knocking the bottom out of the whole seventeenth-century way of looking at human experience. For most contemporaries of Locke, substance meant at least what it had meant to Spinoza, if not to Leibniz: God; and to challenge "substance" seemed to them direct

[1] *Essay*, IV, iv, 12.

atheism. It was not until towards the conclusion of the long controversy between Bishop Stillingfleet and Locke that what was really shocking the Bishop came clearly to light, and that Locke managed to make clear his faith, not only in "God" but also in "substance," although, for his empiricist purposes, he still insisted that our knowledge of substances is confined to "nominal" rather than "real" essences. For Locke, "substance" itself is an undoubted fact. But our knowledge of substance is only partly factual, subject to further testing by sensory experience. From the standpoint of knowledge, substance is not a fact, but an ideal, guiding us as we construct complex ideas and subject them to the further testing of experience.

If by almost discarding substance out of the reasonable part of the world your lordship means that I have destroyed and almost discarded the true idea we have of it by calling it "a substratum, a supposition of we know not what support of such qualities as are capable of producing simple ideas in us; an obscure and relative idea; that without knowing what it is, it is that which supports accidents; so that of substance we have no idea of what it is, but only a confused and obscure one of what it does"; I must confess this, and the like I have said of our idea of substance.

But supposing, my lord, that I should own that we have a very imperfect, obscure, inadequate idea of substance. Would it not be a little too hard to charge us with discarding substance out of the world?[1]

Why is Locke regarded as a "great" thinker? He has no great powers of imagination, poetry, or mysticism; and the many inconsistencies in the *Essay* suggest that he has no great powers in the fields of logic and metaphysics. Many and many a time, he seems to be just muddling through, with little more behind him than "common" sense and "ordinary" experience: just a plain average seventeenth-century English mind, doing its best. In comparison with Spinoza or Leibniz, he is surely nowhere.

In the first place, Locke has qualities of character which make up for these deficiencies, and indeed turn many of them into positive virtues. He is honest with himself as well as with others. He is never specious, brilliant, and shallow. Where there are problems, he faces them, formulates them carefully, works at them until he finds precisely where the difficulty lies. He never conceals, denies, or glosses over his difficulties. If he does not know, he

[1] *Works*, vol. IV, pp. 7–9, cf. 448.

at least discovers plainly that he does not know, and tries to find out why. He takes endless pains, and persists, as in dealing with the problem of free will, until he has at least demonstrated to his own satisfaction that almost every path which can be tried ends in a cul-de-sac. He keeps on inquiring, searching, trying and trying again. When we add to this honesty and this persistency his great powers of judgment, based upon wide and concentrated experience, we have almost a model for empiricists to follow; and it is as the founder of modern empiricism that Locke is chiefly famous.

In the second place, like many great men, Locke sinks himself entirely in his work, and his work is greater than even he himself knew. Many books are biographies of their writers, revealing their early struggles, their mature plans, their deeper hopes and fears. The *Essay on Human Understanding*, however, is not merely a biography of Locke. It is the autobiography of England. Locke has thrown himself so open to the influences around him that he has become a channel for ideas. But they are not *his* ideas, but rather the ideas which express the inner nature of British life, as it struggles through towards reflective self-consciousness. The life-blood which pushes its way sluggishly but powerfully through the intellectual arteries of the *Essay* is so essentially and completely British as to be almost anonymous. Locke is almost typically the unknown British thinker: the thinker who stands, not for himself, but for Britain: slow but powerful, unimaginative but honest, persistent, massive, and sure.

In the third place, Locke's very deficiencies have proved virtues. What makes a thinker "great" is a function, not only of the man himself, but of his effect upon others. And it is in interaction with others, with the readers and students of the *Essay*, that Locke's true greatness has come out. His inconsistencies have stimulated others to be more consistent. His ambiguities have stimulated others to be less ambiguous: to choose and follow one path, where Locke, perhaps, has come to a halt before two. His imperfect empiricism has stimulated others to formulate methods more rigidly empirical or, it may be, to try anew the alternative path of transcendentalism. His inadequate formulation of problems, all real and all fruitful, has stimulated others to improve upon his formulations and to discover more satisfying solutions. In a word, his influence upon students has been such that hardly any persistent reader has been able to lay aside the voluminous *Essay* without having become stimulated to richer thought and deeper insight. Where one reader has admired Spinoza, or two readers have admired Leibniz, twenty readers have interacted with Locke, trying to co-operate with his efforts, and insensibly improving themselves in the process. Of modern philosophers, Locke has proved, through his very deficiencies, one of the most fruitful influences upon subsequent development.

In a word, then, it is as the founder of modern empiricism, as the genuine voice of Britain, and as an exceedingly fruitful stimulus to further science and philosophy, that John Locke is regarded as a truly great thinker.

Chapter VIII

GEORGE BERKELEY 1685-1753

A SOCIETY which bestowed upon Locke the epithet "judicious" hardly knew at first what to make of Berkeley. At
the commencement of the eighteenth century, when clear
and distinct ideas were coming into fashion, when men prided
themselves upon their uncompromising rationalism, when scepticism and cynicism were the only accepted evidence of education
and enlightenment, when corruption was taken for granted, a
character like George Berkeley's was unique. Simple, straightforward, and idealistic, Berkeley was just "good." A good boy, a
good student, a good dean, and a good bishop, he continued to
teach, at sixty, what he had learnt at sixteen, and had never found
occasion to question. Everything he read, and everything he
thought, merely confirmed him in his invincible benevolence.

Finding complete satisfaction in the Christian religion (as by law
established), the young Irishman felt it his mission to extend its
blessings and to remove all impediments to its universal practice.
He conceived the design of conducting a colony of distressed Irishmen across the Atlantic, to found some sort of college in the
Bermudas *ad majorem Dei gloriam*. For such an undertaking, funds
were needed; and, in his simplicity, Berkeley paid a visit to London,
to ask for funds from the British government. To the surprise of
historians, as well as contemporaries, he secured from Sir Robert
Walpole a promise of twenty thousand pounds. For an Irishman to
get money from a British government—and for an idealistic purpose
at that—was something of an achievement. But Berkeley did not
consider that he had done anything wonderful. He expected to meet
with goodness in others, and merely supposed that, the cause being
worthy, Sir Robert had been glad, out of the goodness of his
heart, to promise to supply the needed funds.

The money was, of course, not forthcoming. It was never easy
to get real money from Sir Robert. Berkeley could not understand
it at all. He paid a further visit to London, and after eventually
succeeding in getting to see Sir Robert, actually obtained the first

half of the money in cash, and started out on his long journey. He still supposed that two good men merely had to get together in order to agree, and confidently anticipated that the remaining ten thousand pounds would arrive in time.

The simple truth of the matter was that Berkeley was more than good. He was good-looking, and had charming manners. In London society, where his unique character created something of a furore, his influence was, for the time, unbounded. Everyone was eager to help him; and it was realistic pressure, the only kind of pressure which Sir Robert could understand, from the all-powerful Court ladies which produced, first the promise, and later, the cash. As far as Berkeley was concerned, however, his single-hearted goodness had withstood every trial; and for the rest of his life he was known as "the *good* Mr. Berkeley," or "the *good* Bishop Berkeley."

On the intellectual side, he was well abreast of his contemporaries. Educated at Trinity College, Dublin, he became a Fellow and Lecturer, and remained in close contact with higher education all his life. As a student, he became acquainted with the *Essay* of John Locke, which was then, as indeed later, studied with especial interest at Dublin, for its stimulating and suggestive qualities. Other Irishmen had discovered in the *Essay* ammunition which might be expended in the service of atheism and free-thinking. But not George Berkeley. As *he* read, he could see places where the *Essay* could and should be amended, and its pathways shown unmistakably to lead, not from, but to, God. With his zeal for religion, he set himself, in his early twenties, to point the moral and adorn the deductions which to him seemed inevitable.

Three points especially interested his critical and speculative mind. In the first place, Locke had dealt rather simply with the psychological phenomenon of the third dimension, depth. When we look at an orange, we see it, not as a two-dimensional yellow circle, as we should expect from the standpoint of mathematical physics, but as a three-dimensional spheroid. It has a depth and solidity about it. Locke accounted for this on the basis of sensuous association. When our experiences are repeated, each new perception includes something of the experiences which are past. "Solidity" is primarily an experience which comes when we try to compress an object such as an orange between the hands. In our later experiences, something of the memory of this experience with our hands is retained; so that when we see an orange with our eyes, we seem to *see* it as "solid" and squeezable, although solidity is a tactile rather than a visual experience. Association, with Locke, is at the sensuous level. The orange "looks" solid. The experience is immediate, the factors contributed by memory and the factors contributed by sensation fusing directly with one another.[1]

Berkeley subjected this phenomenon to further experimentation and reasoning, and published, at the age of twenty-four, his *New Theory of Vision*, in an essay still read by students of psychology. He discovered that the perception of visual depth was something more than an illusion, a confusion of seeing with a memory of touching. There are, in the experience of vision itself, a large number of factors which suggest to the mind the unseen third dimension. Minute differences of shading, of size, of the relation of one object to another in the visual field, of clearness and distinctness of outline, are signs and indications which the mind can and does interpret as evidence of distance and depth. In fact, the part played by the mind is so great that, when we look at oranges, tables, houses, human beings, and other solid objects, we realize that we are living in a world of ideas which are, to a far greater extent than had been realized by Locke and his readers, constructed by the mind.

In the second place, Locke had made a determined effort to distinguish between primary and secondary qualities.[2] But his account seemed to Berkeley unsatisfactory. Any competent logician who has ever subjected this account to technical analysis has found it to consist of a number of not very coherent grounds for thinking primary and secondary qualities to be distinct, and has concluded that, as presented by Locke, the evidence is not convincing. Berkeley came to the same conclusion, and went further, suggesting not only that Locke's reasoning was unsatisfactory, but that actually primary and secondary ideas could not be distinguished at all. All ideas are equally primary, or all equally secondary. For himself, Berkeley preferred to treat them all as secondary.

I see evidently that it is not in my power to frame an idea of a body extended and moving, but I must withal give it some colour or other sensible quality which is acknowledged to exist only in the mind. In

[1] Cf. *Essay*, II, ix, 8. [2] Ibid., II, viii, 8–23.

short, extension, figure, and motion, abstracted from all other qualities, are inconceivable. Where therefore the other sensible qualities are, there must these be also, to wit, in the mind and nowhere else.[1]

This means that size, shape, texture, motion, and number are to be regarded as Locke had regarded colours, tastes, and odours: namely, as reactions internal to our selves, rather than as something physically interactive with the forces of the physical environment. Just as we feel that what makes music musical is not its merely physical characteristics, but its interpretation, a constructive activity upon the part of the mind, so we are to regard the primary ideas as mental rather than physical. Indeed, everything loosely called "physical" is now to be regarded as a part of the life of the mind. The whole world of experience is to be regarded as spiritual, in no sense as external and material, but as wholly internal to mind.

In the third place, on examining Locke's account of "real existence," Berkeley was struck by its weakness. "Existence" appears as an idea associated with every sensory and every introspective experience.[2] We do not regard our own selves as originating the ideas which come to us, and consequently Locke, like Hobbes, supposes the original of our ideas to be "some matter without," i.e. a world of physical substances in interactivity with our nervous system and brain. Unlike Hobbes, Locke does not permit himself to accept with full faith this materialist hypothesis, but believes the ideas in our minds to be "copies" of a reality external to our minds. What this external reality or "substance" may be ultimately, he does not know. It falls outside experience. He is quite willing to suppose it may be something beyond both matter and mind, as we know these: something which, in Cartesian terms, can "think" as well as be "extended."[3] But he does not pursue further the pathway thus opened upon vistas which extend beyond a simple materialism. Locke has not a speculative mind. Berkeley, however, *has*, and proceeds to inquire further.

Like many readers of the *Essay* who have not studied closely the elucidations contained in the controversy with Stillingfleet, he

---

[1] *Principles of Human Knowledge*, sect. 10. [2] *Essay*, II, vii, 7.

[3] "Our idea of substance is but a supposed I know not what, to support those ideas I call accidents. . . . There is no more difficulty to conceive how a substance we know not should *by thought* set body into motion, than how a substance we know not should *by impulse* set body into motion. . . . Beyond the simple ideas we receive from sensation and reflection the mind is not able to advance or make discoveries, when it would pry into the hidden causes of those ideas." *Essay*, II, xxiii, 29.

supposes that Locke's reasoning has in effect banished the conception of substance, at least in the sense of material substance, from the world of human knowledge, and that in fact we may conclude that there is no such thing. Locke's position applies to spiritual no less than to material substance; but Berkeley, helped out by his perfectly genuine religious faith, lets go of material substance, but holds fast to the conception of spiritual substance. For him the ultimate substance is "God," and "existence" is to be conceived as essentially spiritual. The original of our human experiences is thus a realm of spiritual substances in interactivity with the ultimate spiritual substance, God. Sensation is doubtless the channel through which communication takes place; but reality is to be understood fundamentally as not material, but spiritual.

To me it is evident that sensible things cannot exist otherwise than in a mind or spirit. Whence I conclude, not that they have no real existence, but that, seeing they depend not on my thought, and have an existence distinct from being perceived by me, *there must be some other Mind wherein they exist.* As sure, therefore, as the sensible world really exists, so sure is there an infinite omnipresent Spirit who contains and supports it.[1]

With these three converging lines of criticism clearly before him, Berkeley set himself to think out an improved version of the *Essay*, and published, at the age of twenty-five, his *Principles of Human Knowledge*, following it up three years later with the three *Dialogues Between Hylas and Philonous*.[2] In these works he undertook to demonstrate, in terms of the techniques made fashionable by Locke, that the world is fundamentally not material, but spiritual. Human beings are essentially spirits, interacting with the Ultimate Spirit, God. This interaction is mediated by sensation, and may be regarded as "direct," i.e. as not requiring the further intermediation of any "unthinking substance" such as "matter," interposed between God and ourselves.

This improvement upon the *Essay*, an improvement consisting, fundamentally, in excluding the hypothesis of a "material world," was motivated by religious considerations. Berkeley's religious convictions were not merely unquestioning. They were direct, simple, and almost unbelievably naïve. He supposed the evils

---

[1] Second *Dialogue Between Hylas and Philonous*.

[2] The much later work *Siris* is more mystical and abandons the earlier position (which is, however, the position by which Berkeley is influential in the history of thought).

of life to originate in "infidelity" or "atheism," and believed "atheism" to rest, intellectually, upon "materialism," i.e. upon a philosophic acceptance of "matter." If, now, he could disprove the existence of matter, would he not have removed the basis of materialism, and indeed of atheism, so that all thinking men would turn naturally to religion, and would share in enjoying and extending its benefits, of whose supreme value there could then be no possible doubt? Such was his hope.

As we have shown the doctrine of Matter or corporeal substance to have been the main pillar and support of Scepticism, so likewise upon the same foundation have been raised all the impious schemes of Atheism and Irreligion. How great a friend *material substance* has been to Atheists in all ages were needless to relate. All their monstrous systems have so visible and necessary a dependence on it that, when this cornerstone is once removed, the whole fabric cannot choose but fall to the ground, insomuch that it is no longer worth while to bestow a particular consideration on the absurdities of every wretched sect of Atheists.

Did men but consider that the sun, moon, and stars, and every other object of the senses, are only so many sensations in their minds, which have no other existence but barely being perceived, doubtless they would never fall down and worship their own *ideas*; but rather address their homage to that ETERNAL INVISIBLE MIND which produces and sustains all things.[1]

His work falls, essentially, into two parts, the philosophy of matter, and the philosophy of spirit. The philosophy of matter is fundamentally negative. Berkeley has to show, if possible, that there is no such thing as matter; at least, that the idea is contradictory and illusory. He has also to unearth the motives which have led men, not, presumably, *all* fools or villains, to invent or accept such a false and contradictory notion. And finally, he has to show that we can get along perfectly well without this idea; that the values of experience are conserved, if not improved, by excluding it altogether from our minds.

In proving these points, Berkeley rests very heavily upon the work of Locke. Locke had asserted, and his readers had believed, that all that the mind knows directly and immediately is its ideas. Idea and mind are, in the *Essay*, correlatives. The function of mind is to perceive; and what it perceives is ideas. It observes their coexistences and sequences, their habitudes and relations,

---

[1] *Principles*, sects. 92, 94.

their agreements and differences, and, on the basis of these observations, it constructs, by further analytic-synthetic procedures, the systematic edifices of ideas known as "science" and "philosophy." It is true that Locke had supposed, and his readers had believed, that these ideas are "copies" of some extra-mental world. But Berkeley saw clearly through the weakness of Locke's reasoning, and concentrated firmly upon the original premisses. If the essence of the mind consists in perceiving, then the essence of ideas consists in their being perceived. They are percepts, phenomena, objects-for-a-mind, essentially intra-mental. They can never, except by abstraction, be regarded as existing "in themselves," out of relation to our perception of them. Experience never presents us with extra-mental things, but always and only with intra-mental ideas; and we may as well realize exactly what this means.

That neither our thoughts, nor passions, nor ideas formed by the imagination, exist without the mind, is what everybody will allow. And to me it is no less evident that the various sensations, or ideas imprinted on the sense, however blended or combined together (that is, whatever objects they compose), cannot exist otherwise than in a mind perceiving them. The table I write on I say exists, that is, I see and feel it; and if I were out of my study I should say it existed—meaning thereby that if I was in my study I might perceive it, or that some other spirit actually does perceive it. There was an odour, that is, it was smelt; there was a sound, that is, it was heard; a colour or figure, and it was perceived by sight or touch. This is all that I can understand by these and the like expressions. For as to what is said of the absolute existence of unthinking things without any relation to their being perceived, that is to me perfectly unintelligible. Their *esse* is *percipi*, nor is it possible they should have any existence out of the minds or thinking things which perceive them.[1]

To say that we eat, drink, and are clothed with—ideas, may sound queer. It may suggest the situation of the fairy-tale Emperor of China, who was clothed only with *ideas*. But Berkeley points out that, by "ideas," *he* does not mean anything unreal and imaginary. He means *real* ideas, actual sensory experiences. When we eat and drink "ideas," this means that we experience actual tactile, visual, and gustatory sensations. The sensations associated with "eating and drinking" are followed by the sensations associated with "digestion." We live in a world of sensations, of experiences as concrete, as direct, actual, and unimaginary as we can desire.

[1] *Principles*, sect. 3.

George Berkeley

Our ideas are to be thought of as entirely detached from anything unideal, anything which falls outside experience, anything as abstract, indirect, and unactual as "material substance." The very notion of such a thing is, in fact, contradictory. If it is an idea, it is, as such, essentially intra-mental, not extra-mental. Or if it is really extra-mental, then it is beyond that human sense-perception which would bring it within our minds. We are trying to perceive the unperceivable: which is absurd.

> Some truths there are so near and obvious to the mind that a man need only open his eyes to see them. Such I take this important one to be, viz. that all the choir of heaven and furniture of the earth, in a word all those bodies which compose the mighty frame of the world, have not any subsistence without a mind, that their *being* is to be perceived or known; that consequently so long as they are not actually perceived by me, or do not exist in my mind or that of any other created spirit, they must either have no existence at all, or else subsist in the mind of some Eternal Spirit —it being perfectly unintelligible, and involving all the absurdity of abstraction, to attribute to any single part of them an existence independent of a spirit. To be convinced of which, the reader need only reflect, and try to separate in his own thoughts the *being* of a sensible thing from its *being perceived*.[1]

It might be supposed, from the above line of reasoning, that Berkeley would proceed to set up a pure phenomenalism, as many later thinkers have done. He might well have argued that we live in a world of sense-phenomena, whose interrelations, observed and systematized by the help of logic and mathematics, constitute science. But in the early eighteenth century, it was still difficult for a thinker to go quite so far. A world of floating adjectives, un-attached to any substance, was enough to give the boldest pause. The world had to be somehow substantial. If material substance, the usual standby, was gone, there was still, especially for a religious thinker, spiritual substance to fall back upon. Without material substance, it is still possible to observe objective sequences of ideas, sequences which we observe and discover, but do not ourselves invent. And this may be enough for scientific purposes. But it is also possible, by attaching the adjectival, phenomenal, modal world of ideas to spiritual substances, to give to our other-wise fleeting experiences a basis, a *terra firma*, without which the seventeenth- and early eighteenth-century mind felt a little at sea.

[1] Ibid., sect. 6.

Here Berkeley's thinking becomes positive. His view is known, not as phenomenalism, but as spiritual realism. With his faith in the reality of spirits he felt, not only that he could get along perfectly well without the peg of "matter" to support his ideas, but that he could do better, infinitely better. With God securely in His heaven, all must be right with the world.

I conclude, *there is a Mind which affects me every moment with all the sensible impressions I perceive.* And, from the variety, order, and manner of these, I conclude *the Author of them to be wise, powerful, and good beyond comprehension.* Mark it well; I do not say, I see things by perceiving that which represents them in the intelligible Substance of God. This I do not understand; but I say, the things by me perceived are known by the understanding, and produced by the will of an infinite Spirit. And is not all this most plain and evident?[1]

Berkeley's philosophy of spirit is almost indescribably bold. He was so sure of himself, and so sure of his God. When he used his powers of reflective introspection, he apprehended the operations of his own mind, busying itself with its store of ideas. And what a busy mind it was, too! Observing, analysing, synthesizing, classifying, inferring, hoping, loving, worshipping. Sometimes arbitrary and playful: putting together ideas which God had not joined, forming complex ideas not found in nature. At other times docile and receptive: following nature, led and guided by the Power behind nature: constructing objective systems, science and philosophy culminating in religion.

What was mind or spirit? There could be no doubt as to its activity and reality. As to its essence, Berkeley accepted what he found in Locke. As an activity, mind expresses itself in willing, in realizing its plans, in constructing ideal systems. Its willing thus depends upon the fundamental activity of apprehending ideas, the content of its plans and the material of its systems. Its essence is thus the activity of perceiving. It is the correlate of ideas, whose essence consists in their being perceived.

I know or am conscious of my own being; and that *I myself* am not my ideas, but somewhat else, a thinking, active principle that perceives, knows, wills, and operates about ideas. I know that I, one and the same self, perceive both colours and sounds: that a colour cannot perceive a sound, nor a sound a colour: that I am therefore one individual principle, distinct

[1] Second *Dialogue*.

from colour and sound; and, for the same reason, from all other sensible things and inert ideas.[1]

As the correlate of ideas, mind is not itself an "idea." It is not an object of perception, something intra-mental. This is true, whether we refer to our own minds, to other persons' minds, or to God's mind. It is not passive, something perceived, but active, what does the perceiving. Mind knows itself, of course, but not by way of perception. Locke had supposed that it knew itself "intuitively" like a truth, as we know, e.g., that red is red, and not blue. Berkeley carries this thought a little further. As he sees it, mind knows itself not as a fact; for facts are ideas and ideas are passive. It knows itself as an activity, as a substance; and substances are known, not by sensation or reflection, but by inference, by intellectual activity: making explicit what is logically implicit in experience, constructing a "notion" or concept, the correlative of the idea or percept.

I have properly no *idea*, either of God or any other spirit; for these being active, cannot be represented by things perfectly inert, as our ideas are. I do nevertheless know that I who am a spirit or thinking substance, exist as certainly as I know my ideas exist. Farther, I know what I mean by the terms *I* and *myself*; and I know this immediately or intuitively, though I do not perceive it as I perceive a triangle, a colour, or a sound. The Mind, Spirit, or Soul is that indivisible unextended thing which thinks, acts, and perceives. I say *indivisible*, because unextended; and *unextended*, because extended, figured, moveable things are ideas; and that which perceives ideas, which thinks and wills, is plainly itself no idea, nor like an idea. Ideas are things inactive, and perceived. And Spirits a sort of beings altogether different from them. I do not therefore say my soul is an idea, or like an idea.[2]

Self-knowledge is altogether different from perceptual know-ledge. It is intuitive and immediate, but "reflex," indirect. What we apprehend directly is the ideas. In apprehending these, we find ourselves necessitated, if we are to complete our understanding of what is so obviously incomplete, to add in something of our own, to frame some rational principle of explanation. If we are to understand the coexistences and sequences of phenomena as observed, we construct a conceptual, analytic-synthetic framework of method, resulting in the systematized experience called "science."

[1] Third *Dialogue*.   [2] Ibid.

We can even, by rational inference, construct ultimate, metaphysical explanations, envisaging nature's ways, for instance, as God's will. This is necessary. The ideas, as given, are not self-subsistent. They cry out for reason to add to them a support, a substance in which they can inhere. Metaphysically, they inhere in God. But they also inhere in *me*. They are *my* ideas. There must therefore be an "I," a "Self" which "has" these ideas, i.e. possesses them by way of perception, of analysis and synthesis, of scientific and metaphysical construction. This I or Self is thus known reflexly and indirectly. It is not a percept, but a "notion."

The being of my Self, that is, my own soul, mind, or thinking principle, I evidently know by reflexion. It is no repugnancy to say that a perceiving thing should be the subject of ideas, or an active thing the cause of them. I have a notion of Spirit, though I have not, strictly speaking, an idea of it. I do not perceive Spirit as an idea, but I know Spirit by reflexion.[1]

Thus we know ourselves intuitively, but indirectly. We look within and observe the operations of remembering, constructing, hoping, etc., and we infer to an active substance which does this remembering, constructing, and hoping. Just what kind of a self we are in detail, we discover by observing our behaviour in detail. In this way we discover whether we are cowardly or brave, atheistical or religious. But the general principle of our selfhood, our reality as spiritual substances, is guaranteed by every idea we perceive, whether in sensation or in reflection. Our *esse* is *percipere*.

Other human selves we know by inference from analogy. In their case, of course, we do not introspect. We depend upon ideas of sensation rather than of reflection. Where we observe certain uniformities and sequences, these suggest to us that, if *we* were involved in such a situation, we should interpret such behaviour as implying the presence of our own selves. In such cases, we seldom hesitate to infer the presence of an active spiritual substance like our own, expressing itself in such-and-such observable ways. And our inference is very frequently verified in further experience.

From what has been said, it is plain that we cannot know the existence of other spirits otherwise than by their operations, or the ideas by them excited in us. I perceive several motions, changes, and combinations of

[1] Third *Dialogue*.

ideas, that inform me there are certain particular agents, like myself, which accompany them and concur in their production. Hence, the knowledge I have of other spirits is not immediate, as is the knowledge of my ideas; but depending on the intervention of ideas, by me referred to agents or spirits distinct from myself, as effects or concomitant signs.[1]

The reality of the Divine Self is known by a similar process of reasoning from analogy. But Berkeley is concerned to show that we know God better than we know other human selves, better even than we know our own selves. A few of the complex ideas we have, such as "triangle" and "centaur," we have ourselves constructed, by such processes as abstraction and synthesis. But most of them do not originate with *our* selves at all. Such complex ideas as "horse," "ox," and "man," and all simple ideas without exception, are just given to us. We did not create them. They did not create themselves. Who, then, did create them? It is plain that they were created by some spirit, a spirit with the power to create simple, as well as complex, ideas; and it does not take Berkeley long to conclude that this Spirit must be none other than the Giver of all good gifts.

We perceive a continual succession of ideas; some are anew excited, others are changed or totally disappear. There is therefore, *some* cause of these ideas, whereon they depend, and which produces and changes them. That this cause cannot be any quality or idea or combination of *ideas*, is clear from the preceding section. It must therefore be a *substance*; but it has been shown that there is no corporeal or material substance; it remains therefore that the cause of ideas is an incorporeal active substance or Spirit.

The ideas of Sense are more strong, lively and distinct than those of the Imagination; they have likewise a steadiness, order, and coherence, and are not excited at random, as those which are the effects of human wills often are, but in a regular train or series—the admirable connection whereof sufficiently testifies the wisdom and benevolence of its Author. Now the set rules, or established methods, wherein the Mind we depend on excites in us the ideas of Sense, are called *the laws of nature*; and these we learn by experience, which teaches us that such and such ideas are attended with such and such other ideas, in the ordinary course of things.[2]

Again, such ideas are often not in our human minds at all. When I leave my study, and turn my attention to other matters, what becomes of the idea of "white paper lying on my desk"? It may

---

[1] *Principles*, sect. 145.   [2] Ibid., sects. 26, 30.

be that someone else is thinking of it for part of the time. But if no human being is thinking of it, what then? It involves an obvious inconsistency, if we suppose an idea, whose very *esse* is *percipi*, to persist in an *un*perceived status. To persist at all, it must persist in some mind. For Berkeley it is again super-evident that what is essentially intra-mental must persist, when not within a human mind, in a superior mind. The world of ideas is thus permanently sustained by God's mind; and God is thus not, like ourselves and our friends, a transient, but a permanent, correlate of ideas.

When I deny sensible things an existence out of the mind, I 'do not mean my mind in particular, but all minds. Now, it is plain they have an existence exterior to my mind; since I find them by experience to be independent of it. There is therefore some other Mind wherein they exist, during the intervals between the times of my perceiving them: as likewise they did before my birth, and would do after my annihilation. And, as the same is true with regard to all other finite created spirits, it necessarily follows there is an *omnipresent eternal Mind*, which knows and comprehends all things, and exhibits them to our view in such a manner, and according to such rules, as He Himself hath ordained, and are by us termed the *laws of nature*.[1]

This raises the further question, the question of the metaphysical status and function of ideas. Psychologically, in relation to my human mind, ideas are percepts, sense-percepts. They are not created by me, but are received through empirical organs of sense. We cannot, however, suppose God to be dependent upon empirical sense-organs. He is not a mere receptor. He is the Creator. What human beings apprehend, under the form of perception, as "ideas," He originates. And here we recall Berkeley's early discovery in connection with our visual experience of depth and solidity. "Depth" is an idea, not given immediately, but suggested to us by certain signs and indications. We interpret these signs and indications, and so arrive at the mind-made idea of "depth." Our ideas are thus largely mind-made, interpretations based upon certain signs and indications.

What is genuinely objective in our ideas is thus not the sensory elaborations characteristic of our human ways of perceiving, but the "signs and indications" upon whose "suggestions" our perceptual processes fabricate the ideas which we all apprehend.

[1] Second *Dialogue*.

George Berkeley

From this metaphysical standpoint, then, we understand that what God creates is precisely these signs and indications. They are God's way of suggesting ideas to us, God's way of communicating with our minds; a kind of sign-alphabet which God uses, in accordance with His own good purposes, in communicating with His creatures.

We should realize, therefore, that our human experience is not merely ours. We are not left blindly to ourselves, but are, if we lift up our eyes, supplied, at every step, with a Divine Guide. The world of nature is an open book; a book which he who runs may read. Science is no mere cataloguing of uniformities and sequences of phenomena which form a closed system of their own, fundamentally cut off from God's wise direction. Such sequences do not, for instance, form a self-sufficient system of "causes" and "effects." The antecedents in such a sequence are as devoid of active force as the consequents; for all are equally "ideas," essentially passive, incapable of "causing" anything whatever. It is as if, when we wrote a message, we supposed the later words to be "caused" by the earlier words; whereas we know, perfectly well, that all alike are caused by the only active power we know, the power of a spiritual substance. Just as we are the causes of the sequences of words which constitute our messages, so God is the cause, the sole and sufficient cause, of the sequences of natural phenomena, which are the letters and words of His messages to us. Rightly understood, science is the registering and deciphering of God's messages; and it should turn us, not from, but to, the ever-present and ever-benevolent Author of our being.[1]

Such is Berkeley's view of reality. The world of sense, in which, at first sight, we seem to live and move and have our being, is a dissolving view, behind which we learn to see a better, brighter, and more rational world, the world of spirits. Ultimately, there exist nothing but spirits or minds, and the mind-made signs whereby we all intercommunicate, under the guidance of our Divine Creator, as we prepare ourselves for participating more fully in spiritual life, with deeper insight into its laws, and with more unhesitating co-operation with our fellow-spirits and our Leader.

---

[1] This mystical view of the ideas which constitute the world of nature, as the "divine alphabet," is implicit in the *Principles*, but is worked out explicitly and in greater detail in *Alciphron, or the Minute Philosopher*, published in 1733. (See especially Fourth *Dialogue*, sects. 7, 11 sqq.). Cf. also *Siris* (1744), especially sects. 252, 254.

This view is plainly in harmony with the good bishop's nature; and we can see in it much to respect, admire, and love. It is a religious philosophy and a philosophical religion. It reconciles tradition and enlightenment, authority and reason, mysticism and science, righteousness and rationalism. Henceforth, it becomes easy to regard philosopher and priest as twin brothers, and laboratory and pulpit as connected by a door which is never closed. Inquiry has become orthodox, and orthodoxy has become sweetly reasonable, following, without fear and without reproach, the new way of ideas. Eternal verities become the mode, and sober Truth dons fashion's latest garb. All is light and joy, amiability and benevolence. Gravity smiles like a little child, and in the midst of eighteenth-century cynicism, the age of innocence is reborn.

The greatness of Berkeley depends, to a considerable extent, upon this position. He is, in the Anglican Church, the most influential of a long line of philosopher-priests. The seed which he planted grew and spread until Anglicanism and British Idealism became almost indistinguishable. They were not merely two flowers upon the same stem, but two halves of the same flower. His influence did much to make religion more enlightened, and enlightenment more religious. Idealism became almost a missionary philosophy, seeking converts in the highways and byways of intellectual life; and its philosophy of "values" always included the values of morality and religion. Even when the universe of discourse was ostensibly scientific, the pontiff was always hovering near, ready to bestow his blessing, and to sprinkle with holy water the growing wings of the spirit.

What made his work especially influential was its simplicity and directness. No erudition was required, no long training in scientific techniques. "It is but looking within," wrote Berkeley; and every parish priest felt himself competent to co-operate in carrying on the good work. And the thought that it is somehow possible to *prove* idealism *true*, and to *refute* "materialism" and "atheism" with weapons drawn from the intellectualist's armoury, has always exercised a fascination over simple souls. This fascination has its dangers, as well as its lure, and this is true in the case of Berkeley himself, as well as of so many of his spiritual successors. It is fatally easy to over-simplify the problem, to grasp with over-confidence at naïve solutions: to feel that, once you have proved the world to be metaphysically "spiritual," you have somehow made a difference to the concrete problems of life. It does make a difference, of course, whether you think of the environment with which you interact as God, as a Divine Leader guiding you by His messengers, or as "things," the blind pressure of circumstances. Idealism changes your attitude towards the problems, and the change is important; but it leaves the problems unchanged in detail; and that may be important too. We may not live by bread alone; but we still need bread.

Be that as it may, the influence of the good bishop succeeded, for many a generation, in making "idealism" accepted as the philosophy of the orthodox; and it is commonly still so regarded. But Berkeley's appeal was not merely to Anglicans. Many of his readers are indifferent both to his personal goodness and to his ultra-refined Christianity. They disregard his religious passages as "a literary convention of the period," and confine themselves to the logic and metaphysics of his position. To such students, it is the "refutation of materialism" which has proved especially fascinating. The argument has been gone over again and again, and each link of the chain severely tested. Is Berkeley right in his view of causation? Is he sound on the subject of abstract ideas? Is he justified in treating all ideas as equally secondary? Might they not, with at least equal logic, be regarded as all primary, and would not this pathway lead to an altogether different metaphysics? If science can do without material substances, can it not do without spiritual substances too? And above all, is not Berkeley's idealism too psychological, too introspective and subjective, too much a matter of simply "looking within"? Does it not rest upon a far too superficial view of "consciousness," "mind," and "spirit"?

Questions like these have led to an immense variety of developments: to a broad cultural spreading of "sound philosophy" among the ecclesiastically educated; to an identification, long current in less religious circles, of metaphysics with introspective psychology; and, in less simple souls, to renewed attempts after a deeper, less orthodox but more independent and scientific attitude towards the interpretation of experience.

Berkeley's work is thus a station upon the main line of modern philosophy. It is important as a junction for travellers by the well-patronized traditional narrow-gauge railway supported by Church and State. But it is important also as opening up new spiritual territory with hitherto unexhausted natural resources.

Chapter IX

DAVID HUME 1711-1776

LIKE many young Scotchmen of ability, Hume sought to advance himself along the pathway of literature and education, with an eye to a professorship in the University of Edinburgh; and his life grew out of his philosophy, rather than his philosophy out of his life. It was the brilliant *Essays* which led to the appointments of his thirties, and doubtless to the librarianship at Edinburgh in his forties, as well as to the subsequent secretaryships in the government service, of his fifties. He was a historian as well as a philosopher, and belongs to the long line of Scottish writers who put "the auld enemy" in her place; and it is the irony of destiny which has made the prejudiced Anglophobe regarded, in Teutonic circles, as *der grösste Denker Englands*.

Hume's patrimony was small, but just enough to live on if he selected his place of abode thriftily. After leaving Edinburgh, where he had been studying at the University since the age of twelve, he took a copy of Locke's *Essay* and went off with it to northern France. There he was able to live inexpensively, to study philosophy, and to pick up a very useful speaking knowledge of French, all at the same time. The reason for taking Locke along was a very simple one. In 1734, Locke was still the latest thing in philosophy; and it was obvious, to any young thinker of ambition, that the way to advancement in philosophy led through the *Essay*. It was to advancement in philosophy that Hume was particularly drawn. He studied to such purpose that, by the age of twenty-eight, he had completed and published Parts I and II of his *Treatise of Human Nature*, and followed this up, in the next year, with the publication of Parts III and IV.

Having thus completed his masterpiece, Hume sat back and awaited fame and fortune. But fame and fortune, then as now, took little interest in an entirely unknown thinker, publishing a heavy treatise upon an abstract subject; and his work, as he put it, fell "still-born from the press." Even Locke had made but little by his *Essay*; and his countrymen, who had not yet digested what

222

Locke had written, showed little inclination to venture upon yet
further journeys into the unknown, especially with a young and
untried guide. Berkeley's work had made an appeal to a well-
established interest; and Berkeley's work was short. But Hume's
appeal was purely speculative; and his book, even for that age, was
repetitious and plaguey long. Obviously, a book which would have
to wait many years for appreciative students. There were, at first,
no readers at all; and the story goes that the circulation of his
masterpiece was confined to the protection of parcels of butter
from the neighbourhood grocery.

Many a man would have despaired and given up. But not David
Hume. Like God after the Creation, he looked upon his work,
and saw that it was good. He set himself to select and rewrite,
in the form of separate *Essays*, the less heavy themes of his *Treatise*,
and such as he judged to be less wholly out of touch with the tastes
of his age. In his thirtieth year, he published Vol. I of these *Essays*,
and in the next year, not only Vol. II, but also—for, joy of joys,
the work was successful—the second edition of Vol. I. A few years
later, he republished these volumes, with the title *Enquiry Concerning Human Understanding*; and, at the age of forty, he published
his *Enquiry Concerning the Principles of Morals*—a *rifacimento* of
Part III of the original *Treatise*.

These works, although inferior in philosophic depth to the work
of his late twenties, which he never surpassed, made him well
known; and from then on his life was both pleasant and easy. His
librarianship at Edinburgh gave him leisure for writing, and the
government appointments of his fifties gave him all the importance
a philosopher could ask for. His happiest years were those spent
in Edinburgh, where eventually, after a tedious and lingering, but
not painful, illness, he passed away, at the age of sixty-five, a
philosopher to the last.

As a thinker, Hume is predominantly critical, sceptical, negative,
coldly academic, building, with superior detachment, upon the
work of men of affairs, like John Locke. His extreme clearness
and leisurely thoroughness have given to his style a smoothness
and an appearance of effortless consecutiveness which have made
more laboured commentators suspect him of superficiality and lack
of genuine depth. He never quotes, and seldom explains. But he
does reason, and reason to the point; and so effective is his reasoning that it is possible for Bertrand Russell, referring to contem-

porary thinkers, to say, "There are only two attitudes towards Hume's arguments: to accept them, or to ignore them."

Actually, of course, there are other attitudes. From the time when Hume's *Dialogues Concerning Natural Religion* were published (posthumously) to the present day, there have been many readers who have rushed into print with refutations. It would be faintly amusing to count up the number of refutations of the essay *Of Miracles*,[1] for example, which have appeared in print; and even the latest *Encyclopaedia Britannica* exhibits a readiness to refute, which mars the objectivity and intelligibility of parts of its article on Hume. There seems to be abroad a wonderful faith in the value of the double negative: a feeling that when No meets No, pious men may come by their own.

There is even, in spite of Russell's dictum, a fourth attitude: the attitude which seeks neither to accept nor to refute, but to understand; and with this attitude, it is possible to regard Hume's work, in its historical setting, as neither eternally right nor eternally wrong, but as an excellent picture of the life and outlook characteristic of eighteenth-century rationalism. From this standpoint, it is possible to bring out the positive features, both social and scientific, which underlie Hume's work, and to realize its inherent greatness, and its place in the main stream of modern philosophy. In what follows we shall first deal with the central doctrines characteristic of Hume's thought, in all their negativity; and shall later proceed to draw together the positive edges and backgrounds of his work, thus filling in the outlines of the complete picture.

Hume's thinking rests very heavily upon a common distinction, the distinction between sense-impression and mental image. When Shakespeare asks "Who can hold a fire in his hand, by thinking on the frosty Caucasus?", he obviously believes that an actual sensation (e.g. of heat) outweighs a merely imagined sensation (of cold). Hobbes had defined this kind of imagination as "decaying sense," and Locke and Berkeley had differentiated sensation and image in respect of objectivity, the impression being forced upon us, while images seem subject to our creative will. Hume drives home this distinction[2] by insisting that (1) impression, and (2) idea or image

---

[1] Published as section x of the *Enquiry*.

[2] *Enquiry*, sect. ii. We may divide all the perceptions of the mind into two classes or species, which are distinguished by their different degrees of force and vivacity. The distinction has enjoyed, in psychology, an honourable history, culminating, perhaps, in the long series of differentiations arranged in parallel

differ in respect of force and vivacity to such a degree that the one can never be mistaken, by a normal man, for the other.

Every one will readily allow, that there is a considerable difference between the perceptions of the mind, when a man feels the pain of excessive heat, or the pleasure of moderate warmth, and when he afterwards recalls to his memory this sensation, or anticipates it by his imagination. These faculties may mimic or copy the perceptions of the senses; but they never can entirely reach the force and vivacity of the original sentiment. The utmost we say of them, even when they operate with greatest vigour, is, that they represent their object in so lively a manner, that we could *almost* say we feel or see it. But, except the mind be disordered by disease or madness, they never can arrive at such a pitch of vivacity, as to render these perceptions altogether undistinguishable. All the colours of poetry, however splendid, can never paint natural objects in such a manner as to make the description be taken for a real landskip. The most lively thought is still inferior to the dullest sensation.[1]

The idea is "a feeble perception, a faint copy of an original sentiment or impression." In fact, ideas are so "faint and obscure" that, whether inadvertently or deliberately, they are easily confused with other ideas which resemble them; whereas the corresponding impressions are so "strong and vivid" that all error or inadvertent mistake is practically excluded. Hume therefore makes it a methodic principle, when faced with a faint, vague, or confused idea, to inquire into its corresponding sentiment or impression, in the firm conviction that this will clear up the obscurity, and remove all doubt and dispute.

If a proper use were made of this distinction, it might render every dispute equally intelligible, and banish all that jargon, which has so long taken possession of metaphysical reasonings, and drawn disgrace upon them. All ideas, especially abstract ones, are naturally faint and obscure: the mind has but a slender hold of them: they are apt to be confounded with other resembling ideas; and when we have often employed any term, though without a distinct meaning, we are apt to imagine it has a determinate idea annexed to it. On the contrary, all impressions, that is, all sensations, either outward or inward, are strong and vivid: The limits between them are more exactly determined: nor is it easy to fall into any error or mistake

columns by William James. Present-day psychologists, while distinguishing the sensory experience according as it is (1) peripherally, or (2) centrally aroused, do not admit Hume's distinction as valid. Apparently they are inseparable, except abstractly, in theory, and are confused, even by experts, in practice.

[1] *Enquiry*, sect. i.

with regard to them. When we entertain, therefore, any suspicion that a philosophical term is employed without any meaning or idea (as is but too frequent), we need but inquire, *from what impression is that supposed idea derived?* And if it be impossible to assign any, this will serve to confirm our suspicion. By bringing ideas into so clear a light we may reasonably hope to remove all dispute, which may arise, concerning their nature and reality.[1]

The principle thus enunciated would be regarded, at first glance, as positive, and even as helpful in the solution of a number of questions. It might be considered analogous to Locke's advice to "think the things," rather than to lose oneself in the logical manipulations of words and external formulas. But, as employed by Hume, its use is largely negative and restrictive. Psychological introspection becomes, with Hume, the chief, if not the sole, method of philosophical inquiry, to the exclusion of dialectical technique and more freely speculative methods. In the name of empiricism, "unprejudiced description of the contents of experience," Hume is rejecting all far-reaching attempts at a deeper explanation. Metaphysics and systematic theology simply disappear. "When we run over our libraries, persuaded of these principles, what havoc must we make? If we take in our hand any volume: of divinity or school metaphysics, for instance; let us ask, *Does it contain any abstract reasoning concerning quantity and number?* No. *Does it contain any experimental reasoning concerning matter of fact and existence?* No. Commit it then to the flames: for it can contain nothing but sophistry and illusion."[2]

This leads us to consider *Hume's theory of belief.* As ordinarily understood, it is on the basis of hearsay, or inference, or some other kind of indirect evidence, that we believe. We believe that the earth is roundish, that Mr. So-and-so holds the world's record for the hundred-yard dash, that the French Revolution is still continuing, that scientific research will find useful answers to many of the questions which perplex us, that war, as a means of settling disputes, will some day disappear from among civilized nations. Hope and fear, self-interest and narrowness of outlook, co-operate in inducing us at times to leap a little blindly and hastily to conclusions, to accept or reject summarily, on insufficient examination of the available evidence. But upon the whole, the ordinary view is that belief represents acceptance after inquiry, after some real

[1] *Enquiry*, sect. ii.   [2] Ibid., Part III, sect. xii.

consideration of the evidence. It is because the reasoning is merely probable, and the evidence insufficient, however carefully examined, to give us the certainty of knowledge, that we say "we believe" rather than "we know." But on the ordinary view, belief rests always upon some rational consideration of the evidence available.

Hume's view of belief is opposed to this. *In*direct evidence, of whatever kind, falls, as he sees it, into the realm of mere ideas, of images, vague, uncertain, easily confused shadows and phantoms. In fact, it is because mankind has based its opinions largely on nothing better that our minds are so doubtful, contradictory, and confused. The vast majority of human opinions are, and always have been, worthless and devoid of validity. Reasoning, however shrewd and persistent, directed upon the feeble and fallacious products of the imagination, is reasoning wasted; and all edifices of thought erected upon no firmer basis than this are subjective shiftings, mischievous superstitions, pseudo-sciences, houses built of playing-cards.

Apply, however, Hume's new method. Discover and bring out into the open the original impressions which are the true sources of these weak and untrustworthy ideas, and all obscurity and confusion will vanish, as morning mists dissolve in the noonday sun. For our impressions are all strong, clear, and distinct. When our minds are filled with an impression, lively, powerful, undeniably what it is, we believe indeed. The authority of sensation is beyond challenge. It produces a conviction in which we can put our whole trust. In sensation, our experience is no longer a matter of trial-and-error. It is immediate. Doubt is lost in certainty. The boundaries between belief and knowledge disappear. We believe, we know that we believe, we believe that we know, we know. Where we have sense-impressions, we have true convictions.

An opinion or a belief may be most accurately defined, A LIVELY IDEA RELATED TO OR ASSOCIATED WITH A PRESENT IMPRESSION. My hypothesis is, that belief is only a strong and steady conception of any idea, and such as approaches to an immediate impression. An idea assented to *feels* different from a fictitious idea. This different feeling I endeavour to explain by calling it a superior *force*, or *vivacity*, or *solidity*, or *firmness*, or *steadiness*. Ideas to which we assent are more strong, firm, and vivid, than the loose reverie of a castle-builder. Belief only changes our manner of conceiving the idea, and renders it more strong and lively. There enters nothing into this operation of the mind but a present impression, a lively idea, and a relation or association in the fancy betwixt the impression and the idea; so that there can be no suspicion of a mistake. Belief is a more vivid and intense conception of an idea, proceeding from its relation to a present impression. Thus all probable reasoning is nothing but a species of sensation.[1]

Hume's theory of belief has found followers among modern psychologists. Like Hume, they challenge the power of reasoning as a factor in belief. Like Hume, they accept the power of the vivid impression. We believe whatever fills our minds, to the exclusion of counter-suggestions. But the power of the impression, which enables it to fill the mind to the exclusion of all else, they explain differently. They explain it as due to instinct, emotion, interest, some organization or disorganization of the nervous system. Hume does not deny the influence of these factors, but insists upon the potency of direct sensation. With his cool, eighteenth-century intelligence, he admits that we may wish or fear to see this or that. But, if we retain our clear-headedness, direct sensation is the ultimate ground of belief. We see what we see, and feel what we feel. Impressions have objective validity. Their content is beyond question.

This view, again, seems at first sight both positive and promising. With thoughts of Locke in mind, we perceive that Hume's "impressions" correspond to the "simple ideas" which are objective and furnish, according to Locke, a trustworthy basis for those mental constructions which we call "science," and indeed for the whole system of conventional institutions upon which civilized life is built. However, before proceeding joyfully along this suggested pathway of progress, let us first note how extremely narrow, for Hume, the scope of our sure belief really is.

Sure belief is limited to our apprehension of the content of our impressions. We feel cold or hot, we see red or blue, we have the impression of hardness or softness. No one can challenge these feelings. When we feel cold, we feel cold, whatever the thermometer may be reading, and whatever other persons may or may not be feeling. But *sure* belief is absolutely restricted to such contents as cold, hot, red, blue, loud, soft, rough, smooth, etc. Any one of these, *A*, is different from any other, *B*. Each is clear, lively, undeniably what it is, and not what it is not. We have here the

[1] *Treatise*, Part III, sects. vii and viii, condensed.

David Hume

alphabet of knowledge. We can distinguish any given letter from any other given letter, and any given grouping of letters from any other grouping. But that is all.

We cannot take a single further step. As to what constitutes a syllable, a word, or a sentence, we are utterly and completely ignorant. If, on the basis of observed uniformities and sequences, we set out to construct a "system," and call the result "science," —if, like Locke, we suppose that, because each direct impression is beyond question, the wholes thus constructed will have objective significance, we are in the position of a child who cannot read, and has been given a box of letters to play with. The child constructs what, to him, look like words and sentences; and, because each letter with which he plays is, *ex hypothesi*, usable for the purposes of literature, he may imagine that his structures, as wholes, are significant. But his "words" may be such compounds as *jrx*, *vlwrk*, *snpb*, *tmqcf*, and his "sentences" may be at least equally meaningless; and this, in spite of the fact that he can really distinguish each letter from each other letter; and, if he should happen, here and there, to hit upon a collection of letters which makes a "real" word, he will not know it. Lockian scientists are thus playboys, and the value of their work is subjective. They are playing a game with rules, and are doubtless getting fun out of it. Science is a more complicated game than checkers or chess, and provides, perhaps, a greater variety of thrills and other satisfactions, both for the players and for all onlookers who take such things seriously. But essentially and fundamentally, such scientists are in the kindergarten class; and their constructions have no objective significance whatever.

Hume's theory of belief, therefore, turns out to be somewhat less promising than we had supposed. It gives us the elements of knowledge, but nothing further. In fact, by denying the possibility of further progress,[1] its chief function, in Hume's hands, is fundamentally negative and sceptical.

Let us now consider *Hume's theory of the self*. Armed with his new theory of belief, Hume investigates the universal belief in a self, and looks for the "impression" from which this idea is derived. Anger, fear, and love are as much matters of direct impression as sensations such as red, loud, or rough. Introspec-

[1] All further progress rests upon "custom" or association of ideas in the mind by "repetition." (*Treatise*, Part III, sect. viii.)

tion provides us with any number of such "states of consciousness," all momentary events, each occupying its brief place in the stream of our experiences. But, in addition to these states of consciousness, which Hume does not call in question, everyone assumes that he has a self: a self which is different from these "states of consciousness," a self which "has" them, and performs operations upon them, observing them, cataloguing them, constructing with them systems called "science."

How do we know that we have any such self? Ordinary experience agrees with Locke that we have an "intuitive awareness" of it. But if we ask how we know our own, individual selves in detail: e.g. how we know whether we are cowardly or brave, lazy or industrious, careless or reliable, it looks as though we have become acquainted with our selves much as other people do, not intuitively, but by observation and inference. Berkeley had noticed this, and had maintained, quite rightly, that the self is not a percept or "idea" at all. If it is not an "idea" but a "substance," we get to know it as we get to know all substances. We watch its behaviour in a variety of circumstances, and use our powers of inference. We construct a hypothesis as to the kind of nature it must have, to account for the behaviour we observe, and we verify this hypothesis. We form a concept or "notion" of the self, and, if we are like Berkeley, we define it as a "spiritual (= non-material) substance."

This position, however, gives Hume pause. Is not "substance" a term of dubious reputation, a member of the intellectual *demi-monde*? Did not Locke leave it in the position of an illegitimate dependant from whom he withholds recognition, a *je ne sais quoi*, "something, I know not what"? And had not the good Berkeley, in excommunicating "matter," in effect expelled "substance" for ever from the pale? Is it not really left in outer darkness, gnashing its teeth, still beckoning feebly towards atheism and all other deadly sin?

Is *self* the same with *substance*? I have a notion of neither, when conceived distinct from particular perceptions. Philosophers begin to be reconciled to the principle, *that we have no idea of external substance, distinct from the ideas of particular qualities*. This must pave the way for a like principle with regard to the mind, that *we have no notion of it, distinct from the particular perceptions*.[1]

[1] *Treatise*, Part IV, Appendix.

Hume decides to look into the matter thoroughly. Is the self known intuitively, or is it not? If Locke is right, we should be able to observe this "self," this permanent identity underlying the flow of successive states of consciousness, directly, as an "impression" or vivid idea. But when we try the experiment of looking within, what do we find?

We have no impression of self or substance, as something simple or individual. When I turn my reflection on *myself*, I can never perceive this *self* without some one or more perceptions; nor can I ever perceive any thing but the perceptions. 'Tis the composition of these, therefore, which forms the self.[1]

We find anger, hunger, fear, hope, and a thousand other such states of consciousness. But do we ever find something different from these, this alleged central core of identity? We do not. Let us make a further effort. Let us interpret our introspections as revealing *Hume*-angry, *Hume*-hungry, *Hume*-fearing, *Hume* as present in each and every state. But, even so, is not the *Hume* in each different state a *different* Hume? The "self," if revealed at all, is revealed as *not the same* from year to year, from month to month, from hour to hour, from moment to moment. We observe the states of consciousness as in temporal succession; but each state is distinct, altogether different from the state which went before and the state which follows after. We observe no central core of personal identity .

Every distinct perception, which enters into the composition of the mind, is a distinct existence, and is different, and distinguishable, and separable from every other perception, either contemporary or successive. The understanding never observes any real connection among objects. It follows, that identity is nothing really belonging to these different perceptions, uniting them together; but is merely a quality which we attribute to them, because of the union of their ideas in the imagination, when we reflect upon them.[2]

The experiment is conclusive. Personal identity is not an "impression," a matter of direct perception, at all. We do not know the self intuitively.

[1] Ibid.   [2] Ibid., sect. vi.

Is the self, then, a "substance," as Berkeley had supposed, known by inference? But, in the light of Hume's introspective experiment, any such inference is, surely, precarious in the extreme. If the trustworthy "impressions," the vivid states of consciousness, are all distinct, all essentially loose and unconnected, except in the sense that one follows another in the temporal order; what are we to think of an inference which goes entirely beyond the evidence, and constructs the notion of a "timeless self," a transcendental identity which somehow connects what experience reveals as *un*connected? Obviously, from the standpoint of empiricism, any such construction must be an abstraction, make-believe, pure fiction.

The identity, which we ascribe to the mind of man, is only a fictitious one, and of a like kind with that which we ascribe to vegetables and animal bodies.[1]

It may be that such a fiction has its practical uses. It is possible that to imagine that a stream of different and distinct states of consciousness is a "spiritual substance," may have value for our social living, for our legal conventions, for our personal hopes and fears. It may be a fiction useful in applying the laws relating to ownership of property, or in regulating city traffic. It may even have value for the purposes of Berkeleian religion. But for the philosopher, such a conception is, and must remain, a fiction. Practice may be for it, but all theory is against it. Negation, utter scepticism, is the only rational attitude here.

I cannot discover any theory, which gives me satisfaction on this head. I plead the privilege of a sceptic, and confess, that this difficulty is too hard for my understanding.[2]

Let us now consider *Hume's theory of causality*. "Every event has a cause"—or so men believe. Bacon had first raised a super- cilious eyebrow, and pronounced the conception of cause to be "unsound," i.e. animistic and unscientific. Berkeley had retained the conception in its animistic sense, as "active force," but had excluded it from science altogether. The sequences of ideas which we observe in nature do not "cause" each other; for each idea is entirely passive, inert, incapable of causing anything. So too the

[1] *Treatise*, Part IV, sect. vi.   [2] Ibid., Appendix.

David Hume

mystic Malebranche had declared that temporal events were, in themselves, all separate and unconnected, incapable of influencing each other directly or indirectly. These views would have resulted in an awkward situation, if Berkeley and Malebranche had not had their God to fall back upon: that Spiritual Substance whose active and creative force brings about, in accordance with His sovereign purposes, the sequences we observe, much as a human being can arrange ideas in his own imagination. Science observes and tabulates these sequences; but to appreciate their full nature and causation requires faith. Hume, whose faith in "spiritual substances" had, as we have seen, disappeared, seems left in a world of events all loose and unconnected, of temporal sequences without foundation or meaning: an uneasy situation.

What is Hume to do? He first realizes the importance of the problem, and then applies his introspective technique to its solution. The problem is important, because causality represents the only way in which men believe it possible to effect a reasonable transition from one event to another.

All reasonings concerning matter of fact seem to be founded on the relation of *Cause and Effect*. By means of that relation alone we can go beyond the evidence of our memory and senses. If you were to ask a man, why he believes any matter of fact, which is absent; for instance, that his friend is in the country, or in France; he would give you a reason; and this reason would be some other fact; as a letter received from him, or the knowledge of his former resolutions and promises. A man finding a watch or any other machine in a desert island, would conclude that there had once been men in that island. All our reasonings concerning fact are of the same nature. And here it is constantly supposed that there is a connection between the present fact and that which is inferred from it. Were there nothing to bind them together, the inference would be entirely precarious. The hearing of an articulate voice and rational discourse in the dark assures us of the presence of some person: Why? because these are the effects of the human make and fabric, and closely connected with it. If we anatomize all the other reasonings of this nature, we shall find that they are founded on the relation of cause and effect, and that this relation is either near or remote, direct or collateral. Heat and light are collateral effects of fire, and the one effect may justly be inferred from the other.

If we would satisfy ourselves, therefore, concerning the nature of that evidence, which assures us of matters of fact, we must inquire how we arrive at the knowledge of cause and effect.[1]

[1] *Enquiry*, sect. iv.

Apart from some principle of connection, experience simply falls asunder into its elements, the altogether distinct and separate "impressions," *A, B, C, D,* . . . In which case, what becomes of the arts and sciences, the human associations and institutions of civilization? All subjective, imaginary, make-believe. Practically important, perhaps, as long as we all play the game and stick to the rules. But if the rules are purely arbitrary, and the game an empty convention, what then? What is an enlightened age to make of civilization, and what is an enlightened philosopher to advise? If there is any validity at all in the conception of causality, it is obviously of the utmost importance that philosophers should discover it.

Hume now invites us to join him in his introspective inquiry. Let us look for the direct "impression," the vivid experience from which this confused and obscure idea of causal connection is derived. Is it a matter of direct sensation, with its basis in visual or auditory experience? Or does it, perhaps, as Berkeley had supposed, fall within the field of inner experience, which Locke called "reflection"? We can be sure that, if there is in our consciousness any such direct impression, it cannot long remain undiscovered.

When we have pushed up definitions to the most simple ideas, and find still some ambiguity and obscurity; what resource are we then possessed of? By what invention can we throw light upon these ideas, and render them altogether precise and determinate to our intellectual view? Produce the impressions or original sentiments, from which the ideas are copied. These impressions are all strong and sensible. They admit not of ambiguity. They are not only placed in a full light themselves, but may throw light on their correspondent ideas, which lie in obscurity. And by this means, we may, perhaps, attain a new microscope or species of optics, by which, in the moral sciences, the most minute and most simple ideas may be so enlarged as to fall readily under our apprehension, and be equally known with the grossest and most sensible ideas, that can be the object of our inquiry.

To be fully acquainted, therefore, with the idea of power or necessary connection, let us examine its impression; and in order to find the impression with greater certainty, let us search for it in all the sources, from which it may possibly be derived.[1]

And first, in the realm of external sensation. Do we see, hear, or

[1] *Enquiry*, Part I, sect. vii.

otherwise directly observe the "active force" supposed to connect
two distinct events? When we observe one event followed by
another, do we immediately suppose that the first has somehow
caused the second? Not without some definite reason, such as
repeated experience. *Post hoc, ergo propter hoc* is a very elementary
fallacy, and we are enlightened, on our guard. When we see the
movement of a billiard ball *A* followed by movement in another
billiard ball *B*: if the two movements are altogether loose and
separate, and there is no observable connection between them, we
do not regard the first as *causing* the second. We suspend judgment, until there is more evidence. If, however, we see the first
ball *strike* the second, and *then* see the second moving, we speak of
the movements as connected, causally connected; because repeated
experience of such sequences leads us to expect the second movement to follow upon the first; especially since such expectations
have always been verified. The ground for our judgment, however,
is not direct sensation, but repeated experience. At no point in our
developing judgment is "active force" a visual sensation, something seen by the eye to reside in *A*, as its size, shape, and colour
are seen to reside in it.

Let us now consider inner experience. When we "will" that
an event should take place, whether in the realm of nature or
in our own imagination, do we apprehend, in our "will," an "active force" capable of producing the result willed? Perhaps. At
any rate, Berkeley thought so. If so, "cause" will be an idea of
reflection, and its "impression" will be our direct experience of
volition.

Let us see, whether this idea be derived from reflection on the operations
of our own minds, and be copied from any internal impression. It may
be said, that we are every moment conscious of internal power; while we
feel, that, by the simple command of our will, we can move the organs
of our body, or direct the faculties of our mind. An act of volition produces
motion in our limbs, or raises a new idea in our imagination. This influence of the will we know by consciousness. Hence we acquire the idea of
power or energy; and are certain, that we ourselves and all other intelligent
beings are possessed of power. This idea, then, is an idea of reflection,
since it arises from reflecting on the operations of our own mind, and on
the command which is exercised by will, both over the organs of the body
and faculties of the soul.[1]

[1] Ibid.

But is Berkeley right? Do we, the first time we will something, apprehend, in our will, the "active force" competent to produce the result willed? When we will to move mountains, to play a perfect game of golf, to project an image of ourselves into the consciousness of some distant friend, so as to induce him to come and speak to us, or when we will that the next card turned up should be odd rather than even, and things of this sort, do we attribute genuinely causative power to our "willing"? Not unless we have further grounds for believing that things and ideas will obey our wills. If repeated experience shows us such obedience, we of course expect the event willed to follow upon our willing. But it is repeated experience, rather than direct insight into "will-power," which leads to such expectations. Apart from such experiences, we should not know what to expect: whether our willing could or could not produce the effect envisaged in imagination. Our form at golf or other games of skill does not always come up to our expectations. Our control over our bodies, and over our ideas too, varies, and varies quite considerably. Here too psychologists seem agreed that "active force" is not a matter of direct experience, but rests upon repeated observation.

As a result of these inquiries, we come to realize that the impression, from which we derive the idea of "cause," is to be sought, not in single experiences of sensation or reflection, but in repeated experiences. In what respect, then, do repeated experiences differ from single experiences of sensation and reflection? Taken individually, experience 3 or experience 4 does not differ from experience 1. But, taken together, there is a cumulative effect. There is an association of ideas, an expectation that *A* will be followed by *B*, which becomes stronger with repetition, and eventually becomes habitual. This association of ideas in our minds, this expectation of ours, is the "impression" from which the obscure idea of cause-and-effect is derived.

There is nothing in a number of instances, different from every single instance, which is supposed to be exactly similar; except only, that after a repetition of similar instances, the mind is carried by habit, upon the appearance of one event, to expect its usual attendant, and to believe that it will exist. This connexion, therefore, which we *feel* in the mind, this customary transition of the imagination from one object to its usual attendant, is the sentiment or impression from which we form the idea of power or necessary connexion. Nothing farther is in the case. Contemplate the subject on all sides; you will never find any other origin of that idea. This is the sole difference between one instance, from which we can never receive the idea of connexion, and a number of similar instances, by which it is suggested. The first time a man saw the communication of motion by impulse, as by the shock of two billiard-balls, he could not pronounce that the one event was *connected*: but only that it was *conjoined* with the other. After he has observed several instances of this nature, he then pronounces them to be *connected*. What alteration has happened to give rise to this new idea of *connexion*? Nothing but that he now *feels* these events to be *connected* in his imagination, and can readily foretell the existence of one from the appearance of the other. When we say, therefore, that one object is connected with another, we mean only that they have acquired a connexion in our thought.[1]

But what have we here? Expectation, based upon association, habit, and custom? Is not this subjective, a matter of the imagination, illusory and fictitious when applied to the external world? It is indeed. Turn it over and over as we will, the empiricist can never find any tie but custom and habit, our human ways of imagining and expecting, to bind together the single impressions, the hot and the cold, the red and the green, the loud and the soft, the angry and the anxious, of which alone we are perfectly sure. Objectively, the world of our experience, whether envisaged as external nature, or as internal reflection, falls asunder into an infinity of simple impressions "conjoined but not connected," associated by us in temporal sequence, but essentially devoid of any objective principle of connexion. All such associations and expectations are all-too-human and individual, and rest upon nothing stronger than repetition, custom, and habit. All our boasted science is infected with this subjectivity. The simple impressions are certain. Their association into our systems is not.

Thus we see that Hume's thought is essentially analytical, critical, and sceptical. Starting with impressions alone as certain, and with belief excluded from the relations of their untrustworthy shadows, the ideas, he finds the notions of a self as possessor of experiences, and of a nature as a causal nexus, belong only to the realm of shadows, their synthesis into something more quasi-substantial being entirely the work of the imagination. He is left with a world atomized into distinct impressions, fundamentally pluralistic, and incapable of objective systematization.

[1] *Enquiry*, Part II, sect. vii.

Upon the whole, there appears not, throughout all nature, any one instance of connexion which is conceivable by us. All events seem entirely loose and separate. One event follows another; but we never can observe any tie between them. They seem *conjoined*, but never *connected*.[1]

As a philosopher, he is satisfied with the degree of enlightenment thus attained, and dissociates himself from the naïve aspirations of less enlightened humanity.

But is this the whole truth about Hume? Many a modern reader, and many a reader in his own time, would say, Yes: Hume's philosophy *is* essentially negative, a perfect demonstration that empiricism leads necessarily to scepticism. And yet, if we read more carefully, more sympathetically, and with due attention to Hume's activities as a historian and public man, we shall find something more, something more positive, more completely in accordance with the practical tendencies of his country and his age.

If social life does not rest upon knowledge, upon theoretical insight and reason, on what does it rest? As Hume sees it, it rests upon repetition, upon custom and habit.[2] British life rests upon British customs and habits, French life upon French customs and habits, German life upon German customs and habits. These customs have grown, by slow repetitions, through centuries of historical evolution and interaction, until they have reached, in part, the level of civilization which Hume finds around him in the eighteenth century. These repetitions, which have thus given rise to national and individual habits of thinking, speaking, and acting, are not, it must be confessed, strictly rational. At the same time, they should not be regarded as purely arbitrary and merely subjective, as whimsical, beyond science altogether. They are traditional. In their way, such traditions are even objective. It is possible to trace their history. Hume did so, in his *History of England*. It is possible to live and act in their spirit. Hume did so, when he represented British interests and traditions at the Court of France. It is possible to discover and formulate the chief features of such traditions. Hume did so, in his philosophical publications. He finds the chief feature of British Justice to be—social utility; and who shall say that he was wrong? He finds in eighteenth-century life in higher social circles a search for enlightenment which was something more than a pose; and who shall say he was mistaken? In the conventional religion of his time he finds a tissue of mixed

[1] *Enquiry*, Part II, sect vii.   [2] *Treatise*, Part III, sects. viii, ix.

David Hume

motives which look a little queer when subjected to rational analysis; and who shall deny the substantial truth of his position? In Locke, we have England stirring uneasily, beginning to wake up, to become reflective, aware of her nature and destiny. In Hume, we have the spirit of Scotland, co-operating practically with the "Southron neighbour" in the furtherance of their traditional destiny, but at the same time rejoicing inwardly, and a little sardonically, in its own superior enlightenment; feeling that in Edinburgh, rather than in London, is to be found the true spiritual home of Great Britain.

In what does Hume's greatness consist? An original thinker he clearly is not. For philosophical pioneering, for years of trial-and-error, muddling through to a hard-won insight, he has no taste. A canny Scot, he leaves such thankless work to the English, to John Locke. He prefers to build upon the foundations constructed by others, with an alteration here and an addition there, no doubt, but, on the whole, his work is in the higher stories, and attracts, for that reason, more attention.

Was he, perhaps, a man of broad and deep experience, giving to his fellow-men of the ripe wisdom which comes from a long and reflective life? No, he was not. Hume's chief philosophical work was completed before he reached his thirtieth year. In fact, his was essentially an academic mind: subtle, dialectical, a little remote from everyday life, fixated, it may be, by the University of Edinburgh, which he had entered at the age of twelve, and to which he returned, as soon as his academic achievements made return possible. Subtle rather than profound, smooth and polished rather than vital, such a writer might well be thought near-great rather than great. It might well be maintained that the legend of his greatness rested chiefly upon the accident of Kant's having come across a German translation of his *Essays* at a moment critical for Kant's philosophical development.

There *are* writers whose importance depends more upon the quality of their readers' response than upon any depth of insight in themselves. And on this side, much has been written about Hume. In relation to Locke, and the "school" of Lockian empiricism, Hume is important. In the first place, his analysis of Lockian empiricism gives pause to almost all readers of the *Essay on Human Understanding*. Many a reader would eagerly cultivate a homestead

239

in the new territory thrown open to settlers by Locke's efforts, if it were not for the suggestion, felt by almost all students of Hume's writings, that Lockian empiricism leads to scepticism. The signpost SCEPTICISM of itself is sufficient to warn off many a youthful enthusiast; and Hume's signpost was very clear, and was placed in a prominent position. His arguments seemed, then as now, unanswerable—except to theological controversialists; and the natural reaction, on reading Hume, was to feel baffled, to withdraw from Locke's guidance altogether, and to hark back to traditionalism of the Scholastic kind, or to mysticism of the Cambridge Platonist sort, or possibly to Descartes and his immediate successors. The reverse side of Hume's signpost read NO THOROUGHFARE; and who wanted to explore what was advertised as a blind alley?

But Hume's signpost had a second arm, pointing, not to Locke, but in a different direction. On the one side, it read DETOUR, and on its reverse, THE NEW PSYCHOLOGY. Hume's new method had opened a pathway towards associative psychology, as a principle of explaining whatever introspective observation seemed to reveal; and Hume's fellow-countrymen were not slow to follow the way thus indicated to them. Thus arose the long and honourable development known as the "Scottish School," aiming at an associative explanation of mental, moral, and economic life; and many subsequent thinkers, by no means all Scottish, owed much to its founder James Mill. John Stuart Mill, Alexander Bain, Huxley, and even writers like G. F. Stout and James Ward, were more influenced than they would themselves, perhaps, have wished to admit. Others, like Reid, seizing upon the certainty granted to the simple impressions, whether of sensation or reflection, and pressing this for at least all it was worth, gradually founded that second development of the Scottish School known as "the Philosophy of Common Sense," which still has its adherents and advocates. For generations, it was felt that Scotchmen had somehow a natural or inborn taste for "the metaphysics," and "the metaphysics" meant for them, not speculative inquiry, but precisely this introspective and analytic psychology, with its reliance upon the laws of association, as upon so much synthetic magic.

In relation to Kant and Kant's work, Hume's influence and importance are known to every German schoolboy. Did not Kant himself write that it was Hume who "awakened me from my dogmatic slumbers"? Has not every reader of Hume, from that day to this, had his attention drawn to the very passages (on Causation) which sounded the alarum? When Kant solemnly suspended all metaphysicians from exercising their functions until they could resolve certain problems, was it not from Hume that these problems took their origin? and has not Hume ever since been read as the great questioner whom Kant "answered"? In relation to Kant, then, Hume has all the glory which awaits the foreign stimulus reduced by Teutonic insight to the position of an *überwundener Standpunkt.*

But apart from these well-known specific developments in the history of philosophy, Hume has two more general claims to greatness; and they are closely connected. In the first place, he is the typical modern sceptic. He represents the questioning mind which asks and asks, and refuses to be put off with soothing noises. No thinker who aspires to be a philosopher can afford to neglect the claims of scepticism. He simply has to face these issues; and Hume's work is a great help towards facing them clearly and honestly. It is no real answer to the sceptic to say "But how do you *know* that knowledge is impossible? Is not that itself, knowledge? Is there not a contradiction between the *form* of scepticism (its general claim to be taken as true) and the *content* of scepticism (its specific claim that there is no such thing as truth)?" This is one of those arguments *ex cathedra* which, given certain assumptions, sound so well in the classroom. But the sceptic questions the assumptions; and the modern thinker has to face this questioning. It is chiefly Hume who forces him to recognize, as in the case of F. H. Bradley, that his own view is not a complete "answer to Hume," but merely an alternative metaphysics, a theoretical possibility, bridging precariously a chasm of doubt.

In the second place, Hume has the mind of a great analyst, and his conclusions rest heavily upon the analytic method. The question whether Lockian empiricism leads to scepticism, about which so much has been written, is relatively superficial. The question, raised by Hume's use of the analytic method, is really more fundamental. For it is the analytic method which seems to reduce Locke's position to scepticism. It is the analytic method which seems to suggest that all empiricism, *interpreted by that method,* can be reduced to scepticism. The question thus forced upon us is technical. We ask, what is the nature, and what are the limitations, of the analytic method itself? Is it really analysis which, when pursued as a method valid in its own right, leads to the impotence of scepticism? Is there some weakness, some one-sidedness, about analysis? Does not analysis, if it is to work successfully, postulate some kind of synthesis? Can we break up the world into little bits, as Hume does, without raising the question as to whether the little bits are not, after all, bits-*of-the-world* we have analysed? Is not analysis itself *our* work, at least partly subjective? These questions raise the technical problem of method, and, until this is solved, the other questions, which influenced so many of Hume's contemporaries and successors, can only receive solutions which are provisional, apparent rather than real.

It is in these directions, then, that we must look for the real greatness of Hume; and, as it takes a great man to understand and appreciate such greatness, and as Kant is precisely such a man, if we wish to appreciate the full import of Hume's work, we cannot do better than study the philosophy of Kant.

Chapter X

IMMANUEL KANT 1724-1804

IMMANUEL KANT, greatest of modern philosophers, was born, lived, and died in the small East Prussian city of Königsberg. A contemporary of Frederick the Great, he too had his Grenadier Guard, his military system, his devotion to duty, and his worlds to conquer. Sergeant Lampe rolled him into bed, and out of bed, every morning and every evening, at the same hour. His day went by clockwork: two hours' study, two hours' lecturing; then study till luncheon. Conversation at luncheon until well into the afternoon. Then his walk—known to this day as the Philosopher's Walk—from precisely the same moment at starting to the same moment at returning. It is said that the inhabitants of Königsberg used to set their clocks by him. Preciseness, orderliness, system at every point. Even his irregularities went by rule. To avoid living too much by rule, he made it a rule to place his handkerchief at the far end of his study: so that, at moments not prearranged in detail, he would have to leave his books—whenever he had to wipe his nose.

What was the reason for this regimentation of his time? It was a matter of health. Of puny size and feeble physique, with one shoulder higher than the other, and with a chest almost concave, Kant, like many another great man, would certainly have died young but for his severe ordering of the details of his living. As it was, while often in pain, and while his mind went towards the end, he lived a longer life, and did more useful work, than the tallest and healthiest goose-stepper of them all.

Of humble origin, and miserably poor, the home-town University meant everything to Kant. He entered it at the age of sixteen, and never left it, except for nine years, when he had perforce to eke out his existence by private tutoring. It was only by the help of a friend that he was able to return and graduate. He graduated, not as a Doctor, but as Master. In his time, it was still possible to take either the M.A. or the Ph.D. degree. The work was about the same, but the fee for the Master's degree was less. It s a little ironical that the man in connection with whose work so many Ph.D. theses have been written himself never took that degree. It was fifteen years after he had entered the University before he graduated; and in the same year he habilitated as *Privatdozent*. This meant that he was entitled to offer lectures. He was given no salary, but received the fees paid by students attending his classes. This, of course, meant that, if he was to live and pay his bills, he would have to be an industrious lecturer, popular both in matter and in manner. He held no salaried position until, at the age of forty-two, he was appointed assistant librarian. At the age of forty-six he was at last elected to a professorship. The chair of logic and metaphysics fell vacant, and to this day it is known as Kant's Chair. Until his retirement, he steadily refused offers of positions elsewhere. A Königsberger born, a Königsberger he remained.

What did this small-town home-body study, and what did he teach? He studied theology, of course, and Latin—also of course. To the end of his life, he could quote the Latin poets—some say Ovid, others Lucretius—to some purpose. But what particularly fascinated him at the University were mathematics and physics. His earlier publications were in the domain of physical science, and the first professorship for which he applied was in the field of mathematics. He also received his initiation into the then fashionable Leibnizio-Wolffian philosophy, and ever afterwards worshipped metaphysics as the Queen of the Sciences, and his chief love.

What of his lighter reading, his social relaxations, and his love-affairs? Detective stories had not then been invented, so our stern Prussian read books of travel, descriptions of places and people he never hoped to see, popular anthropology and sociology. In his luncheon conversations, he avoided philosophers and philosophy, and sought the company of merchants and men of affairs, discussing commerce and travel, and thus enjoying a vicarious life of adventure. In his attendance at evening soirées, when he met the young Fraüleins—the dapper little intellectual was popular with the ladies —he would chat with them on two of their traditional themes, *Kleider und Küche*, clothes and cooking. His social manners, acquired in his private-tutorial years, were considered good; and every one found him attractive.

As to his love-affairs; well, a feeble physique hardly inclines to amorous dalliance. But Kant, like other mortals, was at times smitten. Twice he thought of marriage. But, being Kant, he thought about it in a way peculiar to himself. Did he confide his feelings to the lady? Not noticeably. He withdrew into his study, and went into the mathematical side of the question. Could two live in Königsberg as cheaply as one, one who already lived cheaply, and found it hard enough to make both ends meet? When he emerged, after two weeks' calculating and planning, it was only to find his inamorata carried off in a whirlwind courtship by a Prussian officer with his slogan *Dagewesen*! The second time, the same cause produced the same effect: with this difference, that, when he emerged, he found that the family had meanwhile moved to Hanover, in the extreme west of Germany. And in those pre-train, pre-auto, and pre-airplane days, Space, however unreal in the philosopher's transcendental system, had its way with him, empirically. Kant gave up, and ever after remained a confirmed bachelor: content with his sergeant, his students, and his studies.

The only permanently softer influences upon his life were the memory of his mother, that gentle pietist, and a certain sentimentality which, as with so many in that age of stern enlightenment, made him read the works of the arch-sentimentalist, Rousseau, with passion and utter forgetfulness of self, system, and rule. *Émile* even made him miss his daily walk!

As to his teaching: he was very industrious, and covered a number of scientific fields, from physics and logic to geography and "anthropology," as well as, in later years, works like his own *Kritik der reinen Vernunft*. His most popular lectures were those on *Anthropologie*, a somewhat lighter subject. When published in book form, this was, of all Kant's publications, the nearest to being a "best seller." It is not exactly in the vein: "The French are a polite nation, witty, fond of dancing, and given to gallantry. The English are a nation of shop-keepers, honest, respectable, but uninspired. The Germans are God-fearing, sober and industrious . . .," but comes dangerously close to it. The public, in that age of enlightenment, liked to be well-informed; and this charming little professor, whose personal acquaintance with the world was entirely at second or third hand, gave the public the information which it wanted.

As to the manner of his teaching: professors have two methods with large classes. They may use the straight lecture, in which

The Great Thinkers

they practically dictate their own text-book on the subject under discussion. Books like Prichard's *Kant's Theory of Knowledge* and Jäger's *Aristoteles* originated in this way. The formal reading of the written word is, of course, frequently interrupted by informal comment and illustration. Kant's lectures on *Logik* and *Anthropologie* seem to have taken this form. Or it is possible to take some published work as a text, and confine oneself to comments, references, and suggestions for alternative or further developments of the theme. Lectures on Plato's *Republic*, Locke's *Essay*, and similar philosophical classics, usually take this form. The comments may be partly formal, and partly informal, verging upon the "tutorial." Many, perhaps most, of Kant's classes were taught in this way. He would take in with him, not lecture-notes from which to read, but the text itself, all marked and annotated by himself in the margin, and would take these marks and comments as the starting-points of his less formal discussions. He taught his own *Critique of Pure Reason* in this way. One of the German editors of his *Werke* has published *Reflexionen Kants zur kritischen Philosophie*, i.e. the exact marginal notes which Kant used as reminders in his class-work. It is from these, and from these only, that we know just what Kant personally believed about "things-in-themselves."

In lecturing, Kant's voice was weak, and his delivery unaggressive. In his later years, when his rigid regard for system still kept him to the early morning hours, he was sometimes sleepy, and a little dull. Fichte, the philosophical enthusiast who had travelled across Germany to hear the Master, was distressed and disillusioned. But the classes were attentive and respectful. They never scraped with their feet. Anything that Kant said, they did their best to take down verbatim.

A German Professor's life is in his books. The *Gelehrter* is kindly in his human relations. But it is only in his publications that he becomes really alive. Thus understood, Kant's "life" falls into two sharply distinguished periods, a pre-critical, and a critical, separated by an interval of eleven years during which he published nothing. In a German Professor, such silence is remarkable, to be explained only by a long and arduous inner revolution of his spirit. The turning-point in Kant's life, at which the long interval of silence began, was in his forty-sixth year, at the time when he was appointed to his professorial chair. The appointment came as the climax of his years of steady development along Leibnizian lines: a development

246

marked by commendable industry, ability, and charm. If his development had stopped there finally, we should have had the common phenomenon of a local boy making good locally: with scarcely a hint to any but those wise after the event, that he had it in him to eclipse all other thinkers, and achieve a world reputation.

He lived in an age when, as Hume had discovered, readers liked their philosophy in peptonized cartons, portable, smoothly written, and short. People took their "enlightenment" as the modern man takes his newspaper, with his breakfast. Moses Mendelssohn (ancestor of the famous musician and of the distinguished Beneke family) published a book of popular essays entitled *Morgenstunden,* which are regarded as typical of the period. These are published in a well-known *Bibliothek,* and are still read. Kant, like the rest of his contemporaries, wrote essays, brilliant little treatises, empirical in method, charming in form, and not unrelated to current *Ereignisse.* There are, *inter alia,* a small treatise "On the Beautiful and Sublime," and an entertaining discourse on "Mental Diseases." These are, of course, in addition to more severe theses in the field of natural science. There is also a somewhat longer pamphlet, entitled "Dreams of a Spirit-seer . . .," which comments on the then fashionable mystic Swedenborg, and was written, not only because the theme was timely, but in the hope of thus paying the bill for the mystic's somewhat expensive tomes. The last, more metaphysical, part of this pamphlet it is which, to the wise, contains hints of Kant's future greatness.

The last work of the pre-critical period, Kant's inaugural dissertation as Professor, entitled *De Mundi Sensibilis atque Intelligibilis Forma atque Principiis,* is as devoid of originality and unusual academic ability as the rest of his pre-critical philosophizings. Like Socrates, he taught his students to criticize, to philosophize, to think for themselves. He had no philosophy of his own, and had no expectation of ever developing one. If he had written no more, none but the indefatigable in erudition would ever dream, at the present day, of unearthing the publications which, through so many years, had been the breath of his "life." He would have been labelled "just another professor."

And then Kant read Hume. He soon arrived at the NO THOROUGH-FARE signpost, and saw that the scepticism applied, not only to Lockian empiricists, but also to Leibnizian rationalists like himself. The well-paved highway, upon which all his life he had been accustomed to taking his philosopher's walk, led only to a wilderness of thistles. The Principle of Sufficient Reason proved insufficient to withstand the sceptic's challenge. It could not account for real causes producing real effects. Alas for metaphysics! Hume was right. It was a blow. Kant felt crushed, negated, estopped.

He read again, and noticed the other signpost, with its DETOUR, leading to associative psychology. But this did not satisfy him, as it had satisfied Hume's fellow-countrymen. There *was* Scottish blood in Kant's veins; but he was too much of a Prussian to put up with the easy-going practical compromises of the British. Associationist psychology is merely empirical, a matter of the nervous system, with its contingent reactions to particular stimulations. But Kant, as a Prussian no less than as a Leibnizian, was interested in Reason, with its logical immanence, its perfect universality, and its rigid necessity. As a metaphysician, he was interested, down to the unfathomable depths of his transcendental ego, not in details, but in principles. And when he said "principles," he meant Principles, *a priori* Principles, foundational Principles which made empirical science conceivable, and gave it a rational charter, a basis more reliable than empirical trial-and-error, that groping-in-the-dark which puts its trust in expectation, habit, human and racial customs.

He was in an *impasse*, and he knew it. Alone of the philosophers of his time, he recognized the situation for what it was. The great Leibniz had failed him. Berkeleian idealism? Like Humian psychology, the merest palliative. Hume was in the same *impasse* himself. Everyone was in it. The whole philosophical tradition had come to a dead end. There was no way out.

Since the origin of metaphysics so far as we know its history, nothing has ever happened more decisive to its fate than the attack made upon it by David Hume. He challenges reason, and demonstrates that . . . there is not, and cannot be, any such thing as metaphysics at all.

My object is to persuade all those who think metaphysics worth studying, that it is absolutely necessary to pause and, neglecting all that has been done, to propound first the preliminary problem, *whether such a thing as metaphysics is at all possible.*[1]

In later years, Kant could be philosophical about this blank period in his life. He could write that Hume had "awakened him from his

[1] *Prolegomena*, Introduction.

dogmatic slumbers." But it was many and many a long year before it felt like that.

I freely confess, it was the suggestion of David Hume which many years ago first interrupted my dogmatic slumbers, and gave to my investigations in the field of speculative philosophy a new direction.[1]

At the time, it was a shock, a numbing blow, a sheer impossibility of progress. All his cheerful hopes were blighted, sacrificed upon the altar of the unknowable. He was not "awake." He was not even in the light. He was in the dark, in outer darkness, groping and gnashing his teeth. It was some small comfort to him to realize that everyone else was lost too. It was some slight alleviation of his pain to know that, while all were ignorant, he he was at least not ignorant of his ignorance. He was blind. But at least he saw clearly that he was blind, and that every one of his "enlightened" contemporaries was equally sightless. The abyss of scepticism was engulfing the whole modern world. But he at least was in a position where he could bottom the abyss and investigate its contours. Perhaps a new dawn, a new kind of dawn, would eventually appear. In that case, he might conceivably be in a position to lead the lost world away from its will-o'-the-wisps, and towards the true, hitherto undiscovered source of spiritual illumination.

What does a thinker do, when he finds the ground thus cut away from under him? Does he give up for the time being, and wait, Micawber-like, for something to turn up? Men vary. Many give up philosophizing altogether, and devote their energies to something positive, definite, precise; avoiding ultimate questions as they would the devil—who in very sooth lurks in that abyss. Some devote themselves to secondary issues, engaging in erudite researches, editing philosophical classics, tackling this or that narrowly limited problem for which they feel they have especial qualifications, hanging on by the toe-nails of their technique, in the hope that eventually a rope of salvation will be lowered to those who work. A few remain stunned, stultified, reduced to impotence, nullified. Yet others seek out ways which are new. They grope indeed in the dark, but they keep on groping, pioneering, breaking trails which lead at least to something untried.

Of these last was Kant. Tentatively and industriously, every

[1] Ibid.

working morning for close upon eleven years, he would retire to his study and concentrate. For Kant, to concentrate was something more than to sit-and-think, which is often indistinguishable from mere sitting. He would sit and write, trying to solve this problem and that in the light of Hume's scepticism: expanding Hume, testing his thought in new fields and from new angles; not quite seeing his own way clear; but trying, trying, until he had worked over almost the whole field of knowledge.

I first tried whether Hume's objection could not be put into a general form, and soon discovered that cause-and-effect was by no means the only idea by which the understanding thinks the connection of things *a priori*, but that metaphysics consists altogether of such connections. I sought to ascertain their number, and when I had succeeded in this by starting from a single principle, I proceeded to deduce these concepts, not from experience (as Hume had apprehended), but from the pure understanding. This deduction, which had never occurred to anyone, was the most difficult task ever undertaken in the service of metaphysics; and the worst was that metaphysics (such as it then existed) could not assist me in the least.[1]

Traces of these years are evident in the unpublished papers eventually printed by Reicke, under the title, *Lose Blätter aus Kants Nachlass*. These show Kant at work upon the nature of the imagination, and its powers of synthesis, of groping in the dark until, in the end, the clear light of an intellectual concept illumines its pathway and shows what it was, all the time, working towards. They show him at work upon the nature of causation, upon the nature of logic, and upon many such problems. As with Aristotle, so with Kant. There are many *doublettes*, alternative versions of one and the same problem: obviously so many dialectical experiments, carried out separately and individually, almost for their own sake. In some ways they remind us of Kant's pre-critical publications. There is the same brevity, the same essay-character, the same logical analysis. But they are laboratory sketches, microscope preparations, unfinished, without charm. Kant was wrestling with problems, and had no time for literature. The graces and elegances of authorship were disappearing from his life. But out of these years of wrestling, wrestling technically with problems technically envisaged, there gradually emerged a new Kant, one of the few master-minds of the world. *In diesen Sachen*, says Benno Erdmann, *hat niemand so tief gewühlt, wie er.*

[1] *Prolegomena*, Introduction.

And it was not only with problems that he had to wrestle. Academic circles are critical circles. The criticism is often indirect, not outspoken. But its pressure is felt by all who are sensitive. When a man is appointed to a professorship, and then, for five years, ten years, eleven years, publishes nothing; such a man, however hard he may be working in private, is conscious of the unspoken disapproval of all with whom he works in public. His inner ear hears clearly what he would himself be saying of such a colleague, and his inner voice torments him unescapably. "Why doesn't he *do* something? Now that he has at last obtained promotion, is he going to do nothing more with his chair than occupy it, professing to teach others to think, but himself doing no thinking? Or is he a spent rocket, which has burnt itself out, and has no more stars to give? Has he reached the end, only to linger on, year after year, keeping better men, more productive scholars, out of a University position? If he has struck a snag, why can he not at least formulate his problem clearly, and then proceed, by well-tried academic methods, to work his way towards a definitive solution? Not immediately, perhaps; but surely within a year, or at most two years?"

Such is the voice of academic criticism, all the world over. Every professor who has academic standards feels its force. But especially in Germany is the urge to publish, to have something in proof, to be getting something out, to have off-prints to be sending to friends and colleagues, universally experienced, and experienced not as a luxury, but as a necessity. Academically, the Germans are a nation of writers, of writers even more than of readers. It must have been hard for Kant. No wonder he had so few academic friends. But he set his teeth, and kept to his chosen paths, even when they seemed to be leading nowhere.

My object was not merely to sketch out a plan and leave its completion to others. My heart was in the welfare of the science to which I had so long devoted myself. In truth, it required no little constancy, and even self-denial, to postpone the sweets of an immediate success to the prospect of a slower, but more lasting, reputation.[1]

These years of trial left their mark upon all Kant's subsequent work. One who had been down to the depths with Hume could

[1] Ibid.

never thereafter lose sight of the limitations of knowledge. Is causality a pure myth? Can we never know what causes experience to trace the patterns we observe in it? What is the x, the unknown ground of experience, surely rational, if experience itself contains traces of reason? What is the ultimate nature of things, considered in themselves beyond their merely temporary and transient relation to our sensitivity? Are they, not merely unknown, but for ever beyond human knowledge: absolutely unknowable? Can they be real and rational, and yet beyond, not merely human sensation, but also human logic? Yes, Hume was right. In themselves, things are surely unknowable. To those who have not set their feet where Kant has stood, this seems a hard saying. Such men attempt, rather lightly, to avoid Hume's NO THOROUGHFARE sign, or perhaps take it down and proceed as if it had not been put there for good reasons. But for Kant, the unknowable is very real. It had been his constant wrestling partner for many a long year.

Again, it was the analytic method which had led to Hume's scepticism. Analysis culminates in a number of points, all distinct and unconnected. What becomes of synthesis, the principle of construction which, starting with such points, builds them up into a connected whole? That the imagination is constructive and synthetic is obvious, to Kant no less than to Hume. But is not the imagination, in its syntheses, often groping after something objective, some connection of which reason would approve, something universal and necessary? If this is not grounded in the nature of things-in-themselves, but in the nature of things-in-relation-to-our-sensitivity, upon what, in this relation, does it really rest? Surely upon something more than mere imagination, creative fancy, make-believe, subjective play? Surely science at least attempts to be something more than art?

What of mathematics? What of physics? And what of metaphysics? Are not these more than merely applied disciplines, resting upon repeated observation and sensory demonstration? Is there not a "pure" mathematics? Is there not a "pure" physics? And is not metaphysics essentially "pure," i.e. formal and unmixed with sensory experience? That these disciplines are really synthetic, and that their syntheses do not rest upon expectation custom, and habit, becomes clear when we carry out a few dialectical experiments in each field.

(1) In the field of mathematics. "A straight line is the shortest

distance between two points." *Straightness* is a qualitative concept. *Shortness* is quantitative. No amount of analysis will ever discover shortness as an element in straightness. Straightness means "identity of direction"—as to whether long or short, nothing is said, absolutely nothing. And yet, the proposition which connects straightness with shortness in the field of plane geometry is certain. It is universal and necessary. It rests on mathematical intuition, and it is synthetic.

That a straight line is the shortest path between two points, is a synthetical proposition. For my concept of *straight* contains nothing of quantity, but only a quality. *Shortness* is therefore entirely additional, and cannot be obtained by analysis of the concept *straight*. Here intuition must come to our aid. It makes the synthesis possible.[1]

Our intuition is undoubtedly correct here in connecting two terms which analysis declares to be distinct, "loose and unconnected," as Hume would say. With what right do we so connect them?

(2) In the field of physics. "Every temporal event has a cause." This, as Hume himself had shown, is synthetic. *Event* and *Cause* are two ideas shown by analysis to be distinct and separate, "loose and unconnected." Yet pure physics connects them unhesitatingly in the proposition "Every event has a cause," and regards the proposition as both universal and necessary.

We can say with confidence that certain pure *a priori* synthetical cognitions (pure mathematics and pure physics) are actual and given. Both contain propositions recognized as certain, partly by mere reason, partly by general consent arising from experience, and yet recognized as independent of experience. We have therefore some uncontested synthetical knowledge *a priori*. It is actual, and we ask how it is possible, in order to deduce from the principle which makes the given cognitions possible, the possibility of all other *a priori* synthetical cognitions. It has cost me years of work to solve the problem in its whole universality.[2]

With what right does pure physics effect this synthesis?

(3) Finally, in the field of metaphysics. Metaphysicians, of all people, construct synthetic propositions, which go far beyond what any human being has ever observed, or can ever be expected to observe. "God exists"—or, for the non-theologically minded,

[1] *Prolegomena*, sect. 2.   [2] *Ibid.*, sects. 4–5.

"Reality exists," or "Perfection exists," or "The Absolute exists." The conception of "existence" is understood to add something new and significant to the subject-term "God," or "Reality," "Perfection," etc.[1] Or, to take human beings: for the metaphysician, "Man has a free will," i.e. "Man has the power of being an uncaused cause." That is to say, the physicists' principle "*Every event has a cause*" is denied by the metaphysician, in the case of *human* events, events initiated by *Homo sapiens*. Or we might take a third fundamental proposition which certainly goes beyond human experience, and yet is synthetic: "Man is essentially timeless and immortal." In each case, the propositions are synthetic, and yet are "pure" or independent of sensory experience. With what right do metaphysicians connect terms which analysis reveals as essentially distinct and unconnected? God, freedom, and immortality are commonplaces in the text-books of Leibnizio-Wolffian philosophy, with its well-known divisions into Rational Theology, Rational Cosmology, Rational Psychology, etc. If Hume is right, such books should be "committed to the flames" rather than to the shelves of University libraries. But *is* he right? Or are *they* right?

As Kant busies himself with questions like these, there flits before his mental vision the thought of giving up positive studies altogether and withdrawing entirely into this new field of investigation. Why not occupy himself with this preliminary problem of knowledge? Of knowledge so far as it is more than particular and individual, and professes to be both synthetic and pure, independent of sensation and association? He defines this kind of inquiry as "transcendental," and thus for the first time in the history of modern philosophy there dawns, dimly at first, but with steadily increasing brightness, the conception of a transcendental philosophy.

As soon as I had succeeded in solving Hume's problem, with respect to the whole faculty of pure reason, I could proceed safely, though slowly, to determine the whole sphere of pure reason completely and from general principles, in its circumference as well as in its contents. This is a perfectly new science, of which no one has ever thought. The very idea of it was

---

[1] That the concept of *existence* adds anything to the concept of *God* (or any other concept) is denied on philosophical grounds by both Hume and Kant. But, (1) the (concrete) existence of God is treated throughout by Kant as on a par with (2) the freedom of the will and (3) the immortality of the soul, which constitute for him) typical metaphysical syntheses.

Immanuel Kant

unknown, and nothing hitherto accomplished was of the least use, except it be the suggestion of Hume's doubts. Yet even Hume did not suspect the existence of this formal science, but ran his ship ashore upon scepticism. My object is rather to give the ship a pilot who, by safe principles drawn from a knowledge of the globe, and provided with a complete chart and compass, may steer safely whither he will.[1]

"Transcendental philosophy"—a name to conjure with, as Kant's successors proved. Just what idea did its discoverer form of the land of promise, the homeland of the spirit, flowing with philosophical milk and honey, into which he hoped to lead his metaphysical brethren? It was to be a study, based on principles absolutely certain, of the origin, nature, and limitations of *a priori* knowledge, i.e. of knowledge which was pure and formal, universal and necessary.

From all that has been said we get the idea of a unique science, which may be called the Critique of Pure Reason. It is not a *doctrine*, but a *criticism* of pure reason, and its speculative value is entirely negative, because it does not enlarge our knowledge, but only casts light upon the nature of our reason and enables us to keep it free from error. By *transcendental* knowledge I mean all knowledge that is occupied, not with objects, but with the way in which a knowledge of objects may be gained, so far as that is possible *a priori*. What we propose is not a doctrine of pure reason, but a transcendental criticism, the purpose of which is not to extend knowledge, but to rectify it, and to supply a touchstone of the value of all *a priori* knowledge.[2]

Its problem could be formulated in general terms as "How are synthetic judgments-*a-priori* conceivable?" That is to say, the new philosophers would devote themselves, first, to collecting the facts to be explained, namely, undoubted cases of the synthetic knowledge which Hume had questioned, knowledge which, although synthetic, was also *a priori*, independent of direct sensuous perception. There would be no difficulty about establishing these facts. They were exemplified in the whole of pure mathematics, the whole of pure physics, and the whole of metaphysics. In the second place, the new philosophers would endeavour to construct a hypothesis, an entirely new theory, which would account for and explain these facts. In the third place, they would verify their hypothesis, and exclude alternatives, thus proving their case.

[1] *Prolegomena*, Introduction.
[2] *Critique of Pure Reason* (II), Introduction, sect. 7.

Such an explanation would fall into three parts: (1) a transcendental philosophy of mathematics, (2) a transcendental philosophy of nature, as investigated by physical scientists, and (3) a transcendental philosophy of ultimate nature, as deduced by metaphysicians. No doubt there would also be general considerations and conclusions, involving the construction of a definite programme, towards whose realization Kant might invite the co-operation of his philosophical colleagues.

The general problem once solved in principle, transcendental philosophy would be established as the ideal towards which modern thinkers had been groping their way, hitherto without success. All that would remain would be for men of learning and good will to fill in the outlines, making the whole both in principle and in detail, polished, plausible, and persuasive; and for men of science, their philosophical background and outlook being now taken out of the twilight of uncertainty and perplexity, to devote themselves, with clear insight and absolute confidence, to carrying through their positive researches in properly limited fields. Thus all would work together, in Kant-established harmony, in this best of post-Leibnizian worlds.

Such was Kant's vision. Obviously, everything depended upon the new hypothesis, the explanatory theory which was to make all plain. But how *could* our syntheses be anything more than Hume had said: human, all-too-human, resting upon the nervous system, with its customary and habitual expectation that what had been would be? Kant turned this over and over, in principle and in detailed cases. Could we really know anything whatever about the world, independently of direct or indirect sensuous experience? Empiricists say, "No, No, and again, No. That fire burns, ice cools, bread nourishes, and arsenic destroys, are obviously matters of sensuous experience. You could not deduce them *a priori*, if you tried for a million years." On the other hand, we all believe that seven and five add up to twelve, and that this general statement can be verified, not only in all cases of countable units experienced by human beings up to the present, but in the future, in all cases of countable units, as such. How, how could we possibly know such a statement to be true, especially in unobserved cases?

Kant tried to answer questions of this kind, testing them from different angles, until, at last, it began to dawn upon him that a distinction which he had been using almost unconsciously would solve his problem, yes, would solve all his problems, yes, would solve all conceivable philosophical problems. It was the universal key to philosophy; and Kant could make his colleagues freemen of the new City of Thought, by presenting them with this key. There had been other metaphysical keys forged in the past. Plato, with his distinction between the ideal and the actual, between pure thought or dialectic, "the conversation of the soul with itself," and sensuous experience, had achieved wonders. But the distinction, pushed too far, had been productive of barren abstractions; and, in the hands of followers devoid of metaphysical tact, had been pushed so far that, instead of opening the chambers of the spirit, it had jammed the locks. St. Thomas Aquinas, when in doubt and difficulty, had used a distinction which he had found most helpful: the distinction between the human and the divine point of view. But to use this key successfully, you obviously had to believe in authority, and also, to be born before Hume. Descartes' key, the clear-and-distinct idea, had failed once or twice, in Descartes' own hands; and Leibniz' key, of pre-established harmony and the principle of sufficient reason, had simply melted away before the corrosive logic of Hume's scepticism. A new key was needed, and at last Kant discovered it, in his own possession.

Kant called this key his "Copernican revolution." Physical scientists had tried to explain the interrelations of the heavenly bodies; but their theories were becoming more and more complicated and intricate; until Copernicus' time. Copernicus had suggested that, instead of taking our earth as the centre, with reference to which the motions of the celestial bodies are calculated, we should take the sun, and plot our curves with reference to *that*. This change of standpoint had immensely simplified the astronomic picture, and the science had been able to progress surely ever since. In philosophy, metaphysicians, with their (Aristotelian) ideal of a "science of being *qua* being," had tried to explain experience by making things-in-themselves central, and our minds marginal. Their theories had eventually become so complicated that the best and brightest minds in metaphysics could contradict one another flatly on the most important questions, and no one could really see any way out. Hume's scepticism was entirely justified. Kant's key to the situation was a change in standpoint, a change as revolutionary as that of Copernicus. Take, not things, but mind, as central, and see how immensely the change simplifies the whole picture. Thus reoriented, our problems can be easily understood and completely solved.

Let us make the experiment in metaphysics, of rejecting the assumption that our cognition must conform to the objects, and assuming instead that the objects must conform to our cognition. If our intuition must conform to the objects, I do not see how we can know anything of them *a priori*. If, however, the object conforms to the nature of our faculty of cognition, I can easily conceive the possibility of *a priori* knowledge. I presuppose in myself laws of the understanding which are expressed in conceptions *a priori*. To these conceptions all objects, *to be experienced by me*, must conform.

By this new method we explain the possibility of *a priori* cognition, and demonstrate satisfactorily the laws which lie *a priori* at the foundation of nature (considered as the sum of the *objects-of-experience*)—neither of which was possible according to the method hitherto followed. This attempt to introduce a complete revolution in the procedure of metaphysics constitutes the aim of the *Critique of Pure Reason*.[1]

Take this problem of knowledge, for instance, which, since Hume, has seemed desperate. Let us cease to regard knowledge ontologically, as an apprehension of things in their own ultimate nature. That way failure lies, and scepticism. Human knowledge is a product of two factors, (1) things (no doubt), and (2) mind, in interaction with one another. Of the first factor, things, considered in their own nature, we know nothing. We know only what is filtered through our own minds, and is doubtless conditioned by the nature of those minds. The operations of our sense-organs, and of our mathematical and logical techniques, which give us human science, give us, in that "science," not things-in-themselves, but a mentalized transcript of things. Kant calls this a "phenomenon." For instance: John knows, not Mary, but his idea of Mary: seen through his senses, glorified through his emotions, clarified through his intelligence; but throughout envisaged, not as she may be (perhaps) in herself, from the standpoint of absolute knowledge, but in relation to his own nature. What John knows is thus Mary as a "phenomenon." Our prejudices, our hopes and fears, sometimes even our mathematical and logical patterns, come between us and the object. We see, not the object in its own nature, but what our minds read into it. We know phenomena, not things-in-themselves.

---

[1] *Critique*, tr. Mieklejohn, II, Preface.

Immanuel Kant

The faculty of knowledge is aroused to activity by objects. These, acting upon our senses, partly of themselves produce ideas in us, and partly set our understanding, by comparing, combining, or separating these ideas, to convert the raw material of sensory impressions into that knowledge of objects which is called "experience." Experience is made up of two elements, one received through sensory impressions, the other supplied, on the occasion of these impressions, by our faculty of knowledge. This second element is added by the mind, and is distinguishable from the material to which it is applied. The second element is not empirical, but independent of experience. It is purely formal.[1]

What philosophers can do, and should do, then, is to study this second factor, the nature of our minds. If we can discover the essential nature of our minds, we shall be able to learn more about knowledge, about its framework and structure, than we could ever discover by taking our minds for granted, and puzzling ourselves by projecting what comes from mind into the field of the objects studied.

Kant's philosophy is thus a philosophy of mind, of the subject rather than of the object. It may, accordingly, be regarded as a kind of subjectivism. But there are two kinds of subjectivism, a lower, and a higher. The lower subjectivism, known as "subjective idealism," or "psychological idealism," resolves experience into sensations and associations, explained, it may be, in terms of our nervous mechanisms. From this standpoint, we live, as Hume had concluded, in a closed circle of our own ideas, each in a private world of his own, with no possibility, except through inadequate social conventions, of understanding a public world, such as that presented to us by science.

But it is a higher kind of subjectivism which is associated with the name of Kant. It is known as "objective idealism," or "logical idealism," and its problem is to investigate, not the psycho-physical machinery which underlies our mental processes, but the broad structural features of experience itself. Experience reveals a definite structural pattern. It is systematic, orderly, rational. It constitutes a kind of complex unity, with definite, subordinate laws of its own. It is amenable, through and through, to mathematical and logical reasoning. Hitherto, it had been supposed that this characteristic structure comes from things-in-themselves; that the "laws of thought" are laws for our thinking, because they are the laws of the things which thought thinks. It is because things are

[1] Ibid., Introduction.

259

mathematical and logical that we can analyse and synthesize them; and that is why, when we want to understand anything, we take it to pieces and put it together again; feeling sure that our procedure reveals to us the way things are. It is precisely this sort of supposition which had led, in Hume's hands, to scepticism.

Kant, with his new key, suggests that mathematics and logic are instruments forged by the mind in accordance with its own nature. They are ways of ours for understanding, not things in their own nature, but phenomena, our mental transcripts. We analyse and synthesize phenomena; we add and subtract phenomena; we construct scientific systems of phenomena. We do this because it is of the essence of the mind so to analyse and synthesize, add, subtract, and construct systems. These laws of thought are valid for the things which thought thinks, not in so far as they are things-in-themselves, but in so far as they are thought-by-mind, in so far as they are thinkables, in so far as they are phenomena, sense-data arranged by us into systems.

Kant's transcendental philosophy is pervaded by this higher subjectivism. The philosophy of mathematics becomes a study, not of things, but of the percipient mind. Geometry investigates the nature of space. For Kant, space is no longer, what it was for Newton, a kind of general framework into which things fit, but a formal law of the mind, in its character as percipient. We arrange in two or three dimensions the objects of our perception. When we wish to discuss some subject, we construct a spatial diagram to represent its nature-for-the-purposes-of-discussion. The words we use have meanings primarily spatial, geometric, applied metaphorically but universally, even to things which we feel to be non-spatial. We speak of a friend as having a "broad" mind, a "well-rounded" character, a "lofty" temper. For Kant, then, the philosophy of mathematics becomes a transcendental theory of mind, in its character as percipient. He calls this part of his work "transcendental aesthetic," using the word "aesthetic" in its original sense, as popularized in Germany by Baumgarten, signifying "theory of sense-perception."

In the same way, pure physics is no longer regarded as revealing the structural lines of nature, but rather the structural lines of the inquiring mind: of mind as thinking, as constructing unified systems. Causation is not a way in which one "thing" affects another "thing," but rather a way in which our minds introduce order and rule into the logical system we call "science." So too "objective," in its application to phenomena rather than "things," no longer means "conforming to things in their ultimate nature," but "valid universally for rational intelligences, as such." Kant calls this part of his work "transcendental analytic," using the word "analytic" in the Aristotelian sense, signifying "theory of logic."

The theory of mathematical science thus becomes sense-perception, and the theory of physics becomes logic, in Kant's transcendental philosophy. His new key, thus opening the universal and formal chambers of the mind, simplifies the nature of knowledge. We know, not things, but the phenomena which our minds, when stimulated by nature, construct in accordance with the mind's own laws. Our laws, which express the most general aspects of experience, are the laws of mind, and not of things. They apply to whatever we can think, i.e. to the whole field of experience, and renounce for ever the high ambition of revealing the ultimate nature of things-in-themselves. Mathematics and physics apply only within the realm of the humanly experiencible. Beyond that realm, they are empty of meaning, and their use, as by metaphysicians of the past, becomes a problem.

Kant's solution of the problem resembles Hume's in being largely negative. In relation to things-in-themselves, metaphysics, as a theory of ultimate reality, represents an idle and impossible dream. With his new key, however, Kant relates it to the mind. The speculative use of the understanding has a certain value, even for the scientist. A freer use of logic, without direct reference to sense-data, results, not in "phenomena," or sense-perceivables, but in "noumena" or thinkables, concepts constructed and systematized by logical methods, but which, in themselves, are merely formal patterns, which may, or may not, prove of use to us in arranging our experiences. Their value, for the mind of the scientist, is twofold. This noumenal extension of our thought enlarges our minds, so that they escape undue narrowness. Its audacious guesses suggest alternative possibilities, which go beyond the immediate evidence, but may prove, as in the case of an Einstein, extremely useful for the fresh advance of science.

In the second place, speculation spurs us on to press to the absolute limit of sense-perception, even by highly indirect means, searching for greater unity, more complete orderliness, more comprehensive system. Its value, however, depends, in every case, upon an at least indirect reference to possible sensuous experience, as studied by the methods of science. This part of his work Kant calls "transcendental dialectic," and, while demonstrating the negative value of speculation as applied to things-in-themselves, he emphasizes its positive value as enlarging and stimulating the mind of the scientist, engaged in the widest and deepest possible interpretation of phenomena.

The above represents, in essence, Kant's vision of transcendental philosophy as a whole, and in its chief parts. In working it out, he found his hardest problem consisted in establishing the precise nature of mind. What others called "the general features of reality" would, for him, have to be "the general features of mind," the organizing demands with which the mind faces experience.

The problem fell, as he approached it, into two divisions. In connection with sensuous experience, *space*, regarded by Newton as a pervasive feature of physical reality, became, rather simply, a way in which creatures with sense-organs arrange, in their own minds, the content of their experience. *Time* became, similarly, a way in which we arrange, not merely our sensations, but *all* our experiences, when we reflect upon them, including our logical constructions. In spite of the implied relation to logic, which indicates that time may be a little different from space, Kant treats it as precisely analogous, as a formal law of perception, universal in scope.

(c) Time is the formal *a priori* condition of all phenomena without exception. Space, as the pure form of all external phenomena, is the *a priori* condition only of external phenomena. But all objects of perception, external as well as internal, are determinations of the mind, and, from that point of view, belong to our inner state. And as this inner state comes under time, which is the formal condition of inner perception, time is an *a priori* condition of all phenomena: it is the immediate condition of inner phenomena, and so the mediate condition of outer phenomena. Just as I can say, *a priori*, that all external phenomena are in space, and are determined *a priori* in conformity with the relations of space, so, from the principle of the inner sense, I can say quite generally that all phenomena are in time, and stand necessarily in relations of time.[1]

So far, in establishing the perceptual forms, Kant felt himself on fairly sure ground. A physicist himself, he was well acquainted with the pervasive features of physical reality, and believed that his

[1] *Tr. Aesthetic*, ii, 7.

new explanation was entirely satisfactory. But when he came to the second division of his problem, and sought to establish the formal principles of logical construction, he experienced considerable difficulty. He was trying to break new ground, and to break it in a way which would satisfy, not merely brother logicians, but also his own system-loving Prussian mind.

The general principle was plain enough. Thought unifies and systematizes. Whatever else we look for in the (phenomenal) world we construct in order to satisfy our mind's most fundamental demand, we look for systematic unity. Analysis and synthesis are, by universal agreement, the mind's primary methods. Moreover, as we always analyse into *units*, and synthesize into *units*, it is plain that, for the philosophy of mind, "synthetic unity," as a candidate for the presidential chair, has no competitors. Synthetic unity is therefore declared unanimously elected.

It is only because I am capable of grasping the various determinations in one consciousness, that I can call them all mine; were it not so, I should have a self as many-coloured and various as the separate determinations of which I am conscious. Synthetic unity of the various determinations of perception as given *a priori*, is therefore the ground of that identity of apperception itself, which precedes *a priori* every definite act of thought. Now, objects cannot combine themselves, nor can understanding learn that they are combined by observing their combination. All combination is the work of understanding, and in fact understanding is itself nothing but the faculty of combining *a priori*, and bringing under the unity of apperception, the various determinations given in perception. The unity of apperception is, therefore, the supreme principle of all our knowledge.[1]

But this principle of unity, while occupying a position sufficiently elevated, is terribly formal and general, remote from anything detailed. Kant sought to discover its principal subordinate forms, but had to seek for months and months before he could satisfy himself. Why was this? Let us make a simple experiment, and we shall see.

Take any simple proposition, such as *This rose is white*, and ask what it presupposes. What formal, universal and necessary principles, from the logician's standpoint, does it involve? As a "proposition," it plainly consists of a logical subject *this rose*, a logical predicate *white*, and the symbol of connection *is*. We have here

[1] *Tr. Analytic*, II, ii, 16.

plurality (subject-idea plus predicate-idea), *unity* (the unity of each of these ideas), and *totality* (the complex unity of both ideas in the single proposition). We have further, *identity* (of the subject with itself, of the predicate with itself, of the proposition as a whole), *difference* (of subject from predicate. Not all roses are white; not all white objects are roses), and *organization* (of partly identical, partly different terms into the propositional complex). And further: in so far as we have identity, there is *positive* character; in so far as there is difference, there is *negative* character (whiteness and roseness, so far as different, cannot be identified, but negate one another). And further: we have *relation* (of subject to predicate in the proposition), *system, order, arrangement, duality, mathematical quality, logical quality, quality-in-general, perceivability, thinkability,* phenomenal *reality*, phenomenal *existence*. . . . Such principles for introducing systematic unity into our experience, Kant calls "categories," and regards them as the formal laws of our constructive activity, in so far as we are logical.

Such categories hang together, and are obviously of a piece. Hitherto, as the essential presuppositions of systematic unity, they had been referred to the world, to the nature of things-in-themselves; and different philosophers, as their views of the world differed, had constructed slightly different lists of categories. To the Greeks, with their faith in clear-cut distinctions, categories had seemed to go in pairs. *Motion-rest, Odd-even, Finite-infinite,* were widely accepted among them. The ten categories of the Aristotelian school, *Substance-accident, Genus-species, Place-time, Relation*, etc., seemed to have logical as well as metaphysical status. But, as a rule, a given philosopher's categories were primarily metaphysical in their outlook. Kant, with his new key, relates them all to the nature of the mind. As he sees it, they are the universal principles necessarily presupposed in the attempt to unify, in the way which the logical intelligence can grasp. They originate, not with things, but with the mind, and constitute a relatively simple closed system.

As Kant looked over the list discovered in simple experimentation, such as we have attempted above, he could see, not only that categories hang together, but that some are more fundamental than others. *Quantity, quality,* and *relation* seem especially fundamental. But then, so do *identity, difference,* and *organization.* And where are we to find a place for *substance?* On what principle are such questions to be determined and answered? For a long time, Kant's experimentings, while interesting and suggestive, led to no results which satisfied his mind. At last, he reasoned the matter out in this way: The principle of synthetic unity is the formal principle for unifying our logical thinking. Thinking expresses itself, according to the logicians, in judgments. Find out the different kinds of judgment. Each judgment-type will have its own unifying principle or category; and the problem will be solved. In this way, just as, in discovering space and time, he was helped by the work of the physicists; so in discovering the categories, he will be helped by the work of the logicians, and will not be breaking absolutely new ground after all.

Logic, formal logic. This means, of course, Aristotle, whose "system" was acceptable, not only to medieval Scholastics, but also to Kant and his contemporary "enlightened" thinkers. Now, how does Aristotle, who knew *all* the forms of judgment, classify them? Well, he had not thought of Kant and Kant's problem, and, as it happened, had not reduced them to a single, all-inclusive system after all. However, when it comes to systematic classification, one logician can surely help another. Kant accordingly himself classifies the Aristotelian forms, from his own point of view; and the classification has become almost canonical. Judgments can be classified as Quantitative, Qualitative, Relational, and Modal. Each of these heads can be made to contain three sub-forms. Thus, Quantity contains singular, particular, and universal judgments; Quality contains affirmative, negative, and limitative judgments; etc. There should be one category for each judgment-type; and, as there are twelve types, there will be twelve categories, no more and no less. Under the head of Quantity, there will be *Unity, Plurality, Totality*; under the head of Quality, *Reality, Negation, Limitation*; under the head of Relation, *Substance*-accident, *Cause*-effect, *Community* or *Reciprocity*; and under the head of Modality, *Possibility, Actuality, Necessity*. It gave Kant particular satisfaction to observe that, in this classification, he had got beyond the simple distinction of the ancients. The second category in each group is the negative of its immediate predecessor; but the third is obtained by a synthesis of its two predecessors. His categories are generated, therefore, not as twins, but as triplets. A simple change: but fraught with significance for the further development of objective idealism.

This difficult problem solved to his own satisfaction, Kant was at last prepared to tell the world all about his new metaphysical key, and the age of ultra-enlightenment which was about to dawn for his philosophical colleagues. However, as he thought over what he should say and how he should say it, he found himself checked by two considerations. In the first place, those colleagues of his. Men whose minds are set—and Kant knew how a Prussian's mind could get set—have to have things broken to them gently. They would never be able to appreciate what he had to place before them until he first broke down their resistance by a negative criticism: like Hume's, but extended so as to include unmistakably Leibniz and Wolff. It had taken him ten years or so to convince himself. In the second place, his own experience. Those ten or eleven years of negative criticism had left their mark upon him. He could only get them out of his system by publishing a record of them.

Yes, that would do. He would publish *two* books, a negative work first, criticizing the Leibnizian philosophy. He would call it *The Critique of Pure Reason*, and would break down the uncritical faith in pure reason, which he had himself shared before he had come across Hume. Then the time would be ripe for the publication of a real book, his positive treatise, which he would call his *Transcendental Philosophy*.

The Critique of Pure Reason is the mere criticism of the sources and limitations of pure reason. It is propaedeutic, and its use in regard to speculation is negative: not to extend the bounds of our reason, but to purify it and shield it against error. The sole object of the present essay is a transcendental critique, aiming not at the enlargement, but at the correction and guidance of our knowledge, in such a way as to serve as a touchstone of the worth or worthlessness of *a priori* knowledge.

Such a critique is consequently a preparation for an organon or canon of pure reason, according to which the complete system of transcendental philosophy—the philosophy of pure reason—may one day be set forth. In this philosophy we shall have to do not with the nature of outward objects (which is infinite), but solely with the mind, which judges of the nature of objects *a priori*. The object of these investigations is to be sought not without, but within ourselves, and thus cannot remain concealed.[1]

Accordingly, intoxicated with the enthusiasm which a new baby confers upon its proud and happy father, he set to work. In four

[1] *Critique of Pure Reason*, Introduction, sect. 7.

months' time he had selected and edited, out of the mass of papers he had written in his study during the preceding eleven years, enough to fill a large volume. It was his first big book. And yet, he intended it only as preliminary criticism, to clear the way for his *magnum opus* on transcendental philosophy. Probably, in his enthusiasm, he hardly realized just what he *was* doing.

The Critique of Pure Reason, at first sight, seems negative enough. About half of it is direct criticism of Leibnizio-Wolffian metaphysics; and of the remaining half, about two-thirds of the clearcut analysis gets its point by contrast with "dogmatic" or precritical methods. But, as the ground of his criticism was largely the overwhelming superiority of his new principle, he was unable to keep his positive insights altogether to himself, and the new subjectivism was, in fact, very much in evidence.

So much so that the critics—and who shall blame them?—at first confused it with the lower kind of subjectivism; and the reviewer Garve pronounced the book a work of "idealism"— i.e. "subjective or psychological idealism." This aroused Kant to compose and publish, by way of immediate rejoinder, an altogether unpremeditated book, the *Prolegomena to Every Future Metaphysic* . . . , in which, employing synthetic rather than analytic methods, and writing, perhaps, more intelligibly for his colleagues than in the previous compilation, he expounded for the second time the critical philosophy which was to prepare the world for *objective* idealism. In the second edition of his *Critique*, which was called for soon afterwards, he introduced many alterations, not only speaking more definitely about things-in-themselves (in order to show that he did not doubt, but accepted, their existence), but also transposing a criticism of Wolff's "rational psychology" to a more prominent position, and labelling it "Refutation of Idealism"—i.e. subjective idealism (so that no critic could thereafter be in doubt). However, while his work gradually won its way into almost universal acceptance, he had often to endure hearing it referred to as "idealism" or "subjectivism," without as much emphasis upon its objective and logical quality as he could wish.

Now was the time for his *magnum opus*, the positive exposition of "transcendental philosophy." But he never wrote it. He now discovered that his positive views were sufficiently contained, in principle, and even in detail, in the *Critique*; and he even doubted whether they should be detached from the critical insights to which he had won his way in the long fight with the powers of scepticism. Accordingly, his philosophy never became widely known as "transcendentalism," but only as "formal idealism," "logical idealism," "critical idealism," and, most commonly of all, "The Critical Philosophy."

What did Kant produce during the rest of his life? More "Critiques," of course. Two of them have the word "Critique" in their title; about two others have it in their content. When he turned his eye upon the field of values, especially moral values— Kant was an uncompromising moralist—he found the existing theories (intuitionism, utilitarianism, the dogmatic teaching of the various churches and ethical societies) "a disgusting medley" of motives and appeals patched up from any and every source, however inconsistent. With his new metaphysical key, he proceeded to inquire whether everything in our moral life which goes beyond immediate reaction to stimulation, and claims universality and necessity, might not rest upon some formal demand in the nature of reason itself.

The principle of morality is declared by reason to be a law for all rational beings, in so far as they have a will, i.e. have the power to determine their causality by the conception of "rules," i.e. in so far as they are capable of acting in accordance with practical *a priori* principles. Men, as rational beings, possess such a will; but being creatures affected also with wants and physical motives, their wills are not *holy*—i.e. are not incapable of maxims which conflict with the moral law. In the case of human beings, therefore, the moral law is an *imperative*. The law is unconditioned, and commands categorically. The relation of human will to this law is *obligation*, implying a *constraint* to an action. Human action, thus constrained by the conception of law, is action in accordance with *duty*. Finite rational beings can advance steadily towards holiness of will, and this definite progress of our maxims is called *virtue*.[1]

"Duty" thus claims to be something more than social convenience. Morality, with its "ought," its unhesitating demands upon our obedience, issues commands, unconditional imperatives, "synthetic principles" into whose justification the philosopher of mind might well inquire.

Duty can be nothing less than a power which elevates man above himself (as a part of the world of sense), a power which connects him with an

---

[1] *Critique of Practical Reason*, tr. Abbott, I, i, sect. vii.

order of things that only the understanding can conceive, with a world which at the same time commands the whole sensible world, and with it the empirically determinable existence of man in time, as well as the sum total of all ends (which totality alone suits such unconditional practical laws as the moral). This power is nothing but *personality*, that is, freedom and independence on the mechanism of nature, yet, regarded also as a faculty of a being which is subject to special laws, namely, pure practical laws given by its own reason; so that the person as belonging to the sensible world is subject to his own personality as belonging to the intelligible [super-sensible] world. It is then not to be wondered at that man, as belonging to both worlds, must regard his own nature in reference to its second and highest characteristic only with reverence, and its laws with the highest respect.[1]

Kant, as might be expected, discovers the ground for the unconditional or categorical imperative of morality in the nature of our reason. Reason, turning of itself to social and practical living, can deliver itself of one law, and one law only. We might formulate this inherent moral law as "Be rational," "Live according to Reason and its dictates." The Stoics in the past had so formulated it. But Kant goes further, and invents a variety of formulations which, while all equally grounded in this principle, enable us, as he thought, to pass from the bare precept of abstract reason to the demands of practical life in general, and even in detail, and to solve our moral problems as they arise.

His first formulation is "Act on principles which are universal." This is opposed to older, more metaphysical doctrines, such as "conform to the nature of things," or "to the will of God." It is also opposed to that fashionable psychology which treats human beings like so many amoebas or butterflies, reacting mechanically to each physical stimulus as it occurs. Kant's view is that we should act logically, consistently, on principles which, when technically "universalized," prove non-contradictory, in accordance with the essential nature of mind. Suppose a man tempted to make a promise, with intent to default. He might say, "God would not like this," or "If my associates find me out, they'll never take my word again." Such consideration of metaphysical or social consequences is, from Kant's standpoint, irrelevant. As Kant sees it, a promise with intent to default contains an inherent contradiction. It is not a promise at all. It is illogical, irrational, and conflicts

[1] *Ibid.*, iii.

with the nature of mind-as-such. The man's motive cannot be turned into a logically universal principle.

His second formulation is, "Treat everyone as an end-in-himself, not as a mere means to some end outside himself." This is opposed to the metaphysical view that human beings are means to the realization of some end beyond themselves: such as "God's inscrutable purposes," or the will of some king or dictator, which exploits them in an interest not their own. It is also opposed to the psychological attitude which considers others only as they affect oneself and one's empirical wants. Reflective self-determination, expressing the higher, rational will, is alone moral. Kant urges us to aim at "the perfection of self," on the ground that no one can do our willing for us. We have to live our own lives, ultimately making our own choices. He urges us also to aim at "the happiness of others," i.e. to make conditions, physical, economic, social, and spiritual, conducive to their maximal pleasure, or happiness. This is Kant's substitute for the then fashionable utilitarianism, which aimed at "the greatest happiness of theg reatest number."

His third formulation is "Live in the spirit of membership in the kingdom of ends." This is a social extension of the second formula, and suggests the idea of a community in which each member is a rationally self-determining citizen; where no one imposes or is imposed upon, but all work together, as a community of idealists, making themselves and the world progressively rational, the reflex of a self-determining mind. Kant's thought is extended further, to suggest the notion of a free league of self-determining nations, and a philosophy of law, international and national, based, not upon appeals to pleasure-pain, to economic, or to metaphysical-theological notions, but upon the appeal of a self-determining reason. It leads, further, towards the idealist philosophy of the State, as based upon "objective" or rationally conceived duty and the life of reason, rather than upon subjective pleasure, or external domination; and it has, indeed, many other ramifications. The essential thing about Kant's ethics is his substitution of mind, with its self-chosen ends, for externals, such as pleasure, wealth, or conformity to the will of this or that human or divine being.

The *autonomy* of the will is the sole principle of all moral laws, and of all duties which conform to them. The principle of morality consists in the independence on all matter of the law (namely, a desired object), and in the determination of the elective will by the mere universal legislative form of which its maxim must be capable. The *independence* is *freedom* in the *negative* sense, and the *self-legislation* of the pure, and, therefore, practical reason is freedom in the *positive* sense. Thus the moral law expresses nothing else than the *autonomy* of the pure practical reason; that is, freedom; and this is itself the formal condition of all maxims, and on this condition only can they agree with the supreme practical law.[1]

Such is the theory developed in the *Critique of Practical Reason*, and some three or four minor treatises. Their publication made Kant regarded as a sort of moral dictator in Europe, and various cases of conscience were referred to him for settlement. Philosophers, however, find it interesting for a further, more technical, reason. The reference to persons as *"end-in-themselves"* has a metaphysical ring to it; and Kant does not hesitate to write of the higher self as "noumenal" and "transcendental." It looks as though Kant, having officially, in the *Critique of Pure Reason*, escorted Leibnizian metaphysics down his front steps, is letting it in again by the postern, in his *Critique of Practical Reason*, in the guise of "moral postulates," and replacing it upon its throne.

What philosophers seek to determine is whether, as Kant sees it, the higher self, with powers apparently transcending causality and the space–time world, is just so much make-believe, a useful fiction with a practically beneficial effect on all who believe in it and play the idealist game, or something more—something real, ultimate, the genuine stuff of which metaphysical reality is made. There is no doubt that people can play the game, if they want to, as they play the game of high society and court life. But is there real gold beneath the gilt? Is morality something more than mere posturing? Does it bring us into contact with something truly vital? If it does, does moral experience somehow extend the limits set to the mere scientist, and justify philosophers in constructing metaphysical edifices on this higher ground?

When these ideas of God, of an intelligible world (the kingdom of God), and of immortality are further determined by predicates taken from our own nature, we must not regard this determination as a transcendent knowledge of *supersensible* objects; for these predicates are no others than understanding and will, considered in the relation to each other

[1] *Critique of Practical Reason*, I, i, sect. viii, theorem iv.

in which they must be conceived in the moral law, and therefore only so far as a pure practical use is made of them.

There remains of the notions by which we conceive a pure intelligence nothing more than just what is required for the possibility of conceiving a moral law. There is then a knowledge of God indeed, but only for practical purposes, and if we attempt to extend it to a theoretical knowledge we find an understanding that has *intuitions*, not thoughts, a will that is directed to objects on the existence of which its satisfaction does not in the least depend. These are attributes of which we can form no conception that would help to the *knowledge* of the object. They can never be used for a *theory* of supersensible beings, so that on this side they are quite incapable of being the foundation of a speculative knowledge, and their use is limited simply to the practice of the moral law.[1]

Kant's answer is subtle, but simple. Idealist metaphysics, from the standpoint of scientific knowledge, which confines itself to organizing sense-data into logical systems, *is* a useful fiction. That is to say, it *is* useful, and it *may be* a fiction. The methods of science cannot determine whether there is something real behind it or not. But as men, as minds called upon to act, to take a definite stand in this space–time world, we can and must *believe* more than we can ever *know*. *Faith* enables us to act *as if* ultimate reality consists of minds, centres of spiritual activity, rather than "things." Personally, Kant has that faith. But it is always faith, never knowledge. It can never be proved; it remains his private opinion. His way of expressing this is to say that he "destroys knowledge to make room for faith." As Kant sees it, reason in its practical aspect is superior to understanding in its theoretical aspect. The field of values is not less but more rational than the field of science. Within its phenomenal limits, science is absolute. But truth, goodness, beauty, the self, and God, the values which make life, including the scientific life, worth while, lie beyond those limits. They are not "phenomenal," but something better. They give us a foretaste of the "noumenal" realm, a vital experience of ultimacy.

Kant's third great Critique, his *Critique of Judgment*, is a philosophy of art, and represents a "critical" transformation of an earlier essay of his own. When we stand before art-works, whether these are sublime or merely beautiful, we are conscious of something more than our private, individual, satisfaction. We are drawn out of our everyday selves. There is a sense of something deeper, a

---

[1] *Critique of Practical Reason*, II, ii, sect. viii.

hidden significance coming from some source worthy of admiration, love, reverence. Philosophers have attempted to account for this experience in two ways. Some refer to metaphysics, usually with a little religion thrown in. Plato supposed the artist to be feeling his way, however dimly, towards ultimate reality; and he suggested that, once a committee of experts had finally decided what the ideal patterns were, and how they were to be represented in sensuous image-forms, legislative enactment should forbid further experimentation, as certainly useless, and possible degenerative. In his ideal community, as in ancient Egypt and medieval Europe, the business of art was to be *ancilla theologiae*, a technical amplifier of the (metaphysical-ideal) religion established by law.

Since Hume's *Essays*, it had become increasingly evident that our knowledge of things-in-themselves, no less than of whatever Gods there be, was altogether inadequate; and a more empirical and psychological mode of explanation was beginning to become fashionable. To Kant, in his critical period, it was obvious that such attempts at explanation are subjective, incompetent in principle to explain the sense of objectivity and ultimate significance characteristic of our art-experiences. He therefore takes his metaphysical key, and turns to mind, with its higher subjectivism, as his principle of explanation; and asks what formal features of mind are sufficient to account for the transcendental reference of our experience of art-values.

We have a dual nature, part empirical, part rational. Kant had already appealed to this fact, in accounting for moral feeling, and had not appealed in vain. Empirically, our subjective desires are humiliated before the majesty of the moral law, which bids us do our duty, whether we like it or not. But transcendentally, as noumenal selves, we are elevated to the level of the moral law itself. Synthesis of empirical humiliation with transcendental elation constitutes *reverence* for the law, which the higher self both gives and receives, and for the pure will, which expresses the vital essence of that law.

This formal interrelation of the two sides of our nature, Kant turns to account in explaining artistic, as well as moral, feeling. Art is more playful than morality, less obviously serious. Yet it is essentially significant, purposive. Kant accordingly formulates the principle of beauty as purposiveness: purposiveness in general, rsal purposiveness, with no specific empirical purpose.

...mining ground of the judgment "this is beautiful" is the mere form of purposiveness in the representation by which an object is given to us. It is this formal purposiveness which, so far as we are conscious of it, constitutes the satisfaction which we, without a specific concept, judge to be universally communicable.[1]

For example: a statue representing the human form may symbolize love, strength, vitality, or (better) just ideal quality, underlying what we see. As thus suggestive of higher things (in general), it is beautiful, or possibly even sublime. If, however, it was labelled "Effect of Mr. So-and-so's Physical Culture Course," or "Try Swellins' Muscle Food," this specific, empirical purposiveness would interfere with the general, transcendental effect.

Faced with a work of art, we try to represent this general, transcendental appeal in terms of sensuous images, specific, empirical, distinct. But we fail. Transcendental significance is elusive and suggestive; and our specific imagination, like our scientific understanding, finds itself baffled. Our imagination, humbled as it fails to measure up to the reason's ideal demands, feels reverent; and this is the source of our experience of sublimity.

Kant goes still further. He relates these art-feelings of significance and sublimity to moral feeling, and maintains that art is essentially ancillary to morality. Its function is the stimulation of transcendental feeling, feeling that the world is a place of spiritual values, and that these spiritual values are ultimately of moral significance; art suggests that, behind the veil of space–time phenomena, God and His monads are co-operating, in immortal solicitude, towards the ultimate coincidence of virtue and happiness.

The beautiful is the symbol of the morally good, and it is only in this respect that it gives pleasure with a claim to the agreement of everyone. By this the mind is made conscious of a certain ennoblement and elevation above the mere sensibility to sense-pleasure. In taste, our judgment is self-legislating in respect of the satisfaction associated with its objects. Hence in taste, our judgment of beauty finds itself referred to something within the self as well as without it, namely, to something which is neither freedom nor nature, but yet is connected with the supersensible ground of freedom. In this supersensible ground, the theoretical and the practical reason are bound together in a way which is as yet unknown.[2]

[1] *Critique of Judgment*, tr. Bernard, I, i, sect. 11 (slightly paraphrased).
[2] Ibid., I, ii, sect. 59 (slightly paraphrased).

Immanuel Kant

With the publication of his third *Critique*, Kant's work was practically complete. He had carried through his "Copernican Revolution," placing the thinker in the centre of the scientific, moral, and artistic worlds, and reducing "things-in-themselves" to a marginal shadow, themselves spiritual. He wrote, it is true, further books: composing, under somewhat forbidding social circumstances, the nucleus of what might have been called a "Critique of Religion," and the beginnings of a "Critique of Physical Science." Certain thoughts of the *Critique of Judgment* might well have been expanded into a "Critique of Biological Science." But these "Critiques" remained unwritten. Kant was an old man now. His spiritual arteries were becoming set and rigid, and before long his memory began to lapse, and his mental powers to weaken. It was the end.

His work was done. The "critical philosophy" had been firmly established. The new metaphysical key had been turned in all the locks; and the doors had been opened wide enough for vistas of a new and most attractive avenue, leading apparently straight to the philosopher's *Champs Élysées*, to reveal themselves to all of Kant's younger contemporaries. His greatness, as "the philosophers' philosopher," was universally acknowledged; and the ambition to become recognized as "Kant's Successor" and founder of the new Transcendental Philosophy, the positive idealistic philosophy of mind, seized upon every Teutonic thinker of ability. Kant was the pioneer who had at last worked his way to the end of the rainbow and unearthed the new gold-mine; and his discovery was followed by a spiritual gold-rush.

Chapter XI

POST-KANTIAN MOVEMENTS

IDEALISM, REALISM, PRAGMATISM

I

THE generation which succeeded to Kant's heritage sought to complete his work on its positive side. Fichte, Schelling, Hegel, Schleiermacher, and Schopenhauer were all "transcendental philosophers," philosophers who made "mind" central in their accounts of experience. Not one of them had himself been through the severe training in science, and in scepticism, which had kept Kant cautious and critical. Fichte (1762–1814) was essentially a preacher *manqué*; Schelling (1775–1854), a philosophical Peter Pan, a brilliant intellectual playboy who never grew up; Hegel (1770–1831), a historian who succumbed to the dialectician's standing temptation to pose as a speculative parlour magician; Schleiermacher (1768–1834), a most attractive preacher, always the good boy of the idealist family; and Schopenhauer (1788–1860), by all accounts the *enfant terrible* of the group, if not essentially an *esprit faux*.

None of these thinkers confined himself to repeating the *verba magistri*; for there were a number of sore spots in Kant's work which cried aloud for new treatment. The "deduction of the categories," for instance. This had given the Copernican revolutionist himself almost endless trouble; and the next generation could see—oh, so clearly—that there was really no sound principle for believing in *twelve*, a round dozen, of these categories—or, for the matter of that, in just *twelve* types of judgment. And Kant's neat little arrangement of them, in groups of three each, did more credit, perhaps, to an unsuspected talent for philosophical anagrams than to self-critical philosophical insight. Not one of Kant's successors but could construct a *Wissenschaftstheorie* or Theory of Knowledge (as the now fashionable transcendental philosophizing began to be called) with a more plausible "deduction," and a whole lot more categories.

A second sore spot was Kant's treatment of "things-in-them-selves." The popular view was expressed by Jacobi (1743–1819): "Without the thing-in-itself, I cannot enter Kant's philosophy; but with it, I cannot stay there." To *know* that "things" are "in themselves" unknowable; that they are rational in principle, and the ultimate, ultra-experiential ground of experience, a kind of constant x in our knowledge-equations; is surely, they thought, to know a good deal about the "unknowable." Such knowledge may be formal, but it is none the less universal and necessary; and if it *is* a factor in the experiential equation, surely, by putting the x on one side, and experience on the other, we can at least suggest a tolerable solution of the equation; especially since even Kant allows us to approach pretty closely to this x, in our *value*-experiences. Accordingly, Fichte reads the riddle of life by viewing it as a moral conflict, between the forces of the ideal self on the one hand, and of the not-self, a world of dead, unspiritual "things," on the other. In this ultra-cosmic battle of the spirit against "things," which side, asks the preacher, is young Germany going to take? It is a question of character. Surely, the true German is on the side of the spirit, rather than on the side of Napoleon's big battalions, or England's big business! *Wir alle wollen Hüter sein!*

What kind of a philosophy one chooses depends upon what kind of a man one is. A philosophical system is not a piece of dead household furniture, which one can use or lay aside at pleasure, but is animated by the soul of the man who has it. A man must be born a philosopher, be educated to be one, and educate himself to be one. By no human art can he be made a philosopher. Hence this science expects few proselytes among men whose mental habits have already been moulded; but its hopes are centred in the rising generation, whose native vigour has not yet been impaired by the intellectual laxness of the present age.[1]

Here we see Kant's "practical reason" settling the problems of life, with empirical verification in terms of speculative *Anthropologie*.

Schelling viewed life aesthetically, enjoying both sides of the conflict, as in a drama; taking his seat among the gods of literature, *au-dessus de la mêlée*, and proclaiming, in many a telling phrase, the superiority of the self-conscious artistic standpoint. "So-called dead nature is merely an unripe intelligence." "The creative impulse, without intelligence, is nature; with intelligence, is art."

[1] J. G. Fichte, *Erste Einleitung* (1797) tr. Rand, sect. 5.

"The philosophy of art is the true organon of philosophy."
"Self-consciousness is the luminous point in experience; but it
illumines only forwards, not backwards."

The system of knowledge can be regarded as complete only when it
reverts to its principle. Transcendental philosophy would therefore be
completed only when it also could demonstrate that identity—the highest
solution of its entire problem—in its principle (the *Ego*).

It is therefore postulated, that activity, at once conscious and unconscious, can be shown in the subjective, that is in consciousness itself.

Such an activity can be no other than the *aesthetic*, and every work of
art can only be conceived as the product of such. The ideal work of art
and the real world of objects are therefore products of one and the same
activity. The meeting of the two (of the conscious and the unconscious)
gives *without* consciousness the real, *with* consciousness the aesthetic
world.

The objective world is only the original still unconscious poetry of the
soul. The universal organum of philosophy—the keystone of its entire
arch—is the philosophy of art.[1]

From this standpoint of artistic synthesis, he could create transcendental poetry, or transcendental *Naturphilosophie*, with equal
virtuosity—and with equal superiority to laboratory methods; and
for a time, especially among men of letters, his influence was,
indeed, transcendental.

Hegel viewed experience as the self-evolution of Absolute Mind,
in which the historian, the artist, the priest, the scientist, the
logician, and the transcendental philosopher, taking quasi-parallel
pathways, all go through the same stages; some empirically, in
space–time gropings, others transcendentally, in metaphysically
self-conscious reflection. He had learnt, with unusual dialectical
acumen, to improve upon a technical trick of Kant's, and found it
of the greatest assistance. It was practically a new metaphysical
key, universal in its application, and necessary. No idealist should
be without it.

Kant had almost hit upon it himself. In his logic, he had
generated transcendental triplets, (1) a positive category, (2) its
negation, and (3) the synthesis of the two. But in his critique of
metaphysics, he had fallen back upon the old principle of contradiction, arranging metaphysical positions in parallel columns, under

[1] Fr. W. von Schelling, *System d. tr. Idealismus* (1800), tr. Kroeger, sect. iii.

the heads of "thesis" and "antithesis," which negated each other and simply cancelled out. He had not thought of taking his third step, and effecting a further, ultra-transcendental synthesis. Hegel, however, perfected this technique, and found that, with its aid, the principle of contradiction became like putty in his creative hands.

Mind or spirit, when it is sentient or perceptive, finds its object in something sensuous; when it imagines, in a picture or image; when it wills, in an aim or end. But in contrast to, or it may be only in distinction from, these forms of its existence and of its objects, the mind has also to gratify the cravings of its highest and most inward life. That innermost self is thought. Thus the mind renders thought its object. In the best meaning of the phrase, it comes to itself; for thought is its principle, and its very unadulterated self. But while thus occupied, thought entangles itself in contradictions, i.e. loses itself in the hard-and-fast non-identity of its thoughts, and so, instead of reaching itself, is caught and held in its counterpart. This result, to which honest but narrow thinking leads the mere understanding, is resisted by the loftier craving of which we have spoken. That craving expresses the perseverance of thought, which continues true to itself, even in this conscious loss of its native rest and independence, "that it may overcome" and work out in itself the solution of its own contradictions.

Thought in its very nature is dialectical, and as understanding, it must fall into contradiction—the negative of itself.

The idea as a process runs through three stages in its development. The first form of the idea is Life: that is, the idea in the form of immediacy. The second form is that of mediation or differentiation; this is the idea in the form of Knowledge. The process of knowledge eventuates in the restoration of the unity enriched by difference. This gives the third form of the idea, the Absolute Idea: which last stage of the logical idea evinces itself to be at the same time the true first, and to have a being due to itself alone.

The one single aim, action, and goal of philosophy is to arrive at the notion of its notion, and thus secure its return and its satisfaction.[1]

The technique is known as "Hegelian dialectic," and its invention and universal application made Hegel easily the foremost of Kant's successors; so much so that "objective idealism" is often, even at the present day, known as "Hegelianism," and the later German idealists, one or two of whom, like Adolf Lasson, survived into our own time, were universally known, less as "idealists," and more as "Hegelians."

[1] G. W. Fr. Hegel, *Ency. d. philos. Wissenschaften im Grundrisse* (1817), tr. Wallace, sects. 11, 17, 215.

Schleiermacher, writing anonymously in order not to draw down the wrath of the orthodox, constructed a transcendental philosophy of religion. Addressing his work to *educated* agnostics, he extends and expands the Kantian account of *reverence*. This compound of empirical humility and transcendental elation had been applied, by Kant, to the moral will; and Kant had indeed based his religion also upon morality alone. This view Schleiermacher broadens. He universalizes the principle of reverence, and shows the possibility and necessity of its application over the whole religious field. Religion cannot be intellectual, he teaches; because intellectual concepts are finite, clear-cut, partial, mutually exclusive, confined, in their applications, to the here-and-now, the realm of phenomena —whereas religion is infinite and universal. Religion cannot, however, be moral either; and on the same general grounds. Because moral willings are finite, clear-cut, mutually exclusive, confined, in their applications, to the here-and-now, the realm of space–time action. It follows, then, that the transcendental philosopher must look, for the mental basis of religion, to the only aspect of our mental life which remains, the aspect known as "feeling." For feeling has no boundaries which hem it in, no clear-cut outlines, no mutually exclusive parts. It reaches out to infinity in all directions. It is essentially indefinite and universal. The formal law of human feeling is precisely this reaching out towards the infinite, the feeling of humility, of unsubstantiality, of *dependence*: the need for strength, encouragement, spiritual leadership from a higher source. In feeling, man is made for God. We can verify this law, in its universality and necessity, by reference to all the religions of the world. Eor this principle, and this principle alone, permits us to arrange them all significantly, from the most primitive attitudes which are without a godhead, to the most advanced and sophisticated world-religions, as rungs upon the ladder extending from human experience at its lowest to human experience at its highest and best.

Schopenhauer, regarding this whole idealistic clique of *Universitätsprofessoren* with undisguised contempt, and Hegel, in particular, as an "arch-charlatan," proclaims himself "Kant's true successor," and sets out to found the "philosophy of life." The secret of life is, not morality, or religion, or science, or art. It is not intelligence at all. The secret of life is *life*, *more* life, the *will-to*-life, or will-to-live. This is no self-conscious, dainty parlour performer, arranging its conjuring tricks to amuse a *blasé* audience of well-to-do idlers. It is force, blind force: all-powerful, all-creative, but without purpose, design, or meaning, to be submitted to the languid approval of academic pundits. It is the force which makes the crystal, the storm-clouds, the birds of prey, the beasts of the field, the sex-impulses of man, assume the forms they do.

The double knowledge which each of us has of the nature and activity of his own body, and which is given in two completely different ways, has now been clearly brought out. We shall accordingly make further use of it as a key to the nature of every phenomenon in nature, and shall judge of all objects which are not our own bodies, and are consequently not given to our consciousness in a double way but only as ideas, according to the analogy of our own bodies, and shall therefore assume that as in one respect they are idea, just like our bodies, and in this respect are analogous to them, so in another aspect, what remains of objects when we set aside their existence as idea of the subject, must in its inner nature be the same as that in us which we call *will*.

Whoever has with me gained this conviction will find that of itself it affords him the key to the knowledge of the inmost being of the whole of nature; for he now transfers it to all those phenomena which are not given to him, like his own phenomenal existence, both in direct and indirect knowledge, but only in the latter, thus merely one-sidedly as *idea* alone. He will recognize this will of which we are speaking not only in those phenomenal existences which exactly resemble his own, in men and animals as their inmost nature, but the course of reflection will lead him to recognize the force which germinates and vegetates in the plant, and indeed the force through which the crystal is formed, that by which the magnet turns to the North Pole, the force whose shock he experiences from the contact of two different kinds of metals, the force which appears in the elective affinities of matter as repulsion and attraction, decomposition and combination, and, lastly, even gravitation, which acts so powerfully throughout matter, draws the stone to the earth and the earth to the sun —all these, I say, he will recognize as different only in their phenomenal existence, but in their inner nature as identical, as that which is directly known to him so intimately and so much better than anything else, and which in its most distinct manifestation is called *will*. It is this application of reflection alone that prevents us from remaining any longer at the phenomenon, and leads us to the *thing in itself*. Phenomenal existence is idea and nothing more. All idea, of whatever kind it may be, all *object*, is *phenomenal* existence, but the *will* alone is a *thing in itself*. As such, it is throughout not idea, but *toto genere* different from it; it is that of which all idea, all object, is the phenomenal appearance, the visibility, the objectification. It is the inmost nature, the kernel, of every particular thing, and also of the whole. It appears in every blind force of nature and also in the preconsidered action of man; and the great difference between these two is merely in the degree of the manifestation, not in the nature of what manifests itself.[1]

This will-to-life, the will to assume form at any cost, to compete with all other wills-to-exist, knows no rest, and knows no goal other than its own restless willing and striving. There is no "pre-established harmony," but rather anarchy, universal competition, universal war. Man's life is nasty, brutish, and short. Planning, intelligence, optimism—all essentially self-deceiving, doomed to failure. We desire. What is desire, but pain? We shall not be happy until we attain to our heart's desire. But shall we be happy even then? No. We shall be bored, pained again. Life is a transition from pain to pain, a pendulum-swing from want to *ennui*, from *ennui* to wanting again, and so on, *da capo*, with disease and death waiting for us, certain victors in the restless strife.

"When I think the Absolute, the Absolute thinks in me," wrote Hegel. Yes, says Schopenhauer; this world of ours is born of the Absolute's dreamings, and we are but creatures in them, in the Absolute's uneasy, fitful dreams. For they are not even beautiful dreams. With its universal war and misery, human life is, rather, a cosmic nightmare. And yet, if the Absolute ever ceases to dream, and wakes up—what happens to us? We go out.

It is really incredible how meaningless and void of significance when looked at from without, how dull and unenlightened by intellect when felt from within, is the course of the life of the great majority of men. It is a weary longing and complaining, a dream-like staggering through the four ages of life to death, accompanied by a series of trivial thoughts. Such men are like clockwork, which is wound up, and goes it knows not why; and every time a man is begotten and born, the clock of human life is wound up anew, to repeat the same old piece it has played innumerable times before, passage after passage, measure after measure, with insignificant variations. Every individual, every human being and his course of life, is but another short dream of the endless spirit of nature, of the persistent will to live; is only another fleeting form, which it carelessly sketches on its infinite page, space and time; allows to remain for a time so short that it vanishes into nothing in comparison with these, and then

[1] Arthur Schopenhauer, *Die Welt als Wille und Vorstellung* (1819), tr. Haldane and Kemp, sects. 19, 21.

obliterates to make new room. And yet, and here lies the serious side of life, every one of these fleeting forms, these empty fancies, must be paid for by the whole will to live, in all its activity, with many and deep sufferings, and finally with a bitter death, long feared, and coming at last.[1]

This is not the best, but the worst, of possible worlds. All we can do about it, as individuals, is to view one another with pity, and, for ourselves, to refuse to play the Absolute's game for Him. Let us withdraw from the schemings and contrivings of the world. Let us negate the will-to-live, seeking refuge in the pure contemplation of art, and the cultivation of a superior attitude towards the universal treadmill of ambition and sex, ambition and sex, ambition and sex. Out into the night, for us! The night of Nirvana of cosmic nothingness, of absolute negation. For this is the only alternative which true philosophy, the transcendental philosophy of life, has to offer to those who have lost their illusions.

When through some great and inevitable denial of fate the will is to some extent broken, almost nothing is desired, and the character shows itself mild, just, noble, and resigned. When, finally, grief has no definite object, but extends itself over the whole of life, then it is to a certain extent a going into itself, a withdrawal, a gradual disappearance of the will, whose visible manifestation, the body, it imperceptibly but surely undermines, so that a man feels a certain loosening of his bonds, a mild foretaste of death. A secret pleasure accompanies this grief.

The denial of the will to live, which is just what is called absolute, entire resignation or holiness, always proceeds from that quieter of the will which the knowledge of its inner conflict and vanity, expressing themselves in the suffering of all living things, becomes. When this suffering is directly *felt* by a man himself, it results in perfect sanctification and salvation, the phenomenon of which is the state of resignation, the unbroken peace which accompanies it, and the greatest delight in death.[1]

Such are some of the chief waves in the flood of idealism which the Copernican revolutionist of Könisgberg loosed upon an unsuspecting world. Since then, the tides have ebbed and flowed, more than once. A generation of post-Hegelians has seen the dialectical pendulum swing over into its opposite extreme, with materialism enthroned as the supreme idol of the tribe, and with empirical science and metaphysical agnosticism demanding the loyalty of all good men. Secure in its Kant-derived charter, science for a long

[1] Ibid., sect. 58.   [1] Ibid., sect. 68.

while ruled the phenomenal world with a sceptre of iron, and dismissed from its service the subjective make-believe of metaphysicians of all creeds. But the tide has flowed again. There has been a Back-to-Kant movement, and a Neo-idealist movement based upon the speculative philosophy of Hegel, claiming the field of values, moral, religious, and patriotic, as its special province. *Kulturphilosophie, Lebensphilosophie, Geschichtsphilosophie, Naturphilosophie*—transcendentalism, in many, many forms, still creates for us its brightly coloured soap-bubbles. Man never is, but always is to be, a "rational" animal. So the tides have ebbed and flowed; and under their cross-currents, the sands of modern life have been formed into ridges and channels which must be allowed for by the navigator, although they are omitted from many authoritative charts.

II

Realism, one would think, had been done to death for ever and for ever, by Kant and his successors. But in the middle of the burial service, to the great scandal of the congregation, the alleged corpse sat up and gave notice that the reports of its timely decease had been much exaggerated. Under the forms of positivism and neo-positivism, realism (naïve, innocent, and critical) and neo-realism, it has persisted, sometimes as a despised undercurrent or *überwundener Standpunkt*, and sometimes, especially since the Great War, as the true and dominant philosophy of the modern age.

Realism holds that physical things exist in their own right, prior to and independently of our awareness of them. This realistic hypothesis covers the relevant facts of experience and explains them better than any rival hypothesis.[1]

Realism is hard to kill. Its roots go very deep. Realists are always conscious of powerful allies, such as Aristotle and "sound" philosophy on the one hand, and commonsense and the factuality of everyday experience, on the other. Faced with idealism, however triumphant—and after Kant it has been (more than once) almost disgustingly cocksure of itself—the realist repeats a couple of well-tried formulas, to save himself from being hypnotized. To those who urge "Take Mind, not Things, as central," he replies

[1] Durant Drake, in *Contemp. Americ. Philos.*, I, 284.

"*Clever, but does it work?* Does it make any difference to a single genuine problem? What the world calls 'things,' the idealist insists upon our calling 'ideas.' But is not the rose, whatever name we give it, the selfsame rose, with the selfsame thorny environment?" The realist admits that, to regard life as fundamentally "spiritual," fits in with the usages of traditional religion. But he insists that the real problem goes deeper than linguistic niceties and emotional subjectivities. In this way, he succeeds in keeping his realism stern and pure.

In the second place, he carries the war into the enemy's country. "On your view," he says, "*we eat, drink, and are clothed in—ideas.* If you are not saying that, then what, in the name of truth, clearness, and honesty, *are* you saying?" A question easy to ask, but not easy to answer, at least to a realist's satisfaction. For the rest, in recent times realists have convinced themselves that their views are natural to humanity, *eine unausrottbare menschliche Glaube*, and are particularly adapted for use by physical scientists. They have, further, developed a psychology all their own, an "objective" psychology, and a technical logic which, having engulfed mathematics as well as itself, is so puffed up that its three leading volumes, with their rigid formalism, practically insist upon the rest of the world standing to attention and presenting arms.

Convinced of the essential soundness of his own position, how does the realist feel about the work of Kant? Of course, he interprets it realistically. Like Berkeley's philosophy, although the technique differs somewhat, it is, as he sees it, "spiritual realism," a view which maintains a doctrine as to the nature of reality, the doctrine that reality is spiritual, consists of units or monads which are spirits. That Kant is a realist at heart is easy to demonstrate. In relation to the content of experience, the sense-data or "given" qualities of red, blue, hot, cold, etc., Kant is an avowed realist, quite as much as Locke or any modern realist. The difference of one sense-quality from another is "given" to us, not, as one might think, by "mind," but by "things-in-themselves." Kant says so, in so many words. Of course, it is true that Kant thinks of "things" as ultimately monadic minds; but then, it is not as *our* mind, but as something *external* to our mind, that they affect our sensibility in this way and that, so that we feel hot or cold. Our sensibility is passive rather than active, in this receptivity. It is active, in so far as we use selective attention, or construct scientific systems out of our data. But as far as the data themselves are concerned, we attend to what is there to be attended to. We apprehend what is there to be apprehended. It is given to us, and we receive it. This doctrine is pure realism, and that Kant teaches precisely this is beyond dispute.

"Well," it will be objected, "so far as the content is concerned, we will grant Kant's alleged realism. But the distinctive feature of Kant's philosophy is his *formal idealism*, his view that the synthetic forms of experience—space, time, causation, and the rest of the categories—are *not* given to us, but are *created by the mind*, in its search for systematic unity and scientific order. Realists suppose we somehow apprehend these as part of the nature of *things*. Kant does not suppose they come from *things*, but from the *mind*. Kant is, therefore, not a realist."

To this objection, the realist replies, unabashed, as follows: How do we know which "form" to apply? Why arrange experience *A* spatially or temporally, experience *B* causally or substantially, experience *C* under the form of plurality or totality? Kant says, "We use our judgment." Quite so. How true! And on what do we rely, when we "use our judgment"? On (*a*) sensation (says Kant), verifying or throwing doubt upon our selection of this or that formal principle of arrangement; and (*b*) upon the *x*, the unknown but rational ground, which makes our experience the thing it is. Again, how true! But do not both these factors, asks the realist, come, in the end, even for Kant, from "things-in-themselves"? Of course they do. Sensations are "affections of our sensibility *produced by things*," and the *x*, the unknown constant in experience, is precisely, the "thing-in-itself." In relation to our experience, then, these synthetic forms—space, causality, and the rest—are all "empirically real," as Kant says, for a Kantian no less than for a realist.

And further: what are these forms, considered apart from the guarantee of experience? Kant says, we don't know, and can't say: except that they are somehow grounded in the nature of reality, of things-in-themselves. In so far as we don't know, Kant calls them "transcendentally ideal,"—i.e. ideas of ours, whose explanation is problematic. For himself, Kant regards them as *mind*-made, *self*-derived, rather than *thing*-derived. But his "mind" or "noumenal self" is precisely as real, as final, and as ultimate a principle of explanation for what he does not know as are the realist's "things," however interpreted. In fact, Kant's "mind" is his interpretation of the realist's "things." The logic of the two positions is identical.

What Kant is trying to do is to discover the "categories," the most general features of experience, and explain them in terms of "mind." What the self-styled realist is trying to do is to discover the "categorial features," as S. Alexander calls them, the most general features of experience, and explain them in terms of "reality," i.e. in terms of "matter" or "physical material" such as space–time, or possibly "neutral reality"—which is neither mind nor matter, but the matrix out of which both "emerge." Kant's "mind" is, in strict logic, in exactly the same position as the realist's "reality." It is that whose fundamental features the philosopher is seeking to enumerate, to interrelate, and to comprehend in a single, unified world-picture. It is not created, but discovered by the philosopher, and accepted with "natural piety." Whether he calls himself an "idealist" or a "realist" is thus a difference within the general field of realism; the difference between two explanatory hypotheses: the difference between "spiritual realism" and "physical realism." All thinkers, as such, are trying to explain the nature of "reality," and thus are, in strict logic, "realists," whatever the specific principle of explanation they may adopt in detail.

After the above demonstration,[1] it will readily be seen that modern realists are in no danger of permitting Kant or any other idealist to hypnotize them into viewing "mind" as necessarily central in experience. The realist school is thriving at the present day, and is developing all sorts of hypotheses in order to account for the data and "categorial features" of experience, and their "emergence" in the precise forms which scientists and philosophers regard as verified. Most members of the school are definitely *physical* realists, laying great weight upon the methods and results of physical science, and treating reality as constructed out of "space–time" or some such modern formula for "matter." But others have developed the "neutral monism" of Mach into a neutrality so very neutral, so very much neither mind nor matter but a common matrix, as to reduce it, without remainder, to logic. E. B. Holt is the best-known of the neo-realists of this type; but

[1] Idealists do not accept this "demonstration." As they see it, there is an essential difference of opinion as to the nature and function of "mind." For idealism, this is in no sense a "physical object," one "thing" in a world of "things," but something *sui generis*.

all believers in a realm of "essences" find themselves in much the same boat; and to a modern reader with a sense of humour, it is easy to see how a thinker like Bosanquet could bring himself to write on *The Meeting of Extremes in Contemporary Philosophy.* When we come across an idealist talking with pathetic earnestness about "the material substratum of the physical world," or a realist constructing the physical, as well as the mental environment out of pure logic, without a particle of old-fashioned "matter" in its composition, we begin to ask ourselves whether, in some sudden flurry of modern life, the lid has blown off the box of labels, and some of them are sticking to the wrong persons. Or is it that we are all "practical" nowadays, like liberal politicians addressing conservative constituencies, and vice versa?

Of all the forms of modern realism "positivism" is, perhaps, the most in favour with the enlightened public which reads such works. The general idea of positivism is associated with the names of August Comte (1798–1857) and Herbert Spencer (1820–1903), but they have large numbers of followers at the present day. A positivist is a professing empiricist. His aim is to describe and depict the world of human experience as simply, directly, and completely as possible. He has, as he says himself, no *a priori* bias whatever, and no metaphysics or other form of transcendentalism at all. He reports the "facts" of experience, and reads into them nothing which is not there. He reports to persons of well-trained mind, who can see for themselves that what he reports is so. What he writes is interesting, informative, up-to-date, and absolutely reliable; and anyone who can read the *Encyclopaedia* (latest edition) with enjoyment, will find that "positivism" will partly duplicate and partly intensify that enjoyment.

How does a positivist philosopher differ from a scientist? For scientists, too, are often referred to as "positive." He differs as a great mind, which can take in several fields, differs from the specialist mind which can handle only one thing at a time. The positive scientist occupies himself with a highly specialized field, a little bit of physics, chemistry, microbiology, or what not. The positive philosopher is like Bacon. He "takes *all* knowledge for his province," and is equally good in all parts of his field. He does far more than transpose the reports of individual scientists. He synthesizes their reports, surveying wide and varied fields of investigation, and checking the narrowness of A by reference to

B, *C*, and *D*. His philosophy is thus a "synthetic philosophy."

Philosophy may still properly be the title retained for knowledge of the highest generality. Science means merely the family of the Sciences— stands for nothing more than the sum of knowledge formed of their contributions; and ignores the knowledge constituted by the *fusion* of these contributions into a whole. As usage has defined it, Science consists of truths existing more or less separated and does not recognize these truths as entirely integrated.

The truths of Philosophy thus bear the same relation to the highest scientific truths, that each of these bears to lower scientific truths. As each widest generalization of Science comprehends and consolidates the narrower generalizations of its own division; so the generalizations of Philosophy comprehend and consolidate the widest generalizations of Science. It is therefore a knowledge the extreme opposite in kind to that which experience first accumulates. It is the final product of that process which begins with a mere colligation of crude observations, goes on establishing propositions that are broader and more separated from particular cases, and ends in universal propositions. Or to bring the definition to its simplest and clearest form: Knowledge of the lowest kind is *un-unified* knowledge; Science is *partially-unified* knowledge; Philosophy is *completely-unified* knowledge.[1]

His generalizations, while always, of course, scientific—for are they not based upon the reports of undoubted scientists?—are broad and deep indeed. He synthesizes all the reports of all the scientists into a single world-picture, and establishes the most widely based, the most sweeping, and the most fundamental generalizations or laws which the human brain can be expected to conceive. The last word in science, the surest and deepest and latest thing in philosophy—no wonder that the many forms of positivism, from "general science" to disquisitions upon the ultimate significance of the human venture to understand its world, have been wider and more popular in their appeal than the intricate metaphysics of a Kant or a Hegel.

What is the fundamental law which the positivist philosopher discovers? Well, that varies with the particular positivist philosophers. Comte, in his *Philosophie positive*, sees everywhere evidence of a fundamental law of the human mind, the *Law of the Three Stages*.

[1] Herbert Spencer, *First Principles* (1862), sect. 37.

The law is this: that each of our leading conceptions—each branch of our knowledge—passes successively through three different theoretical conditions: the Theological, or fictitious; the Metaphysical, or abstract; and the Scientific, or positive.[1]

In the history of the developing individual, in the history of the race as a whole, in the history of each branch of science and art, we can trace three typical stages. First in the order of time comes the *theological stage.* Primitive man, young children, the arts and sciences in their beginnings, view everything in a personal way as guided by powerful spirits, gods, and explain what takes place as "God's Will," or some personal equivalent. Second comes the *metaphysical stage.* More sophisticated man, later adolescents, the arts and sciences in their early modern form, substitute general principles, impersonal causes and "absolutes," for the animistic "gods" of the earlier stage of development. They explain events as due to "the principle of pre-established harmony," or "the essential nature of a self-caused substance," or some similar metaphysical principle. Third and last comes the *positive stage.* Truly modern men, with a genuinely adult mind, and the arts and sciences which have grown up and abandoned their leading-strings, describe and depict what experience reveals to them, without any teleological or metaphysical bias. They are complete and radical empiricists; and this stage of positive description of what *is*, represents the latest and finest flower of the human spirit, an everlasting flower, which will never go to seed, but will bloom throughout eternity, in harmony with science and nature, and closely allied with a self-conscious sociology, a self-directed and controlled economy of human life.

Herbert Spencer, in his *Synthetic Philosophy*, sees things a little differently. For him too there is one fundamental law, and for him too it is a Law of Evolution. But Comte's three stages mean nothing to Spencer. Spencer's "Law" is a formulation of what he takes to be the essence of the "evolution" studied, in some of the sciences, by their specialist representatives. By widening their generalizations so as to take in all the arts, and also social life, he sees everywhere a "struggle for existence" (i.e. for food and reproduction), associated with "the survival of the fittest" (i.e. the fittest to survive in this space–time "struggle"), and the move-

[1] A. Comte, *Cours de Philosophie Positive* (1830–42), tr. Martineau, i.

ment of Evolution in every field of human experience to be "from the homogeneous to the heterogeneous," i.e. in the direction of ever greater complexity.

The formula finally stands thus: *Evolution is an integration of matter and concomitant dissipation of motion; during which the matter passes from an indefinite, incoherent homogeneity to a definite, coherent heterogeneity; and during which the retained motion undergoes a parallel transformation.**

* The definition of Evolution needs qualifying by introduction of the word "relatively" before each of its antithetical clauses. The statement should be that "*the matter passes from a relatively indefinite, incoherent homogeneity to a relatively definite, coherent heterogeneity.*" . . .[1]

The views of Comte and Spencer, and of their present-day followers, are clear and distinct. Being associated with modern democratic movements, and a little hostile to anything savouring of "old families" and "vested interests," and depicting the ventures of modern life as a suitable compound of universal enlightenment and universal democracy, with appropriate opportunities, intellectual, economic, and social, for all intelligent readers, positivist treatises have had widespread influence and far-reaching success. Authors of this class are not, as a rule, original thinkers They are popularizers of science posing as its champions. Like Bacon, they are journalists of science posing as leaders. Professional scientists and philosophers feel a little doubtful of the quality of their work, and especially doubtful as to whether it is really "scholarly."

But such treatises are always interesting; and the general reader is not only flattered by finding that he can understand them, and that they suggest all kinds of interesting and comforting ideas to him. He also absorbs a certain amount of information which, in its own way, is doubtless of value to him. "Popularizers" are always liable to professional criticism; but, if they do succeed in making science and the scientific point of view more popular, there is a place for such writers; and along with much which is perhaps misleading, on the whole, positivism seems to have come to stay as a feature of present-day life. It changes, as the work of the scientists, upon whom the journalist depends, changes. But in spirit, it remains popular, and occupies a place which is, no doubt, legitimate.

Certain developments are not in any sense "popular." What is called "neo-positivism" or "logical positivism," the work of

1 Spencer, *First Principles*, sect. 144.

Carnap and his school, while owing lip-allegiance to the general gospel of empiricism, with its aim of unprejudiced description and explanation of experience, is really highly technical. It is concerned with the analysis of concepts, as used by scientific workers in a variety of fields; and its analysis is in terms of a specific and ultra-technical logic. It does not hesitate to accept what fits in with its techniques, and to reject what does not so fit in, and is in a fair way to becoming, not a general survey of contemporary thought on its logical side—which is what it claims to be—but just one more specialized school of interpretation, caught up in the intricacies of its own system.

Such, then, is the nature of modern realism, as a general movement with many undercurrents, some of them highly specialized, but all drawing from the same general source.

III

Pragmatism is an unwanted child which has come of age and repudiated its parents with a vengeance. Historically, its lineage goes back to Protagoras and the Greek Sophists. Hence its alias of "humanism." In modern times, there are traces of it in the work of a number of the Great Thinkers, and there is a bar sinister connecting it with the work of Kant. Kant popularized the doctrine of the "priority of practical reason," as solving (*ambulando*) problems where speculative reason could only look on both sides and claim world-championship in modern fence-sitting. From this Vaihinger deduced, in his *Philosophy of As If*, the principles of his pragmatism, known under the alias of "fictionalism." In this work, which its parent disowned until it had demonstrated its *Lebensfähigkeit* beyond the possibility of doubt, Vaihinger shows that scientists, like lawyers, aim, not at absolute truth, but rather at establishing working hypotheses, which are frequently acknowledged fictions. Meanwhile, independently in America, the work of Pierce, James, and Dewey was establishing the vigorous school of pragmatism, acknowledged under its own name, although here too it had an alias or two, notably the alias of "instrumentalism." The work of Schiller in England, and of Boutroux in France, is also associated with the pragmatist movement; but its acknowledged leader is John Dewey.

In general, the school eschews metaphysics as such, and, after making the (usual) profession of "radical empiricism," seeks to describe experience exclusively in biological and social terms. With self-conscious rectitude, it withdraws the hem of its skirts from anything savouring of vested interests, especially from historical idealism and historical realism, and demands a new deal, a complete "reconstruction in philosophy." From the pragmatist standpoint, idealism, with its "transcendental subject" and "transcendental object" and "transcendental theory of knowledge," has withdrawn so far from the actualities of human experience as to eke out a precarious existence in a twilight realm (entitled "transcendental"), in which, with abstract and unreal mental counters, it plays an unending parlour-game of "Mental Teasers," occupying itself with a set of mind-made puzzles essentially incapable of solution, and essentially without influence upon the "live options" of genuine experience. From this standpoint, idealism, in so far as it is "transcendental," is little more than "the systematic misuse of a terminology invented for that precise purpose." In so far, however, as idealism is genuinely empirical, and occupies itself with here-and-now problems, performing this action, completing this business deal, acquiring this skill, it has a genuine place in modern biological and social existence; and pragmatism, as guided by Dewey, claims to be precisely *empirical idealism*.

What is historically known as "realism," while equally unreal in its endeavours after an absolute knowledge in which it avows its essential disinterestedness, suffers from an over-developed technique of its own. As Bertrand Russell, one of the leaders of the modern school, himself says, "It is a sort of intellectual game of chess, played for its own sake. Its presuppositions are selected and accepted, because they make possible the largest number of logical consequences." As the pragmatist sees it, realism over-emphasizes the importance of the "exact" sciences of mathematics and physics, and looks askance at the newer and more concrete disciplines of psychology and sociology. The logic in which realists profess belief is highly technical, and, as the pragmatist diagnoses the case, is infected with the malignant disease of abstract disinterestedness, complicated by faith in the possibility of absolute knowledge. In general, historical realism is declared to be too remote from the concrete realities of life-as-it-is-lived. As contrasted with this, the pragmatist assumes the point of view of biology, behaviourist psychology, and descriptive sociology, and keeps his mathematical and physical techniques where such techniques should be kept, in his laboratory annex. Pragmatism, as guided by Dewey, thus claims to be *concrete realism*, that is to say, a form of realism which is more true to the realities of actual experience than the historical movement which, in its abstract and technical arrogance, has usurped the name of "realism."

To say that pragmatism is an idealism which is empirical, a realism which is concrete, and that it has lost its illusions in relation to "absolutes" and explanations which are not fundamentally biological or social-psychological, is perhaps a negative line of approach. Can we state its nature more positively? Dewey claims that pragmatism is the national philosophy of America, of the New World, with its admittedly concrete objectives, its admittedly novel methods, its whole-hearted acceptance of the facts of life, and of the essential limitations of biological and social organisms living out their own life-cycle in a largely hostile environment. The aim of pragmatism is to aid in the maximal realization of the potentialities for biological and social living resident in the human social organism—not in "pure contemplation" or "withdrawal from the struggle for existence," but in the closest and most direct interactivity with its fellows and with its environment. The method of pragmatism is the only method suitable for such organisms engaged in such interactivity: the method of trial-and-error, not controlled by the dead hand of the past, but experimenting with the creation of a new future.

Industrial civilization presents philosophers with a challenge. One of its tasks is to discover the full meaning of the experimental methods by which the advances of natural sciences have been made secure. Ideas must be developed after the model and pattern of what competent inquirers actually *do* in the attainment of knowledge of facts and principles. The accomplishment of this task signifies a new logic in investigation and criticism of social institutions and customs. For this area, in which men concretely live, is hardly touched as yet by the experimental habit of mind.[1]

In relation to the schools—the established institution for making possible such a future—realism, as the pragmatist views it, has aimed at building up, block by block, in courses of study taken in sequence, with "passing" at the end of one year taken as the

[1] John Dewey, "Philosophy," in *Whither Mankind?* (ed. Beard, 1930), p. 327.

necessary prerequisite to starting upon the next year's course, a systematic body of objective knowledge in the pupil's nervous system. So many years in Grammar School, followed by so many years in High School, followed by so many years in College, and so many years in Graduate or Professional School, are supposed to prepare the pupil to be a Latinist, a Mathematician, an Engineer, or what not. The pragmatist believes that, by this method, realism is building up "vested interests" in this or that out-of-date culture, which interfere with anything so modern as efficiency and creative intelligence. It involves teaching laboriously immense amounts of alleged information whose value is relative, chiefly, to the dead-and-gone past, and the creation of an academic, backward-looking attitude on the part of the memory-trained pupil, which unfits him for living in the present. As the pragmatist sees it, a present-day student, who seeks to evaluate the language and customs of bygone ages in relation to present-day problems, should be able, if taught efficiently, i.e. by "doing" rather than by passively listening and memorizing, to get more out of two years' active study in the pragmatist spirit than out of a dozen or more years spent in the realist treadmill. The forward-looking, problem-solving attitude is worth any number of walking encyclopedias, when it comes to the sciences, the arts, and indeed to life generally. Alert and adaptable, knowing how to discover rather than how to repeat, how to do rather than how to use words, the modern pragmatist throws himself upon his new problems with new methods. He acts, and he gets results.

Idealism, as the pragmatist sees it, has tried to use school subjects, not objectively and for their own sake, but in order to develop the personality of the student. But then historical idealism has tried to develop a personality which is transcendental, interested, not in the here-and-now problems of day-to-day living, but in abstract spiritual contemplation, and quasi-mystical exaltation. This, to the pragmatist, seems a terrible mistake. He teaches his pupils, on the contrary, to be alive, up-to-date citizens of the modern world, solving the problems of the present by techniques adapted to the present, and living in a *milieu* where everything comes to him who acts, and acts efficiently and quickly. "Thrice blest is he who has his motive just; But four times he who gets his claim in first." But realist and idealist of the transcendental pattern tend to believe in processes of evolution which are lengthy, tortuous, and slow. The pragmatist is more impatient, and desires to "scrap" inefficient social institutions, as a modern manufacturer scraps outdated factories, and designs new techniques adapted to the new situations of our own times.

In fact, only pragmatism, with its gospel of efficient social action, is in harmony with modern life, and attuned to its spirit. Otherworldliness, such as is characteristic of idealism, and that overvaluation of objectivity and system for its own sake, which is characteristic of realism, are, as the pragmatist sees it, simply behind the times.

The spiritual elements contained in the religions, arts, literature, moralities, and polities of our traditional inheritance should be restated: revised so that they bear an operative relation to the state of affairs through which they are realizable. By the same movement of thought, existent conditions cease to be taken as fixed, changeable only by some external and accidental intrusion; they cease to be models and measures of conduct. In this way pragmatism affords illumination and direction to our confused civilization.[1]

Action, creating the future, co-operative social action, creating and controlling the instrumentalities of economic and social living, not only in principle, but in detail, is the only formulation of life-as-it-is-lived which is true to the facts as we know them at the present day. In recent times, the tempo of life has been speeded up to such an extent that our panting nervous systems, with their inherited instinct-patterns, toil after it in vain; and only pragmatism, with its essentially forward-looking attitude, is equipped to catch up with the present, and to co-operate in creating and controlling the future.

Finally, in its latest developments, pragmatism has begun to discover, like other schools, that it is evolving a metaphysics all its own: no metaphysics of transcendental, abstract contemplation, whether of the self or of "being *qua* being," but the metaphysics involved in social activity, the metaphysics of social living itself.

Apparently we do encounter one "absolute" in the philosophy of experimentalism. That is the conviction that man should face his world with courage and hope and seek to find solutions to his specific problems

[1] John Dewey, "Philosophy," in *Whither Mankind?* (ed. Beard, 1930) p. 328, condensed.

as they confront him in experience. Even Dewey, who more than other experimentalists has opposed fixed beliefs, absolute ends, unchanging hierarchies of values, seems to recognize that there is something final about the attitude and disposition with which man should approach experience. He condemns all flights from the responsible task of seeking to understand and control the events, natural and social, in which our lives are implicated. In the *Quest for Certainty* he says we can dispense with all fixed beliefs about values "save the one value of the worth of discovering the possibilities of the actual and striving to realize them."

It would seem that the devotion of the experimentalist to the democratic principle is on the same general level as his faith in experimental method. Democracy is not a cult; it is a principle. It contributes a sense of direction, it affords an indispensable orientation to the social situation.[1]

Pragmatism thus comes into line with other post-Kantian movements. Still thoroughly alive and growing, but developing an armour-plate shell of logic, psychology, and metaphysics; hardening, perhaps in spite of itself, into "just another system."

Since the time of Kant, philosophy, taken by and large, has been an affair of co-operative movements: social and intellectual enterprises carried through by a number of thinkers grouping themselves together and working out the presuppositions and consequences of a particular set of principles, rather than an affair of individual great thinkers. Of course, representatives of each such movement can and do point with pride to their own leaders as "great thinkers." This is only to be expected. Among idealists, for instance, it used to be considered good practice to maintain stoutly, in the face of the enemy, that Hegel was their great leader. But since the Back-to-Kant movement, it has been almost universally felt that Kant is the real landmark, and Hegel merely an important member of the school which Kant's work called into being. Every now and then some one thinker, like Bergson, has been acclaimed, in all countries interested in philosophy, as one of the Great Ones. But in every case, his vogue has soon passed; and until centuries of interaction with the thought of such men have had time to elapse, so that students will have a real perspective for judgment, it is perhaps best for us post-Kantians to close on a note of modesty. As Wundt has put it, *wir sind alle Epigonen*.

[1] J. L. Childs, *Education and the Phil. of Experimentalism* (1931), pp. 120–2, condensed.

We have, in fact, nothing to compare with the Platonists, Aristotelians, Cartesians, Leibnizians, and the Kantians, of the past. We have, instead, groups and sub-groups of "realists," "positivists," and the like. In these groups we are engaged in working out co-operatively both principles and details of the cultural heritage which has come down to us. We are trying to understand, to integrate, and to apply this to the improvement of our science, our conduct, our economic and social living, our art and our religion: making, unmaking, and remaking the web of our human destiny.

Conclusion

The Great Thinkers whose work we have been studying constitute a sort of cultural mountain range. Plato and Aristotle, Locke, Kant, and the rest, can be regarded as the chief peaks of human reflection upon the human venture. We have now explored the whole range and have scaled, one by one, the highest peaks. We have projected ourselves wholeheartedly now in this direction, and now in that, and, by merging ourselves with the inmost self of each Great Thinker, have experienced within ourselves his enthusiasms, his visions, and the attractiveness of his conclusions. We have thus stimulated, stretched, and expanded our own capacity for philosophic reflection. So far, so good. But what (we ask) comes next?

Some of us will be content with what we have achieved. In fact, we shall select the insights acquired in company with some one thinker: Plato or Kant, Aristotle or Locke, Berkeley or Hume We shall feel spiritually at home with the insights of some one philosopher, and shall feed our own inherent tendencies upon his reasonings. Satisfied with these fruits of our venture into the noumenal realm, for the rest of our lives we shall apply ourselves, without further questioning, to the phenomena of nature, to practical experience, to good citizenship.[1]

Others of us will also be content with what we have achieved. But our achievement will be, not the selective choice of some *one* set of insights, but rather the broad general toleration which comes from appreciating and understanding *the complete range* of human power of interpretation. Regarding nothing human as alien to our spirit, we shall exemplify the position of "humanism," the position of the educated man who has made himself at home everywhere in the world of human culture. Such a man accepts as final the contentions of no one school, but keeps his heart and mind open to all influences, whether ancient or modern, which can claim the loyalty and esteem of educated men and women. Wherever he can feel that there is something of positive value to make his own, and to make available to others, he will feel that his attitude should be one

[1] Cf. Plato, *Republic*, 498a.

of acceptance: critical acceptance if you will, but acceptance rather than rejection.[1]

Yet others will look for something different. They will inquire how far it is possible to synthesize the messages of the different Great Thinkers, to fuse them into one quintessential message. Can we not (they will ask) formulate the nature of the human venture, and in the light of the thinkers' message determine the capacities, the functions, and the limitations of human reflection? Or if it is too much to expect that these can be determined in a way that will be final—for human evolution is still proceeding—will it not be possible to illumine, to give both background and outlook to, our continuing researches, as we construct a theory of knowledge, a theory of conduct, a theory of art, a theory of religion? Can we not in this way do something to determine the directions for carrying on philosophical inquiry? To technical philosophers, the "what next?" may be expected to take some such form.

For myself, in so far as I am a member of the cultural world of today, I find myself adopting the general position of "humanism." I try to hold in balance the rival claims of realism, of idealism, and of pragmatism. My natural bias is toward the position historically known as transcendental idealism. But I am unable to believe that any one -ism is "absolutely right," and its alternatives "eternally wrong." I prefer to think that theories are made for life, rather than life for theory; and in defining philosophy as "reflective living," I do not forget that the place assigned to "reflection," even where living is imperfect, is always adjectival.

In so far as I am a writer on philosophical topics, I find that study of the Great Thinkers opens vistas, frequently in novel directions, and that I cannot afford to ignore any of the vistas thus opened to me. These keep my mind open; and in approaching the technical solution of present-day problems, I find it helpful to work out the implications, for my problem, of each of the major points of view. In a word, the lesson of the Great Thinkers to me is the continuing value of openness, of positive enthusiasm, and of balance.

[1] Cf. Warner Fite, *Moral Philosophy*, and Philip Wheelwright, *Critical Introduction to Ethics*, ch. VII.

Index of Names

301

Index

Index

London, 199, 206-7, 239
Longinus, 57-8
Lose Blätter aus Kants . . ., 250
Lucian, 6
Lucretius, 244
Lyceum, 9-10, 34, 36, 50, 55
Lycurgus, 2

Macedonia, 30, 32, 36
Mach, E., 287
Macrobius, 5
Magna Graecia, 2
Malebranche, 106, 163, 178, 233
Malmesbury, 171
Marcus Aurelius, 75
Mary, 116-19, 121-4, 130, 134, 136, 146-7, 159-63, 258
Medea, 8
Meditationes (Descartes), 92-101
Mendelssohn, M., 247
Metaphysica (Aristotle), 35, 49, 53
Micawber, 249
Michelangelo, ix
Mill, James, 240
Mill, John Stuart, 240
Miltiades, 15
Monadologie, 142, 144-51, 153-8, 162
Morgenstunden, 247

Napoleon, 277
Natorp, P., 60
Neokantian, 60
Neoplatonist, 56
New Theory of Vision (Berkeley), 208
Newton, 282
Nicias, 28
Nirvana, 283
Nouveaux Essais . . . (Leibniz), 143-4
Novum Organum (Bacon), 169-71

Occasionalists, 164
Oedipus, 8
Œuvres philos. (Leibniz), 144
On Civil Government (Locke), 179
Oriental, 56
Ovid, 244
Oxford, 174, 177

Paris, 85, 92, 93, 197, 199
Parmenides, 21, 23, 25
Parmenides (Plato), 4, *n.* 1
Pericles, 1, 6, 15
Persia, 55, 56

Phaedo (Plato), 4, 30, 59, 75
Phaedrus (Plato), 4, 14, 25
Philo Judaeus, 110
Philosophie des "Als Ob" (Vaihinger), 292
Pierce, C. S., 292
Plato, Ch. I, ix, 30-4, 36, 47, 49, 53-7, 59-60, 62-4, 69, 72, 75-7, 97, 246, 257, 273
Platonists, Cambridge, 177, 240
Platonopolis, 3, 56, 82
Plotinus, Ch. III, ix, 108, 110, 137
Pope, A., 158
Porphyry, 57-9
Prichard, H. A., 244
Principia Philosophiae (Descartes), 93
Principles (Berkeley), 209-13, 217, 219
Prolegomena . . . (Kant), 248-51, 253, 255, 267
Protagoras, 10-12, 292
Protrepticus (Aristotle), 32, 42
Prussia(n), 244-5, 248, 263, 266
Punch, 182
Pythagorean(s), 2, 19, 21-3, 31

Raphael, 71
Reflexionen Kants . . ., 246
Reicke, O., 250
Reid, Th., 240
Rembrandt, ix, 71
Renaissance, 110
Republic (Plato), ix, 1, 4, 7, 9, 14, 18-21, 24, 26-7, 29-30, 246
Rome, 55, 56, 82, 83, 198
Rosicrucians, 139
Ross, W. D., 33
Rousseau, 245
Rubens, 71
Russell, Bertrand, 223-4, 293

Santayana, G., 6
Schelling, 276-8
Schiller, F. C. S., 292
Schleiermacher, 276, 280
Scholastics, 35, 45, 83, 139, 174, 177, 240
Schopenhauer, A., 9, 276, 280-3
Schubert, 71
Scottish School, 240, cf. 222, 239-40, 248
Shaftesbury, 174
Shakespeare, ix, 8, 9, 71, 104, 224
Shaw, G. B., 6, 8-9, 71

Index

INDEX OF SUBJECTS

Index

Apprehension, simple, 87–91
A priori, 147, 153, 162, 253, 255–9, 262–3, 266, 268, 288
Arbitrariness, 165–6
Aristocracy, 1, 55
Art(ists), 5, 9, 11, 22, 41, 48, 57, 60–74, 78, 102, 126, 162, 272–4, 277–8, 283
Artificer, Divine, 30, 47–8
Artisans, 15, 48
Aspiration, 46, 99
Association, 150–1, 207–8, 229, 236–7, 240, 248, 259
Atheism, 23, 103, 108, 202–3, 207, 211, 220, 230
Atoms, 149–50
Attribute, 90, 106, 126–9, 165
Authority, 83, 97, 145, 167, 171–2, 179–80, 220
Autonomy, 269–71
Axioms, 89–90, 153, 170, 176

Beauty, 12, 14, 22, 32–3, 48, 60–74, 79, 81, 177, 273–4
Being, 21–37, 51–2, 63–4, 95–6, 151, 212–13
Belief, 92–4, 176, 226–9, 233

Categorial . . . Reality, 287
Categorical Imperative, 268–70
Categories, 30, 32, 51, 194, 264–5, 276, 278, 286–7
Causa sui, 131–2, cf. 143–4, 153, 198, 290
Causation, 232–8, cf. 23, 34, 36, 47–8, 115, 127–8, 130, 150, 153–4, 156, 200, 217, 219, 221, 241, 250, 252–4, 260, 271
Certainty, 91–3, 100, 200–1, 227
Change, 18, 49, 100, 131, 146–8, 150, 152
Chaos, 5, 12, 23, 24, 73, 172
Character, 18, 26
Christianity, 7, 9, 35, 50, 56, 82–3, 123, 206, 221
Church, 83, 145, 163, 220–1
Citizen(ship), 9–10, 13–18, 22, 33, 136, 295
Civilization, 7, 198–9, 228, 234, 238, 294
Clubs, 10, 13
Cogito, ergo sum, 95–7, 107
Commonsense, 240, cf. 46, 48, 88, 179. 203, 284

Commonwealth, 173
Communication, 218–19, 274
Community, 14–15, 17, 18, 20–1, 23–4, 74–5, 270
Concepts, 39–40, 50–2, 89, 127, 151, 215, 230, 250, 261, 280
Concrete experience, 184, 186, 188, 193–4
Conflict, 69, 79, 82, 287
Confusion, 225–7
Connection, 234–8, 250, 252–3
Consciousness, 46, 49–50, 67, 96–7, 117, 146–8, 188, 195, 221, 230–1, 235, 263, 278
Consent, 179–80, 253
Conservatism, 12, 139, 146
Consistency, 151, 173, 202, 269
Constitution(s), 2, 3, 33, 34, 183
Construction, mental, 201–2, 217
Contemplation, 43–4, 49, 53, 62, 69, 95, 97, 122, 198, 283, 295
Contract, Social, 172
Contradiction, 151, 269, 279
Co-operation, 12, 24, 26, 28, 152, 156–7, 163, 180–1, 296–8
Correlate of Ideas, 215, 218
Courage, 2, 10, 27, 28, 72 *n.*, 74
Creativity, ix, 3, 9, 13, 22, 25, 30, 39, 40, 41, 52, 63, 65, 69, 70–1, 73–5, 77, 79, 143, 154–5, 166, 209, 217, 286–7, 296
Creator, 77, 111, 166, 217–19
Criterion of truth, 91
Critical philosophy, 107
Criticism, 13, 15–17, 25, 30, 32, 97, 121, 178–9, 184, 251, 255, 266,
Custom, 229, 237–8, 248, 252

Data, 191–2, 196–7, 285–7
Death, 1, 7, 68, 149, 172, 282–3
Definition, 27–8, 61–2, 64, 105, 165, 171
Degeneration, 69
Deliberation, 33–4
Democracy, 1, 36, 55, 179–80, 291, 297
Demon, malignant, 94, 97, 100
Description, 184, 288, 290
Desire(s), 11, 49, 115, 136, 157, 282
Deus ex machina, 5, 160
Dialectic, 1, 6–7, 11–12, 15, 20–2, 30, 53, 57, 60, 63, 69, 257, 279
Dictator, 2, 30, 54, 271
Discovery, 31, 76, 84–6, 95, 102, 166, 176, 185, 287

305

Index

Index

Index

Matter, 63–5, cf. 31–32, 36–39, 41–2, 45–8, 76, 101, 105–6, 109, 126–9, 163–4, 210–11, 214, 230, 288, 291

Meaning, 48, 52, 226, 261

Mechanism, 18, 101–2, 104, 156–7, 162, 164

Medium, sensory, 38, cf. 200

Memory, 39–40, 42–3, 45, 87, 93, 118, 207–8, 216, 225, 295

Metaphysics, 166–8, 261, 272–3, cf. 19, 25, 31, 34, 36, 40, 45, 49–50 51, 63, 68, 76, 80, 106, 110–12, 116, 129, 133, 144, 149–50, 164, 216, 221, 226, 240–1, 244, 248, 250, 252–4, 258, 264, 290, 296–7

Method, analytic, 241–2, 252

Method, Cartesian, ix, 84–93, 99–102, 107, 118, 184

Method, Hume's, 225–7, 234, 240

Method, Locke's, 184

Method, scientific, 170–1, 272

Method, Spinoza's, 108–9, 117–18, 121–2, 123–4, 133

Mind, 93–102, 126–9, 151–2, 191–4, 215–19, 257–63, 266, cf. 18–19, 26, 30, 41, 51, 72, 105, 109, 118, 120, 140, 145, 163–5, 186–8, 197–8, 208–12, 214, 221, 224–5, 230, 232, 273, 279, 285–7

Mode, 112–15, 118–19, 122–5, 127, 130–4, 136, 147, 159, 161, 201–2, cf. 213

Modernism, 11–12, 93, 95, 97, 106–7, 110, 139, 155, 159–60, 163–5

Monad(s), Ch. VI, 142, 146–9, 151–60, 167, 274, 285

Morality, 1, 33, 73–5, 102–3, 126, 156–7, 268–71, 274, 280

Motion, physical, 186–7, 235

Mysticism, 76–82, 122–5, 133–5, cf. 21, 56, 60, 66, 74–5, 109–10, 117, 129, 131, 137, 158–9, 219–20, 240

Narrowness, 102–4

Nature, 258, cf. 2, 18, 30, 41, 43, 47–50, 61, 67, 69, 71, 75–6, 89–92, 104, 110–12, 114, 123, 127, 131, 156–7, 160, 162, 179, 201, 216–17, 219, 277

Negation, 43, 64, 81–2, 124–5, 132, 229, 232, 238, 266, 283

Nisus, 43, 62, 66

Non-being, 46, 63–4

Notion, 50, 215–17, 230, 279

Noumena, 261, 271–3, 286

Objectivity, 261, cf. 46–7, 52–4, 56, 60–1, 78, 87–8, 90–2, 94, 100, 187, 213, 218–19, 228–9, 237, 273

Observation, 32, 34–5, 52, 183, 188, 201–2, 216–17, 230, 253

One, the, 25, 55, 77–8, 81

Ontology, 96, 99

Opinion, 118, 159, 227, 272

Optimism, 157–8, 167–8

Organization, 44–5, 159

Originality, 57, 63, 109–10, 137, 144, 166, 239, 247, 291

Orthodox(y), 220–1, cf. 280

Other persons, knowledge of, 215–17

Pantheism, 111–12

Parallelism, 127–30, 163

Participation, 22, 26, 28–9

Particulars, 33, 36, 124

Perception, 37–8, 40, 42–3, 96–7, 100–2, 117, 147–50, 152, 200, 207, 212–18, 225–6, 231, 263

Perfection, 157–8, cf. 23, 43–6, 48–9, 51–2 (cf. 58), 66–7, 71, 98–100, 123, 125–6, 131, 153, 254, 270

Personality, 1, 5, 25–6, 118, 268–9, 295

Phenomena, 258, 260–2, cf. 18, 35, 49, 52, 90, 219, 281

Phenomenalism, 213, cf. 259–62

Philosophers, 9, 14, 17, 20, 23, 35, 43, 46

Philosophy, ix, 2, 20, 22–3, 25, 34, 36, 43–4, 71, 93, 95, 277, 279, 289

Philosophy, transcendental, 254–62, 266–8, 275–84

Physics, 18–20, 23–4, 34, 93, 100–2, 128, 149–50, 153, 164, 171–2, 244, 252–3, 260–1

Picture-thinking, 115–16, 160, 173, 279

Plan, Divine, 2, 71, 90, 131, 156, 162

Play, 165–6, 252, 273

Pleasure, 195, 270, 274

Pluralism, 31, 146, 175, 237

Poetry, 11–15, 22, 60, 104, 225, 278

Politics, 1–2, 15, 34, 36

Popularizers, 291

Positivism, 34, 52, cf. 94, 103, 284, 288–292, 298

Post-Kantian Philosophy, Ch. XI

Potentiality, 40–4, 45–7, 60, 64

Index

Index